ESSENTIAL REFERENCE FOR DRAWING THE BODY

ANATOMY FOR ARTISTS MADE EASY

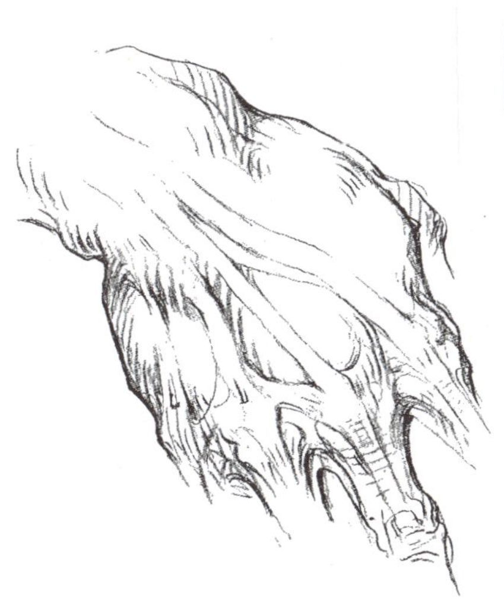

Publisher and Creative Director: Nick Wells
Project Editor: Laura Bulbeck
Art Director: Mike Spender
Digital Manager: Chris Herbert

Special thanks to George Bridgman (1865–1943) on whose book *Constructive Anatomy* (John Lane/Bodley Head, 1920) this new edition is based.

FLAME TREE PUBLISHING
6 Melbray Mews, Fulham, London SW6 3NS
United Kingdom

www.flametreepublishing.com

First published 2015

15 17 19 18 16
1 3 5 7 9 10 8 6 4 2

A CIP record for this book is available from the British Library upon request.

Images used in this book were created by **George Bridgman** who was an instructor in drawing, and lecturer on the construction and anatomy of the human figure, at the Art Students League, New York. He was also the author of such books as *The Book of a Hundred Hands*, *Bridgman's Life Drawing* and *Features and Faces*.

ISBN: 978-1-78361-602-2

Printed in China

ESSENTIAL REFERENCE FOR DRAWING THE BODY

ANATOMY FOR ARTISTS MADE EASY

TEXT & IMAGES
GEORGE BRIDGMAN

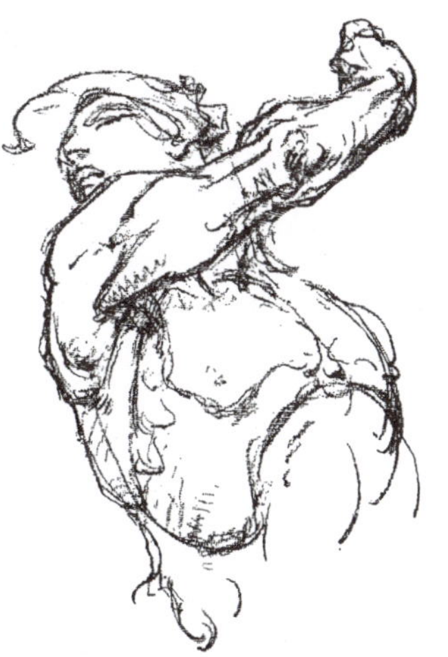

REVISED BY
JAKE JACKSON

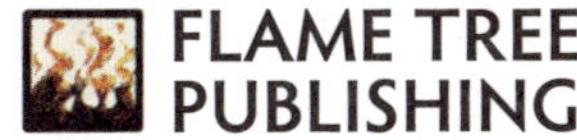

CONTENTS

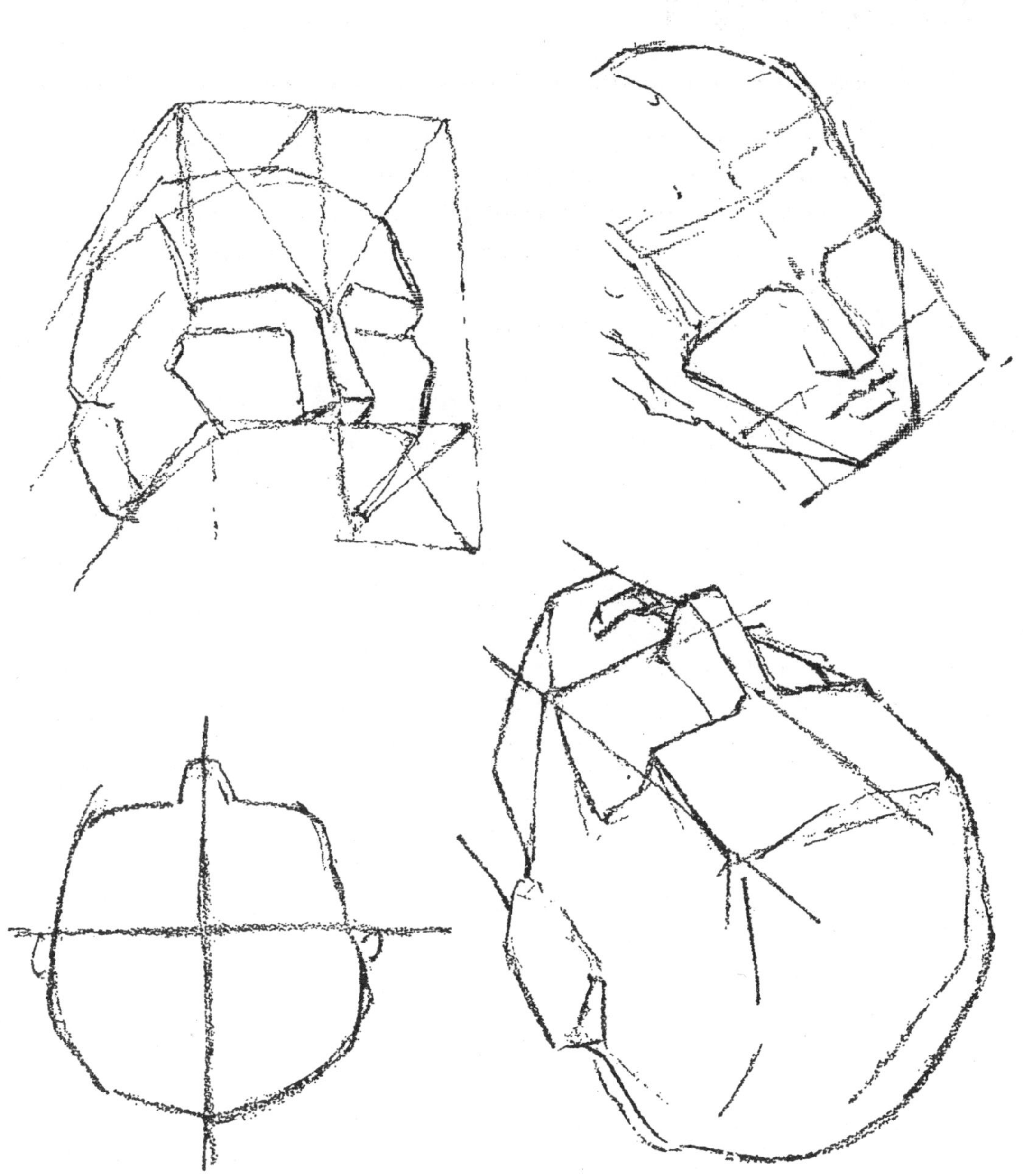

ANATOMY: FOREWORD

An anatomy book fulfills a variety of needs, but essentially addresses the requirement for all artists of figurework: how to construct the human body. Once we learn the components it becomes relatively easy to create work without reference, especially useful for commercial illustration, manga and comics and all forms of digital art.

With hundreds of drawings, ***Anatomy For Artists Made Easy*** shows you how to break the body down into **blocks**, and makes it easier to understand how those blocks **rotate**. The emphasis is on the movement of blocks together, which create the flowing lines of the body itself.

George Bridgman, the originator of this material, was a New York art teacher at a time of the great flowering of illustration in the early twentieth century; as the world of fine art moved from the representational to the abstract it opened up the market for illustrators just at the point where paper pulp became more affordable. This led to a golden age of illustrated hardback books, pulp magazines such as ***Weird Tales*** and laid the path for the first mass market comics, to the manga books of today.

Anatomy For Artists Made Easy, whether you want to learn technical terms for muscles, bones and tendons, or just copy these elegant and powerful drawings, is an invaluable tool for all artists.

Jake Jackson, 2015

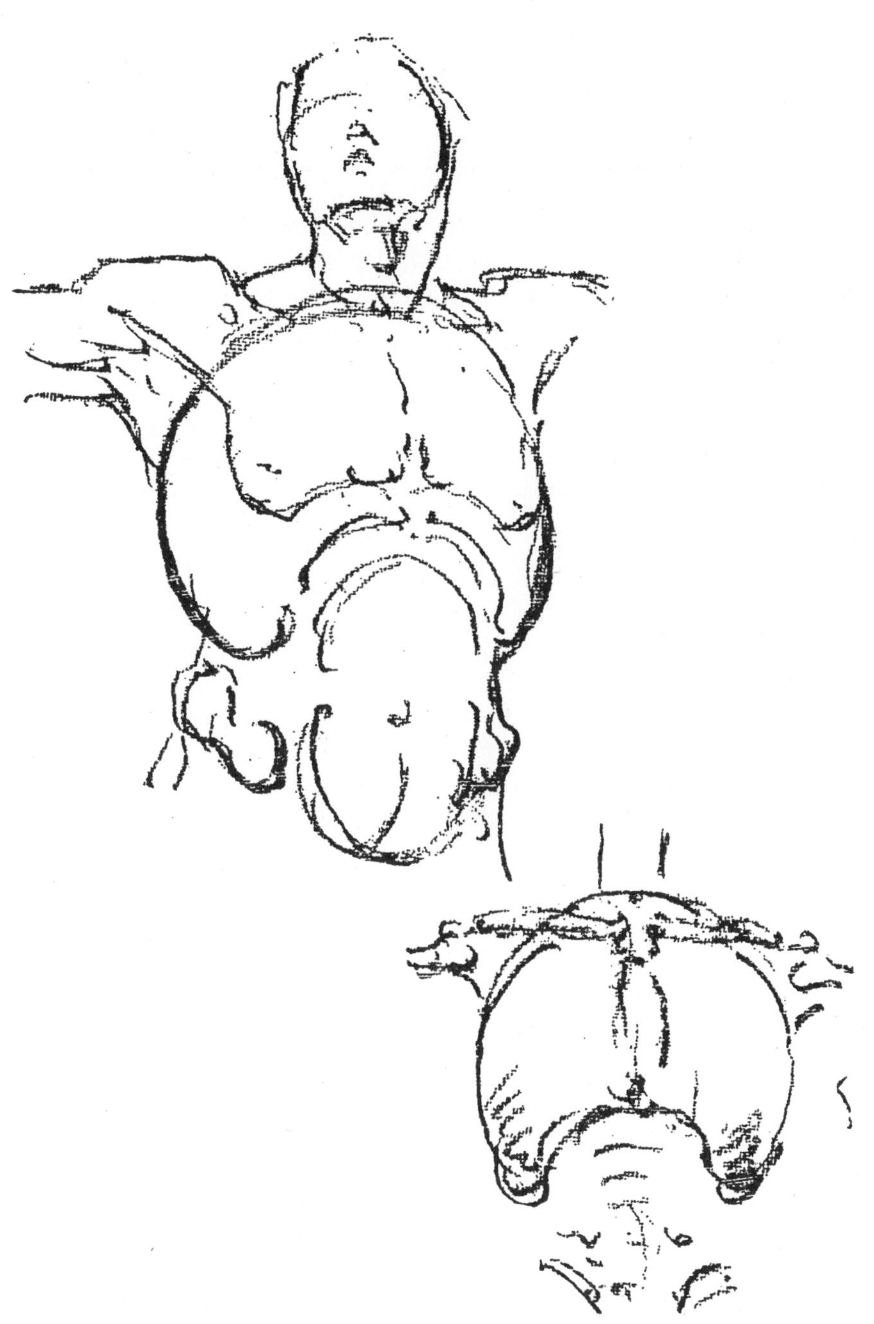

ANATOMICAL NAMES

Anatomy drawings (with the mechanics of the skeleton and the muscles that govern movement) are essential to a clear understanding of the human body. In this book parts of the body are identified with their medical and technical names.

GENERAL

Abductor	Drawing away (from median line)
Adductor	Drawing toward (median line)
Anterior	In front
Brevis	Brief, or short
Extensor	Extender
External	Outside of
Flexor	Bender
Infra	Below
Internal	On inner side
Longus	Long
Minimus	Smallest Pronator
	Turning face down
Posterior	Behind
Rectus	Straight
Semi	Half
Supinator	Turning face up
Tertius	Third
Vastus	Vast, or large

BONES

Calcaneum	'From *calx*, heel'
Carpal	'From *carpus*, wrist'
Clavicle	'Key, collar bone '
Coccyx	Cuckoo (beak of)
Cuneiform	Wedge-shaped
Digit	Finger
Femur	Thigh
Fibula	Flute
Frontal	In front
Humerus	Bone of upper arm
Inferior	'Below, lower '
Malar	'From *mala*, cheek '
Mastoid	Nipple-shaped
Maxillary	Jaw
Metacarpals	Beyond the wrist
Metatarsal	Beyond the instep
Nasal	Nose
Occipital	'From *ob*, over against, and *caput*, head; so back of head '
Os innominatum	Bone without a name
Os magnum	Great bone
Parietal	'From *paries*, wall '
Patella	Little pan
Phalanges	Ranks of soldiers
Pisiform	Pea-shaped
Radius	Spoke (of wheel)
Sacrum	Sacred (used in oracles)

Scaphoid	Boat-shaped
Scapula	Spade; shoulder blade
Semi-lunar	Half-moon
Sternum	Breast bone
Superior	'Above, upper'
Tarsal	Instep
Temporal	'Time'
Tibia	Shin
Trapezium	Table
Trapezoid	'Like a table – two sides parallel, two not'
Ulna	Cubit

MUSCLES

Abductor	Drawing away (from median line)
Achilles' tendon	The tendon by which Achilles' mother held in dipping him into the River Styx to make him invulnerable
Anconeus	Donkey's foot
Anticus	(Adjective) in front
Biceps	Two-headed
Brachialis	Pertaining to arm
Coraco-brachialis	'From *coracoid* (beak-like) process of *scapula* to *brachium*, or arm'
Deltoid	Like 'Greek letter *delta*, triangular (equilateral)'
Fascia	Band
Gastrocnemius	Frog's belly
Gluteus	Buttocks
Gracilis	'Slender, graceful'
Lata	Broad
Major	Greater
Masseter	'Chewer, masticator'
Maximus	Greatest
Medius	Middle-sized
Minimus	Smallest
Minor	Lesser
Oblique	Slanting
Pectoralis	Pertaining to breast
Peroneus	Pin-another name for *fibula*
Plantaris	Of the sole of the foot (compare *palmaris* of the hand)
Rectus abdominis	Straight muscle of abdomen
Rectus femoris	Straight muscle of the *femur*
Semi-membranosus	Half membranous (broad, flat tendon)'
Semi-tendinosus	Half tendinous
Serratus	Saw-toothed
Soleus	'Sole fish, or flounder'
Sterno-cleido-mastoid	'Attaching to *sternum*, *clavicle* and *mastoid* bones'
Temporal	Pertaining to *temporal* bone
Tensor	'Tightener, or holder'
Teres	Round
Thyroid	'Shield (and *eidos*, like); so shield-like. (So all words ending in -oid.)'
Thyroid cartilage	Adam's apple
Triceps	Three-headed
Vastus externus	Great muscle outside
Vastus internus	Great muscle inside

ANATOMY: INTRODUCTION

The drawings presented here show the methods that have proved simplest and most effective in constructing the human figure.

The eye in drawing must follow a **line** or a **plane** or a mass. In the process of drawing, this may become a moving line, or a moving plane, or a moving mass. The line, in actual construction, must come first; but as mental construction must precede physical, so the concept of mass must come first, that of plane second, that of line last.

Think in masses, define them in lines. Masses of about the same size or proportion are conceived not as masses, but **as one mass**; those of different proportions, in respect to their movement, are conceived as **wedging into each other**, or as morticed or **interlocking**.

The most effective way of describing this is **wedging**.

GENERAL ANATOMY

Bones constitute the **pressure system** of the body. In them are expressed, therefore, laws of architecture, as in the dome of the head, the arches of the foot, the pillars of the legs, etc, and laws of mechanics such as the hinges of the elbows and the levers of the limbs.

Ligaments constitute the retaining or tension system, and express other laws of mechanics. Muscles constitute the contractile or **power system**; they produce action by their contraction or shortening. In **contraction** they are lifted and bulged, while in their relaxed state they are flabby and soft. Muscles, attached to and acting on the bony and ligamentous systems, constitute the **motion system**. In the muscles are expressed, therefore, laws of dynamics and of power.

For instance, for every muscle pulling in one direction, there must be the corresponding muscle pulling in the opposite direction. **Muscles are** therefore **paired, throughout the body**. Every muscle on the right side must be paired with one on the left; for every flexor on the front there must be its corresponding *extensor* on the back.

Muscles express also laws of **leverage**; they are large in proportion to the length of the lever they move. Those of the individual fingers are small and can fit in between the bones of the hand. They grow larger as we ascend the arm, the leverage being longer and the weight greater. The muscles of the forearm are larger than those of the fingers; those of the arm larger than those of the forearm, while the muscles of the shoulder are larger still.

MASSES AND MOVEMENTS OF THE BODY

The masses of the head, chest and pelvis are unchanging. Whatever their surface form or markings, they are as **masses** which can be conceived as **blocks**.

The conception of the figure must begin with the thought of these blocks in their relation to each other. They are to be thought of first as one thinks of the body of a wasp, with only **one line connecting them**, or without reference at all to connecting portions.

Ideally, in reference to gravitation, these blocks would be **balanced symmetrically** over each other. But rarely in fact, and in action never, is this the case. In their relations to each other they are limited to the three possible planes of movement. They may be:

- **Bent** forward or back in the sagittal plane
- **Twisted** in the horizontal plane
- **Tilted** in the transverse plane.

Invariably all three movements are present, to different degrees.

In these various movements, the **motion of the spine** provides the greatest limitation. The spine is the structure that connects each part of the body with another. It is a strong column occupying almost the **centre** or **axis of the body**, of alternating discs of bone and very elastic cartilage. Each segment is a joint, whose lever extends backward to the long groove of the back. Such movement as the spine allows, the muscles also allow, and are finally connected by the wedges or lines of the actual contour.

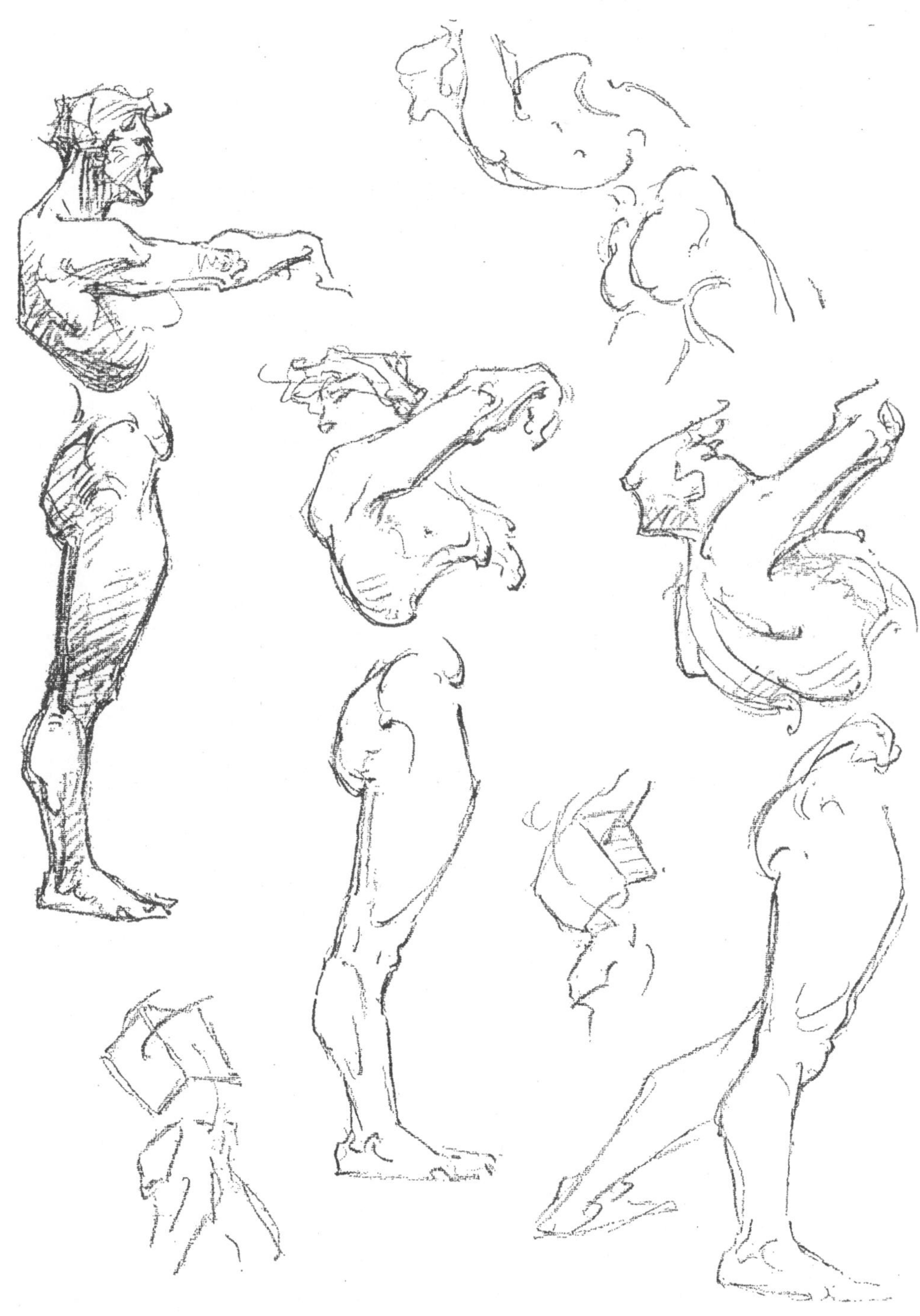

CONSTRUCTION

MASSES AND MOVEMENTS OF THE BODY: TILTING OF THE MASSES

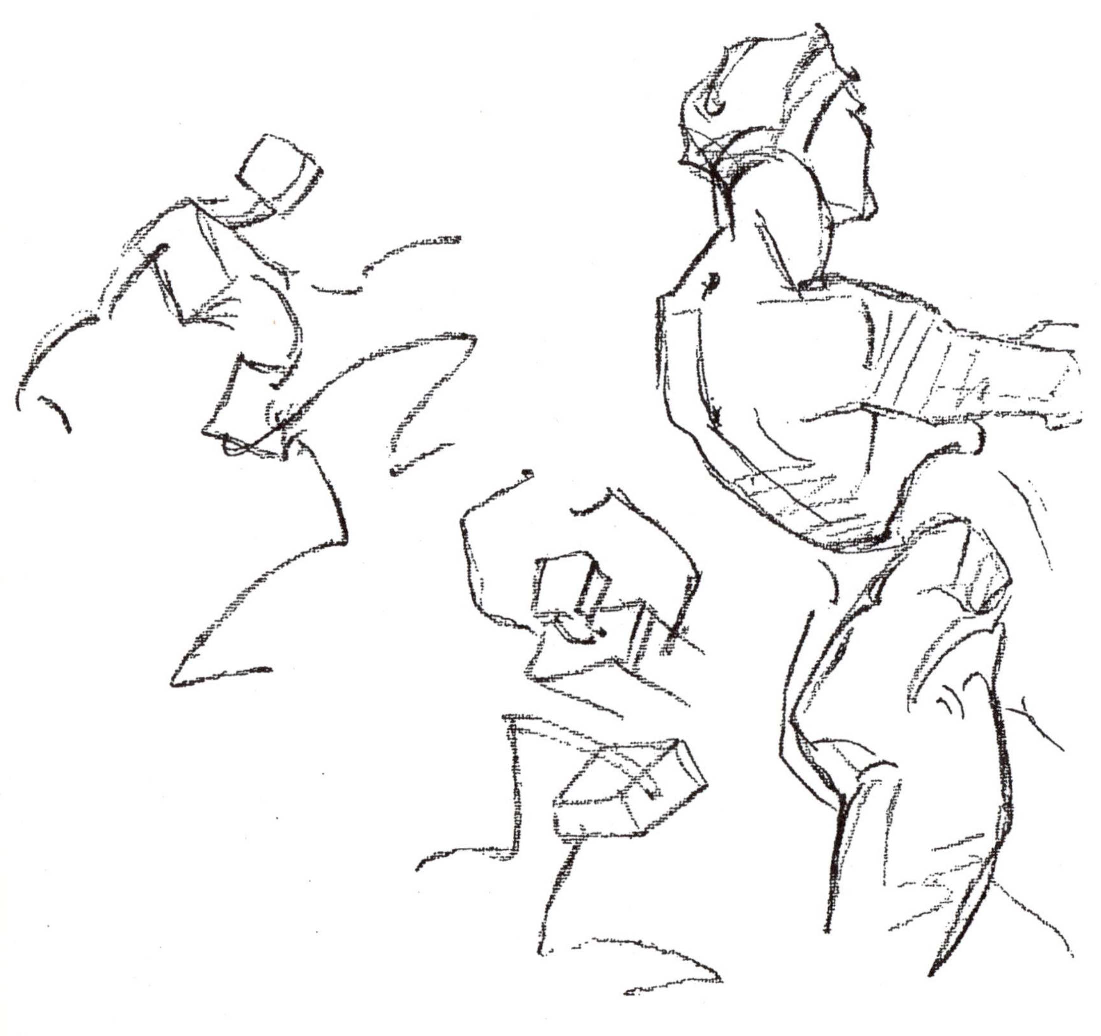

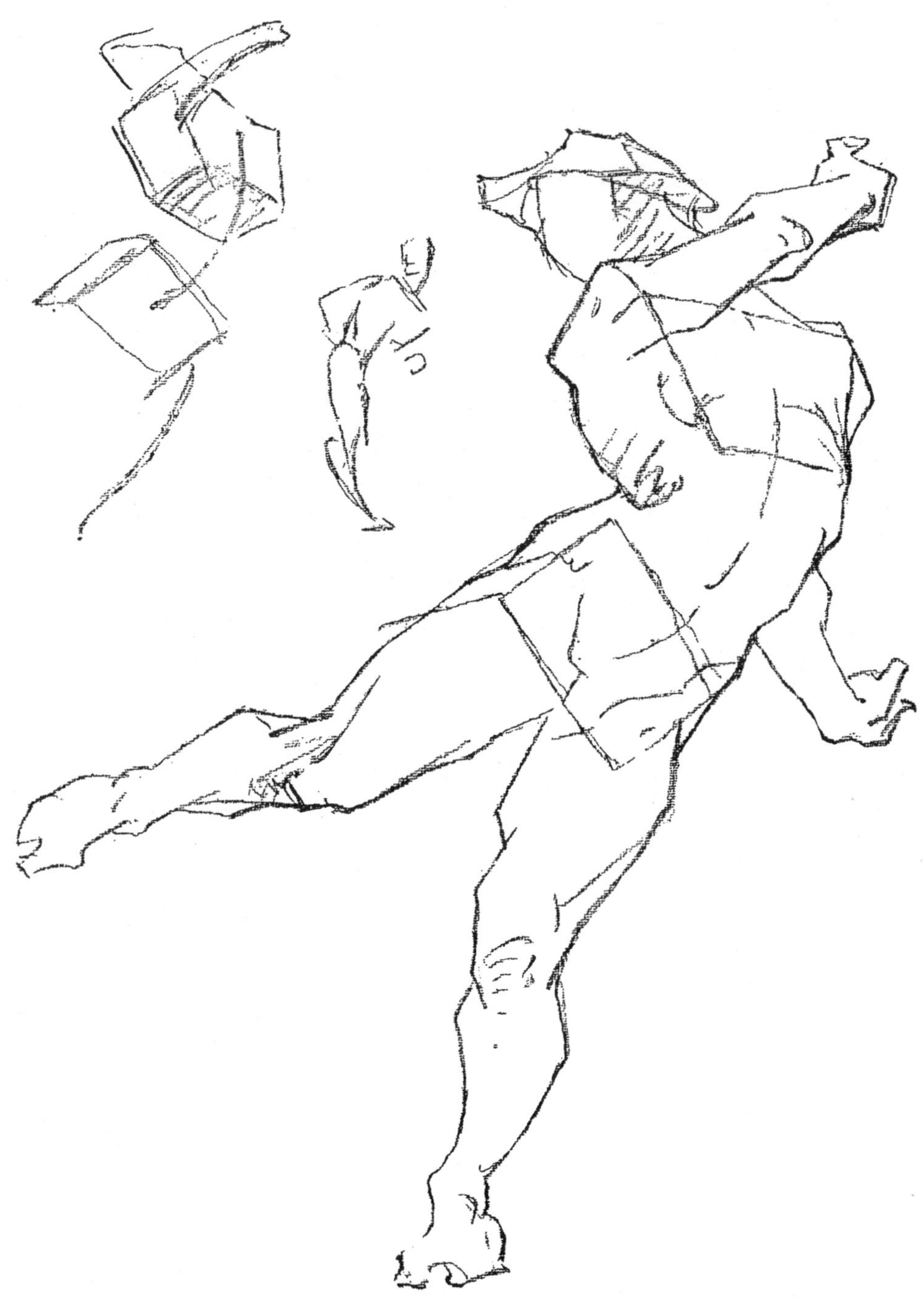

CONSTRUCTION

THE HORIZONTAL AND VERTICAL PLANES

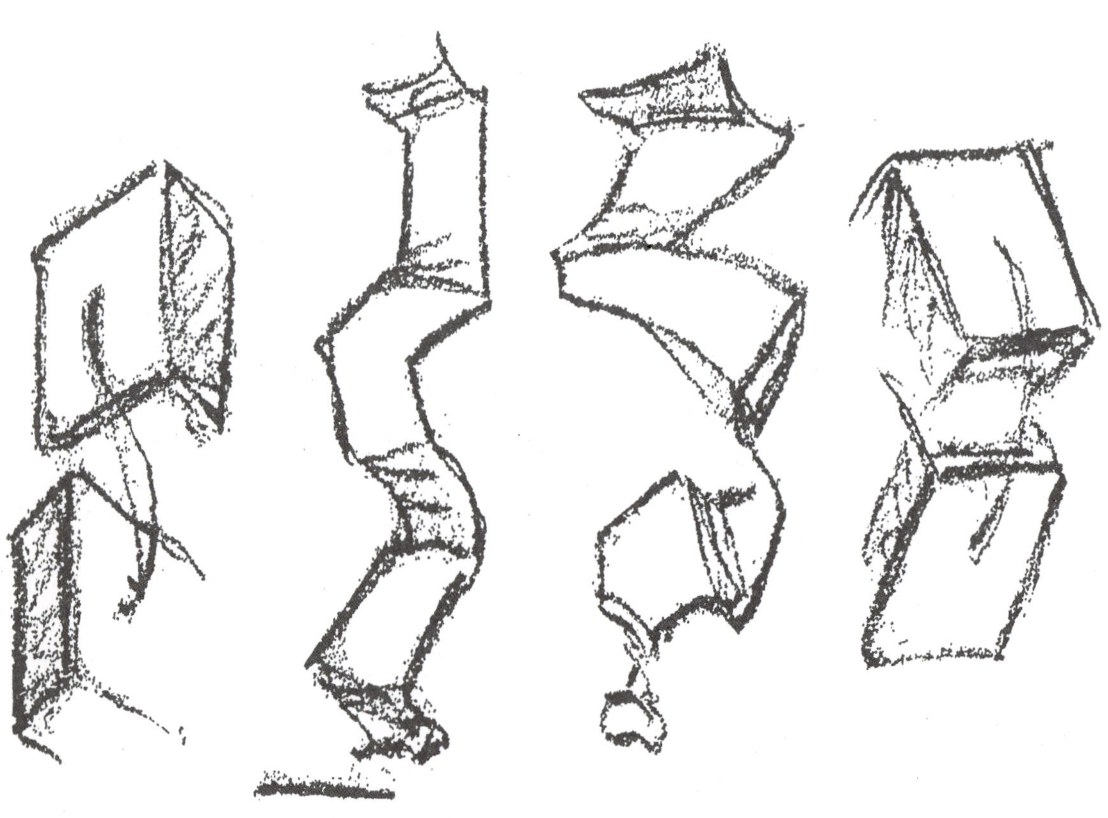

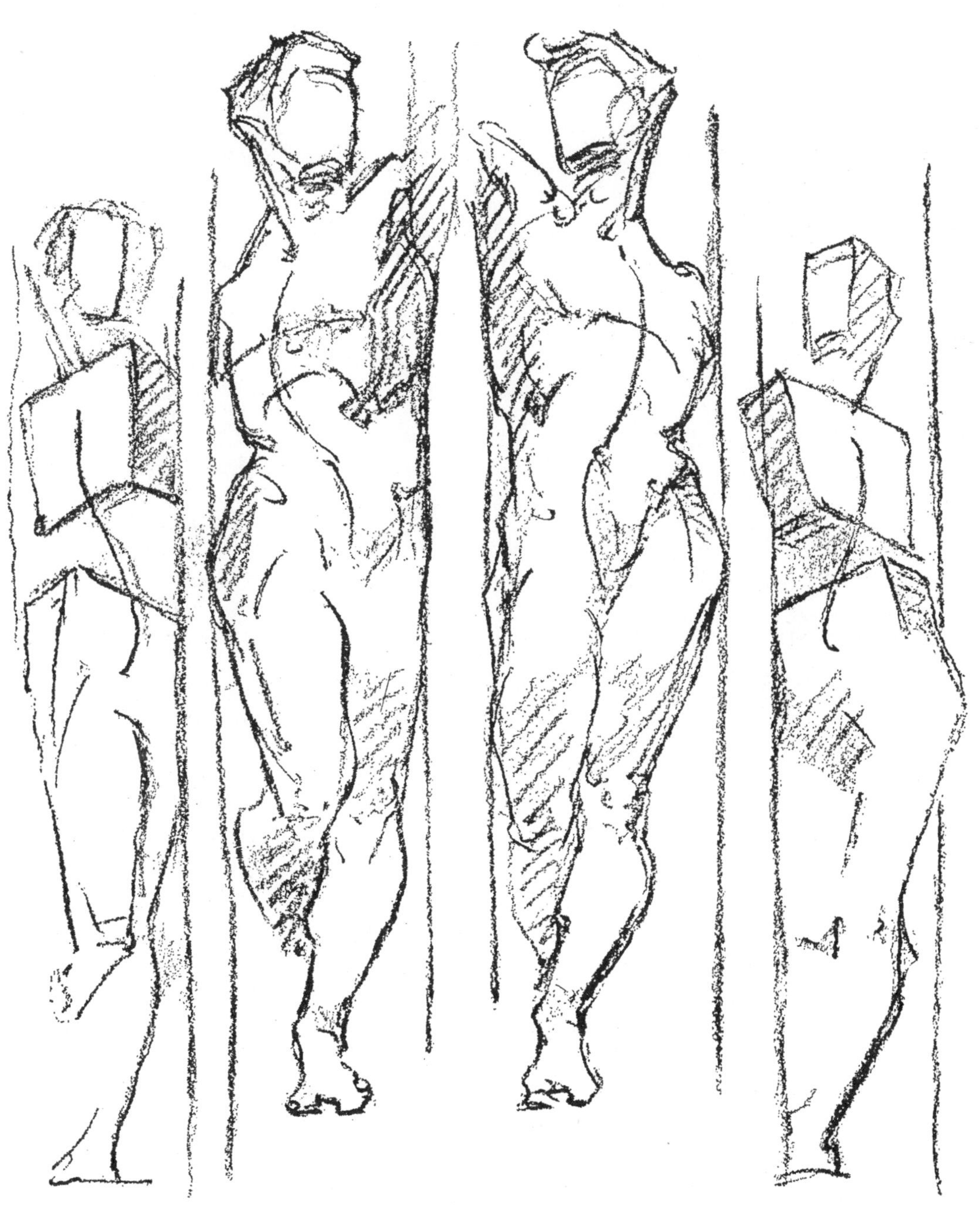

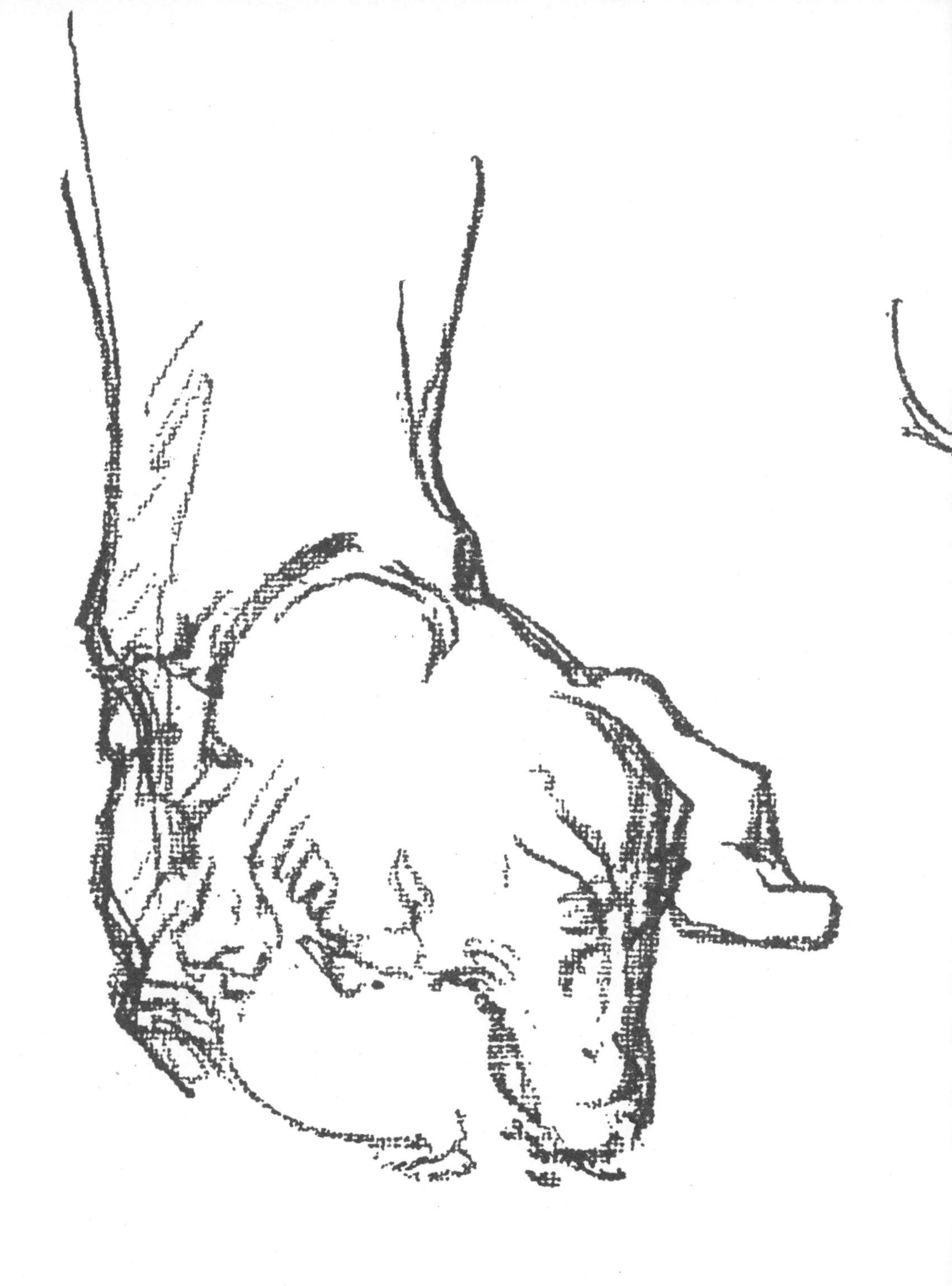

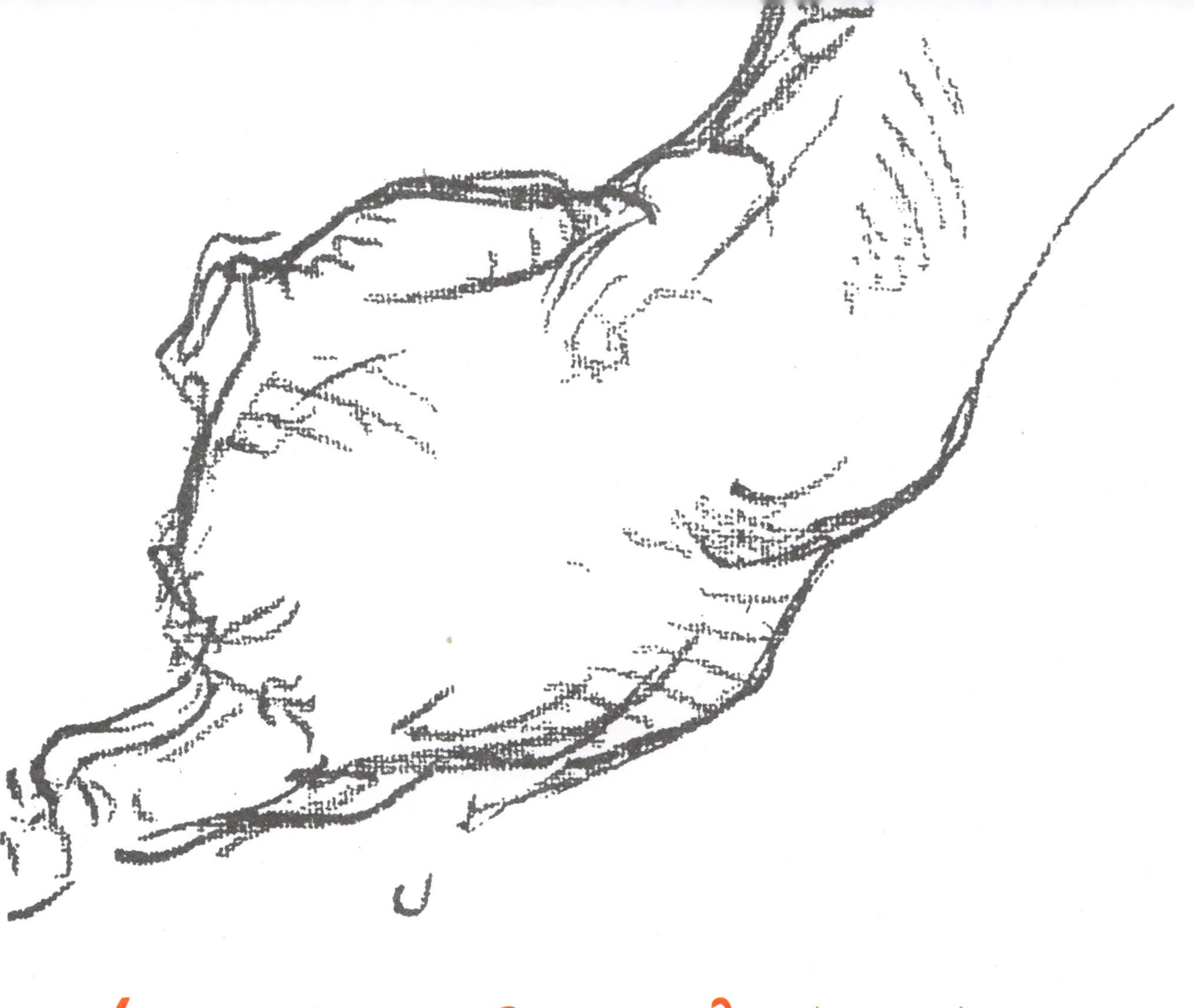

Hands & Wrists

ANATOMY OF THE HAND

In the hand are four bones, continuous with those of the fingers, called *metacarpals* (*meta*, beyond, *carpus*, wrist). They are covered by tendons on the back, and on the front by tendons, the muscles of the thumb and little finger, and skin pads.

ANATOMY

There is a very slight movement like opening a fan between these bones. They converge on the wrist bones and are morticed almost solidly to them. The hand moves with the wrist. The dorsal tendons converge more sharply than the bones. The short muscles of the hand, crossing only one joint, the knuckle, and moving the fingers individually, lie deep between the metacarpal bones and so are called *interossei*. They are in two sets, back and front, or ***dorsal*** and ***palmar***.

The *palmar interossei* are **collectors**, drawing the fingers toward the middle finger, and so are fastened to the inner side of each joint except that of the middle finger itself. The *dorsal interossei* are **spreaders**, drawing away from the centre, and so are fastened to both sides of the middle finger and to the outside of the other joints.

In the thumb and little fingers the muscles of this set are called ***abductors***, and being in exposed positions, are larger. That of the first finger forms a prominent bulge between it and the thumb; that of the little finger forms a long fleshy mass reaching to the wrist.

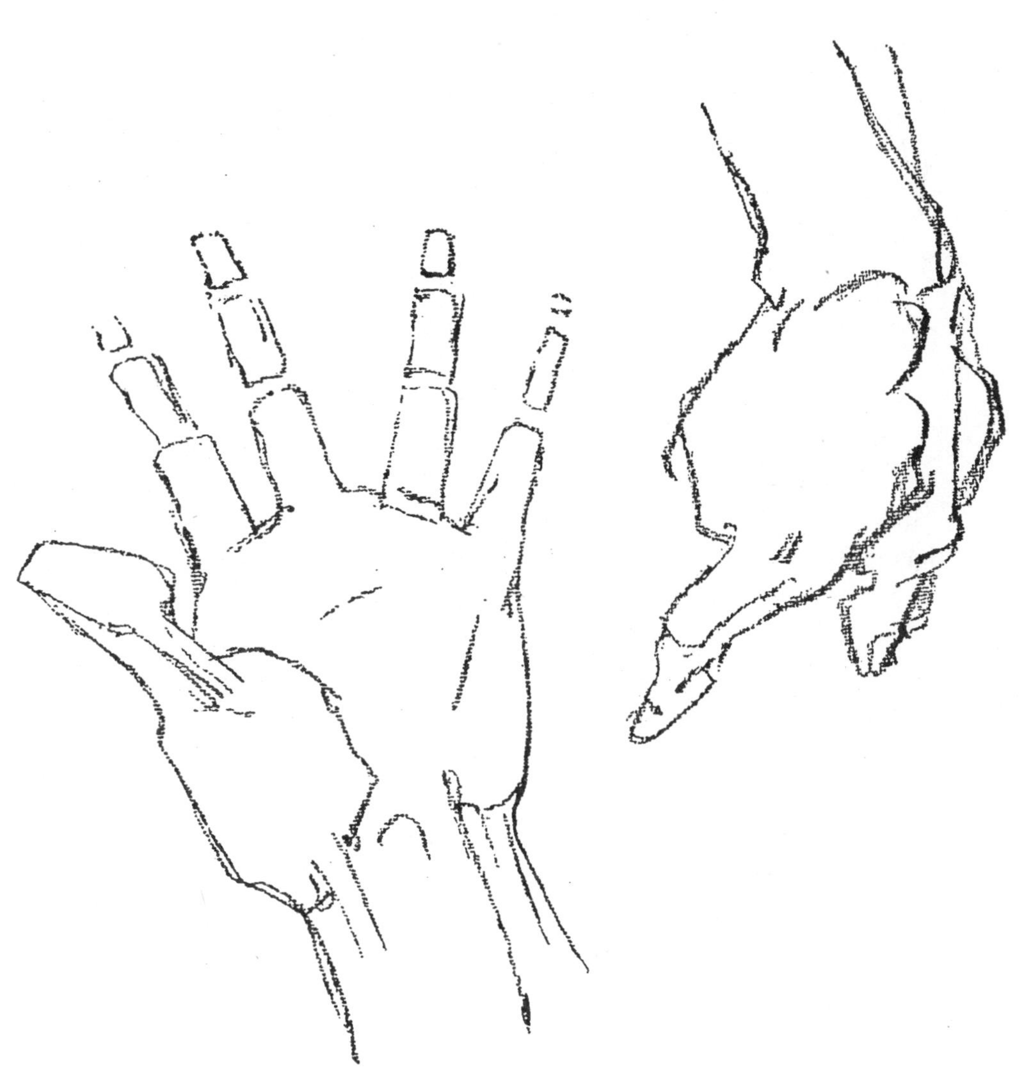

MASSES

The masses of the hand are two to one greater than that of the hand proper, the other that of the thumb.

The **first** of these is beveled from knuckles to wrist on the edge; from wrist to knuckles on the flat side, and from first to little finger from side to side. It is slightly arched across the back. Somewhat more arched are the knuckles, concentric around the base of the thumb.

The **second** knuckle is larger and higher than the rest; the first is lower on its thumb side, where it has an overhang, as has also the knuckle of the little finger, due to their exposed positions.

Belonging to the hand is the **pyramidal mass** of the first segment of the **thumb**, which joins on at an angle, never quite flat with the hand, and bending under it to more than a right angle with its flat surface.

The thumb may be drawn in until only its root bulges beyond the lateral line of the hand, and may be carried out to a great angle with it. In this latter position its first segment forms a triangle whose base is the side of the hand, equal to it's length; whose height is, on the *palmar* surface, equal to the width of the hand, and on the dorsal surface, almost as great.

On the **little finger side**, the form is given by the *abductor* muscle and the overhang of the knuckle, by which the curve of that side is carried well up to the middle of the first segment of the finger. The pad of the palm overlaps the wrist below and the knuckles above, reaching to the middle of the first segment of the fingers.

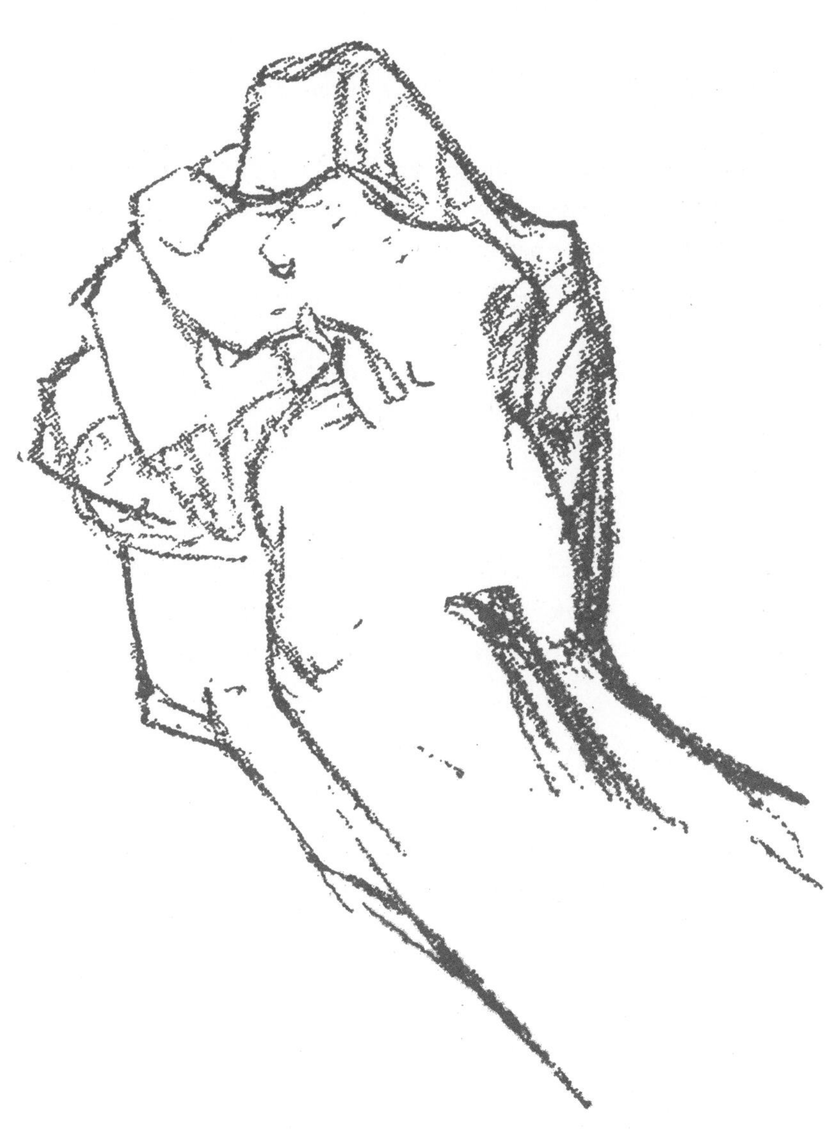

ANATOMY OF THE WRIST

Morticed with the bones of the hand are the bones of the wrist; the two make one mass and the hand moves with the wrist. Eight bones (*carpal* bones) in two rows make the arch of the wrist; in size they are like deformed dice.

The two pillars of this arch are seen on the ***palmar* side**, prominent under the thumb and the little finger. The latter is the heel of the hand but the arch is thicker and a bit higher on the thumb side.

Under it passes the long flexor tendons to the fingers and thumb. The dome of the arch is seen on the back with an apex at the trapezium under the first finger. It is crossed by the long *extensor* tendons of the fingers, which converge on its outer half.

MASSES OF THE WRIST

Its width is twice its thickness. It is narrower both ways where it joins the arm, giving an appearance of construction. There is always a step-down from the back of the arm, over the wrist, to the hand.

MOVEMENTS

Being solid with the hand, the wrist moves with the hand on the forearm. Its movement is like that of a boat in water; easily tipping

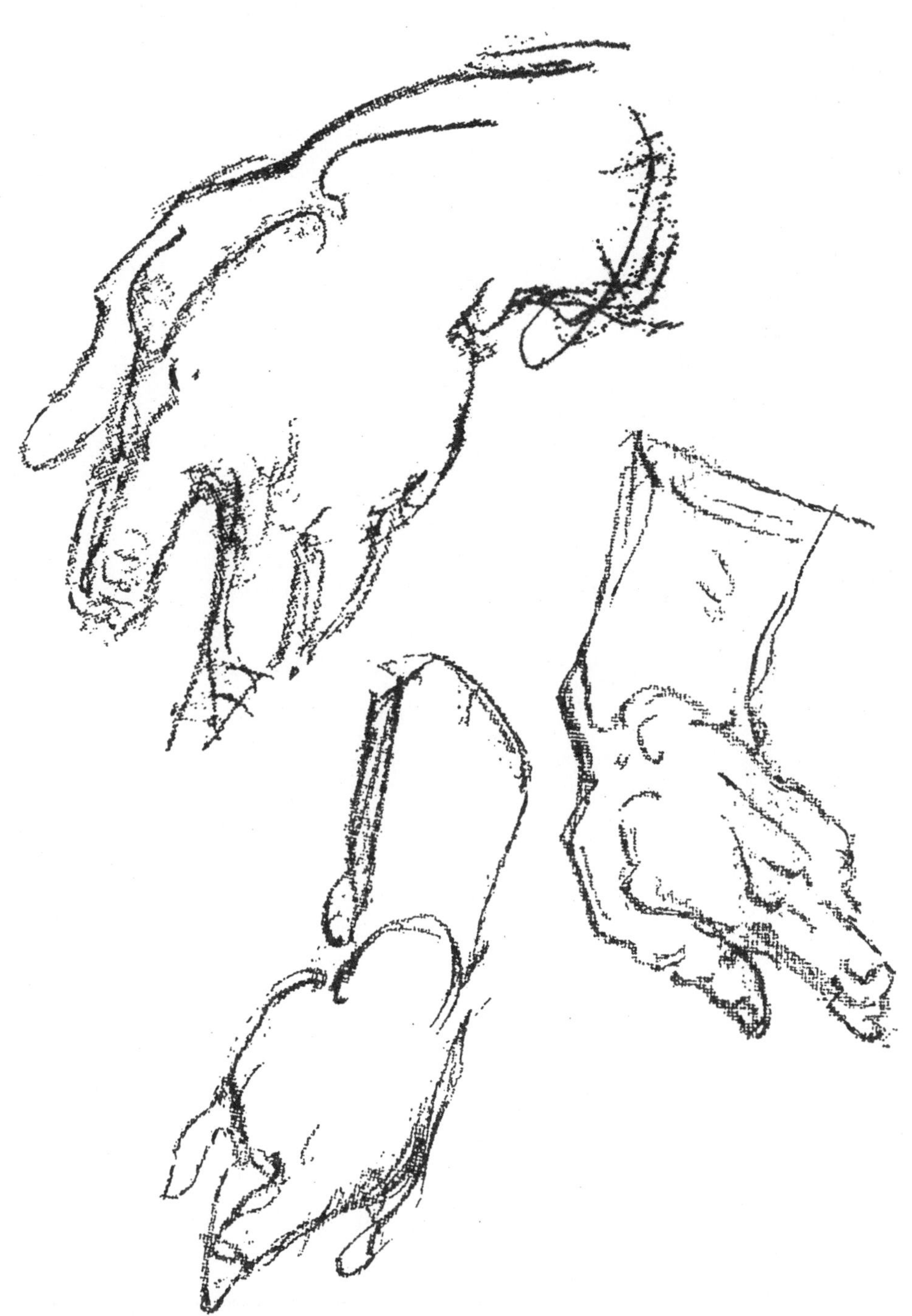

sideways (**flexion** and **extension**) with more difficulty tilting endways (**side-bending**) which in combination give some **rotary movement**, but having no twisting movement at all. This movement is accomplished by the forearm.

The inset of this boat-shaped joint with the arm gives the appearance of constriction. The prow, under the thumb, is higher than the stern under the little finger. When fully extended, the back of the hand with the arm makes almost a right angle; when fully flexed, the *palmar* surface makes almost a right angle; the total movement therefore is slightly less than two right angles.

When the **wrist is fully flexed**, it forms at the back a great curve over which the *extensor* tendons are drawn taut, so much so that the fingers can never be closed when the wrist is fully flexed. In this position the *flexor* tendons are raised prominently under the skin.

When hand and arm lie extended along a flat surface, it is the heel of the hand that is in contact, the arm bones being lifted from the surface. To the four corners of the wrist are fastened muscles; two in front (*flexor carpi radialis* and *flexor carpi ulnaris*) and two behind (*extensor carpi radialis* and *extensor carpi ulnaris*, the former being double).

By their contraction **the wrist is moved in all directions**, except twisting, which movement is produced not in the wrist but in the forearm. Only the tendons cross the wrist, the muscular bodies lying in the forearm.

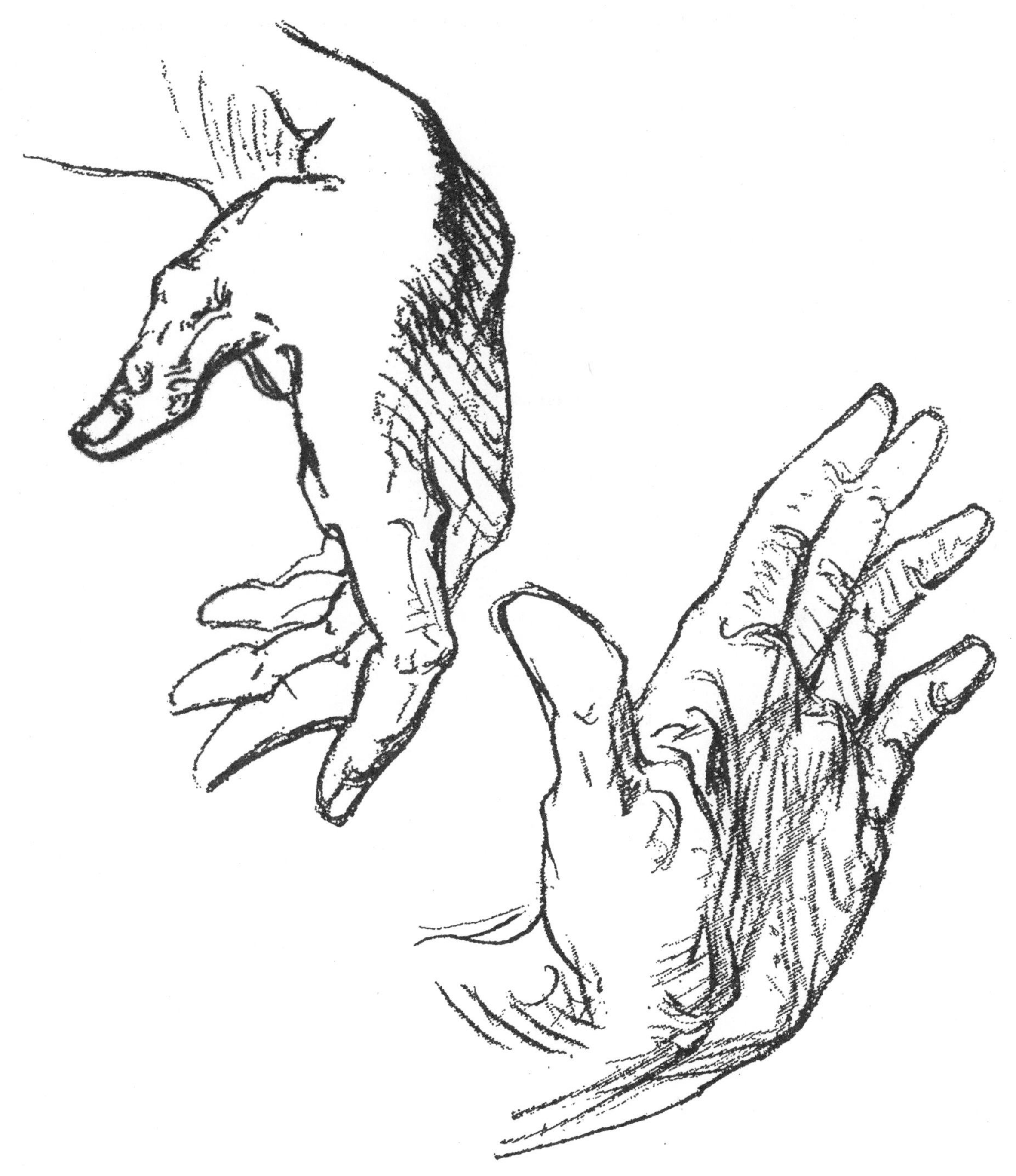

THE HAND

Some fist shapes for reference.

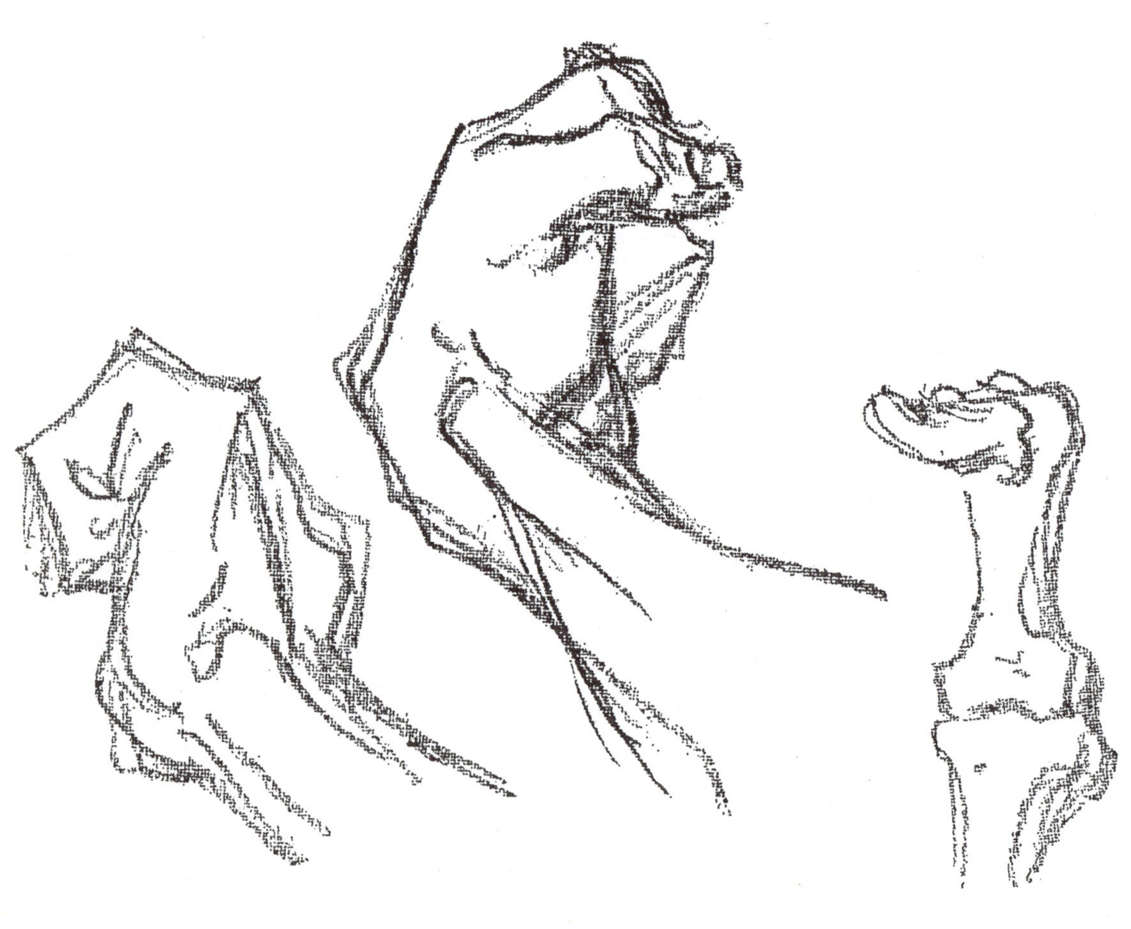

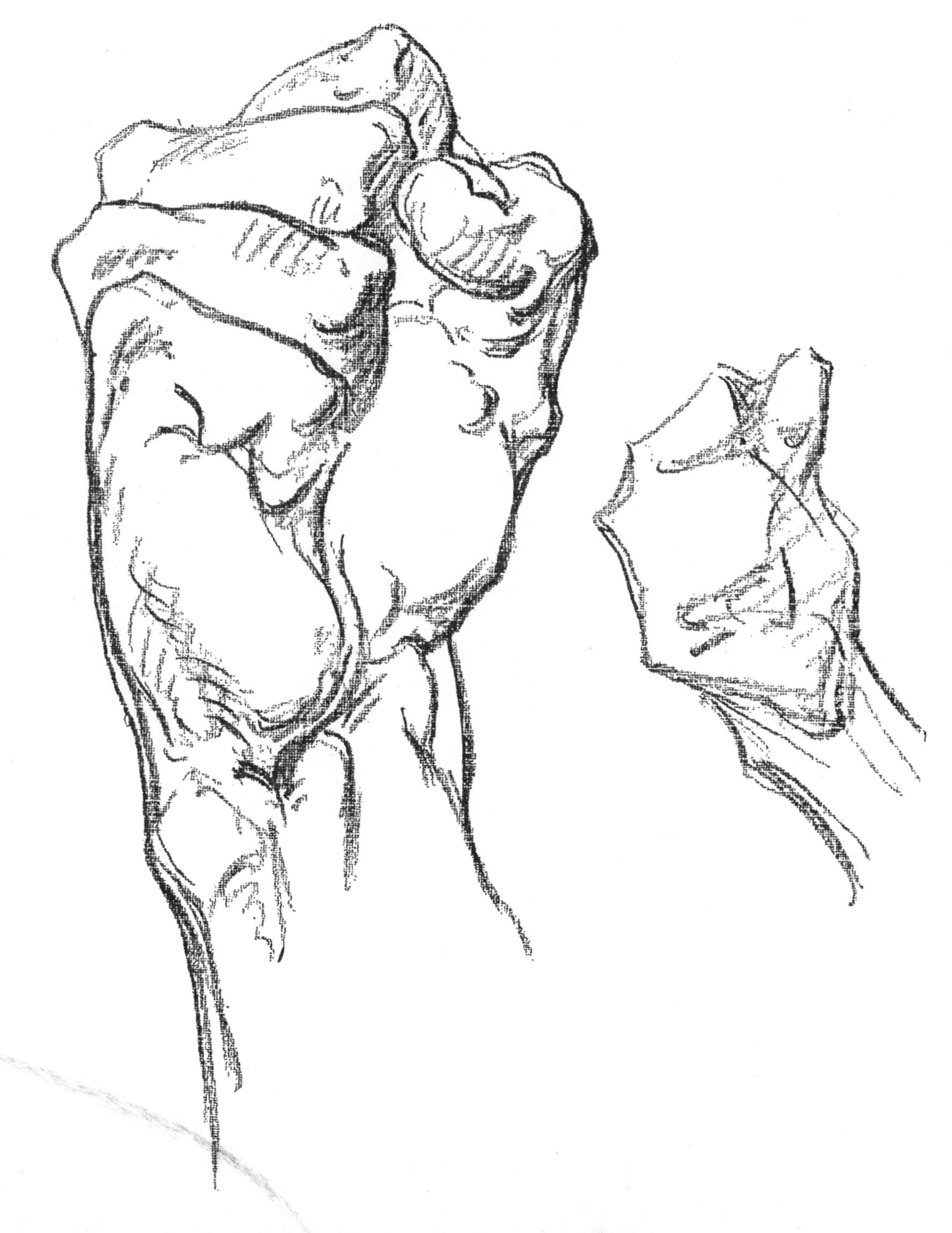

THE HAND

Some open hand shapes for reference.

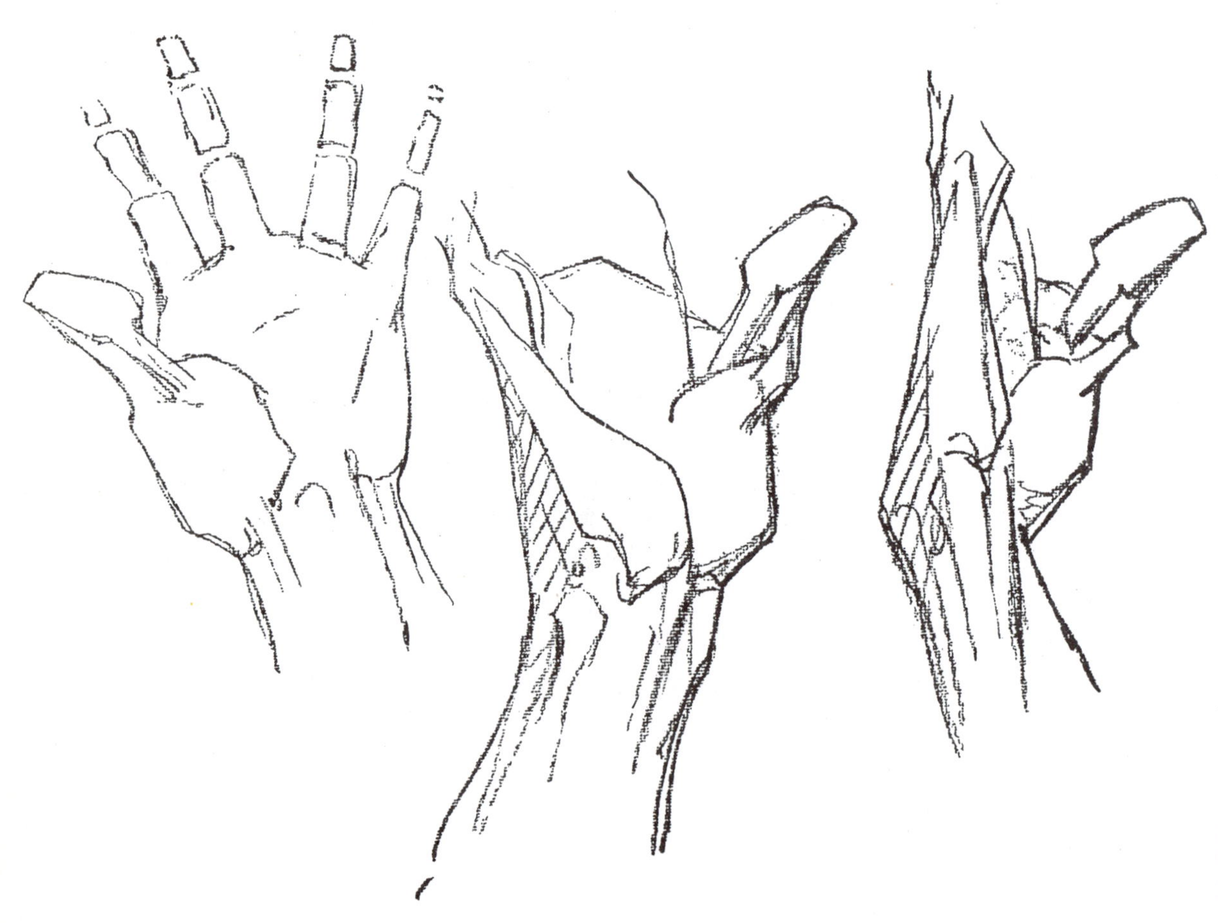

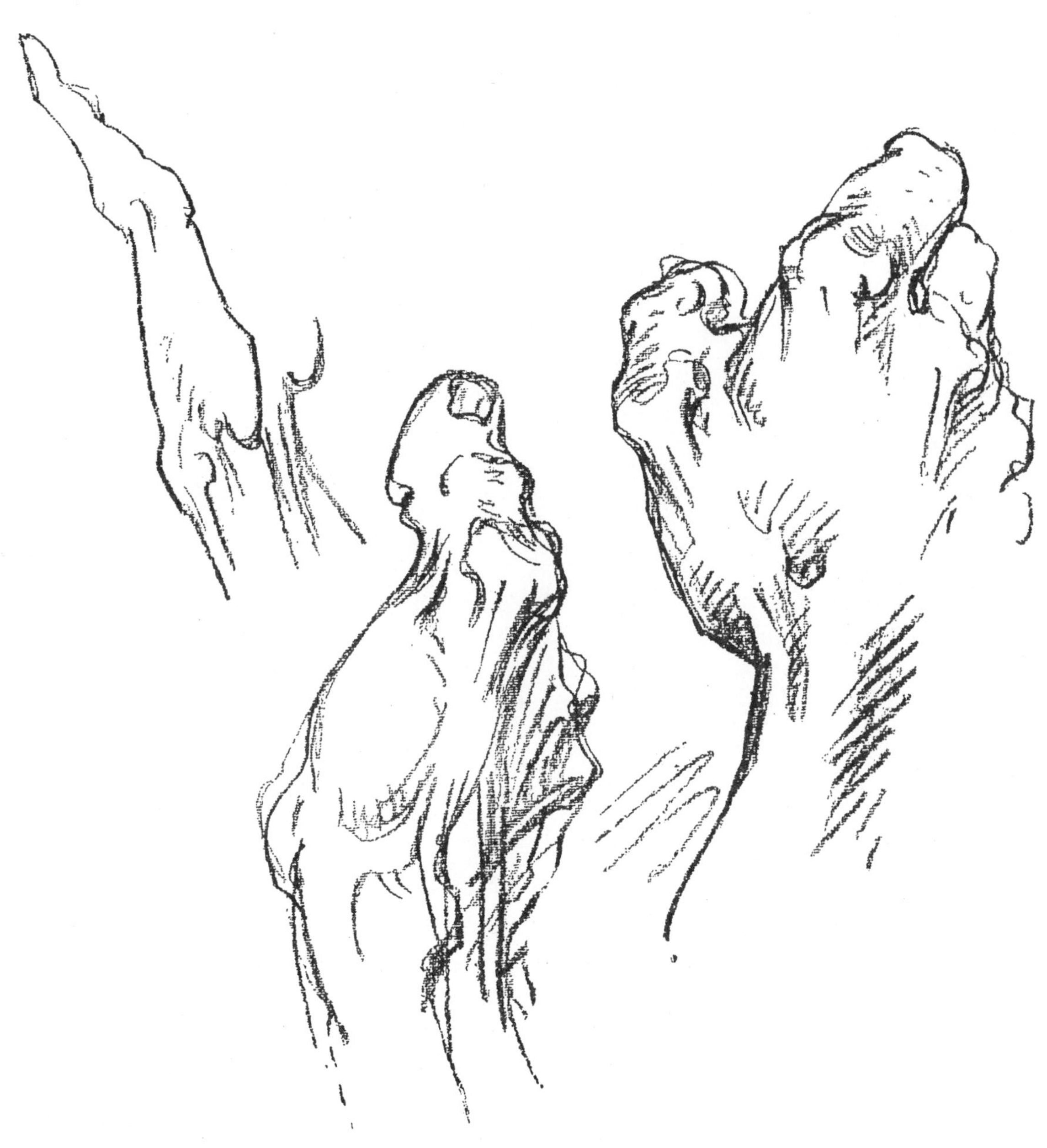

THE HAND

MUSCLES OF THE HAND: FRONT PALM VIEW

① *Abductor pollicis.*
② *Flexor brevis pollicis.*
③ *Abductor transversus pollicis.*
④ *Lumbricales.*
⑤ *Annular* ligament.
⑥ *Flexor brevis minimi digiti.*
⑦ *Abductor minimi digiti.*

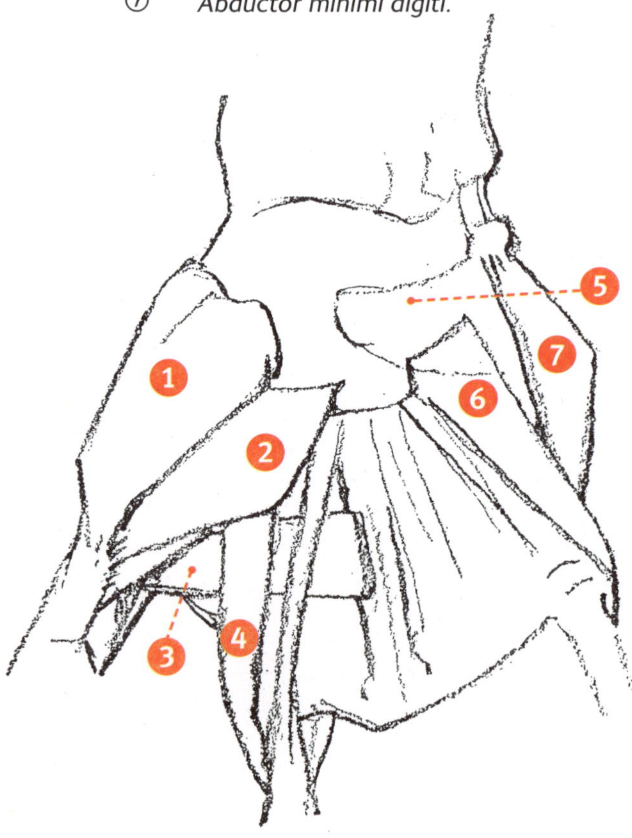

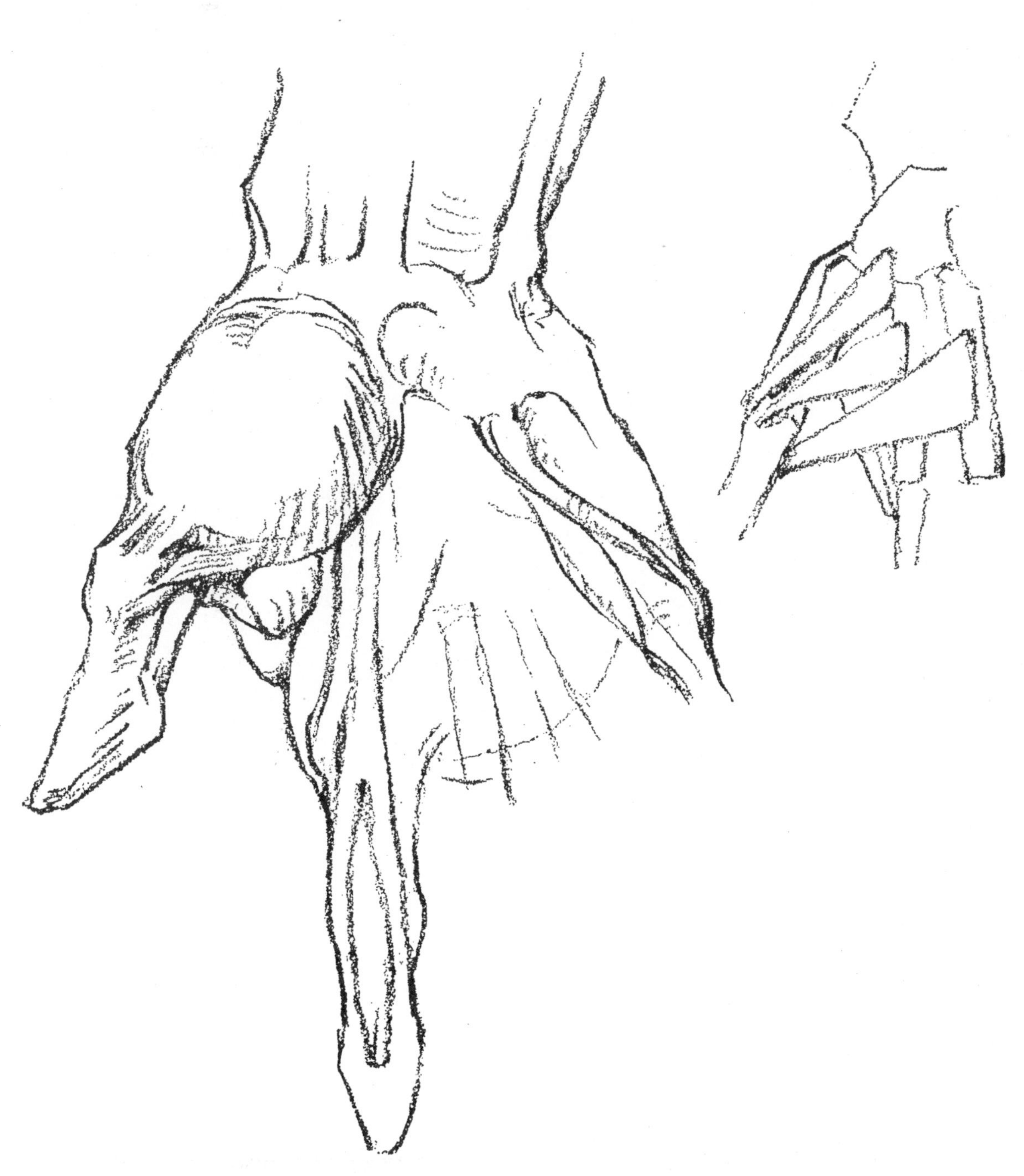

THE HAND

Some hand to finger shapes for reference.

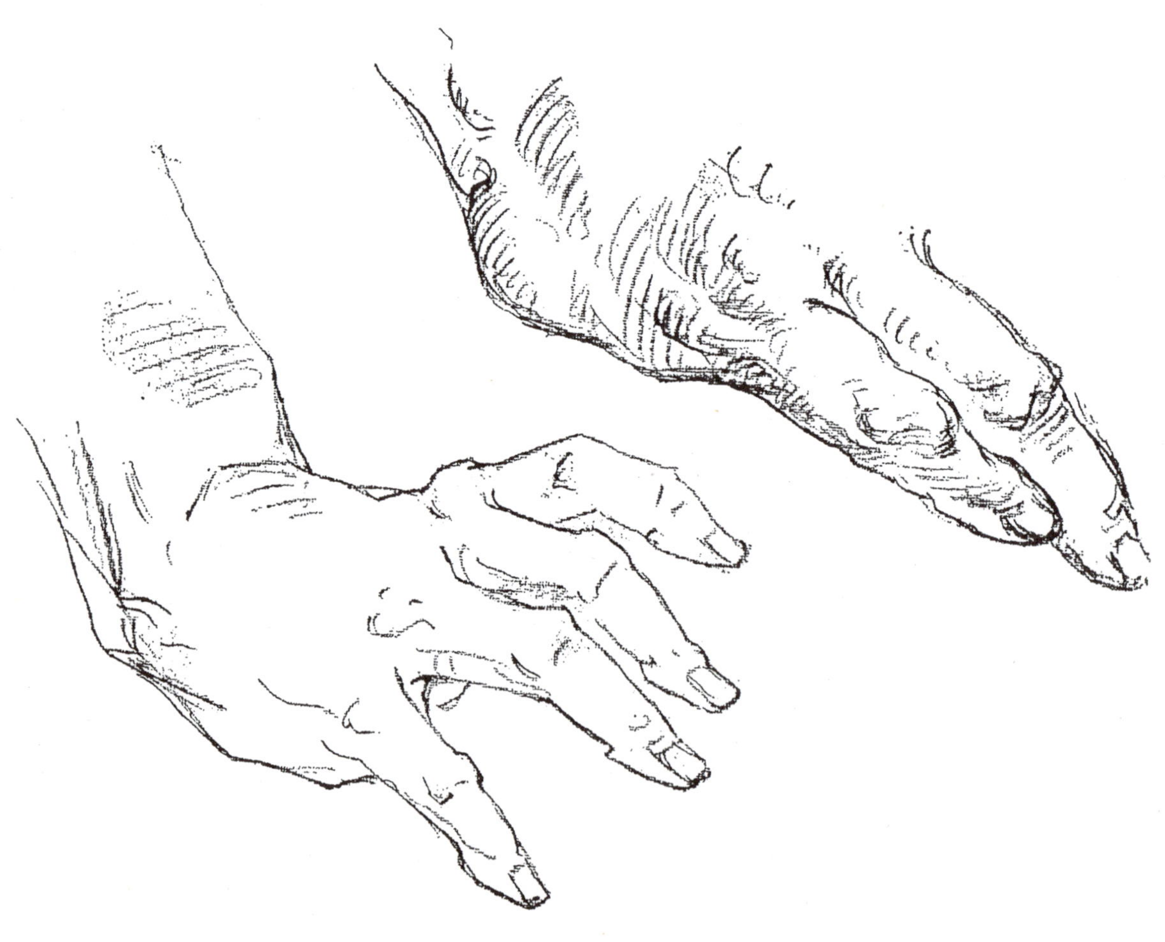

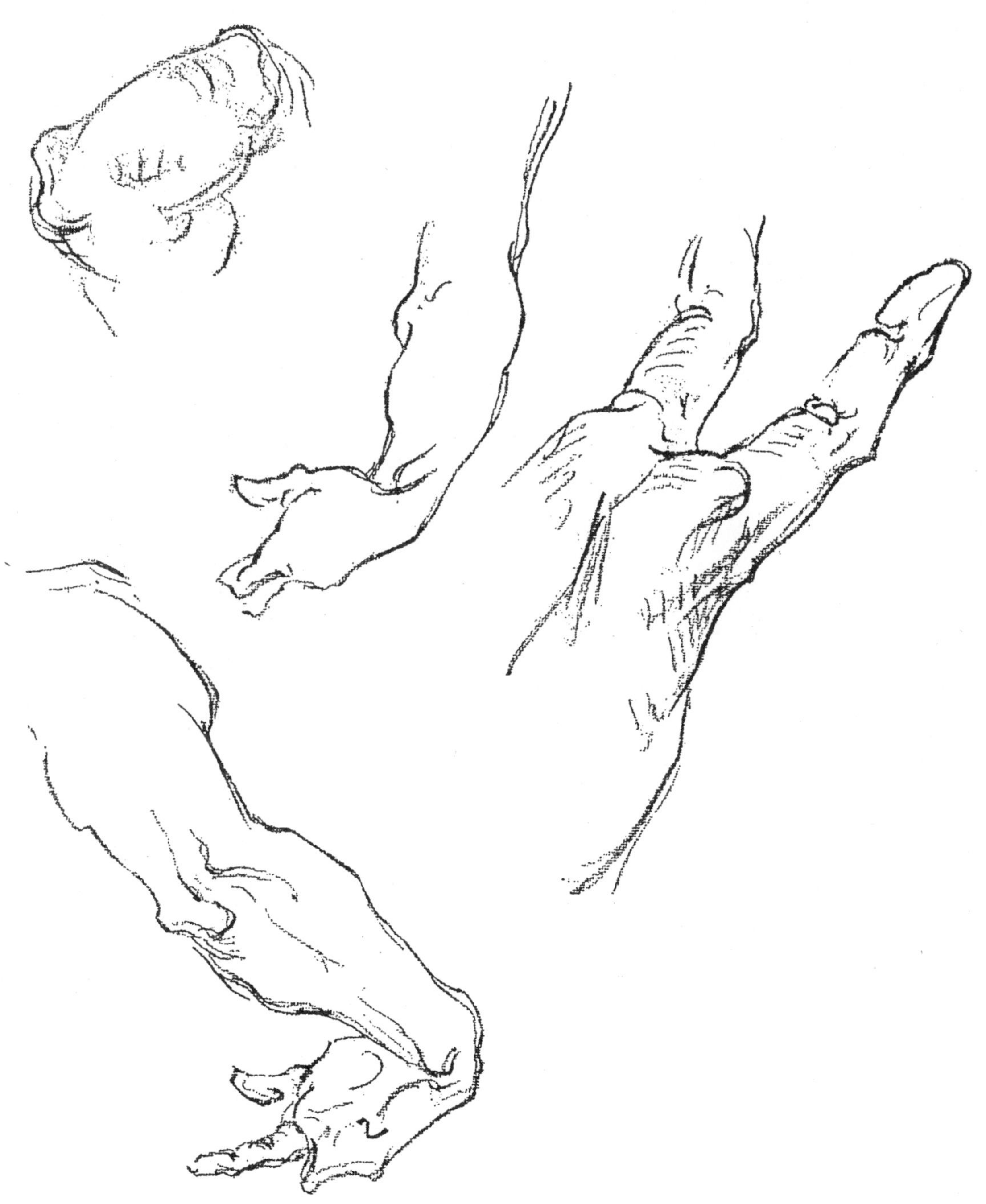

THE HAND

MUSCLES OF THE HAND: BACK VIEW

① First *dorsal interossei.*

② *Abductor pollicis.*

③ *Dorsal interossei.*

④ Tendons of *extensor communis digitorum.*

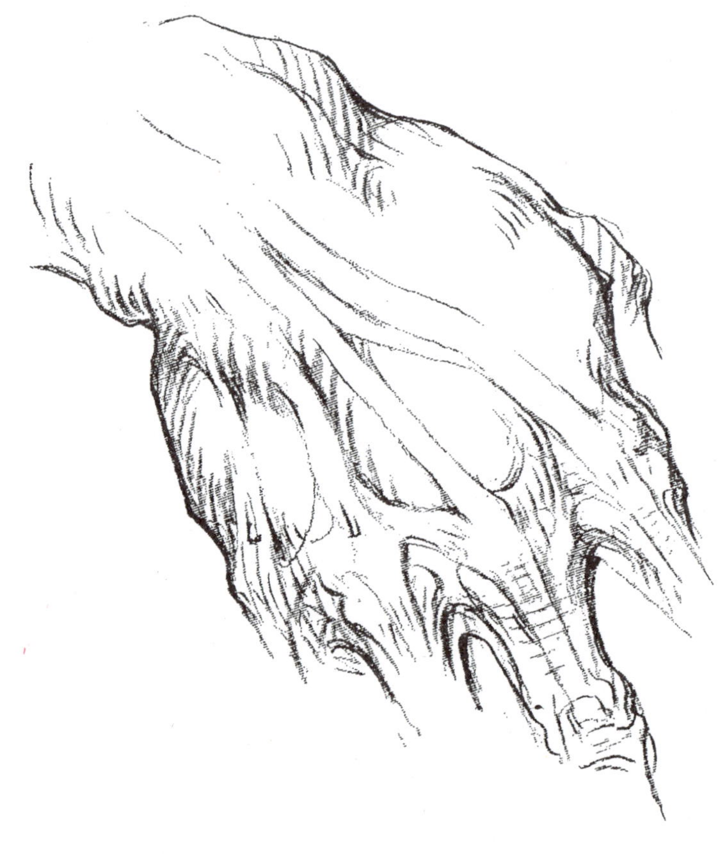

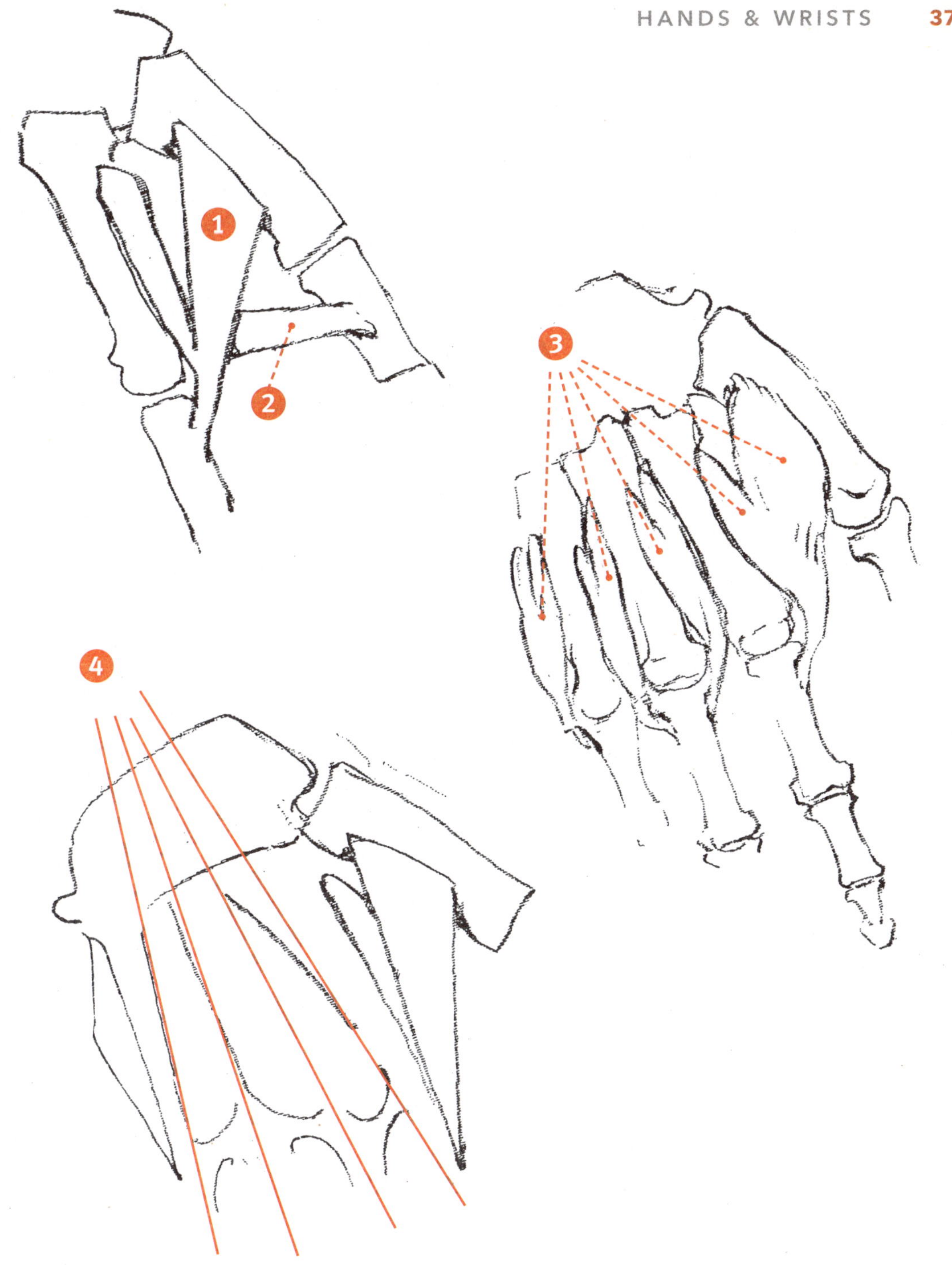
1
2
3
4

THE HAND

WEDGING OF THE WRIST: THUMB SIDE

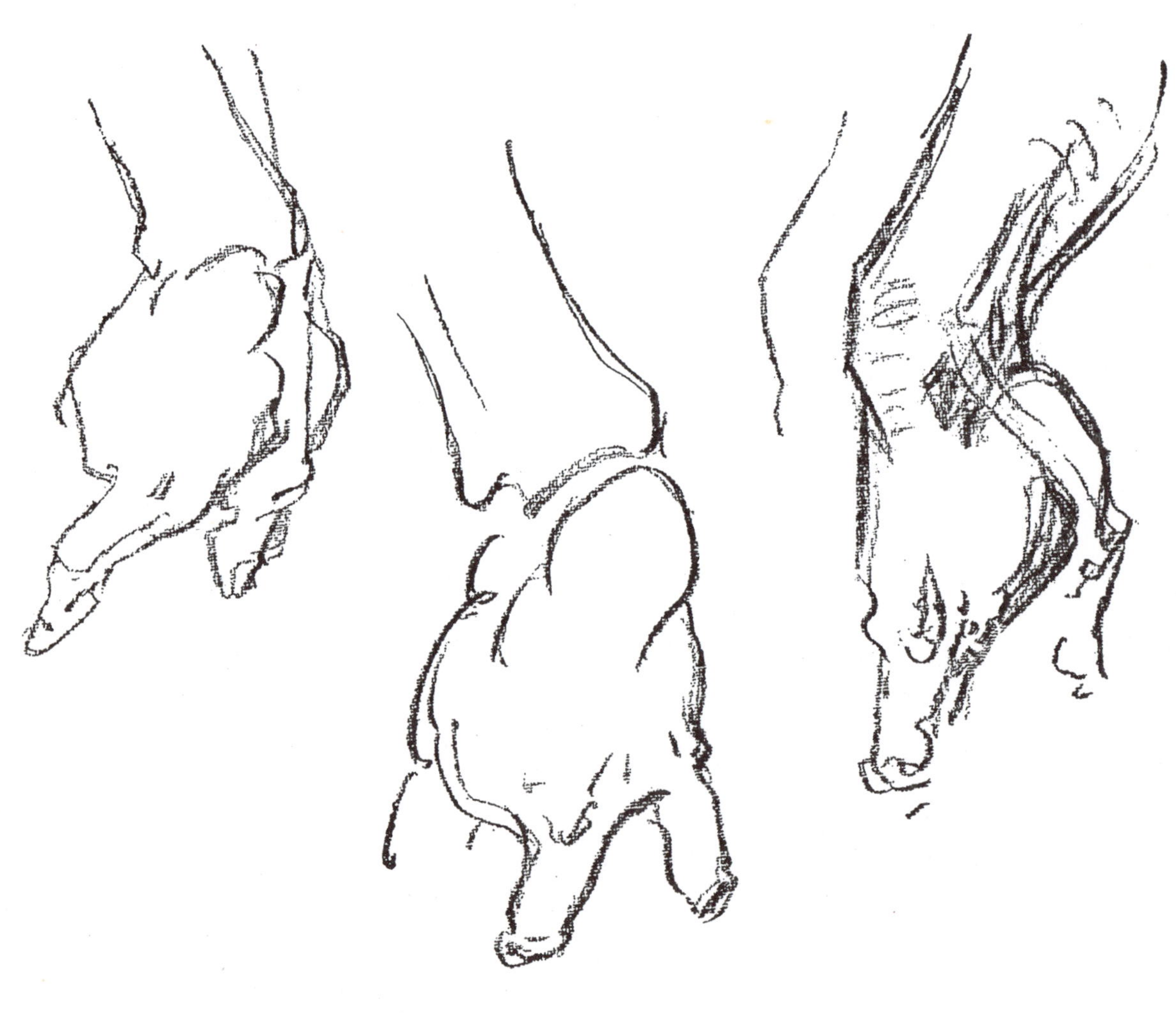

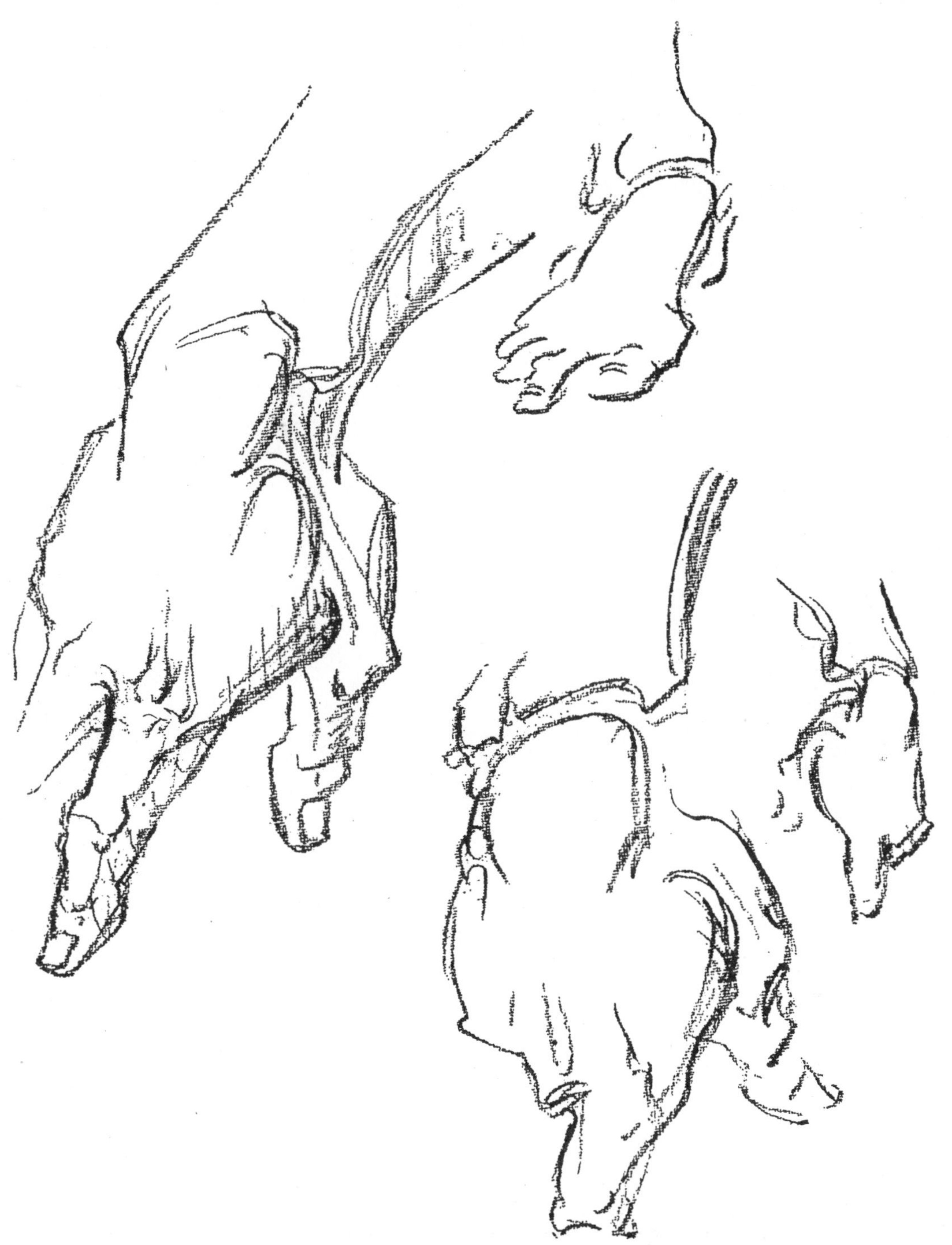

THE HAND

WEDGING OF THE WRIST: LITTLE FINGER SIDE

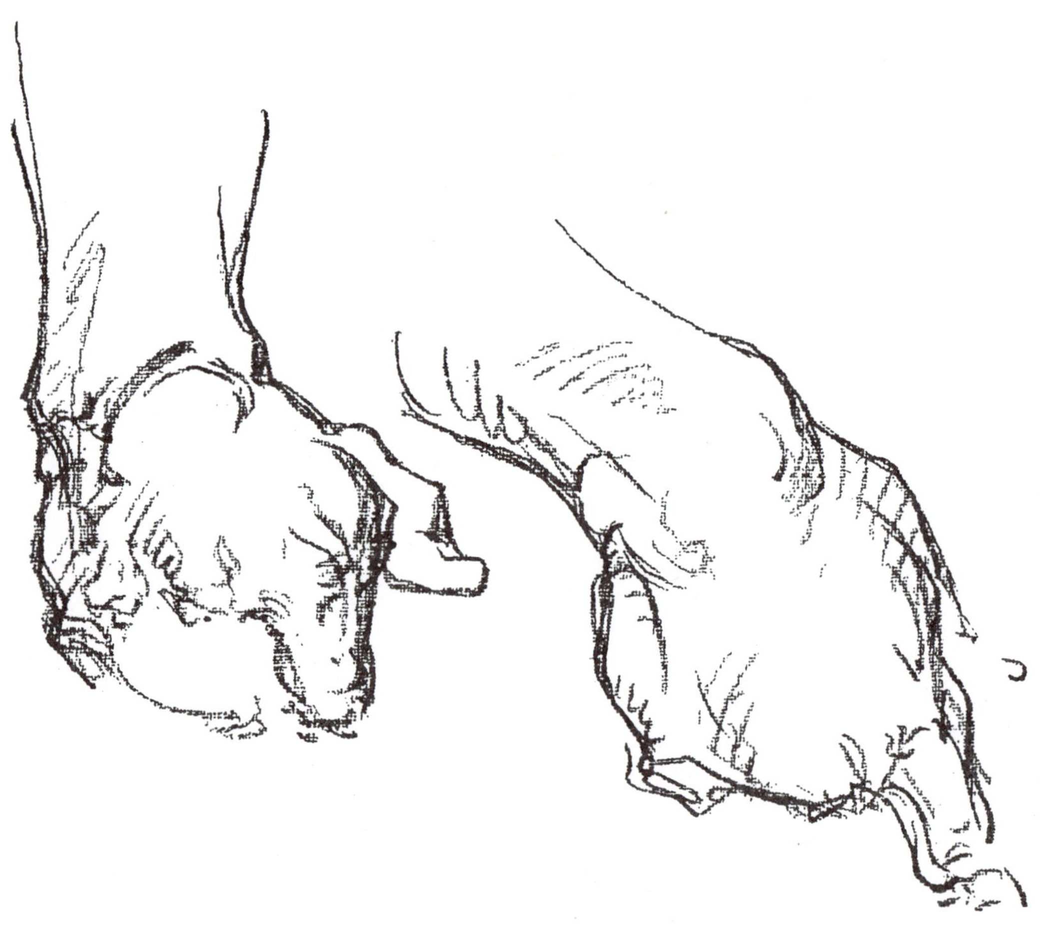

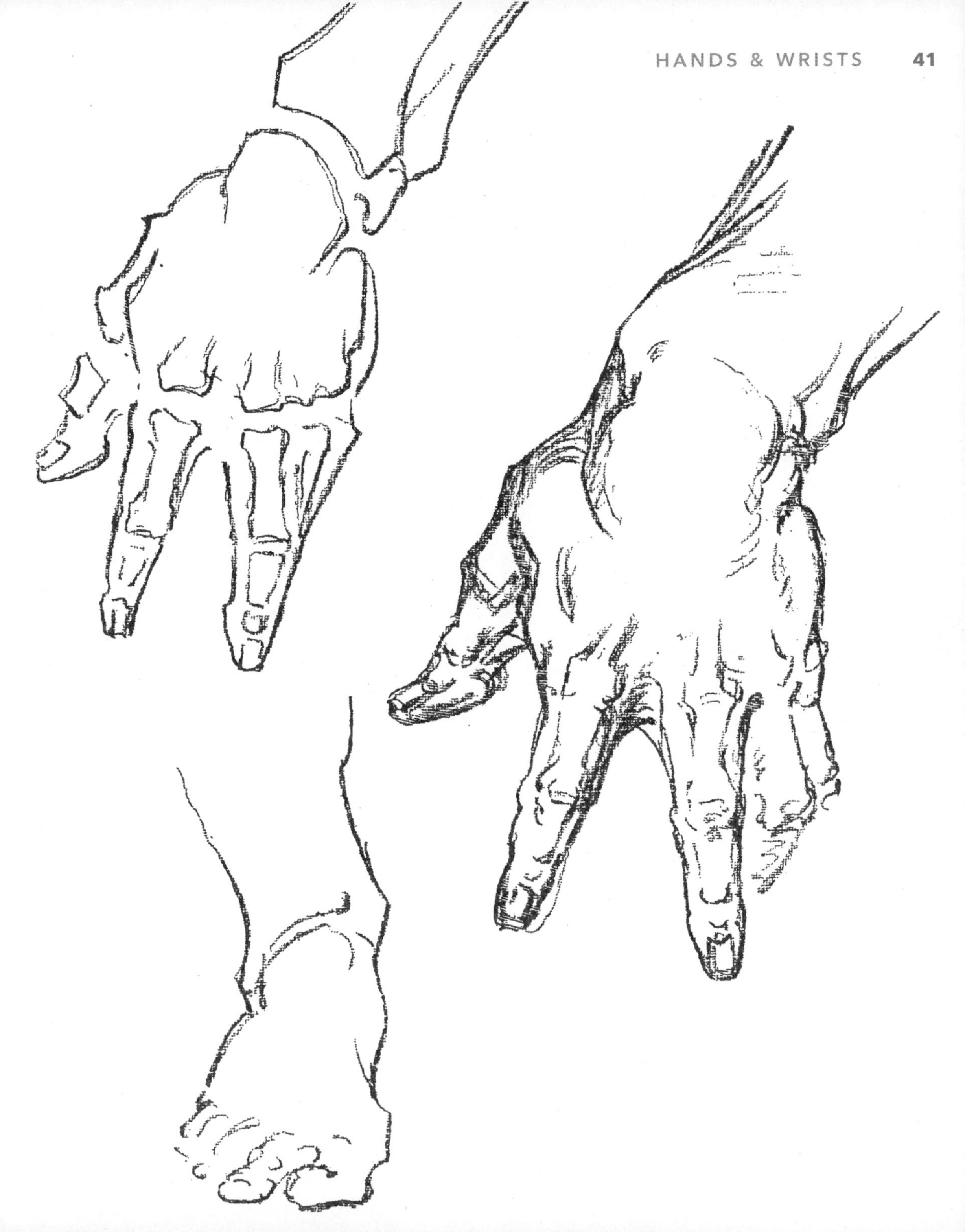

THE HAND

CONSTRUCTION

In the hand as in the figure there is an action and an inaction side. The side with the greatest angle is the action side, the opposite is the inaction or straight side. With the hand turned down (prone) and drawn toward the body, the thumb side is the action side, the little finger the inaction side. The inaction side is straight with the arm, while the thumb is almost at right angles with it.

The **inaction construction** line runs straight down the arm to the base of the little finger. The **action construction** line runs down the arm to the base of the thumb at the wrist, from there out to the middle joint, at the widest part of the hand; thence to the knuckle of the first finger, then to that of the second finger, and then joins the inaction line at the little finger.

With the hand still prone, but drawn from the body, the thumb side is the inaction side, and is straight with the arm, while the little finger is at almost right angles with it.

The inaction construction line now runs straight to the middle joint of the thumb, while the action line runs to the wrist on the little finger side, thence to the first joint, second, and so on.

These **construction lines, six in number**, are the same with the palm turned up, according as it is drawn in or out. They place the fingers and indicate the action and proportions of the hand.

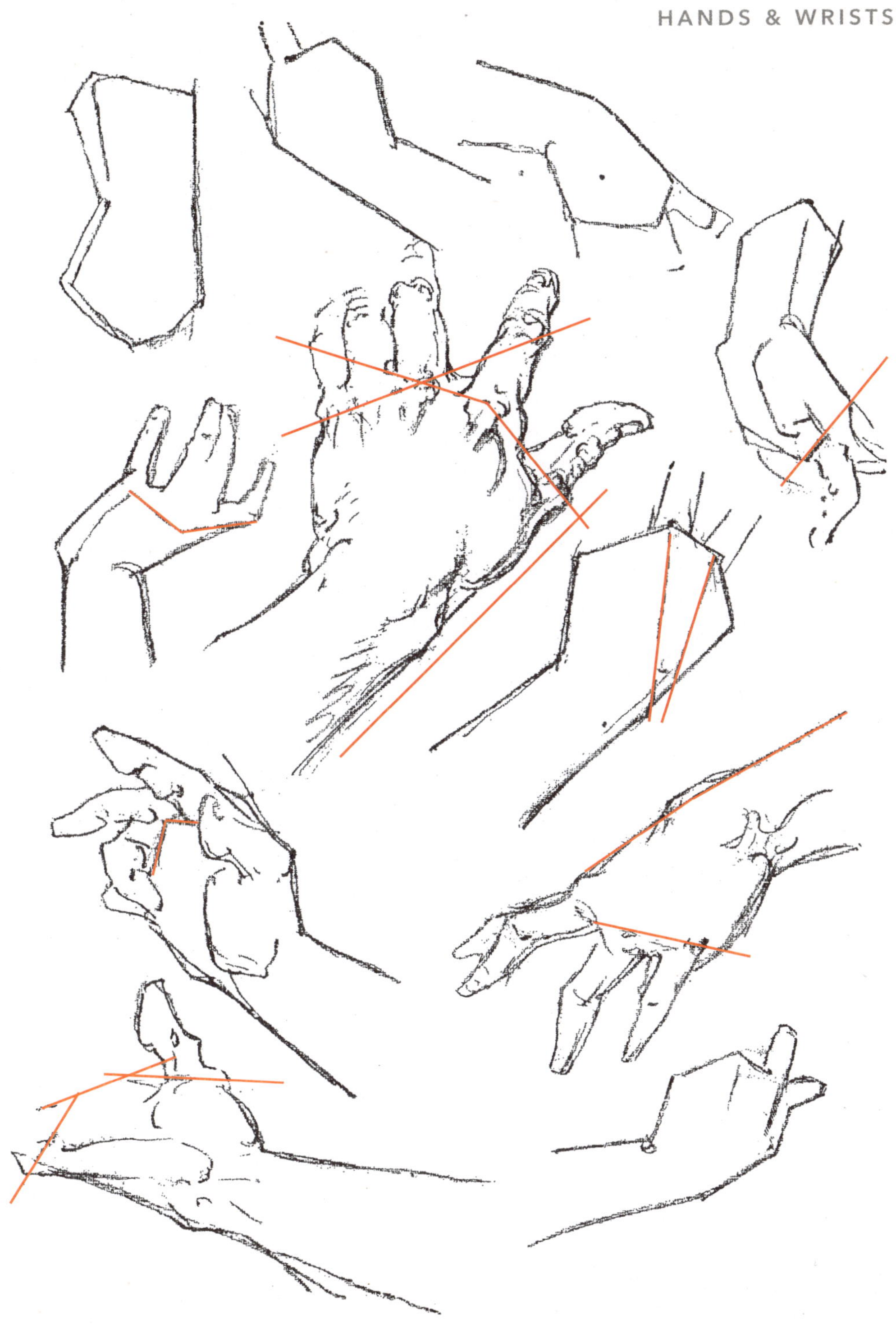

THE HAND

Some examples for reference.

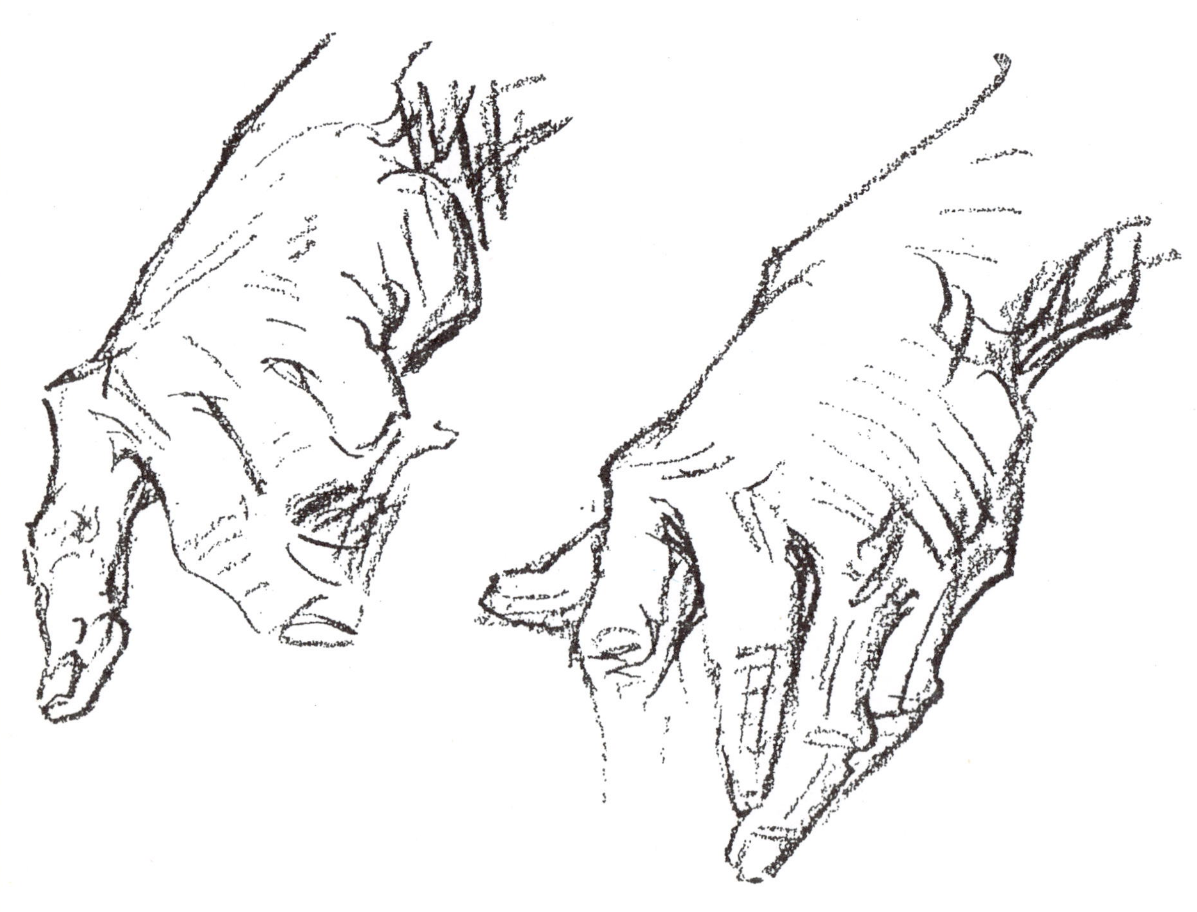

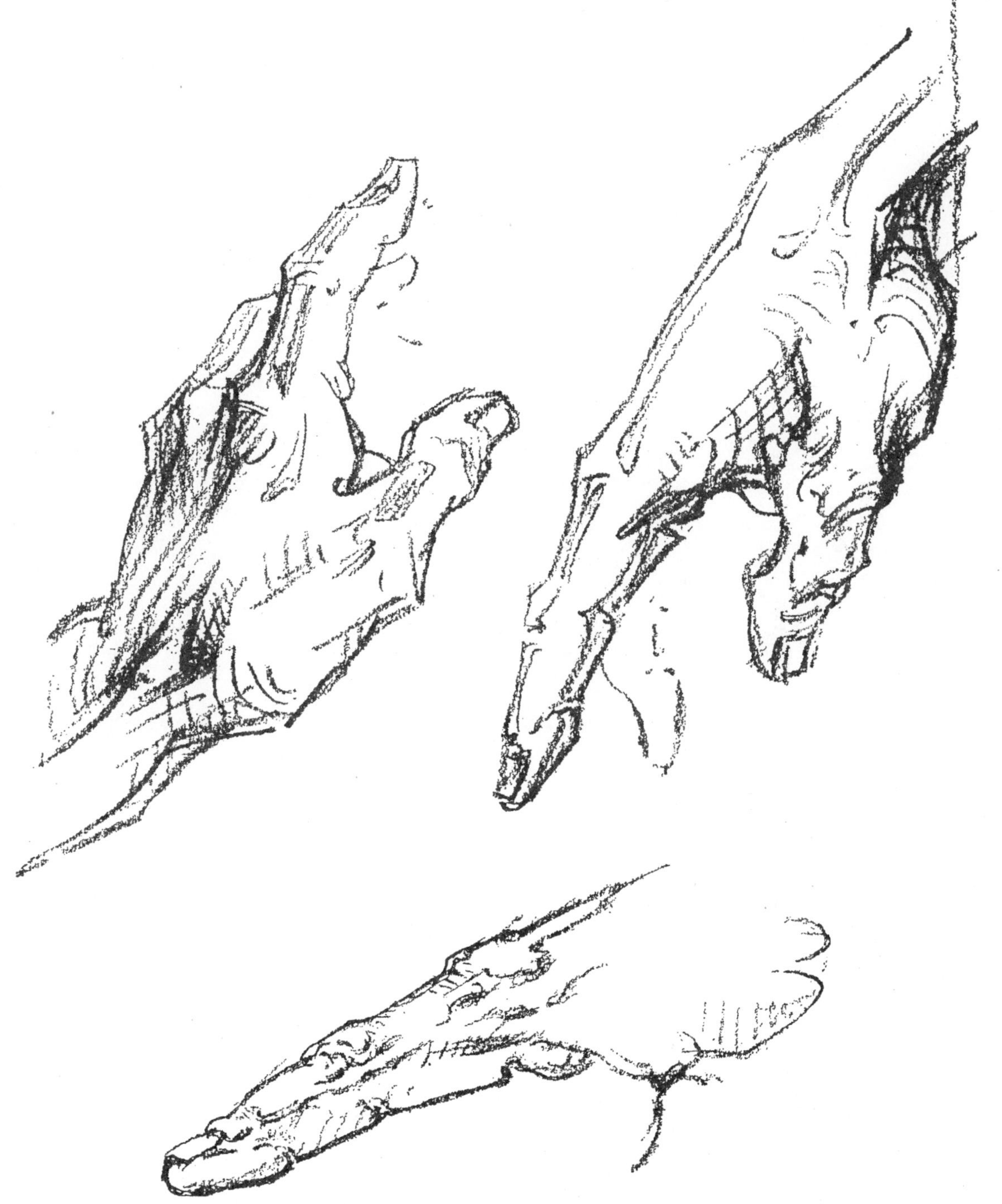

THE HAND

More examples for reference.

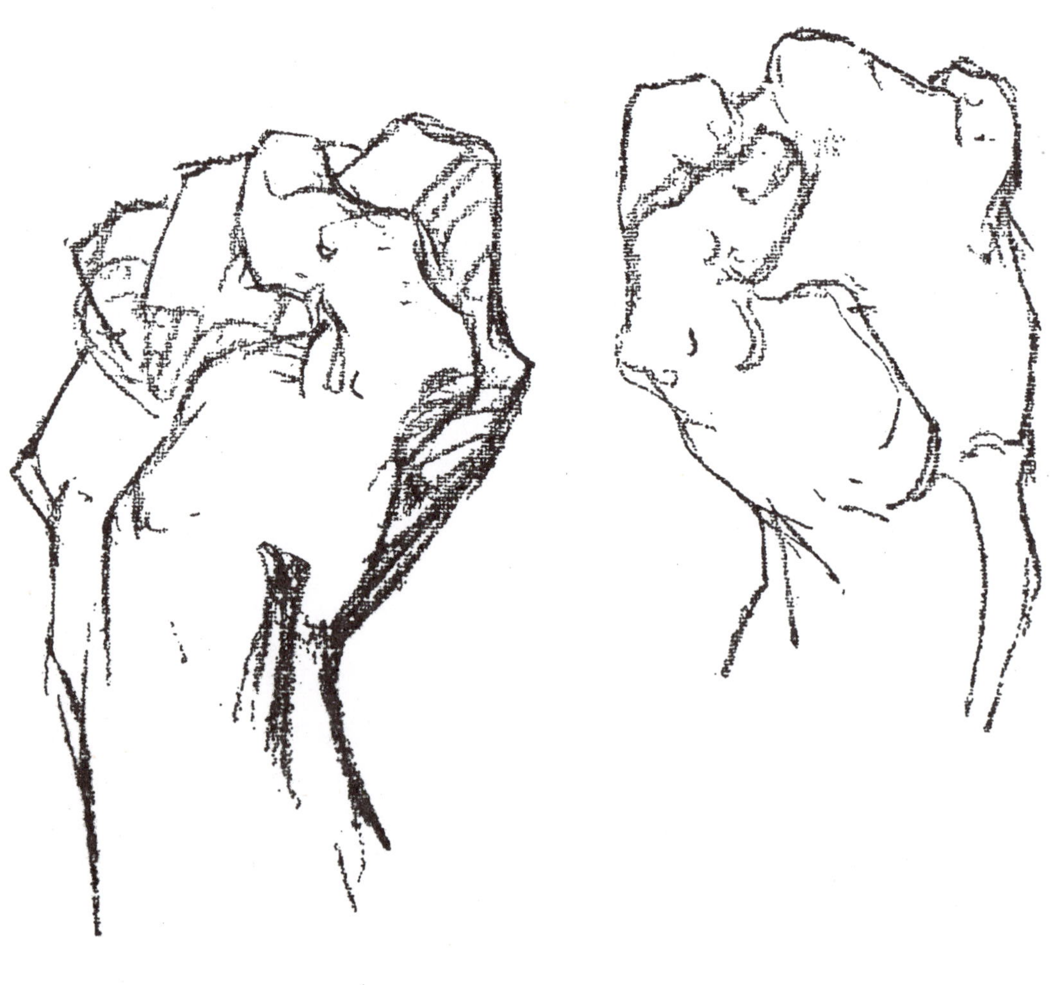

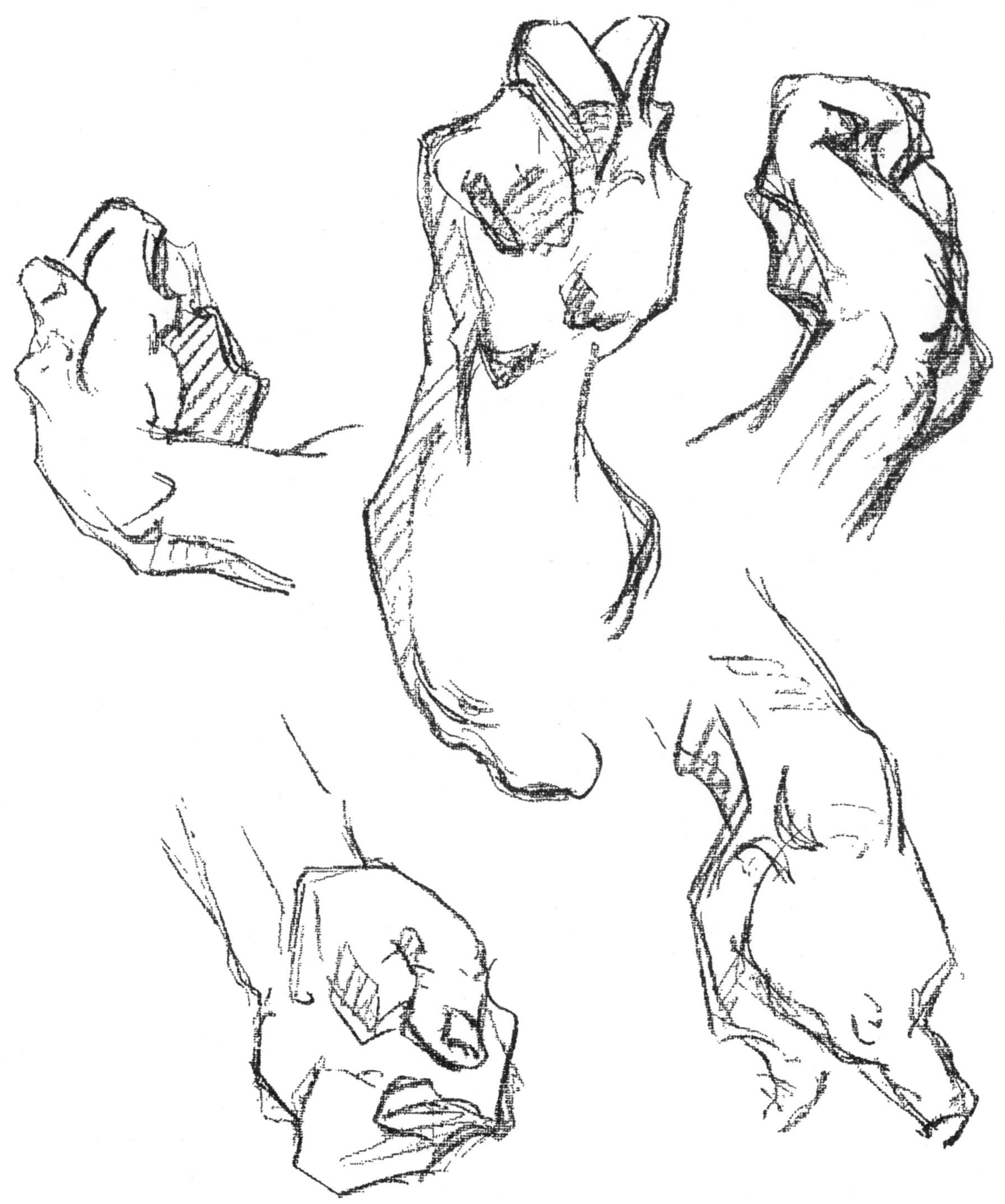

THE HAND

More examples for reference.

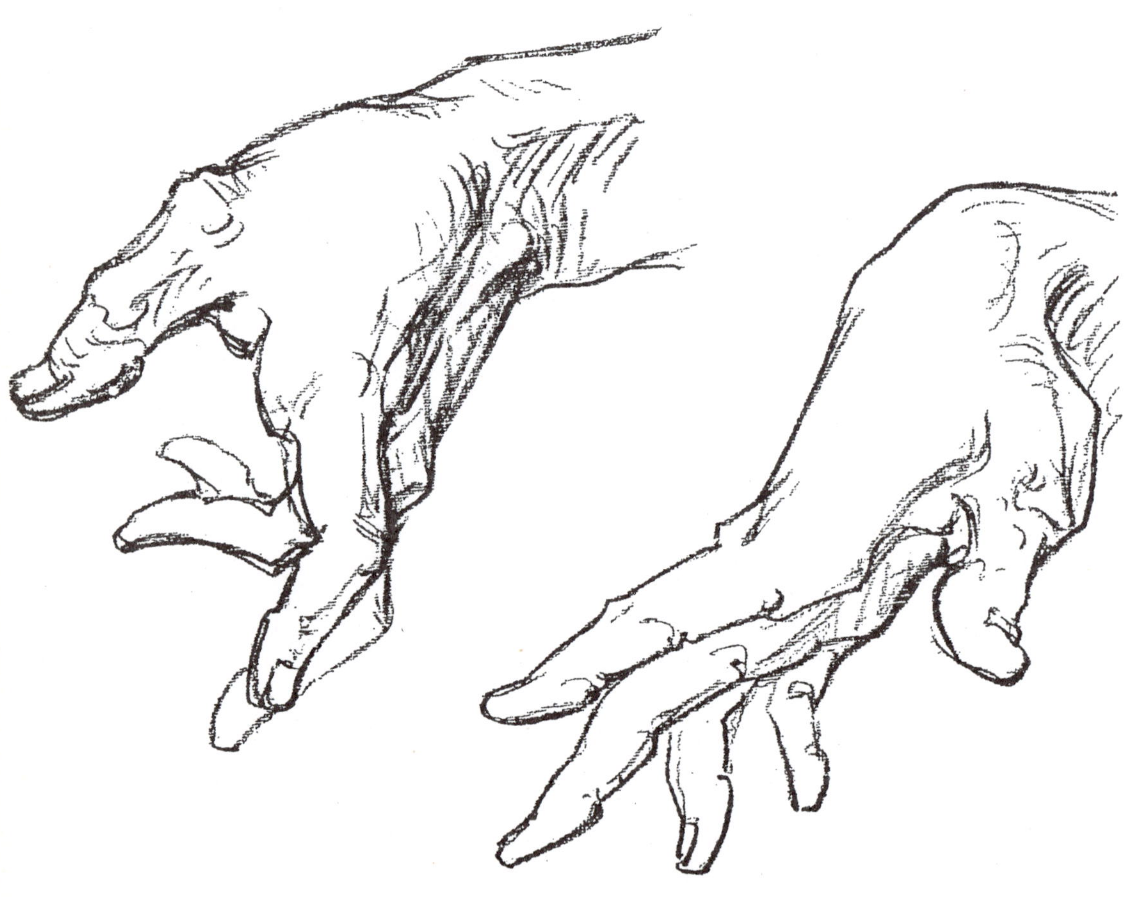

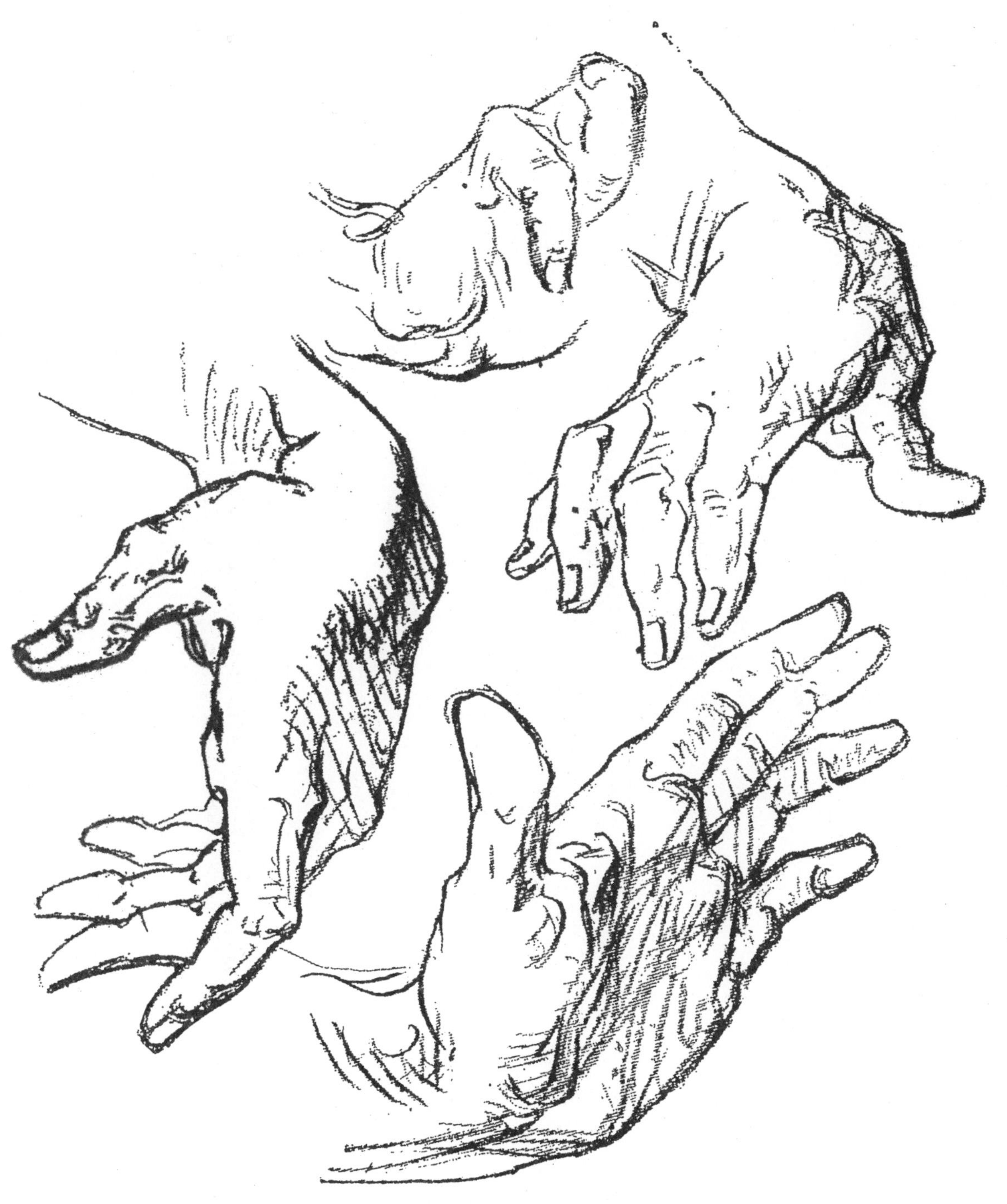

THE HAND

TURNING OF THE MASSES OF THE HAND AND WRIST

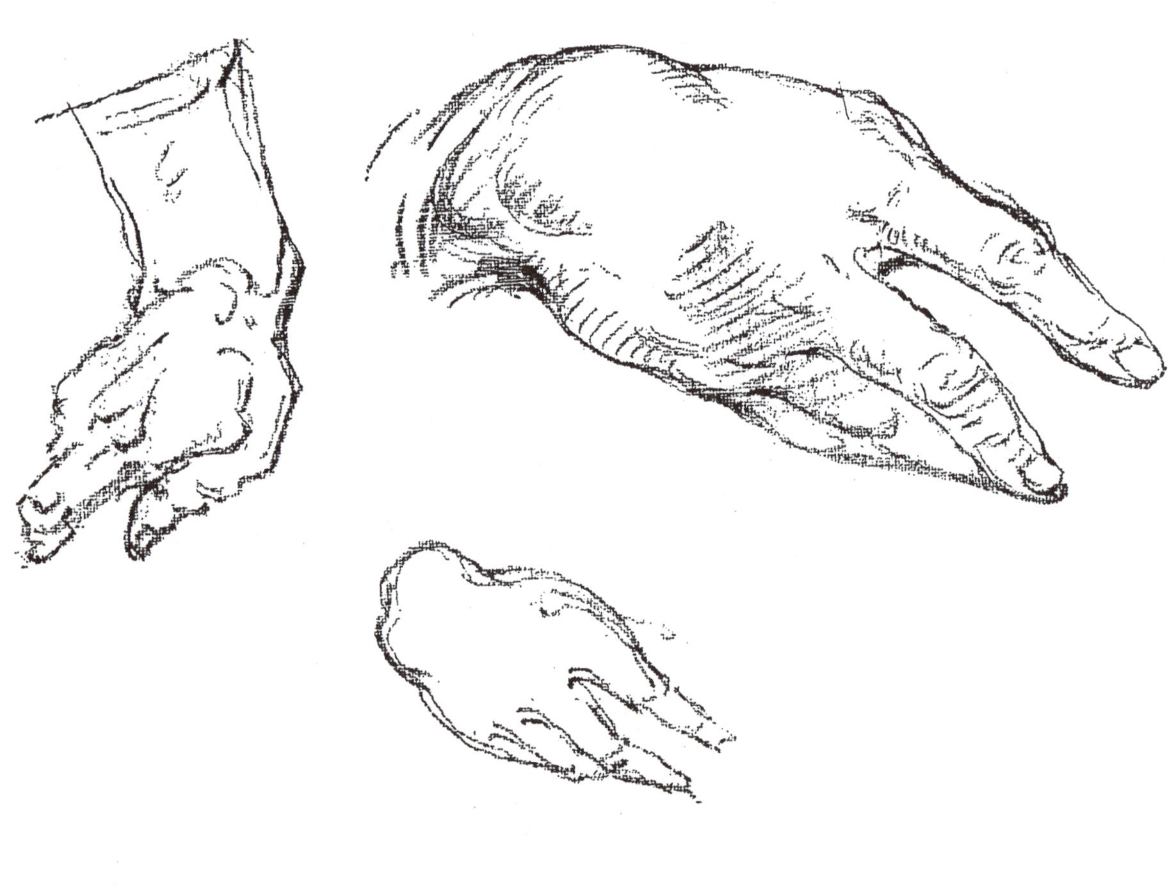

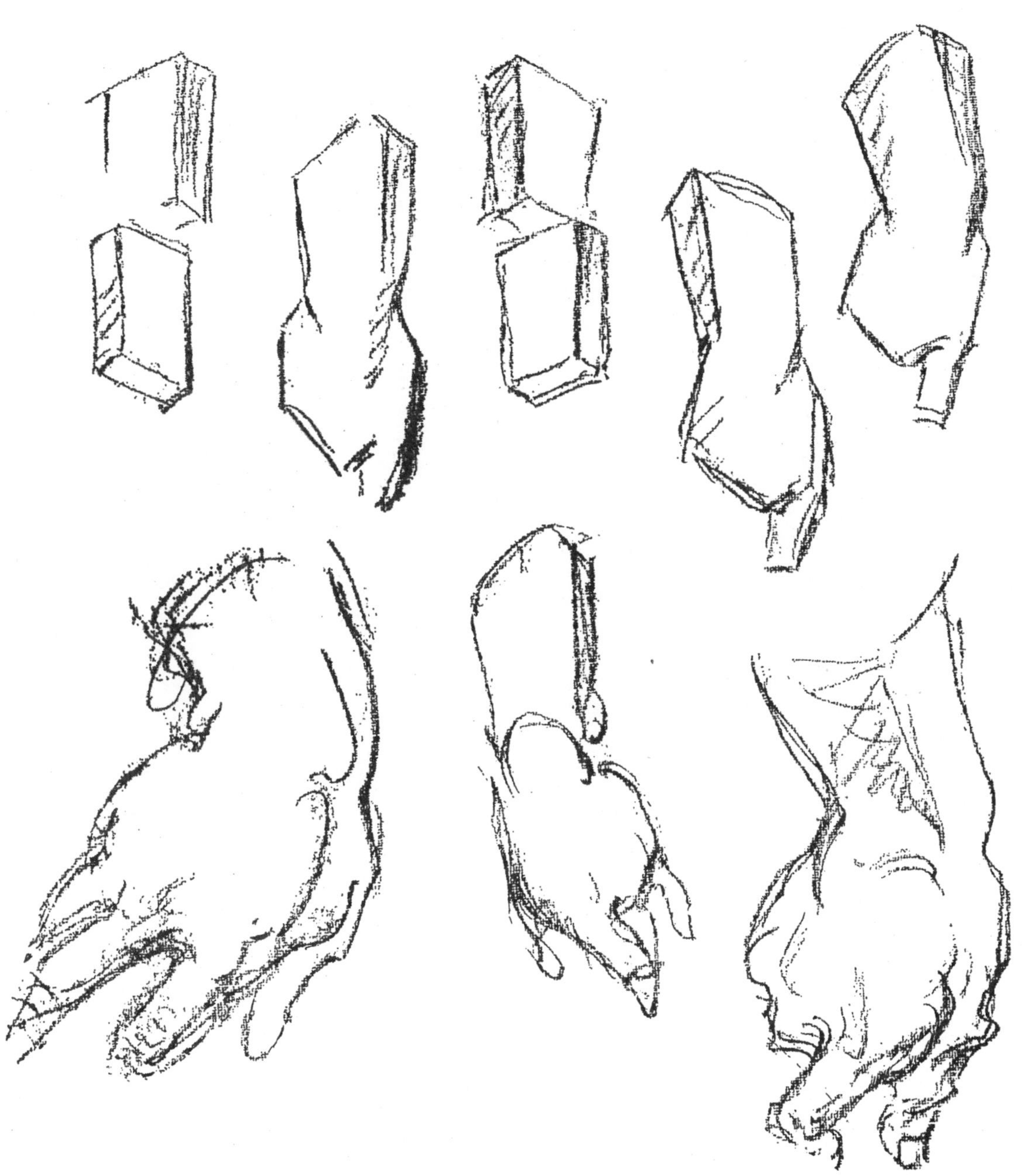

THE HAND

MASSES OF FINGERS, HAND AND WRIST:
STEP-DOWN, WEDGING, INTERLOCKING

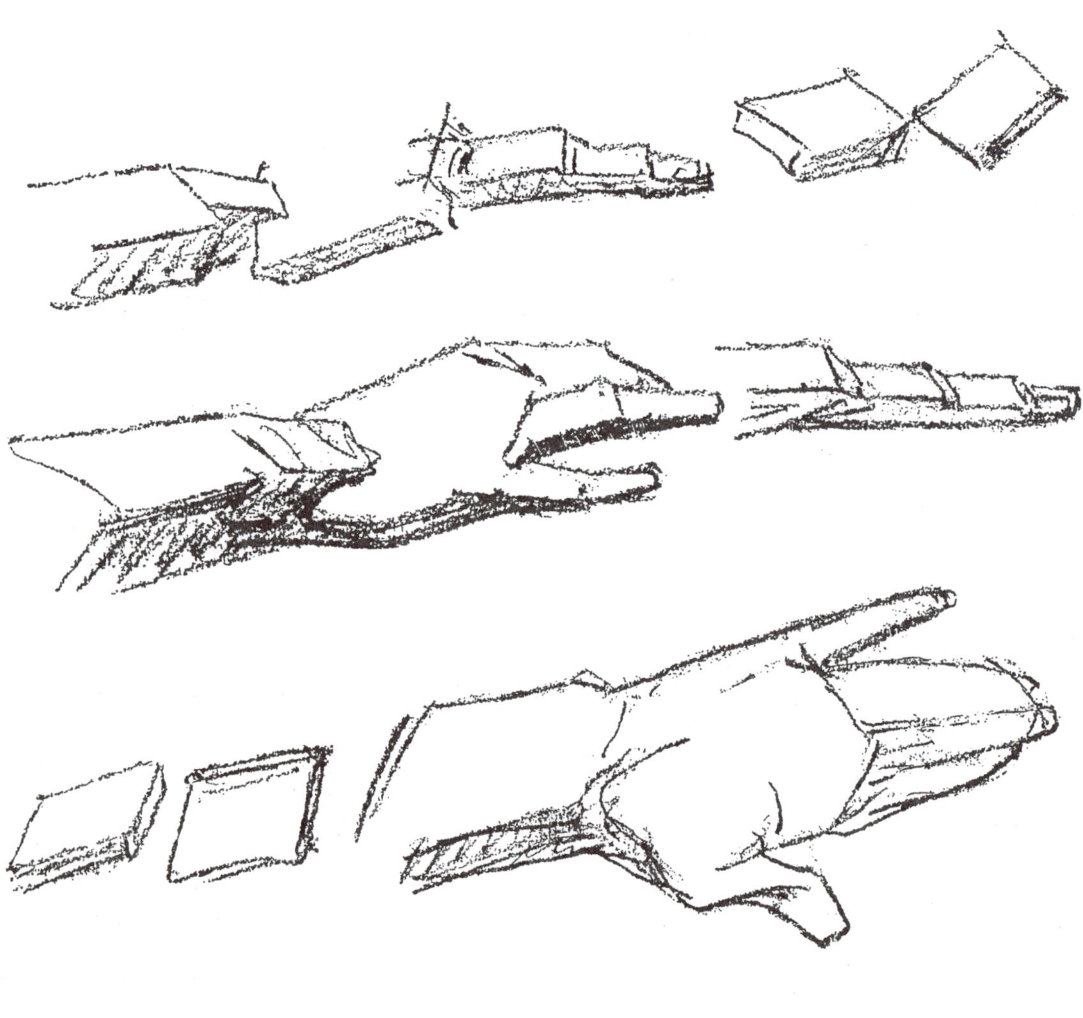

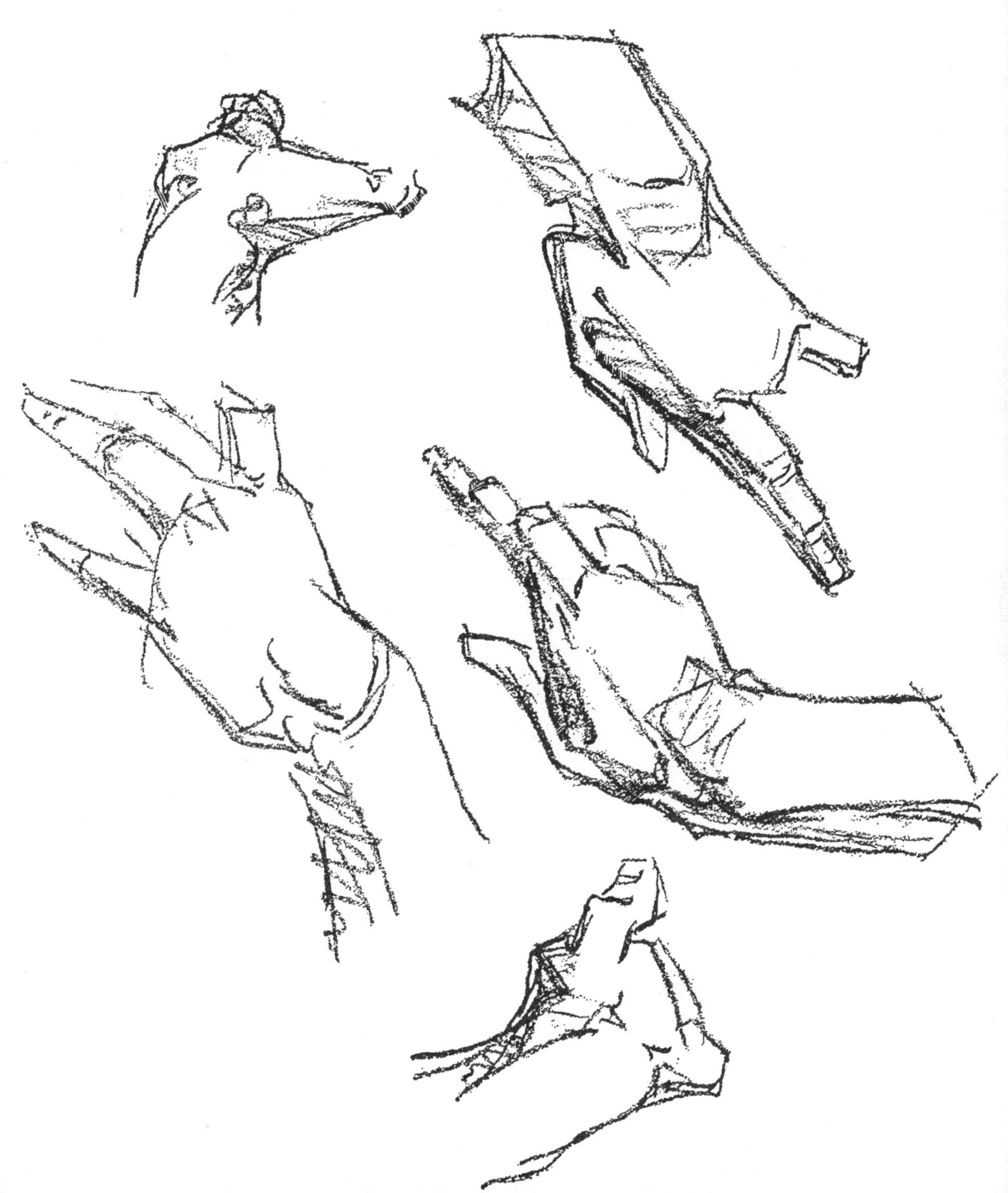

THE HAND

INTERLOCKING OF HAND AND WRIST: LITTLE FINGER SIDE

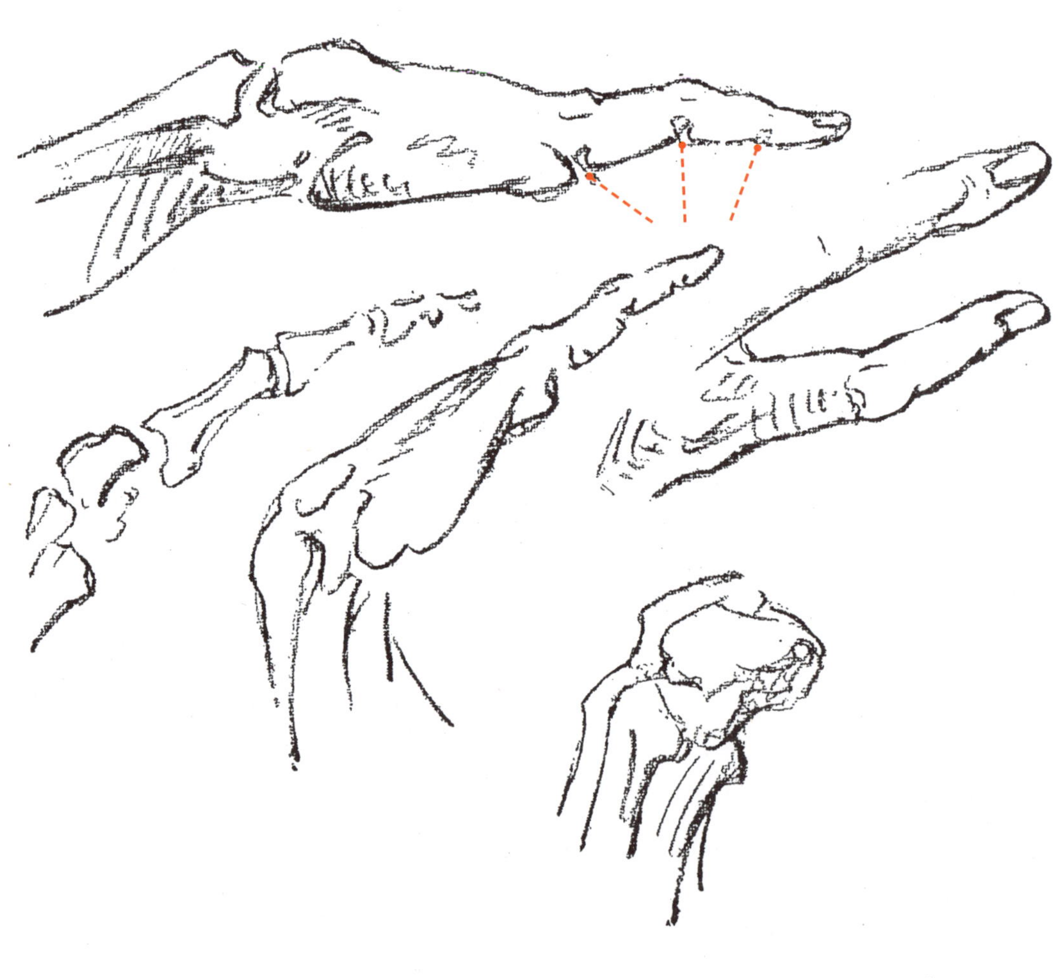

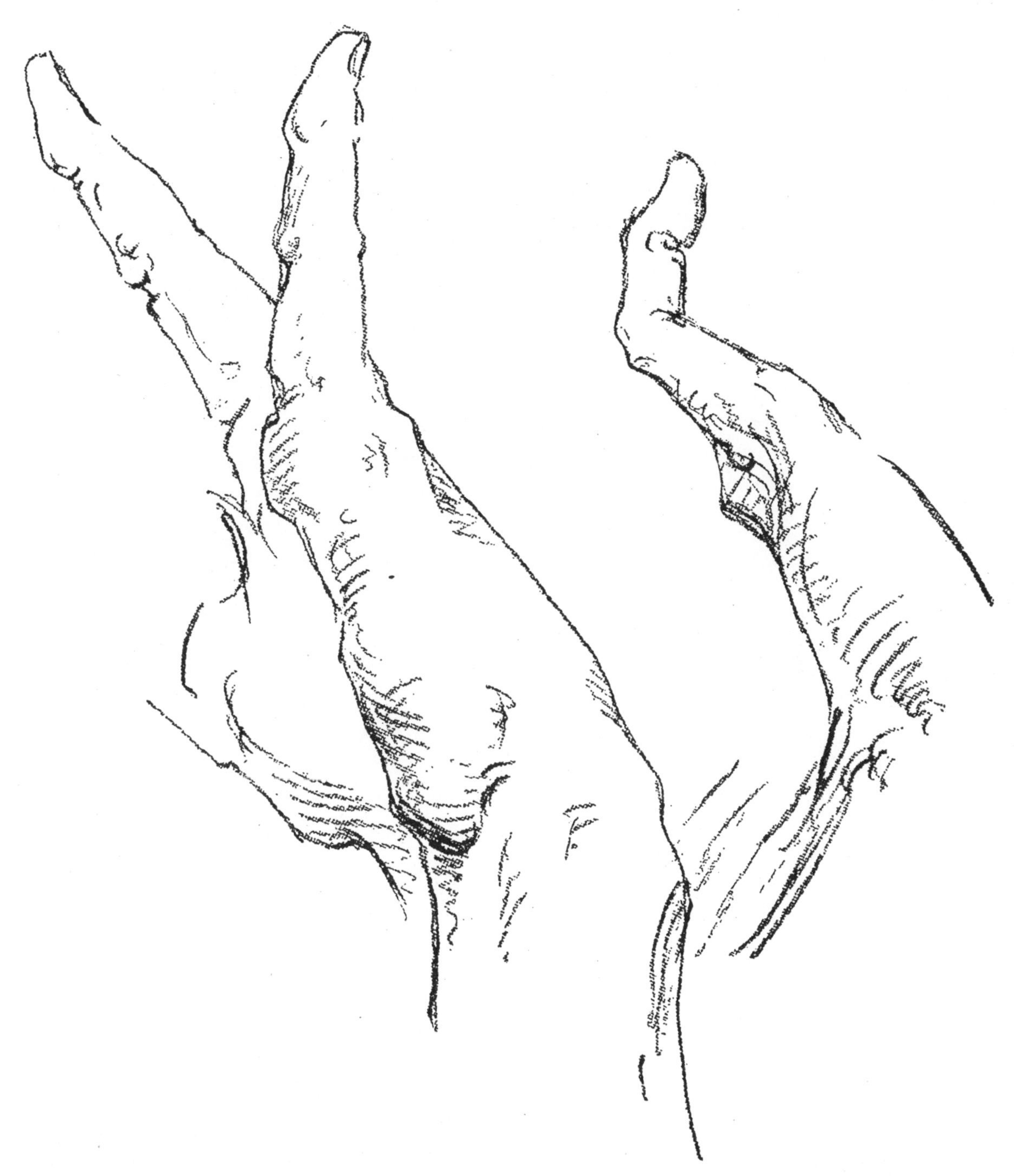

ANATOMY OF THE THUMB

Drill master to the fingers, the hand and the forearm, is the thumb. The fingers, gathered together, form a corona around its tip. Spread out, they radiate from a common centre at its base; and a line connecting their tips forms a curve whose centre is this same point. This is true of the rows of joints (knuckles) also.

Bent, in any position, or closed as in clasping, the fingers form arches, each one concentric on this same basal joint of the thumb. Clenched, each circle of knuckles forms an arch with the same common centre. **The mass of the thumb dominates the hand**. The design and movement of even the forearm is to give the most unhindered sweep to the thumb; while, through the biceps muscle, its movement is seen to begin really at the shoulder.

ANATOMY

The thumb has three segments and as many joints. Its bones are heavier than those of the fingers, its joints more rugged. Its last segment has a nail and a heavy skin pad. The middle segment has only tendons. The basal segment is a pyramidal mass of muscle reaching to the wrist, the 'line of life' of the palm, and the base of the first finger.

The superficial muscles of this mass are a fat one, a broad one, and a thin one. The fat muscle hugs the bone (*opponens*), the broad one forms the bulk of the pyramid (*abductor*) and the thin one lies inside, toward the index finger (*flexor brevis*).

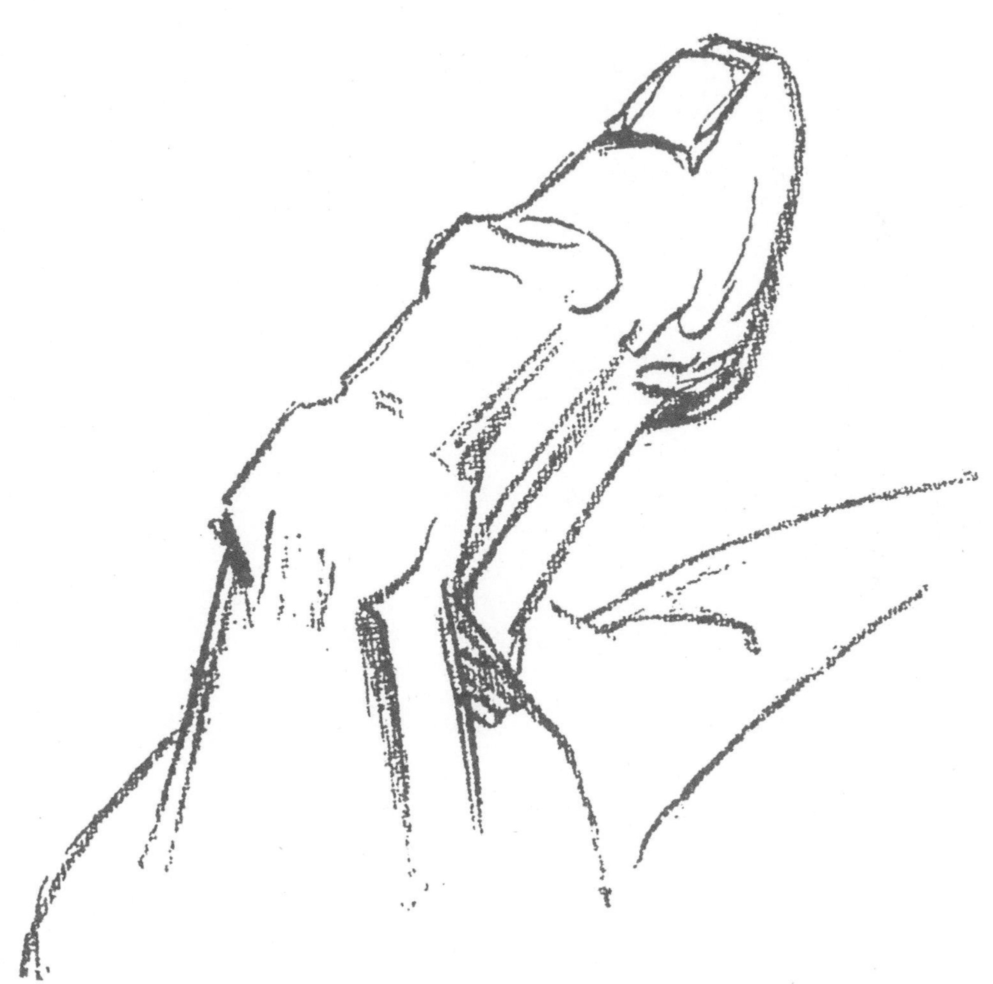

Between the thumb and first finger the skin is raised into a web, which is bulged, especially when the thumb is flattened, by the *adductor pollicis* muscle.

MASSES

The thumb is pyramidal at the base, narrow in the middle, pear-shaped at the end. The ball faces to the front more than sideways. It reaches to the middle joint of the first finger. The last segment bends sharply back, carrying the nail. Its skin pad, broad at the base, gives it an appearance not unlike a foot, expressing its pressure-bearing function.

The middle segment is square with rounded edges, smaller than the other two, with a small pad. The basal segment is rounded and bulged on all sides except where the one is superficial at the back.

MOVEMENTS

The last joint has about one right angle of movement, in one plane, and may by pressure be twisted toward the fingers. The heavy middle joint moves less freely, also limited to one plane. The joint of the base is a saddle joint, with movement like one in a saddle, that is, with easy bending sideways, less easy forward and back; which two in combination give some rotary movement, but giving a twisting movement only with difficulty and strain.

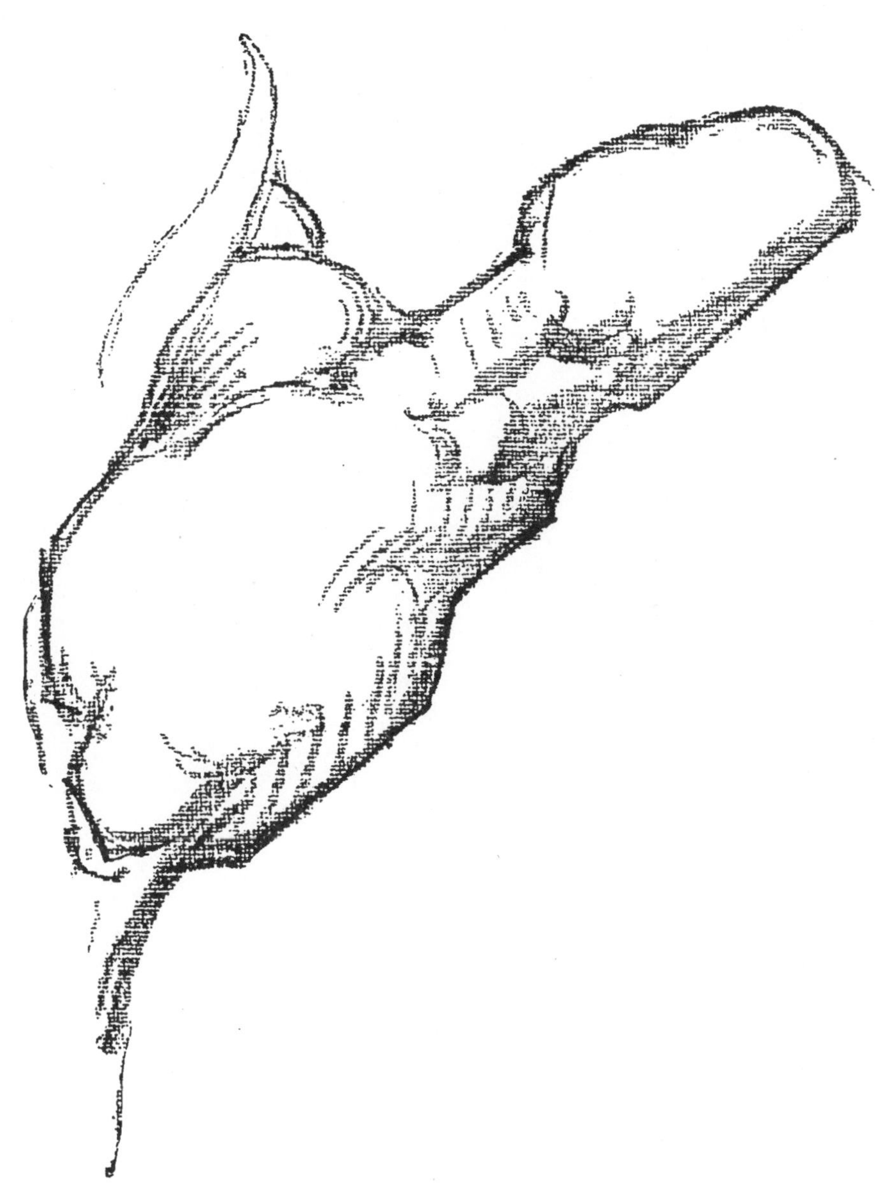

THE THUMB

EXTENSORS OF THE THUMB

① *Extensor ossis metacarpi pollicis.*
② *Extensor brevis pollicis.*
③ *Extensor longus pollicis.*

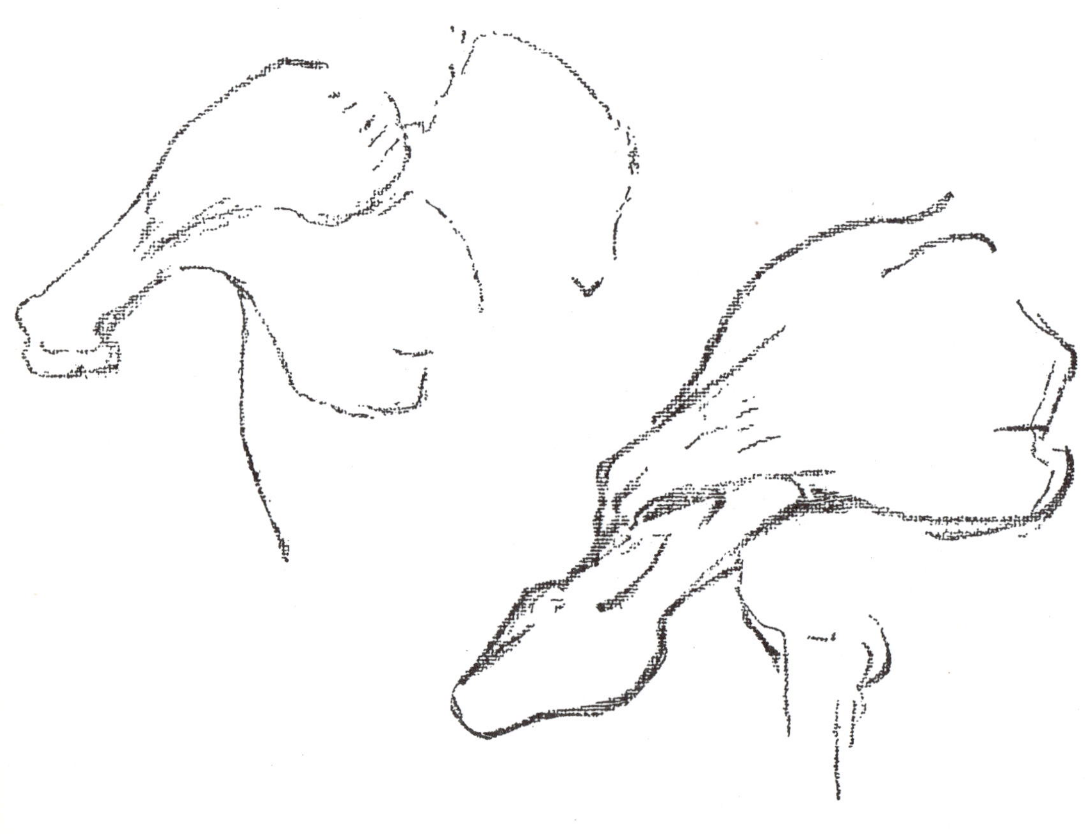

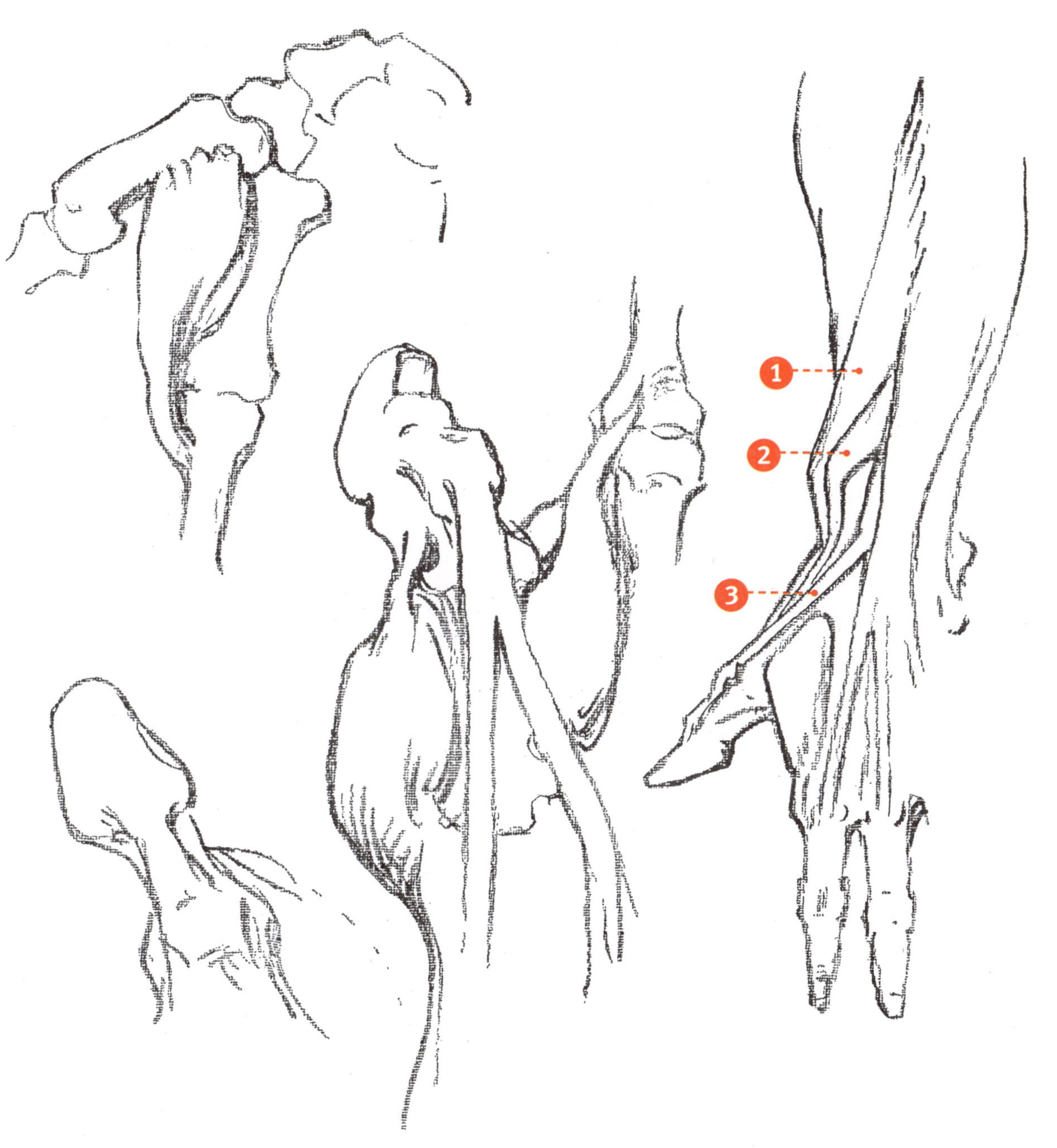
1
2
3

THE THUMB

MUSCLES OF THE THUMB: FRONT PALM VIEW

① *Flexor* brevis *pollicis.*
② *Abductor pollicis.*
③ Apponens *pollicis.*

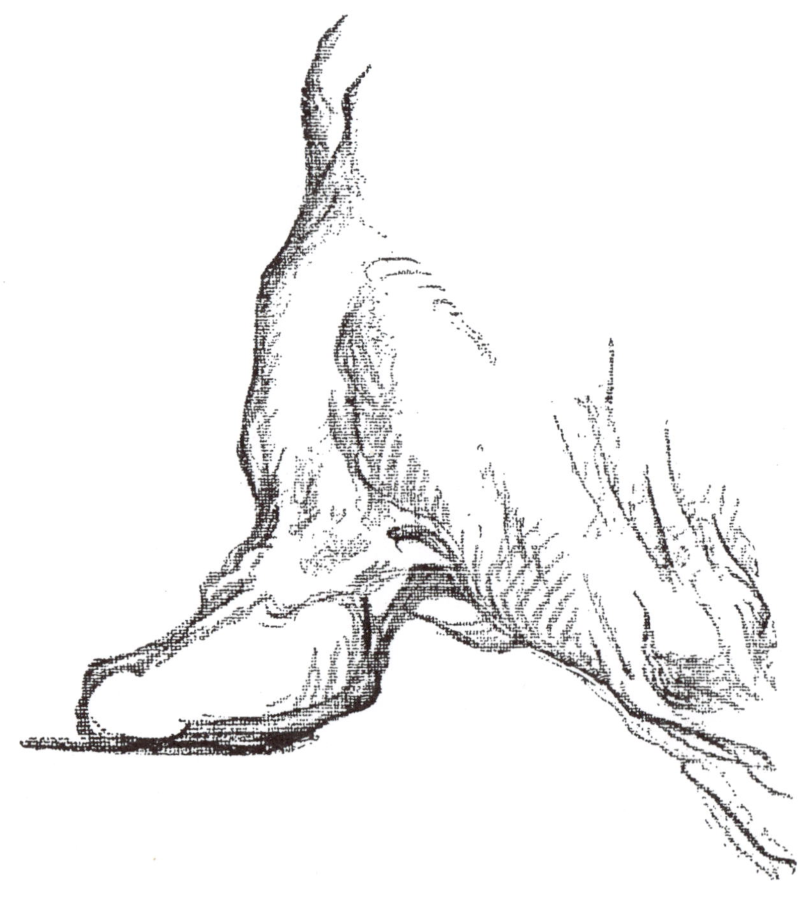

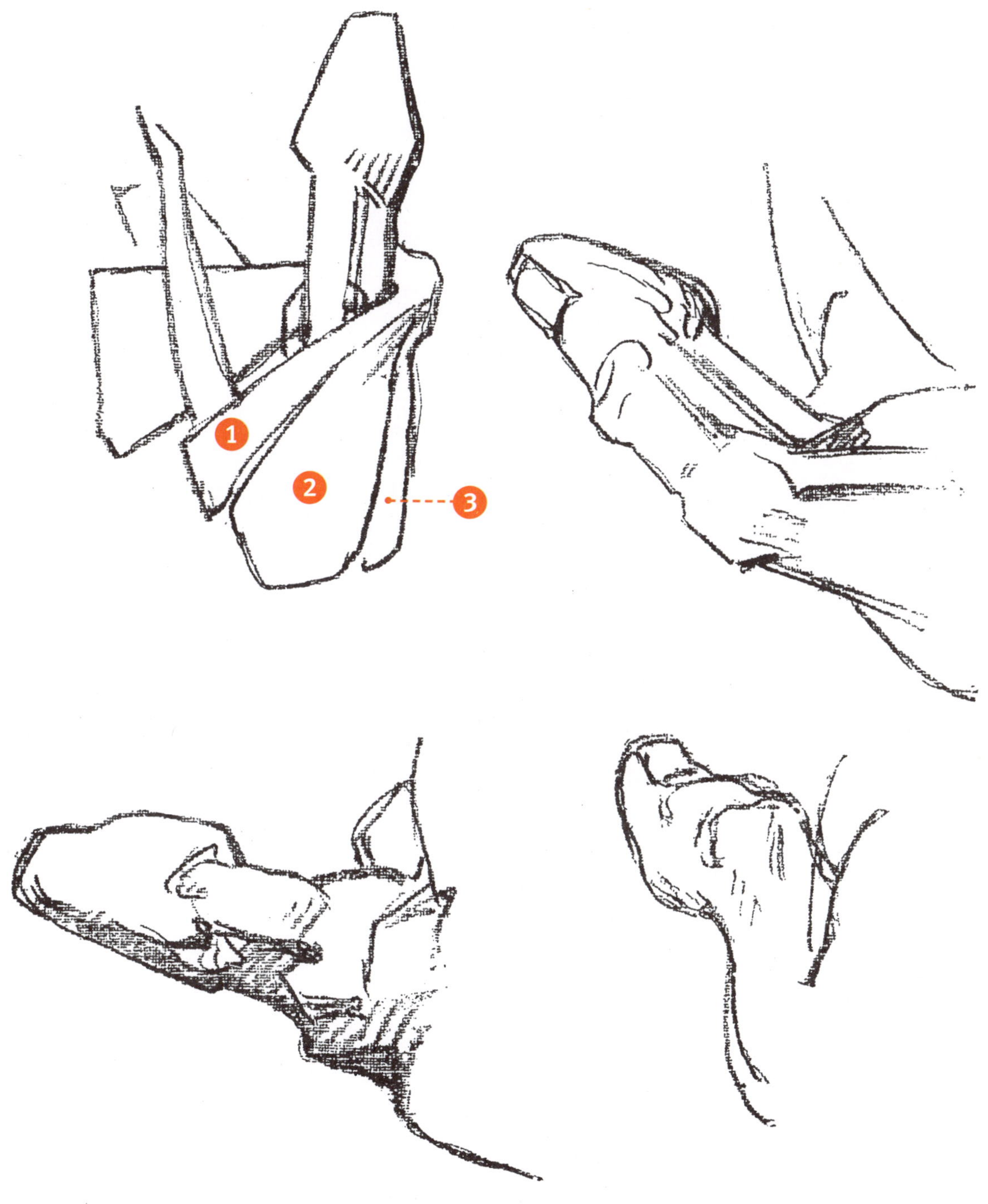
1
2
3

THE THUMB

Examples for reference.

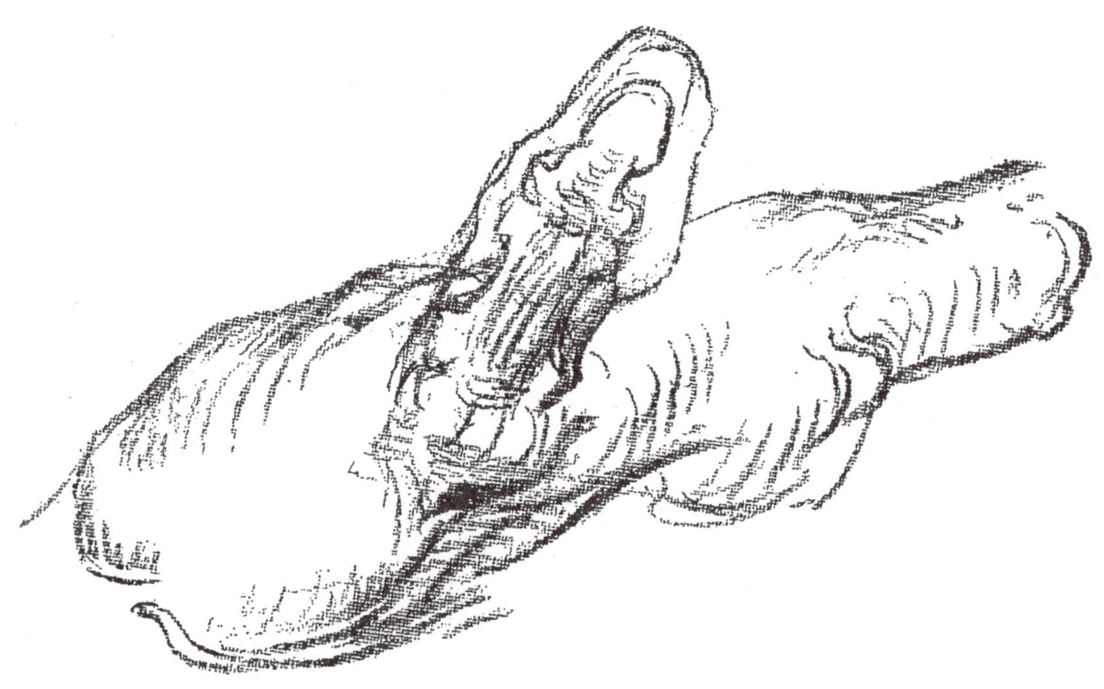

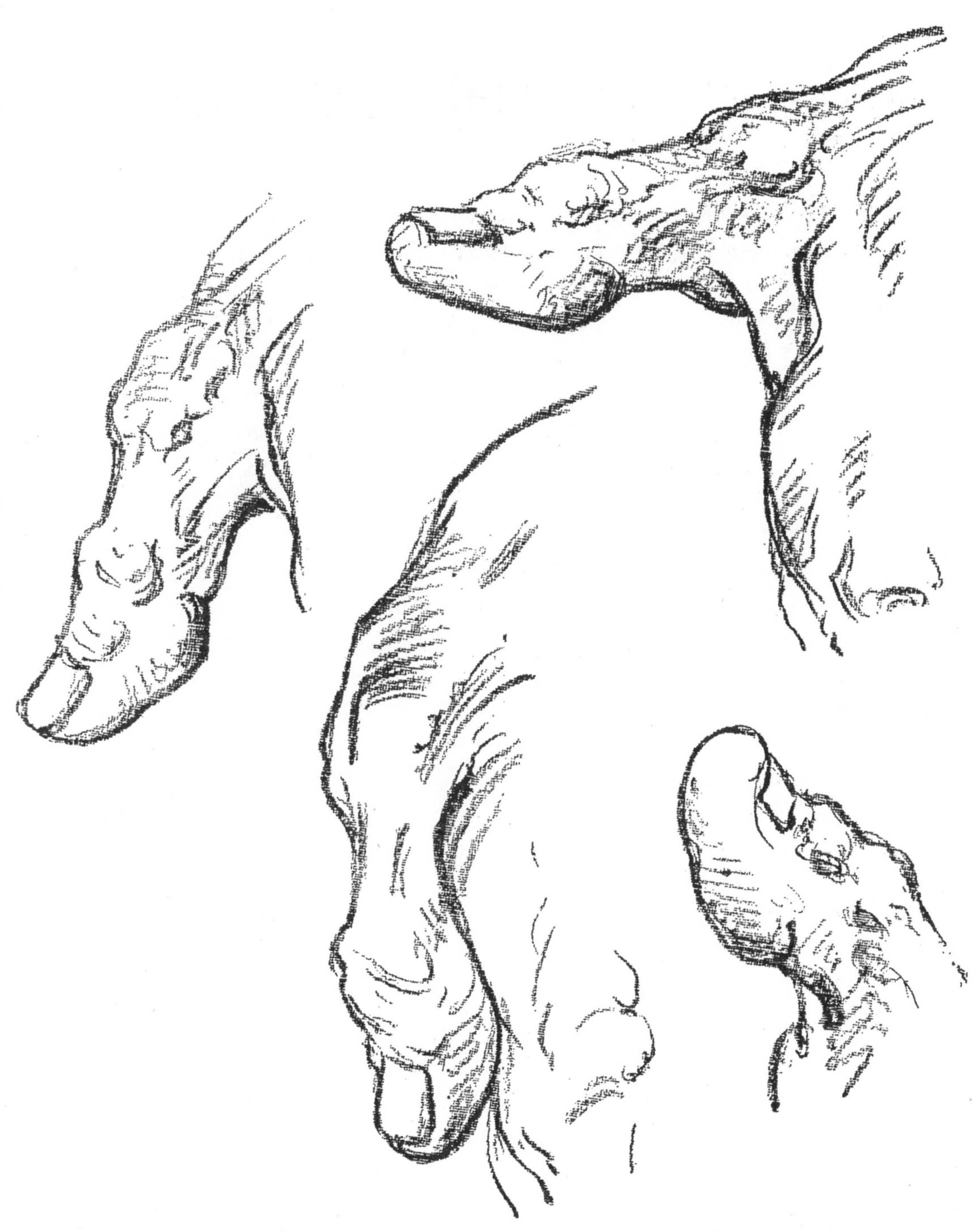

ANATOMY OF THE FINGERS

Each of the four fingers has three bones (*phalanges*, soldiers). Each *phalanx* turns on the one above, leaving exposed the end of the higher bone. There are no muscles below the knuckles; but the fingers are traversed by tendons on the back, and are covered on the front by tendons and skin pads.

The middle finger is the longest and largest, because in the clasped hand it is opposite the thumb and with it bears the chief burden. The little finger is the smallest and shortest and most freely movable for the opposite reason. It may move farther back than the other fingers, and is usually held so, for two reasons; one is that the hand often 'sits' on the base of the little finger; the other is that being diagonally opposite the thumb it is twisted farther backward in any outward twisting movement, and so tends to assume that position.

MASSES

All bones of the body are narrower in the shaft than at either end, especially those of the fingers. The joints are square, the shafts smaller but square, with rounded edges; the tips are triangular. The middle joint of each finger is the largest. In the clenched fist it is the end of the bone of the hand (*metacarpal*) that is exposed to make the knuckle. The finger bone (first *phalanx*) moves around it, and bulges beyond. The *extensor* tendon makes a ridge on the knuckle and connects it with the first *phalanx*; but on the middle and the last joints the tendon makes a depression or groove in the

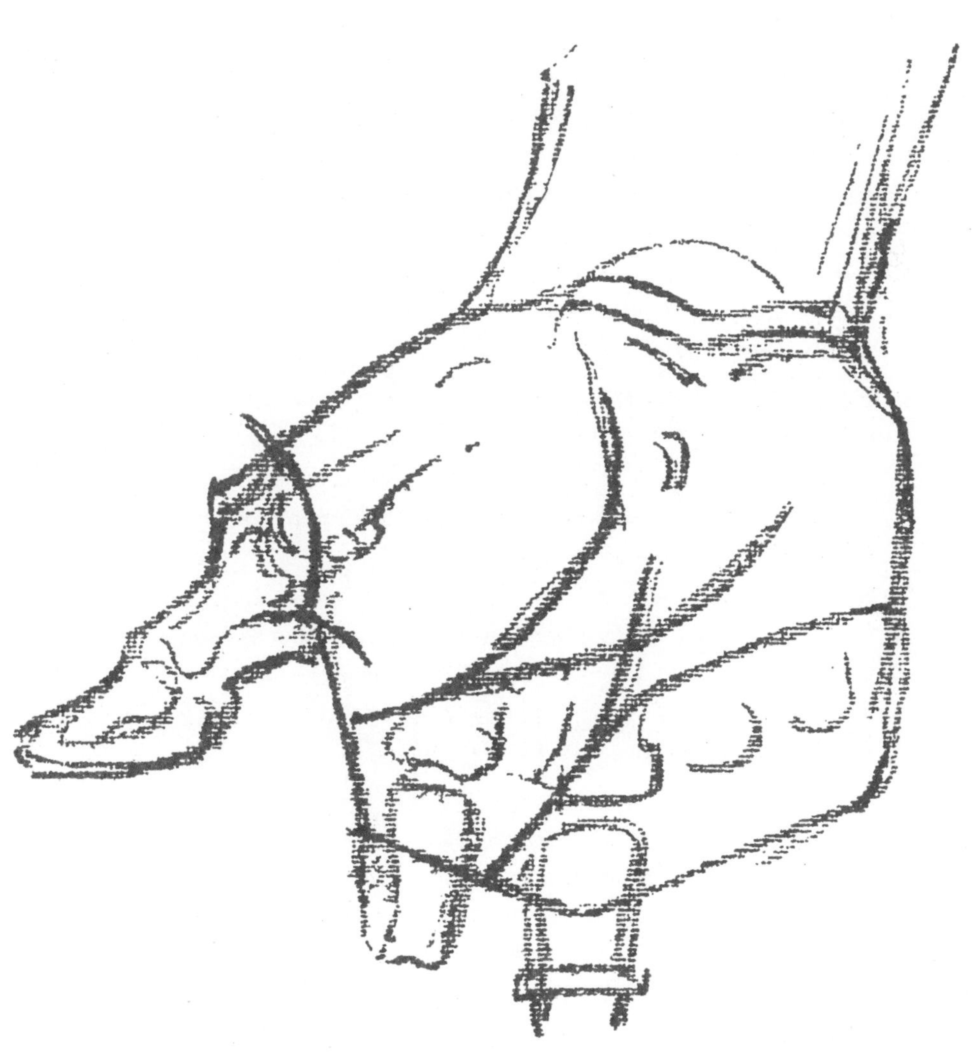

centre of the joint. The masses of these segments are not placed end to end, as on a dead centre, either in profile or in back view.

In the back view, the fingers as a whole arch toward the middle finger. In the profile view, there is a step-down from each segment to the one beyond, bridged by a wedge. A series of wedges and squares thus marks the backs of the fingers.

Into the square of the knuckles a blunt wedge is seen to enter from above. From it a long tapering wedge arises and enters the square of the middle joint, from which a blunt wedge also reaches backward. Another tapering wedge arises here and moves half way down the segment. The whole finger tapers from the middle joint, to become embedded in a horseshoe form holding the nail. This form begins back of the root of the nail and bevels to below its end, at the tip of the finger.

The whole last segment is a wedge. The *palmar* webbing opposite the knuckles, which reaches to about the middle of the first segment of the finger, in front, bevels backward and points to the top of the knuckle in the back. The segments of individual fingers are of different lengths, those of the middle finger being longest. From tip to base, and on into the bones of the hand, the segments increase in length by definite proportions.

MOVEMENTS

Each joint moves about one right angle except the last, which moves slightly less; and limited to one plane, except the *basal*, which has also a slight lateral movement, as in spreading the fingers.

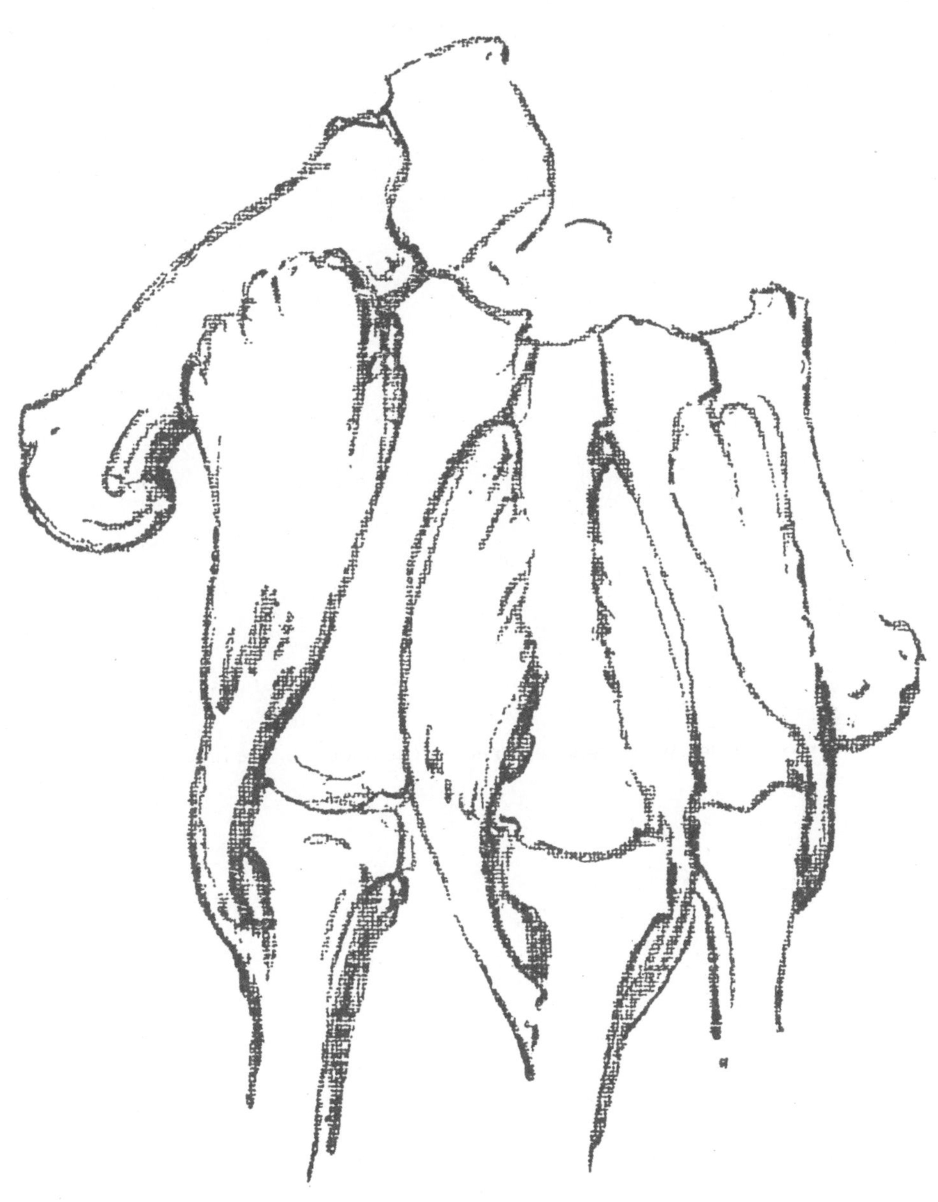

FINGERS

PAD BETWEEN THUMB AND FIRST FINGER

① First *dorsal interosseus.*

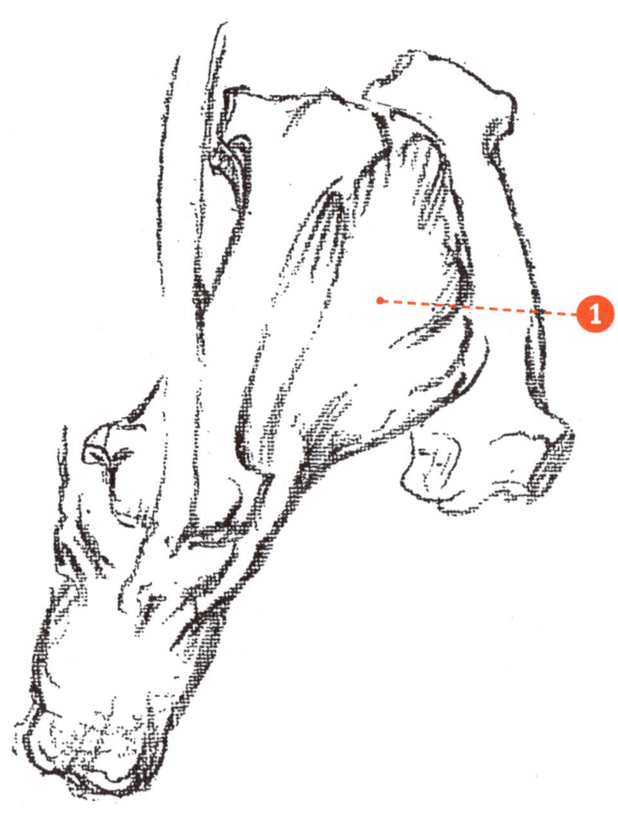

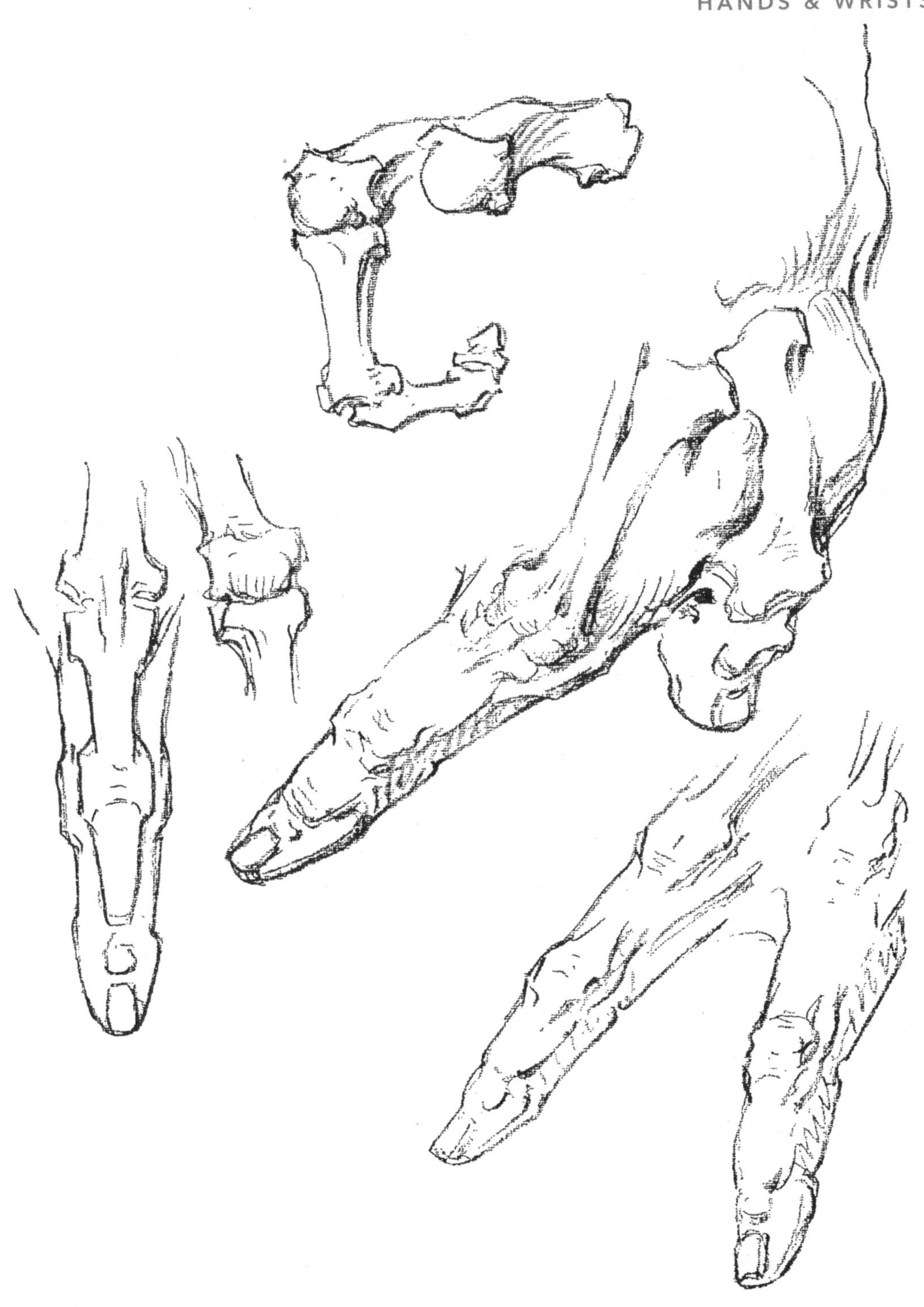

FINGERS

MECHANISM OF THE FIRST FINGER

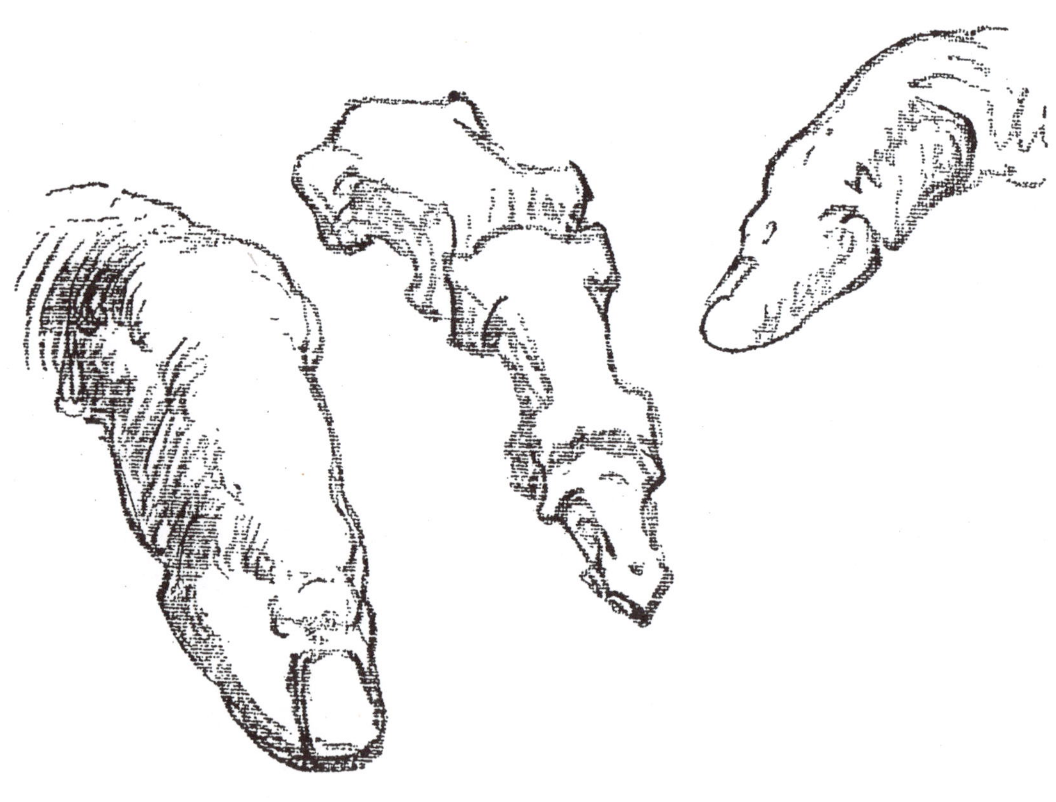

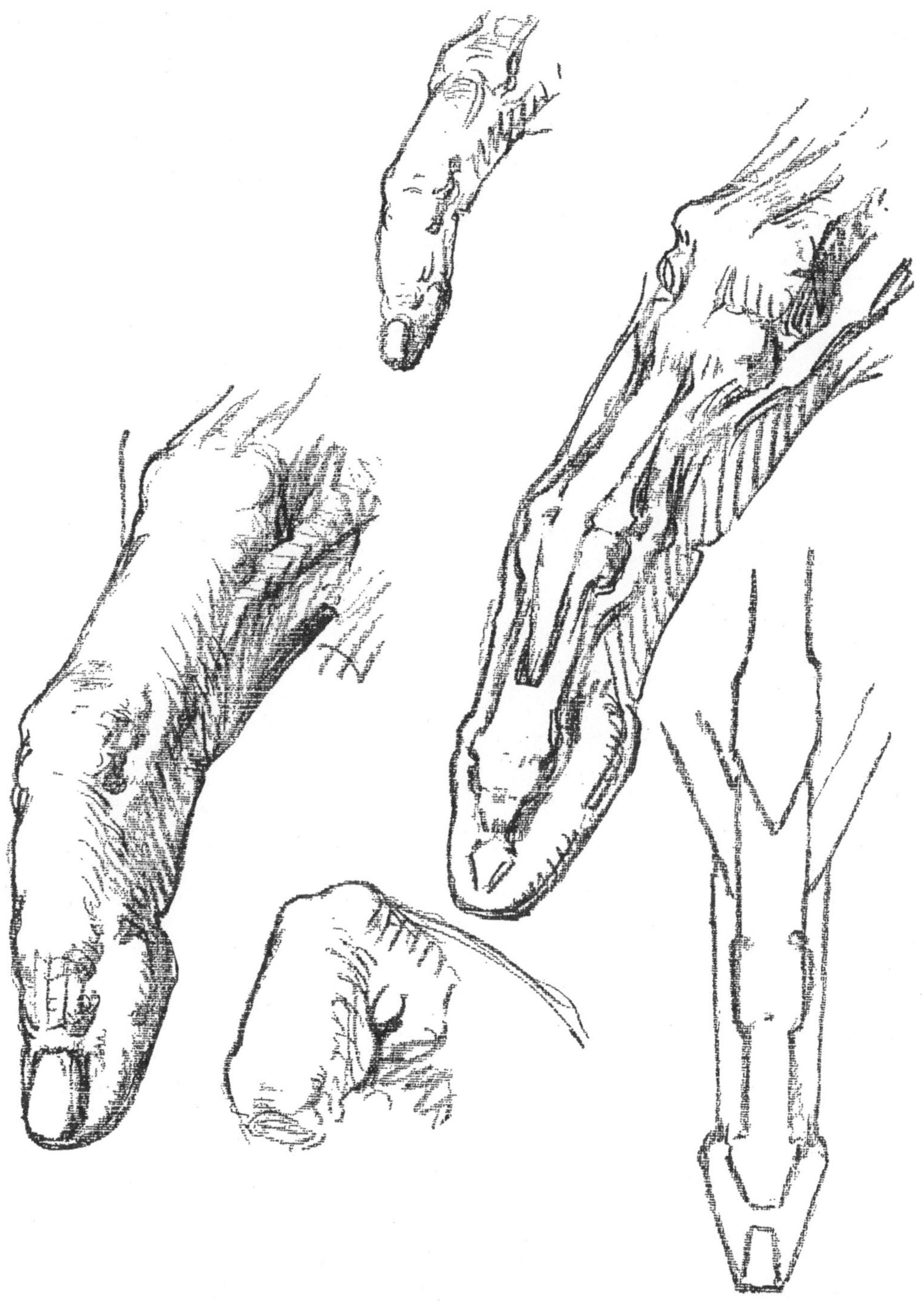

FINGERS

CREASES

While the segments of any finger, seen on the back, are of different lengths, the pads seen on the *palmar* side are of the same length, including the pad of the base which is part of the palm, so that the creases between them are not all opposite the joints. The reason is immediately seen when the finger is viewed closed on itself. The creases are then seen to form a cross, the pads to meet in the common centre, filling in the four sides of a diamond.

In the **first finger** the creases are:

- Short of the last joint
- Opposite the middle joint
- Half way between middle and basal joint, opposite the basal knuckle (above the joint proper, which is considerably beyond the point of the knuckle).

In the **second finger** they are:

- Opposite the last joint
- Beyond the middle joint
- Midway between middle and basal joint, opposite basal joint.

In the other fingers they vary in different individuals. The creases are all transverse except that opposite the *basal* joint, which forms one long wavy crease on the palm; and those next beyond, on first and little fingers, which slope down on the outside, in the spread fingers making a curve around the base of the thumb.

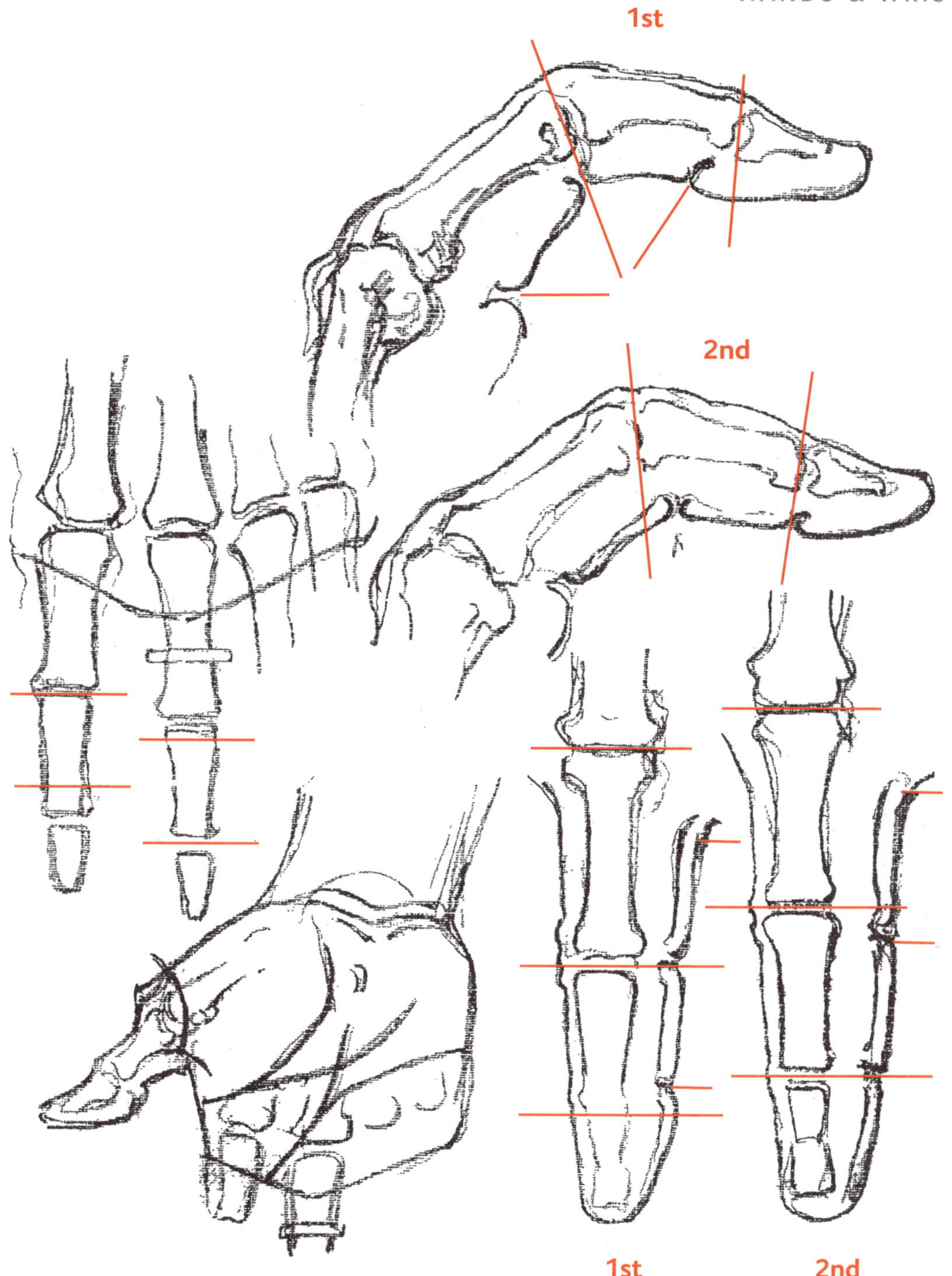
1st
2nd
1st
2nd

FINGERS

① *Dorsal interossei* of the hand.
② Tendons, finger, *dorsal* side.
③ Tendons, finger, palm side.

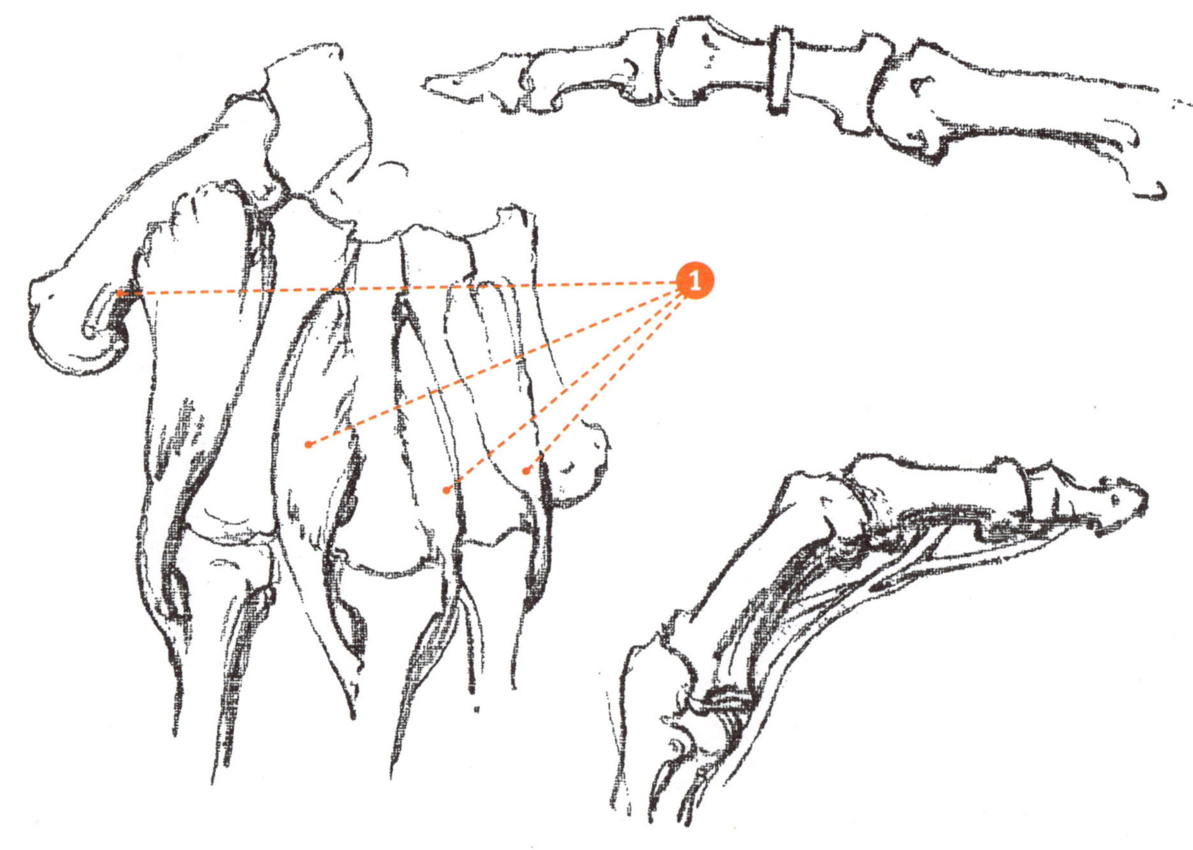

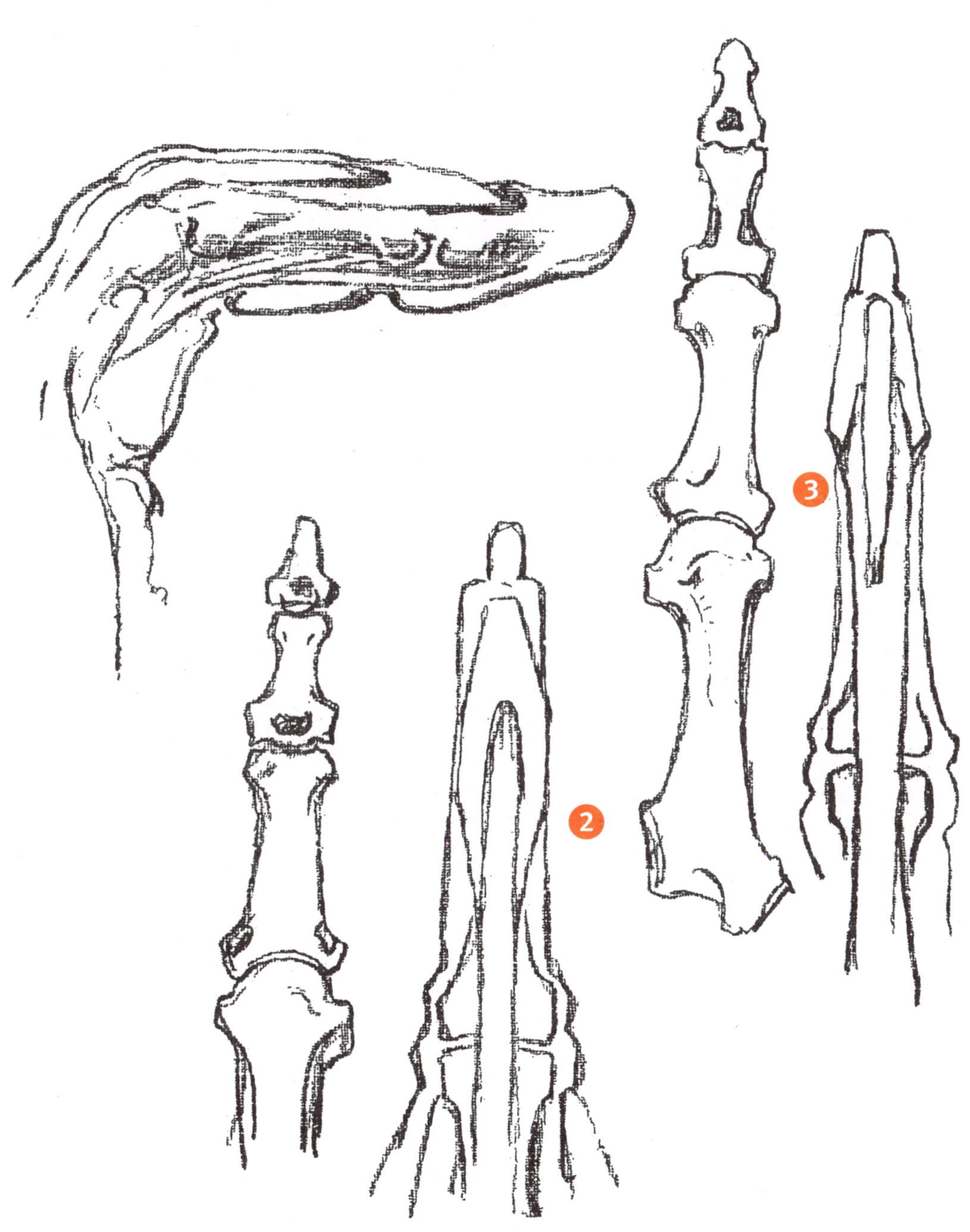
2
3

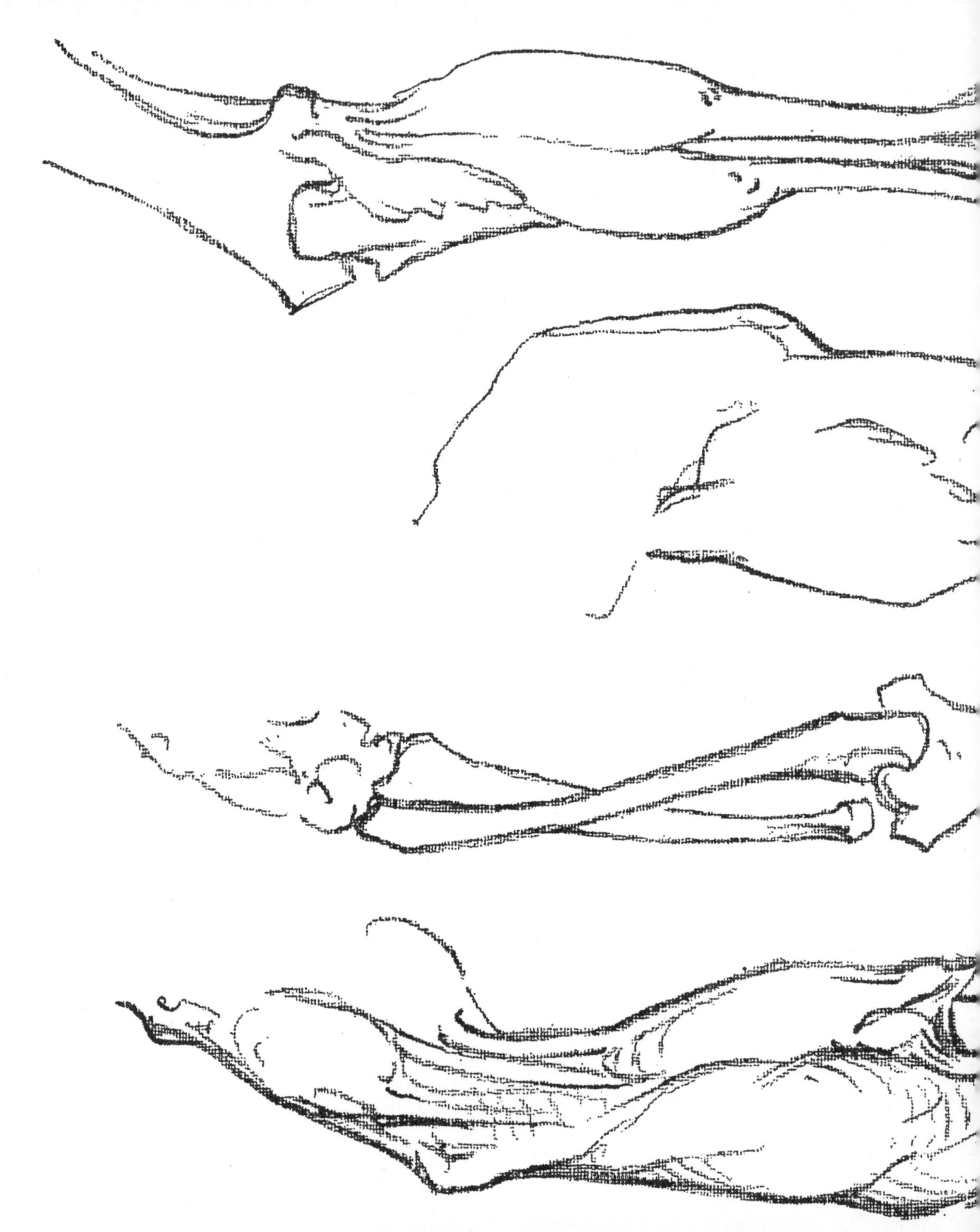

The Arm

ANATOMY OF THE FOREARM

In the forearm are two bones, lying side by side. One is large at the wrist, forming two-thirds of the joint; the other is large at the elbow, where it also forms two-thirds of the joint. They are joined at their sides and move like a long piece of cardboard folded diagonally. The one that is large at the elbow is the *ulna*. It forms a hinge joint and moves in the bending of the elbow. The other slides as the hinge moves.

ANATOMY AND MOVEMENTS

This second bone is the *radius*, or turning bone; it is large at the wrist and carries the wrist and hand. Diagonally opposite the thumb, on the *ulna*, is a hump of bone which is the pivot for both the *radius* and also the thumb. Muscles must lie above the joint they move, so that the muscles that bulge the forearm are mainly the *flexors* and *extensors* of the wrist and hand.

Overlying them and reaching higher up on the arm are the *pronators* and *supinators* of the *radius*. The *flexors* and *pronators* (*flexor*, to flex or bend; *pronator*, to turn face down, or prone) form the inner mass at the elbow, the *extensors* and *supinators* form the outer mass. Between them at the elbow lies the *cubital fossa*. Both of these masses arise from the condyles of the *humerus*, or arm bone. These are the tips of the flattened lower end of that bone.

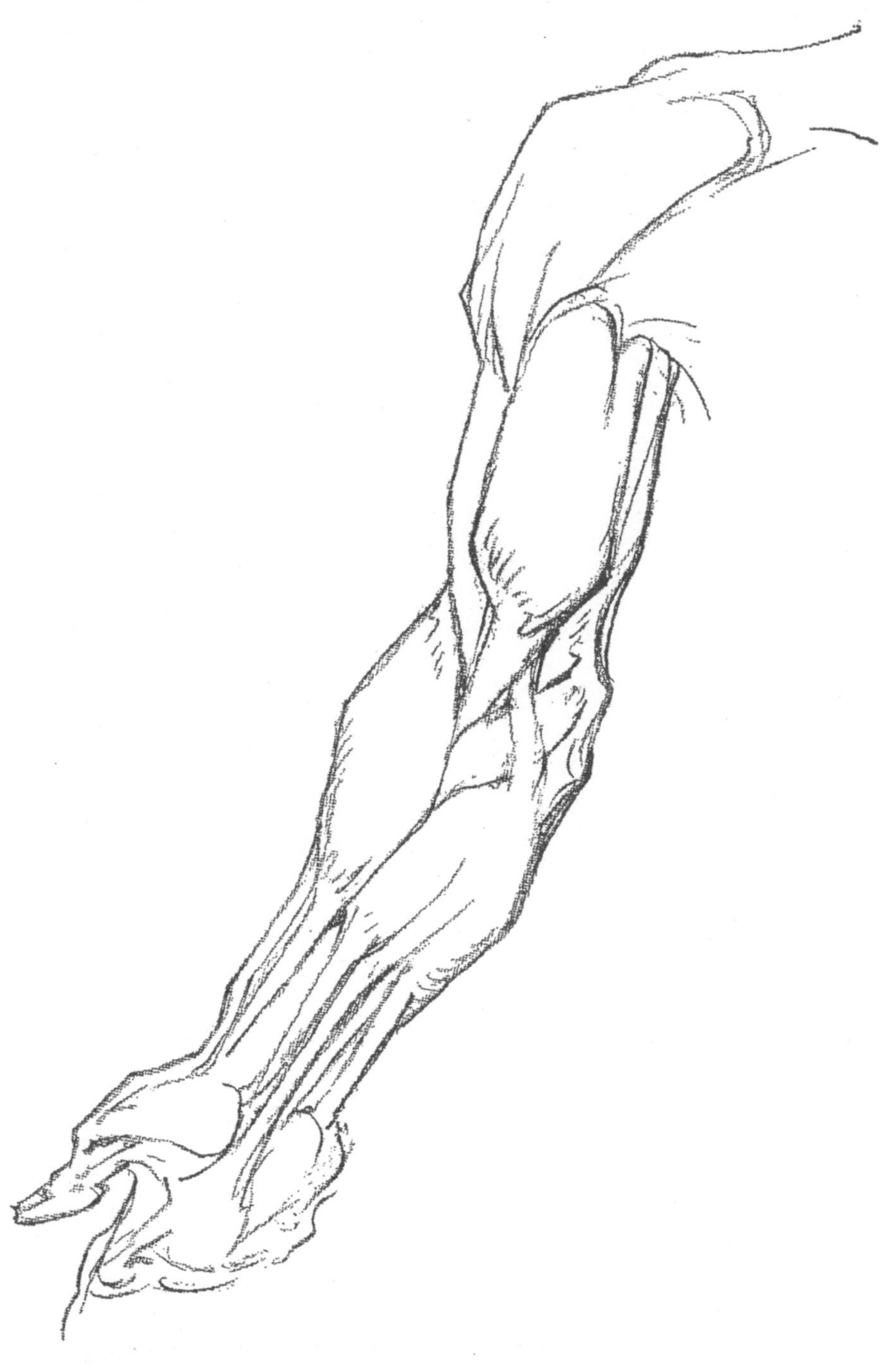

From the inner condyle, which is always a landmark, arises the *flexor-pronator* group. This is a fat softly bulging mass which tapers to the wrist, but shows superficially the *pronator teres* (round), whose turning function requires it to lie diagonally across toward the thumb side.

The outer condyle is hidden by its muscular mass when the hand is turned out. This mass is the *extensor-supinator* group, which bulges higher up, and becomes tendinous half way down. It is dominated by the *supinator longus*, which rises a third of the way up the arm, widens as far as the elbow, tapers beyond, and loses itself half way down the forearm. In turning, this wedge follows the direction of the thumb, and overlies the condyle when the arm is straight with the forearm.

From the back view, the elbow is seen to have three knobs of bone; the two condyles above referred to, and between them the upper end of the *ulna*, forming the elbow proper, or *olecranon*. The latter is higher when the arm is straight and lower when it is flexed. The overlying muscular masses meet over half way down, so that the *ulna* forms a thin dagger of bone pointing to the little finger.

MASSES

The masses of the forearm will be described in connection with those of the arm and shoulder.

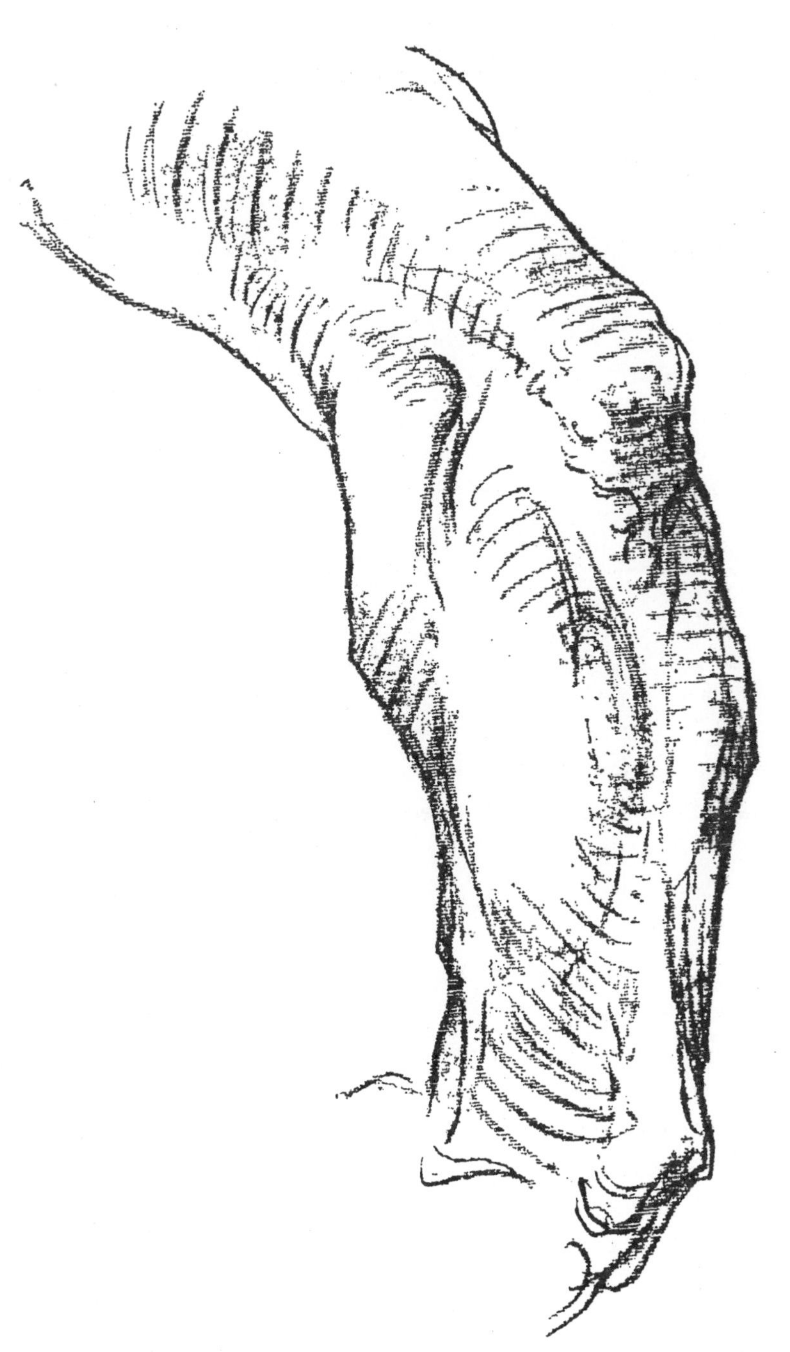

ANATOMY OF THE ARM

The bone of the upper arm is the *humerus*. The part facing the shoulder is rounded and enlarged to form the head, where it joins the shoulder blade. The lower end is flattened out sideways to give attachment to the *ulna* and *radius*, forming the *condyles*. The shaft itself is straight and nearly round, and is entirely covered with muscles except at the *condyles*.

On the flat front side of the condyles, reaching half way up the arm, is placed the broad, flat and short *brachialis anticus* muscle; and on top of that the thin, high and long *biceps*, reaching to the shoulder; its upper end flattened as it begins to divide into its two heads. One head passes to the inside of the bone and fastens to the coracoid process, under the shoulder; the other passes outside, grooving the head of the *humerus*, and attaching to the shoulder blade above the shoulder joint, under the *deltoid* or shoulder hood.

On the back, behind the flat surface made by the two condyles, arising from the central knob or *olecranon*, is the *triceps* (three-headed) muscle. Its outer head begins near the condyle, and occupies the outer and upper part of the back surface of the *humerus*. The inner head begins near the inner condyle and occupies the inner and lower portion of the bone. The middle head reaches diagonally in and up to the back of the shoulder blade.

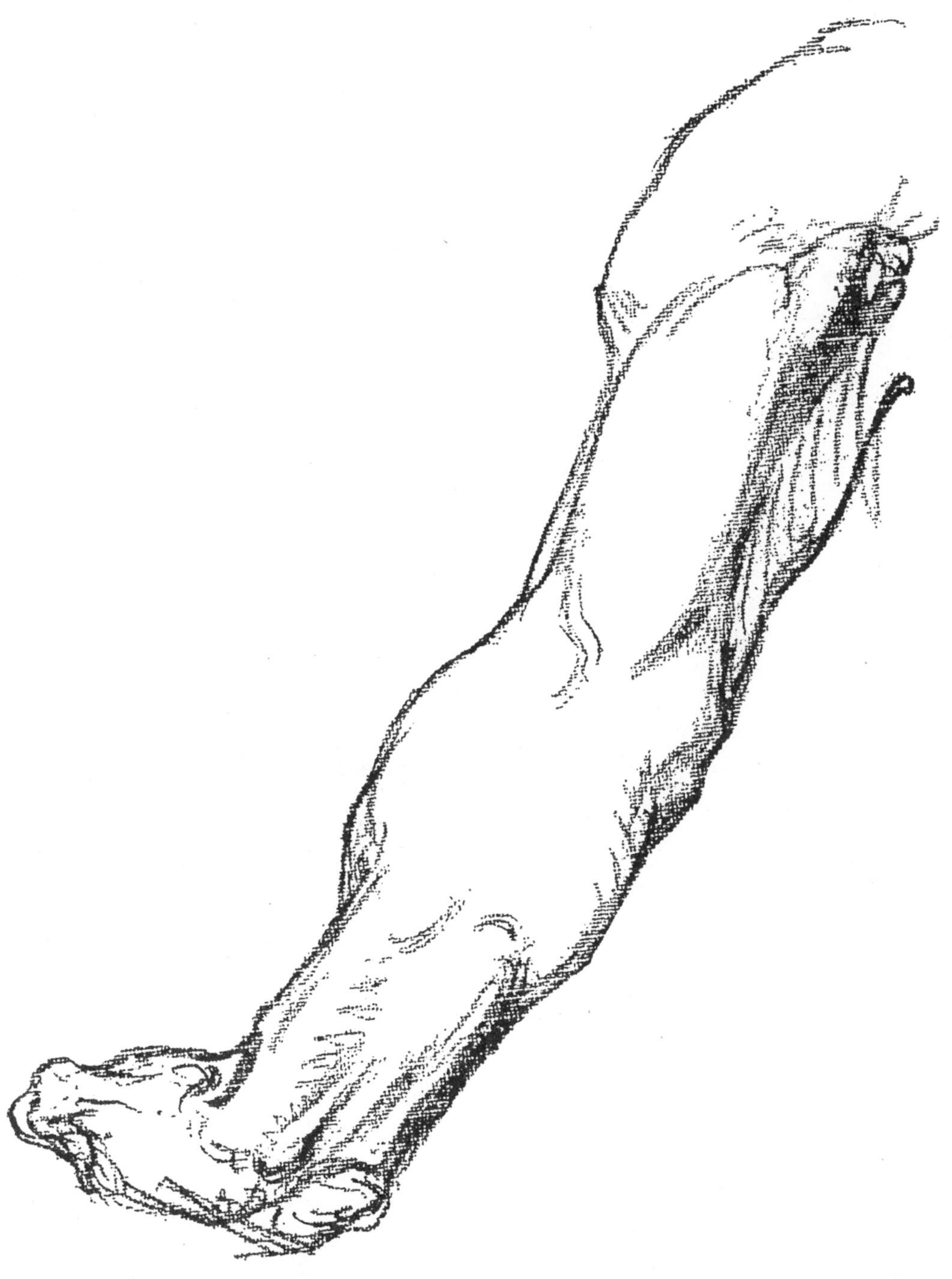

These all converge on the broad flat tendon from the *olecranon*, forming a wedge surrounded by two wings of muscle.

The triceps also is overlaid by the *deltoid* above. Between *biceps* and *triceps* are grooves. The inner condyle sinks into the inner groove below, and it is filled out above by the *coraco-brachialis* muscle, entering the armpit. The outer condyle sinks into the outer groove below, while midway of the arm the apex of the *deltoid* muscle sinks into it, overlying the upper ends of both *biceps* and *triceps*.

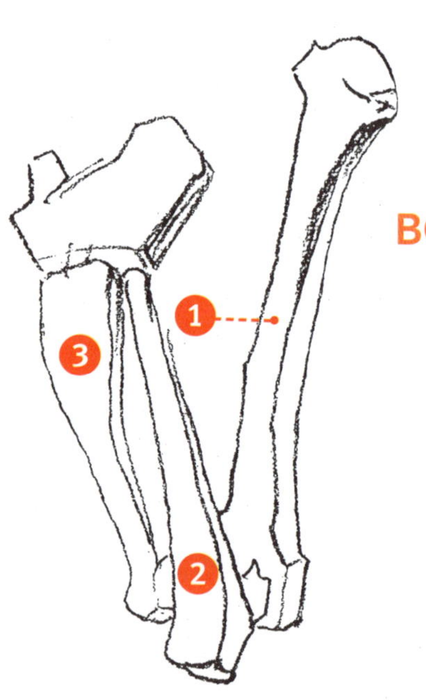

BONE OF THE ARM

① *Humerus*.

BONES OF THE FOREARM

② *Ulna* (little finger side).
③ *Radius* (thumb side).

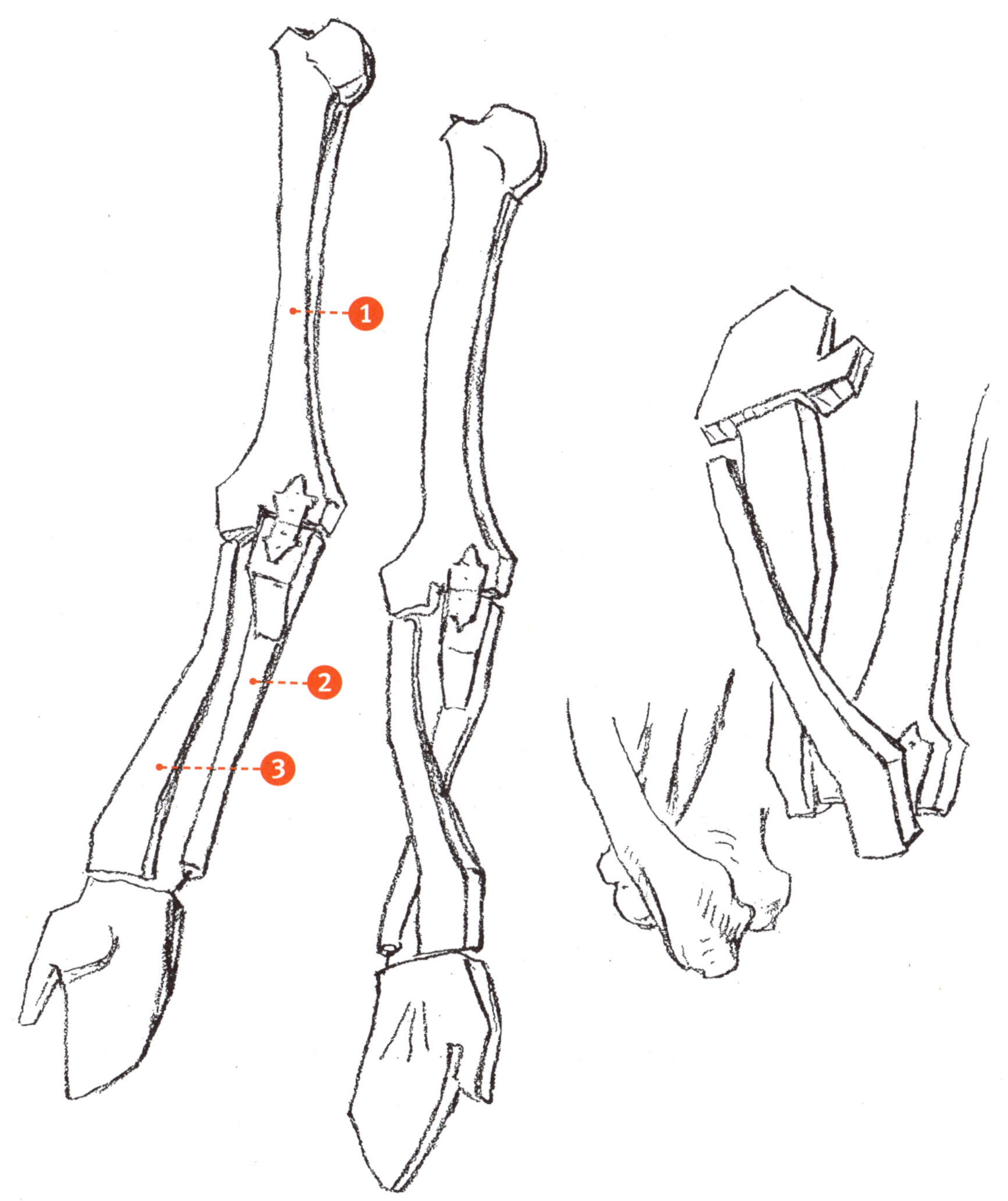
1
2
3

THE ARM

BONES OF THE UPPER LIMB

- *Humerus* – arm.
- *Radius* – forearm, thumb side.
- *Ulna* – forearm, little finger side.

MUSCLES OF THE UPPER LIMB: FRONT VIEW

① *Coraco-brachialis.*
② *Biceps.*
③ *Brachialis anticus.*
④ *Pronator radii teres.*
⑤ *Flexors*, grouped.
⑥ *Supinator longus.*

Coraco-brachialis:
From *coracoid* process, to *humerus*, inner side, half way down.
Action: Draws forward, rotates outward, *humerus*.

Biceps:
Long head from *glenoid* cavity (under *acromion*) through groove in head of *humerus*; short head from *coracoid* process; to *radius*.
Action: Depresses shoulder blade; flexes forearm; rotates *radius* outward.

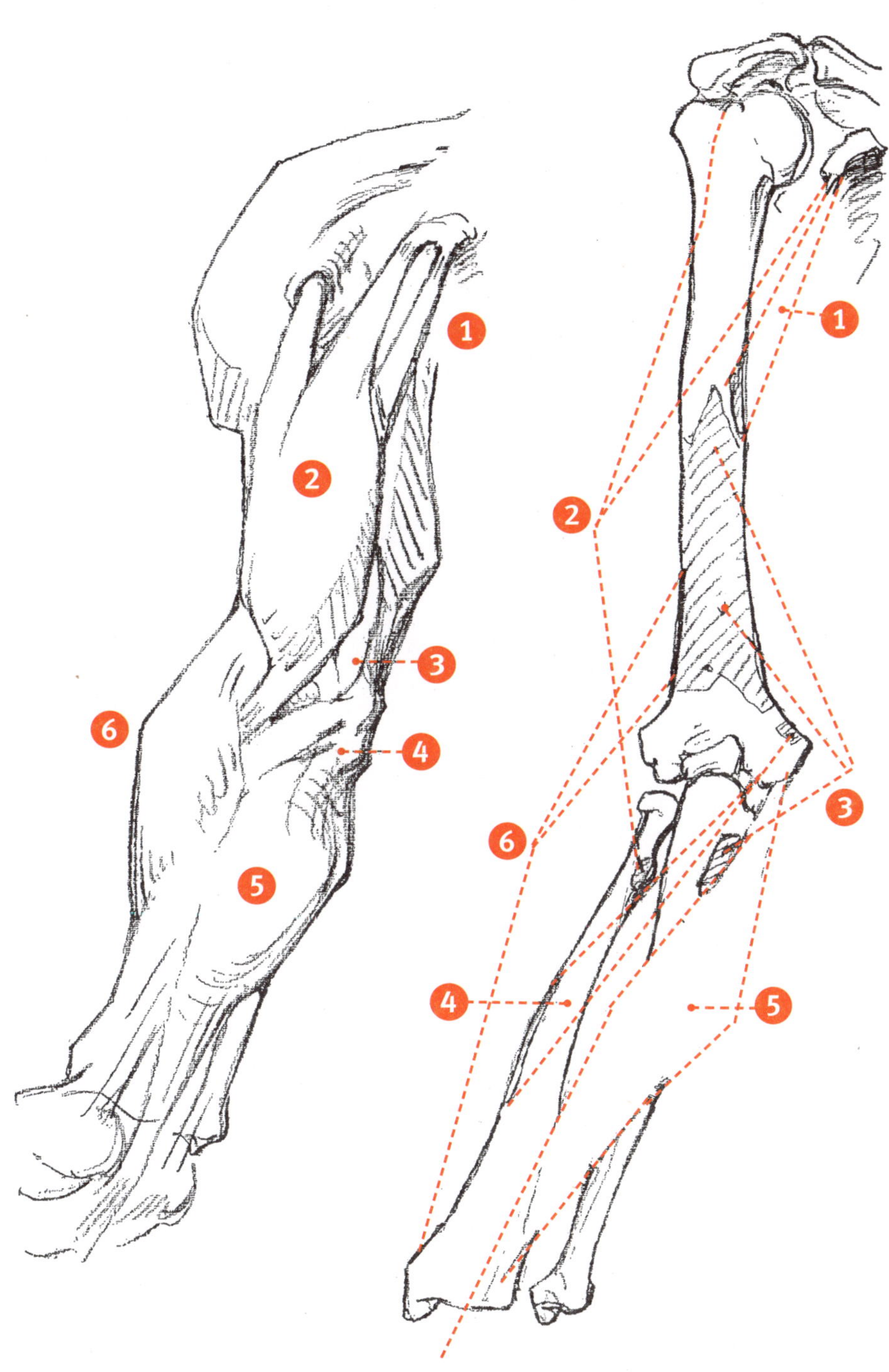
1
2
3
4
6
5
1
2
3
6
4
5

THE ARM

SUPINATION AND PRONATION OF THE FOREARM: FRONT VIEW

① *Supinator longus.*

② *Pronator radii teres.*

③ *Flexors*, grouped.

Supinator Longus:

From external *condyloid* ridge to end of *radius*.

Action: Supinates forearm.

Pronator Radii Teres:

From *internal* condyle and *ulna* to *radius*, outer side, half way down.

Action: Pronates hand and flexes forearm.

(***Flexor*** group, *see* page 108)

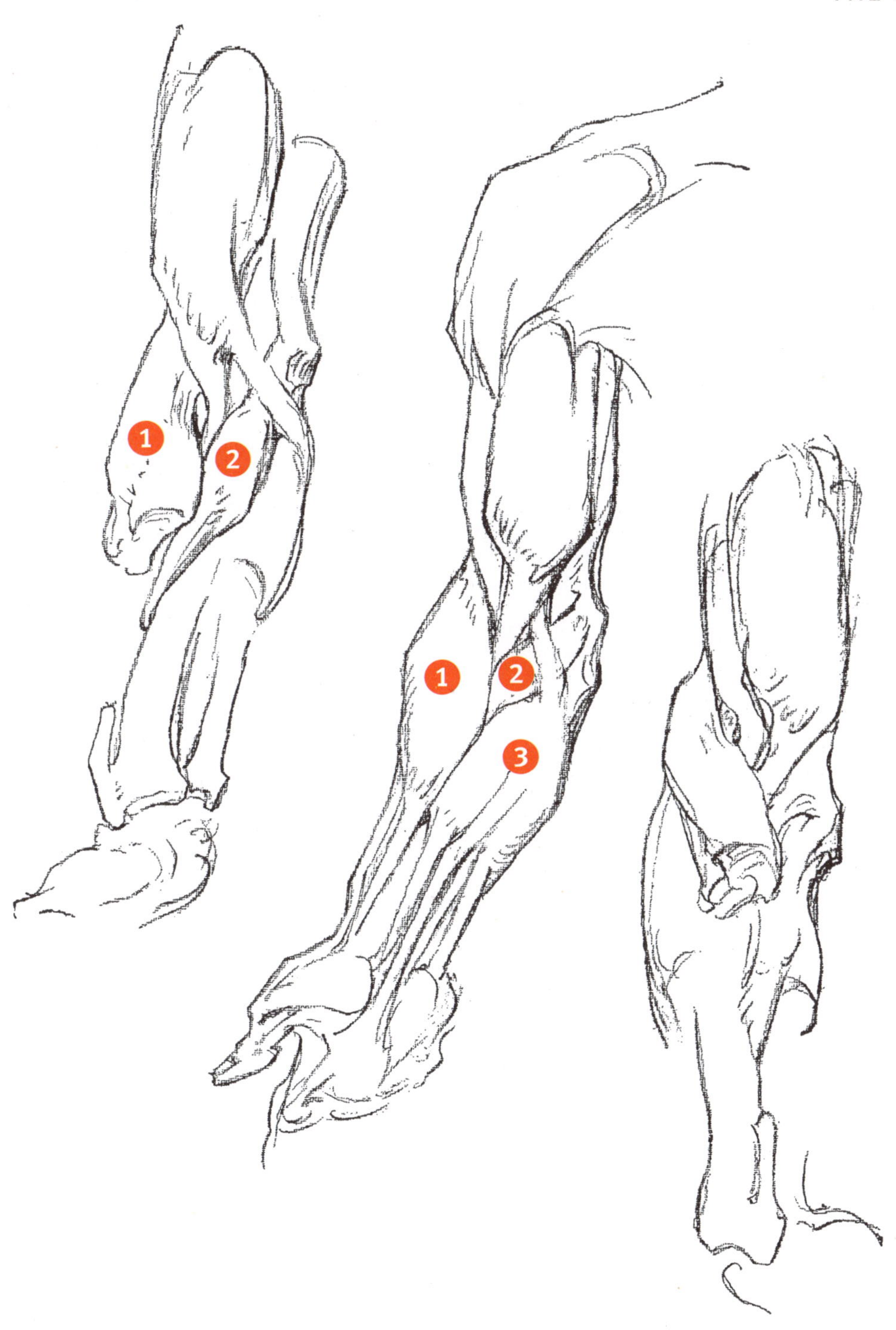
1
2
1
2
3

THE ARM

MASSES OF THE ARM, FOREARM AND WRIST:
WEDGING AND INTERLOCKING

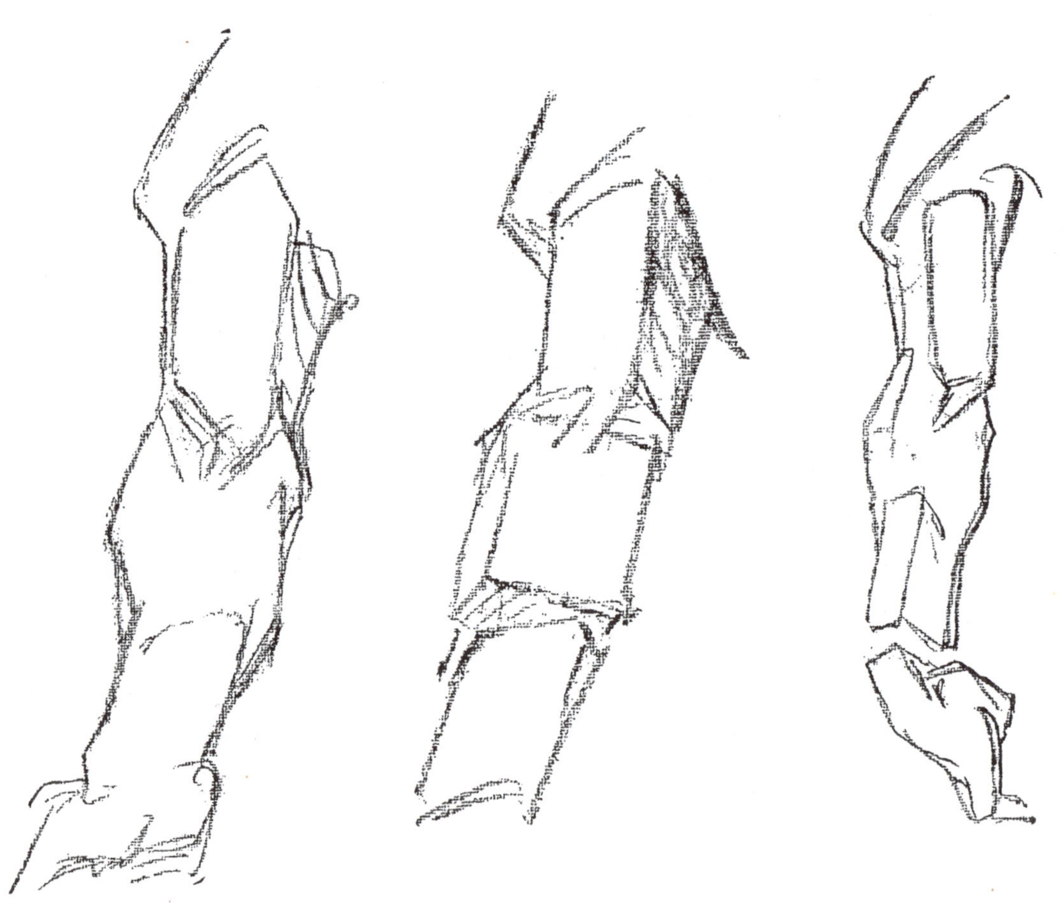

THE ARM

MUSCLES OF THE ARM: LATERAL VIEW (THUMB SIDE TOWARD THE BODY)

① *Coraco-brachialis.*
② *Biceps.*
③ *Brachialis anticus.*
④ *Supinator longus.*
⑤ *Extensor carpi radialis longior.*
⑥ *Pronator radii teres.*
⑦ *Flexors*, grouped.

Brachialis Anticus:
From front of *humerus*, lower half, to *ulna*.
Action: Flexes forearm.

Extensor Carpi Radialis Longior:
From external *condyloid* ridge to base of index finger.
Action: Extends wrist.

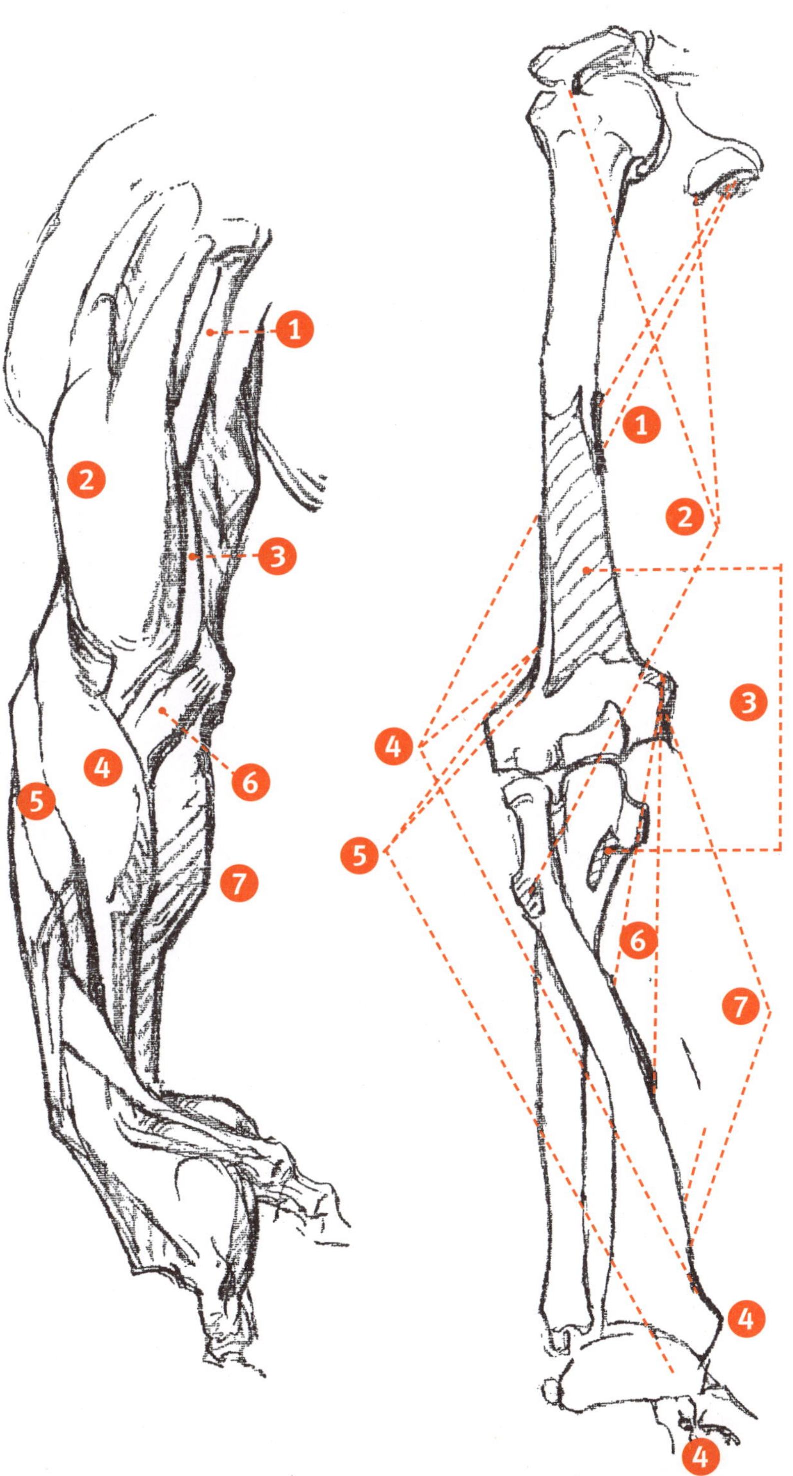
1
2
3
4
5
6
7
1
2
3
4
5
6
7
4
4

THE ARM

TURNING OF THE HAND ON THE FOREARM AND THE FOREARM ON THE ARM

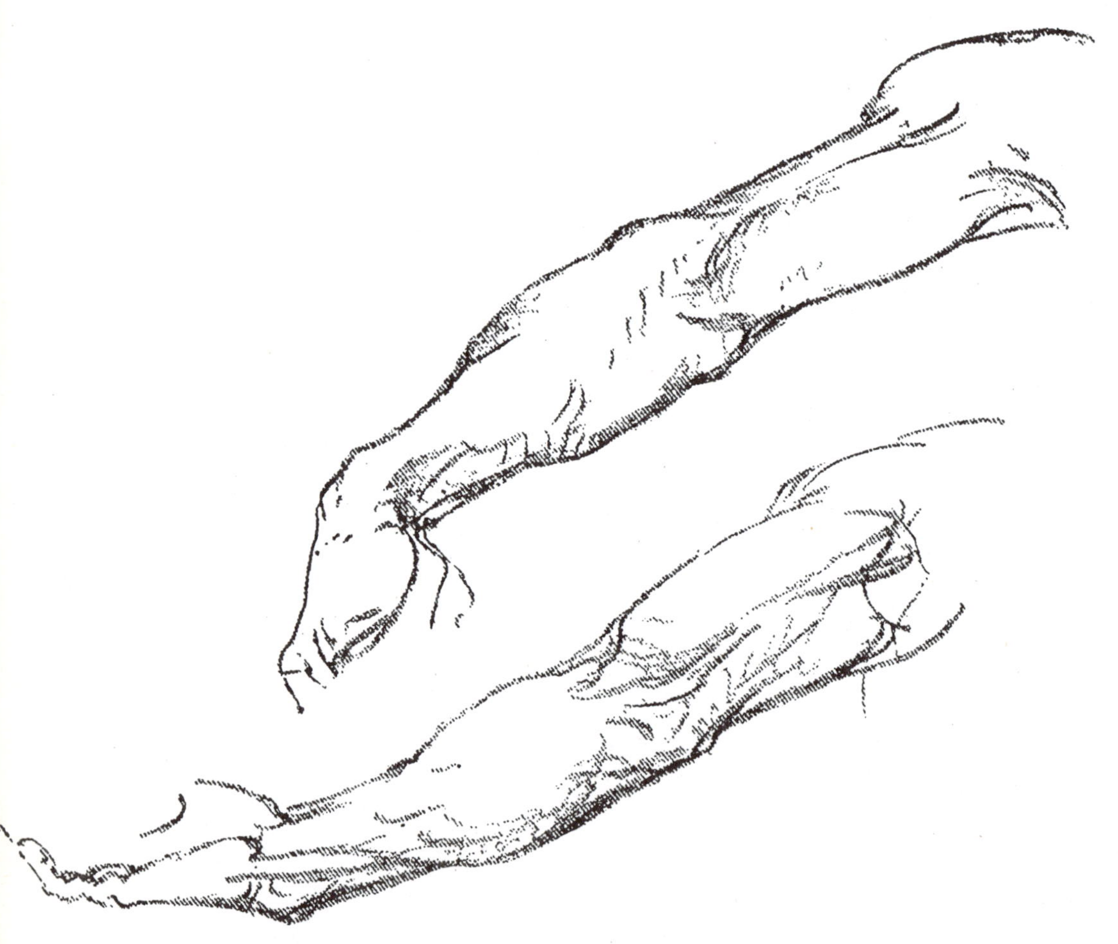

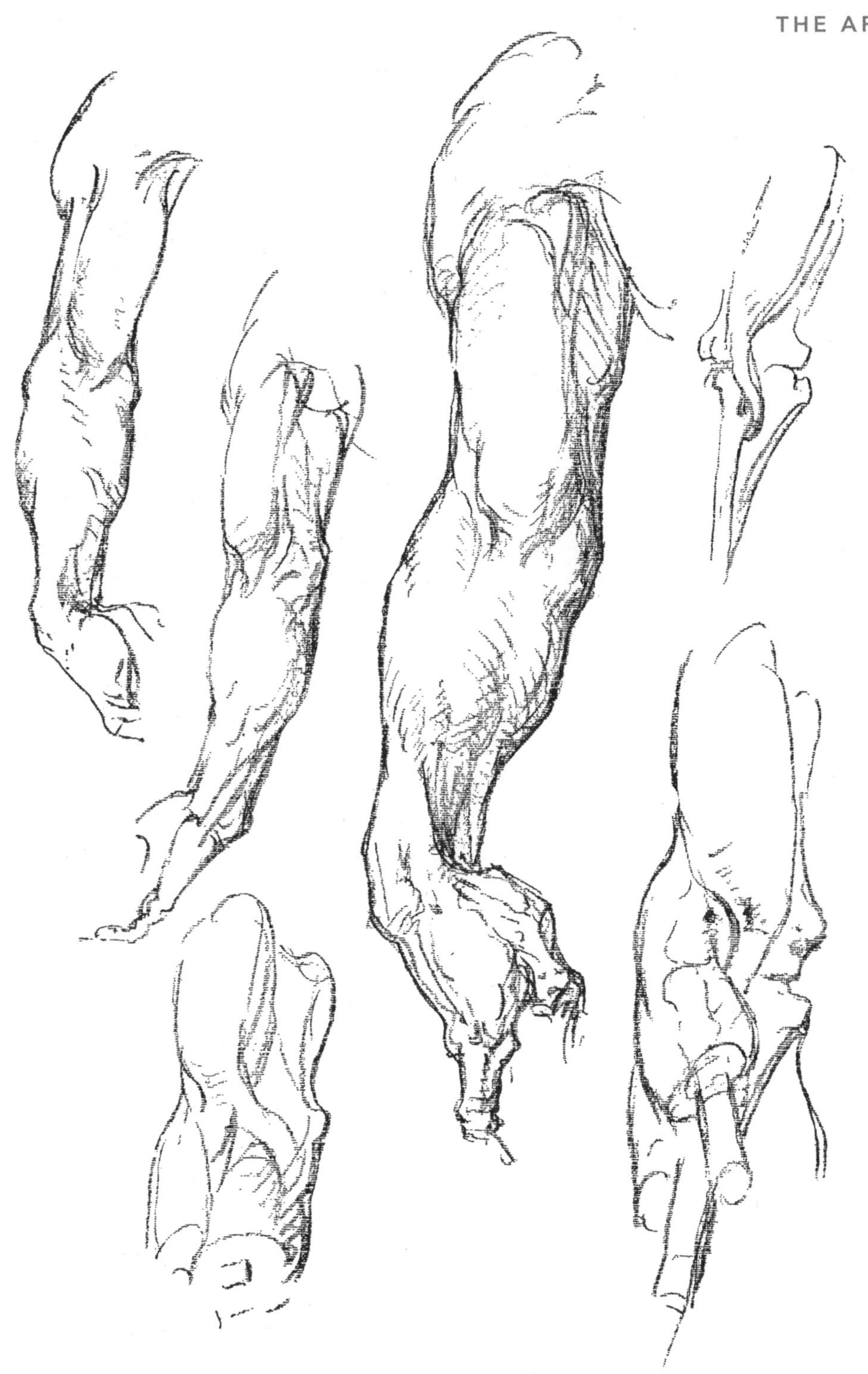

THE ARM

MUSCLES OF THE UPPER LIMB: OUTER VIEW

① *Triceps.*
② *Supinator longus.*
③ *Extenso carpi radialis longior.*
④ *Anconeus.*
⑤ *Extensors*, grouped.

Anconeus:
From back of external condyle to *olecranon* process and shaft of *ulna*.
Action: Extends forearm.

EXTENSOR GROUP

FROM EXTERNAL CONDYLE OF HUMERUS

Extensor Digitorum Communis:
From external condyle to second and third *phalanges* of all fingers.
Action: Extends fingers.

Extensor Minimi Digiti:
From external condyle to second and third *phalanges* of little finger.
Action: Extends little finger.

Extensor Carpi Ulnaris:
From external condyle and back of *ulna* to base of little finger.
Action: Extends wrist and bends down.

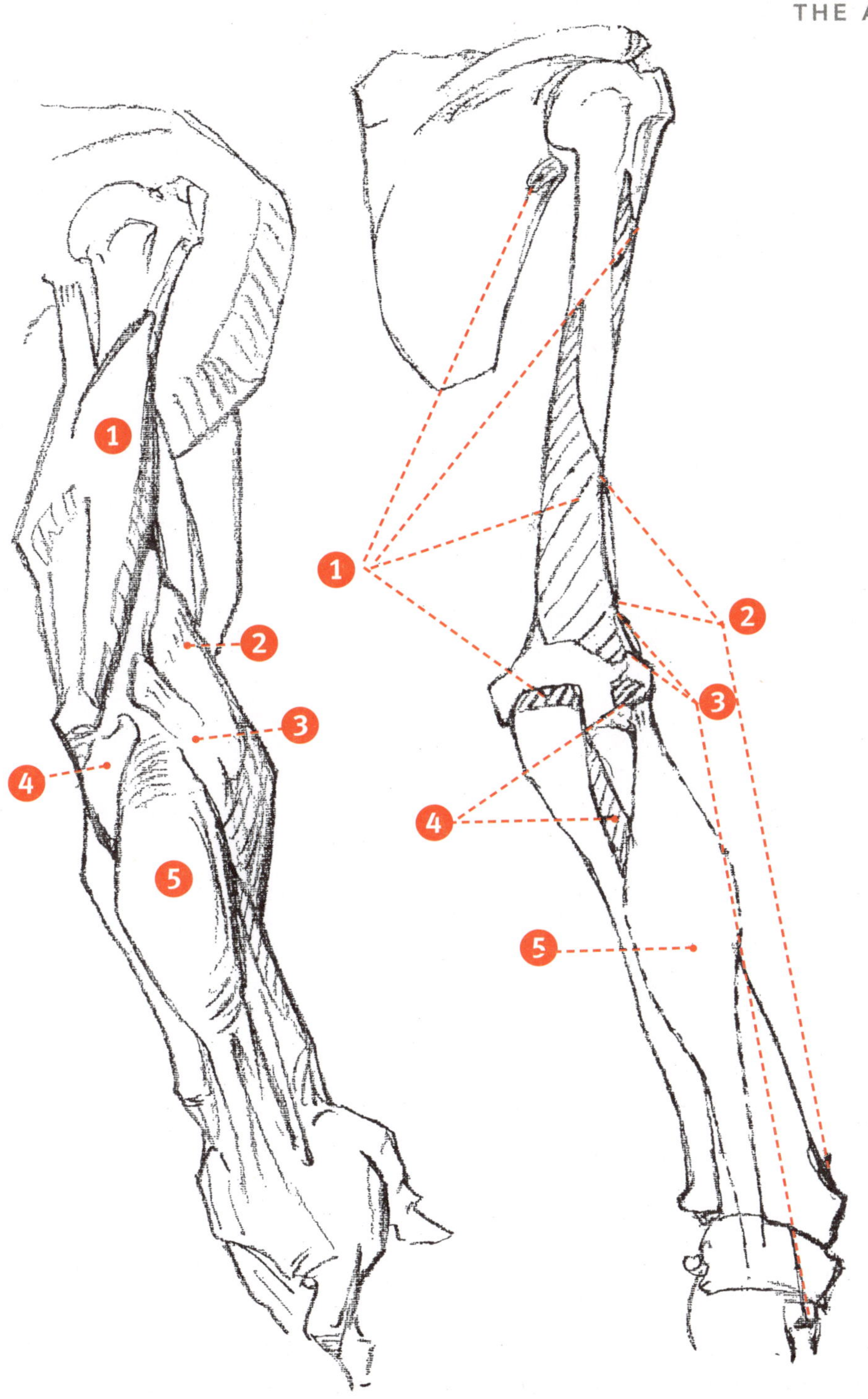
1
2
3
4
5
1
2
3
4
5

THE ARM

MUSCULAR MASS OF FOREARM: BACK VIEW

① *Extensor carpi ulnaris.*
② *Extensor communis digitorum.*

(***Extensor*** group, *see* page 98.)

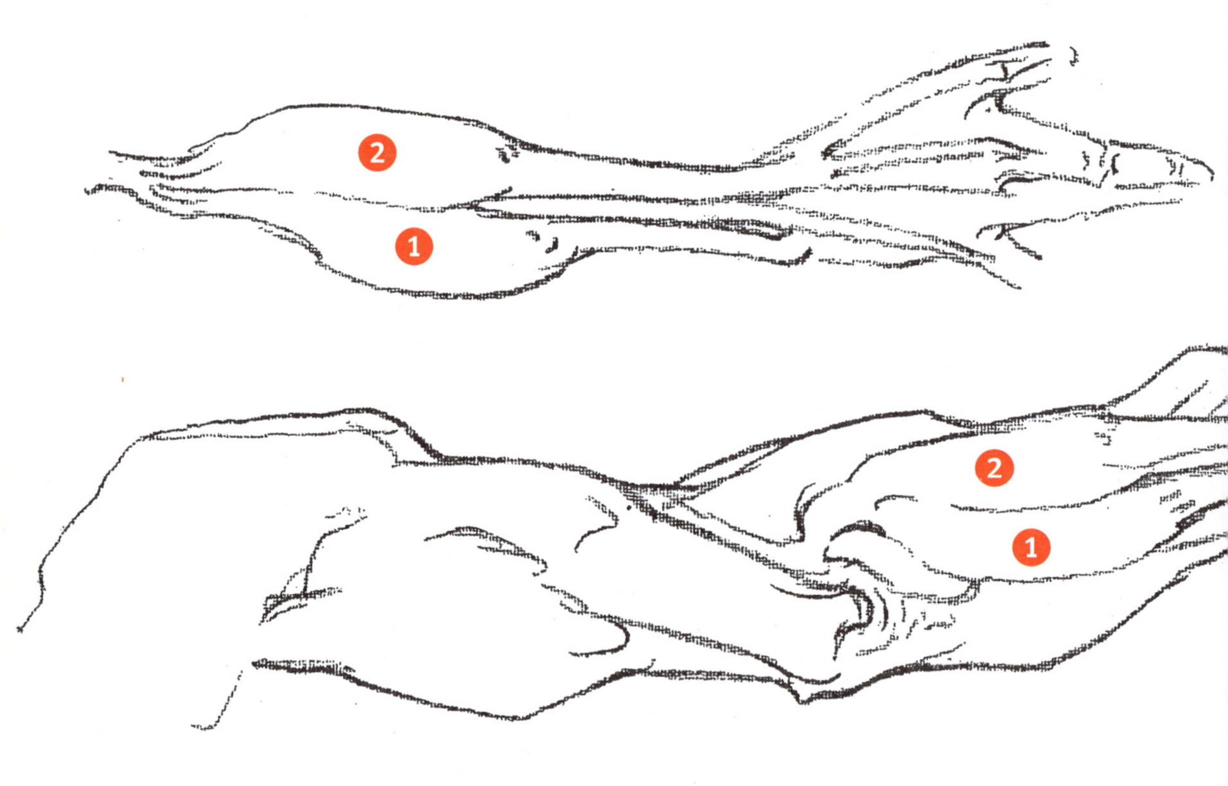

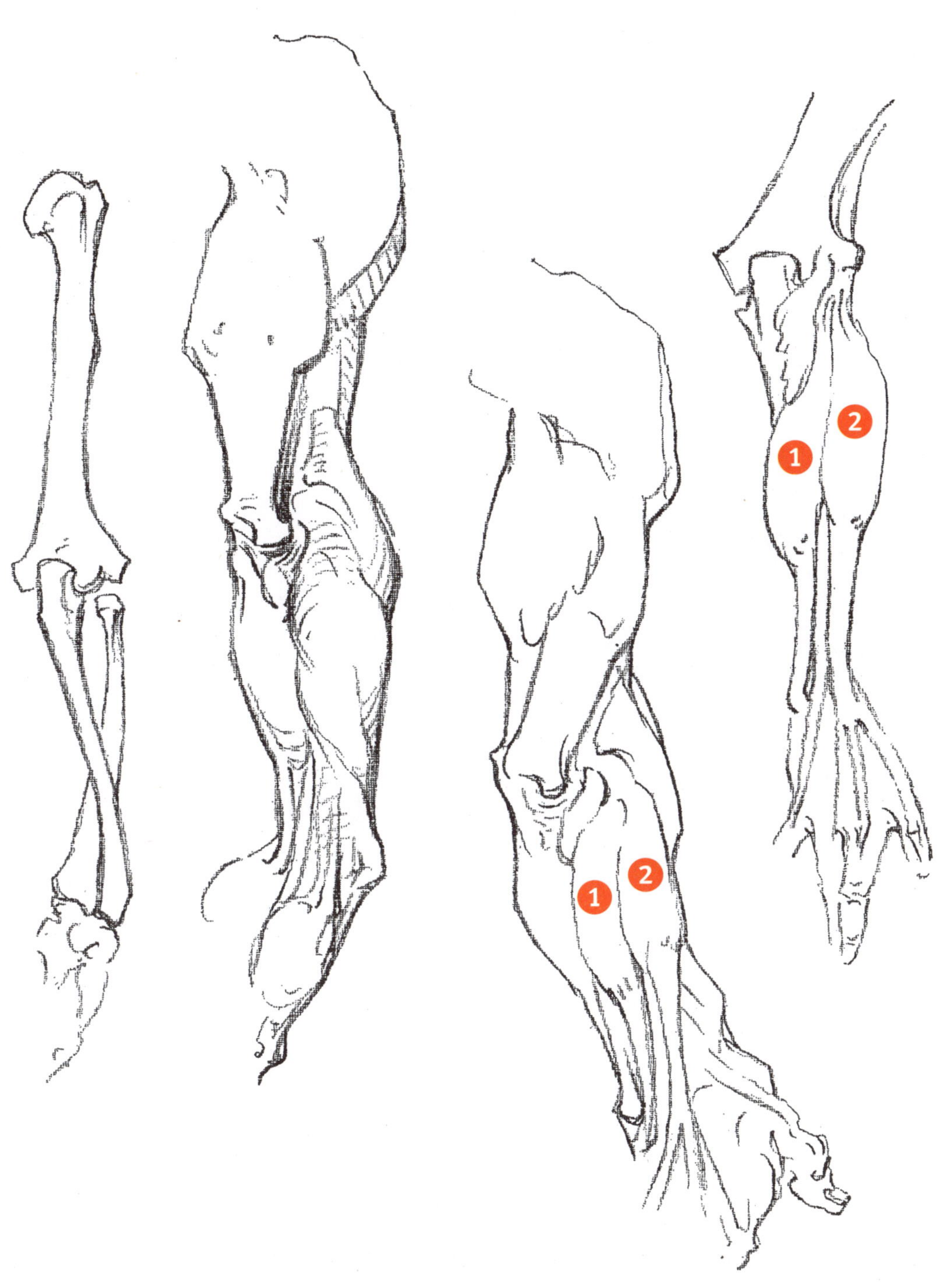
1
2
1
2

THE ARM

WEDGING OF THE ARM INTO THE FOREARM: BACK VIEW

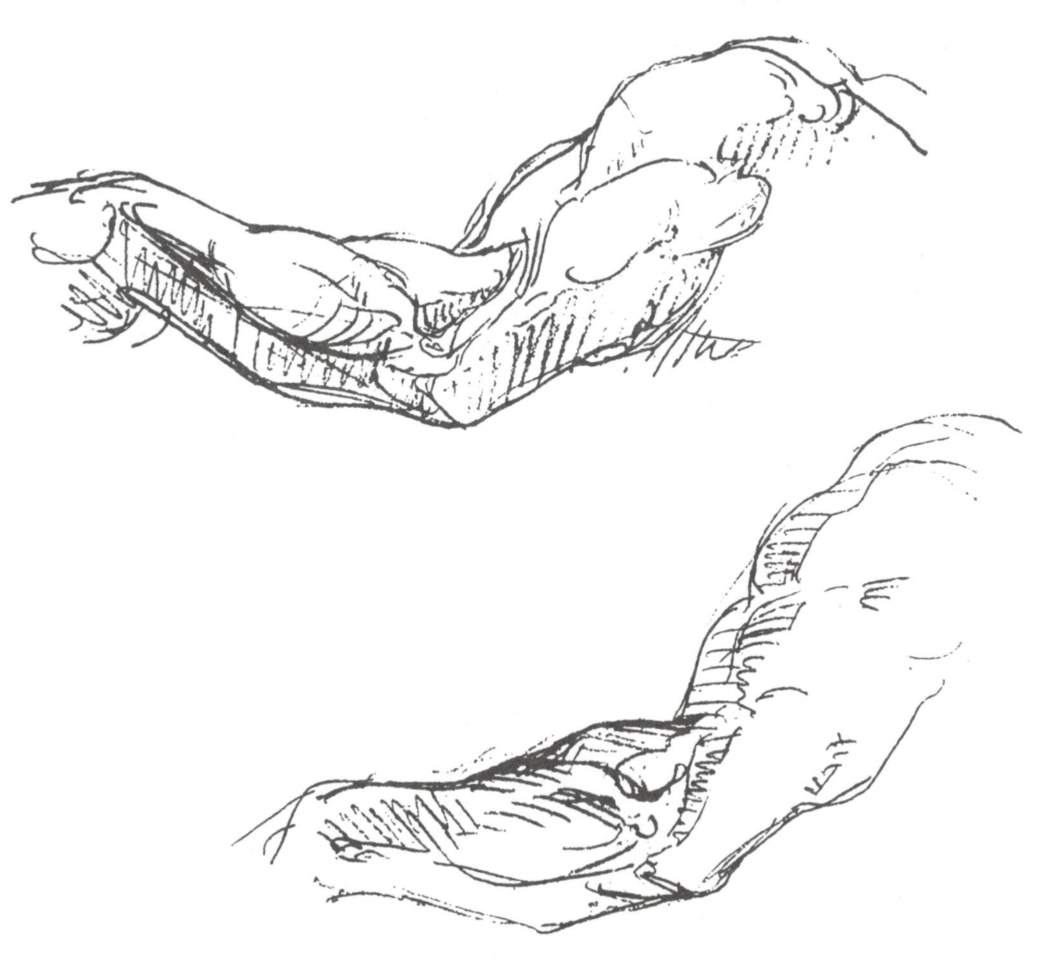

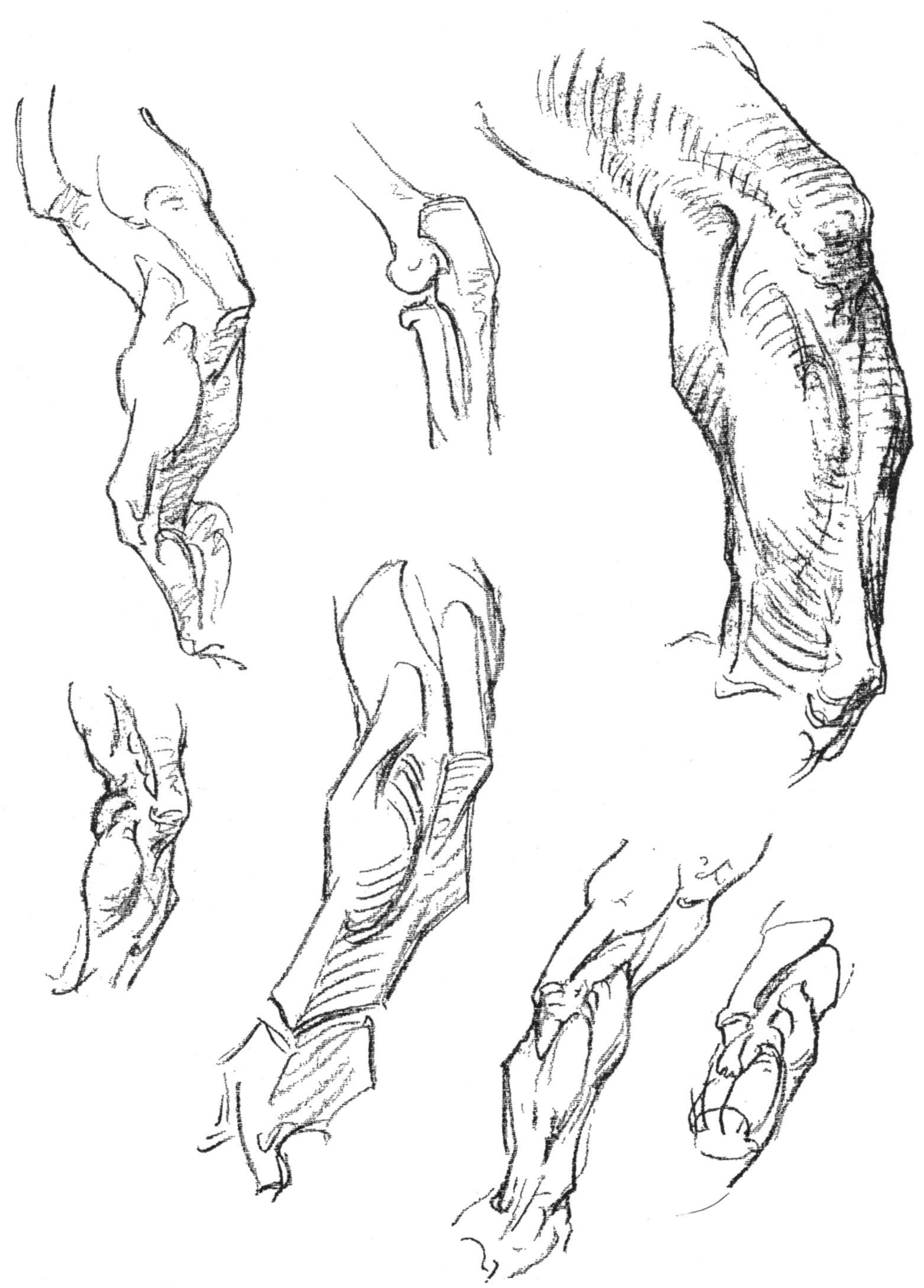

THE ARM

WEDGING OF ARM INTO THE FOREARM AT THE ELBOW

① *Biceps.*
② *Triceps.*
③ *Supinator longus.*
④ *Flexors.*
⑤ *Extensors.*

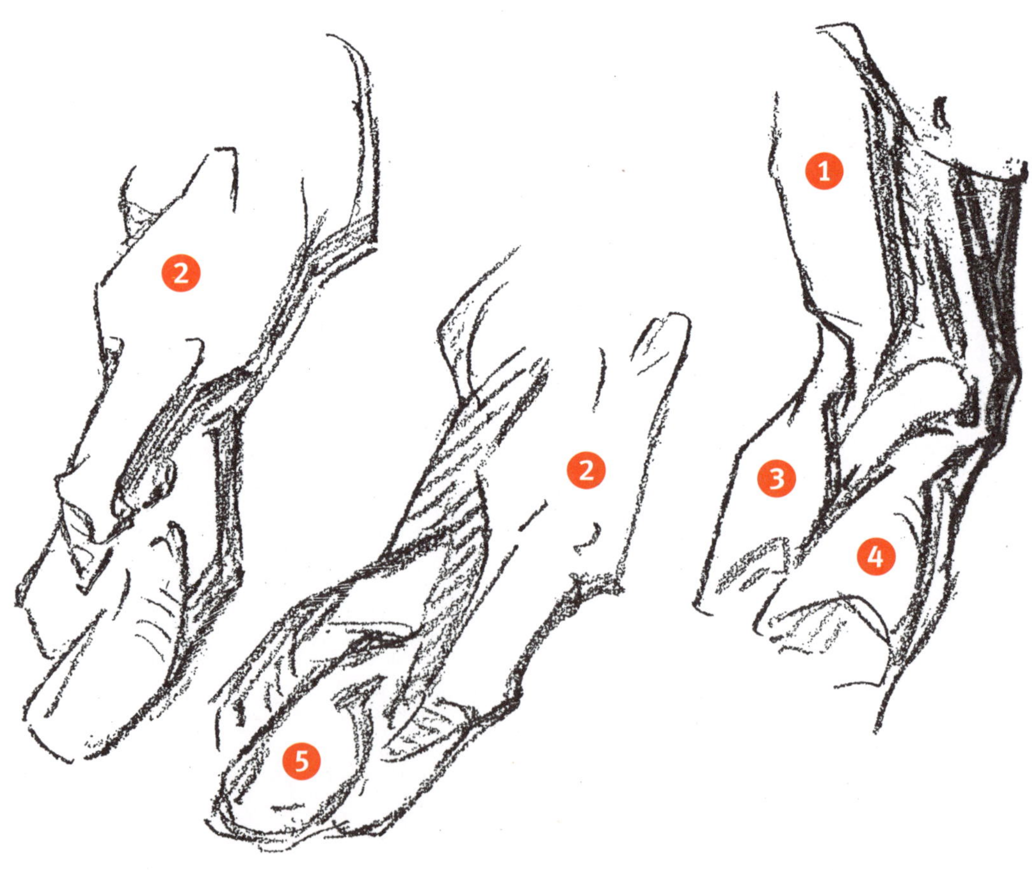

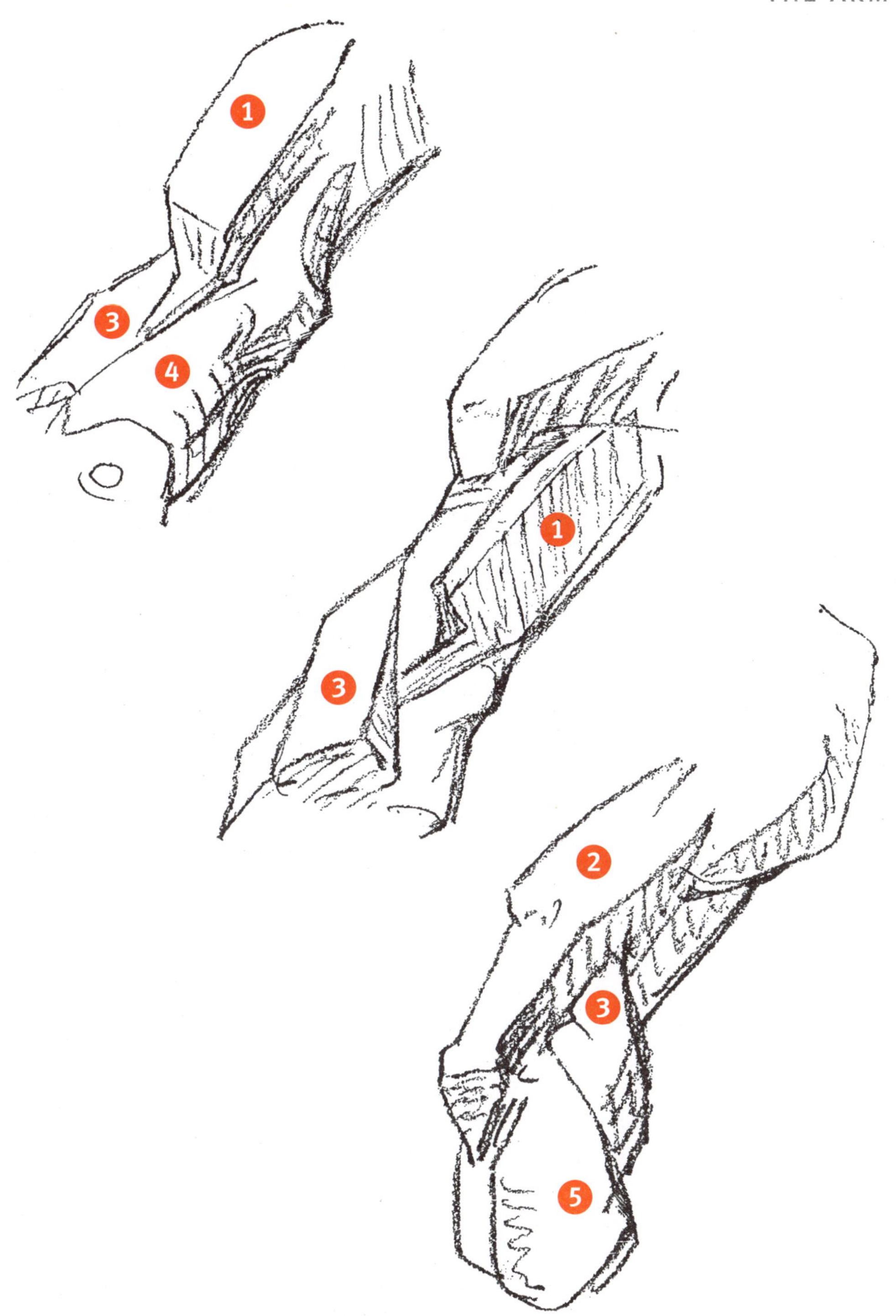
1
3
4
1
3
2
3
5

THE ARM

Examples for reference and study.

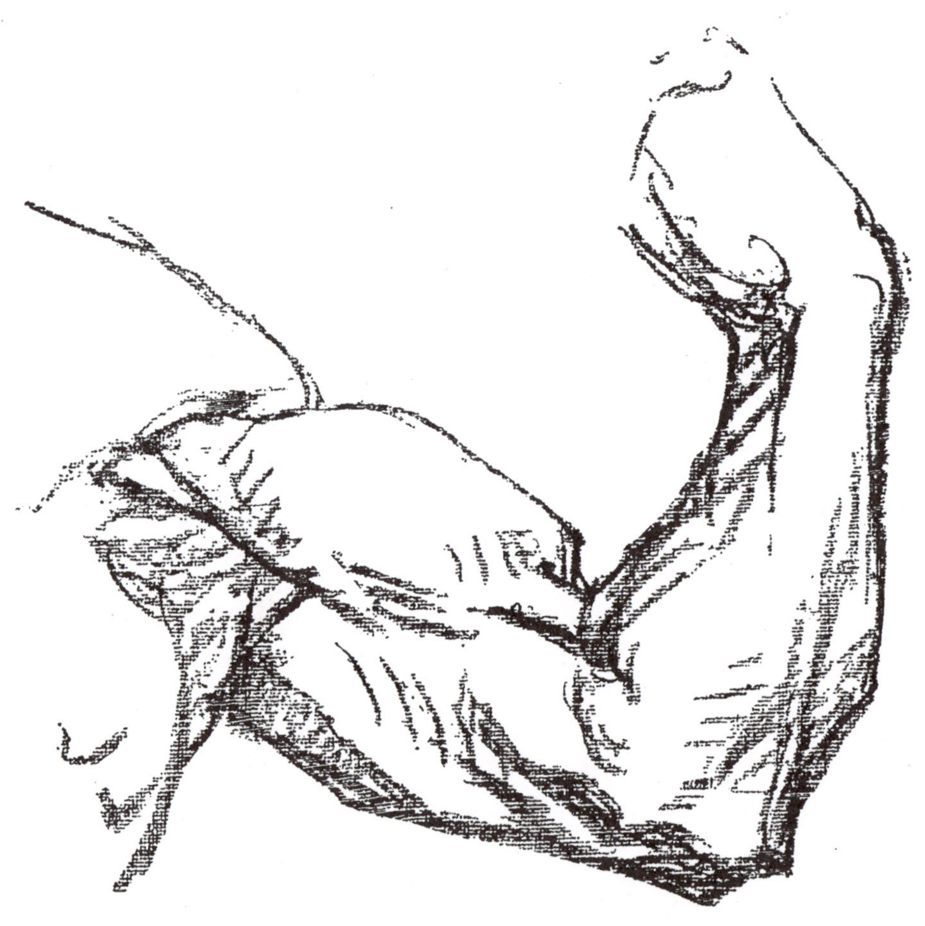

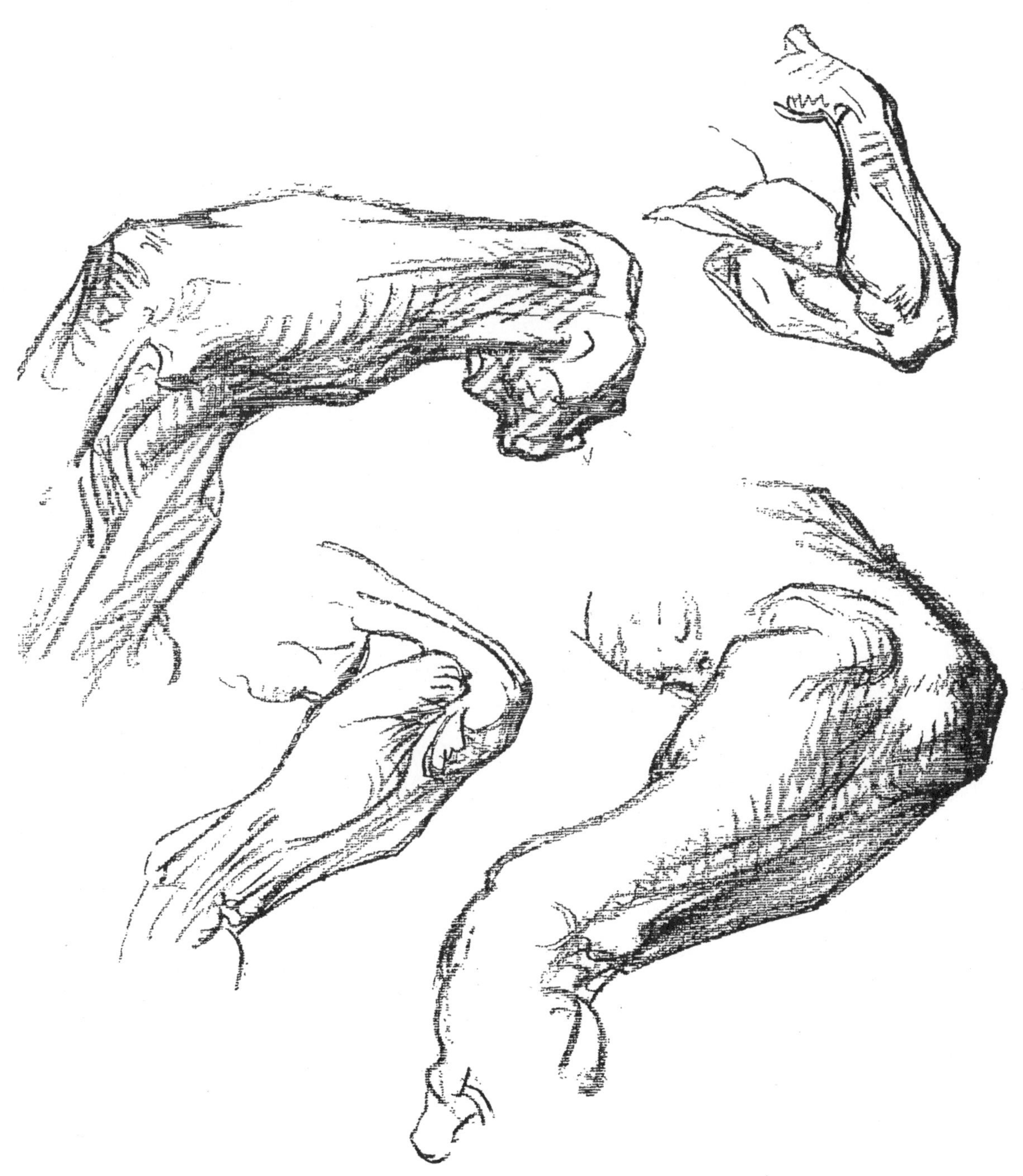

THE ARM

MUSCLES OF THE ARM:
INNER VIEWS

① *Triceps.*

② *Biceps.*

③ *Supinator longus.*

④ *Flexors*, grouped.

⑤ *Pronator teres.*

FLEXOR GROUP

FROM INTERNAL CONDYLE OF HUMERUS

Flexor Carpi Radialis:

From internal condyle to first *metacarpal.*

Action: Flexes wrist and bends up.

Flexor Carpi Ulnaris:

From internal condyle and *olecranon* to fifth *metacarpal*, base of little finger.

Action: Flexes wrist and bends down.

Flexor Sublimis Digitorum (flexor sublimis perforatus):

From inner condyle, *ulna* and *radius* to second *phalanges* of all fingers; perforated to admit passage of *profundus* tendons.

Action: Flexes fingers and hand.

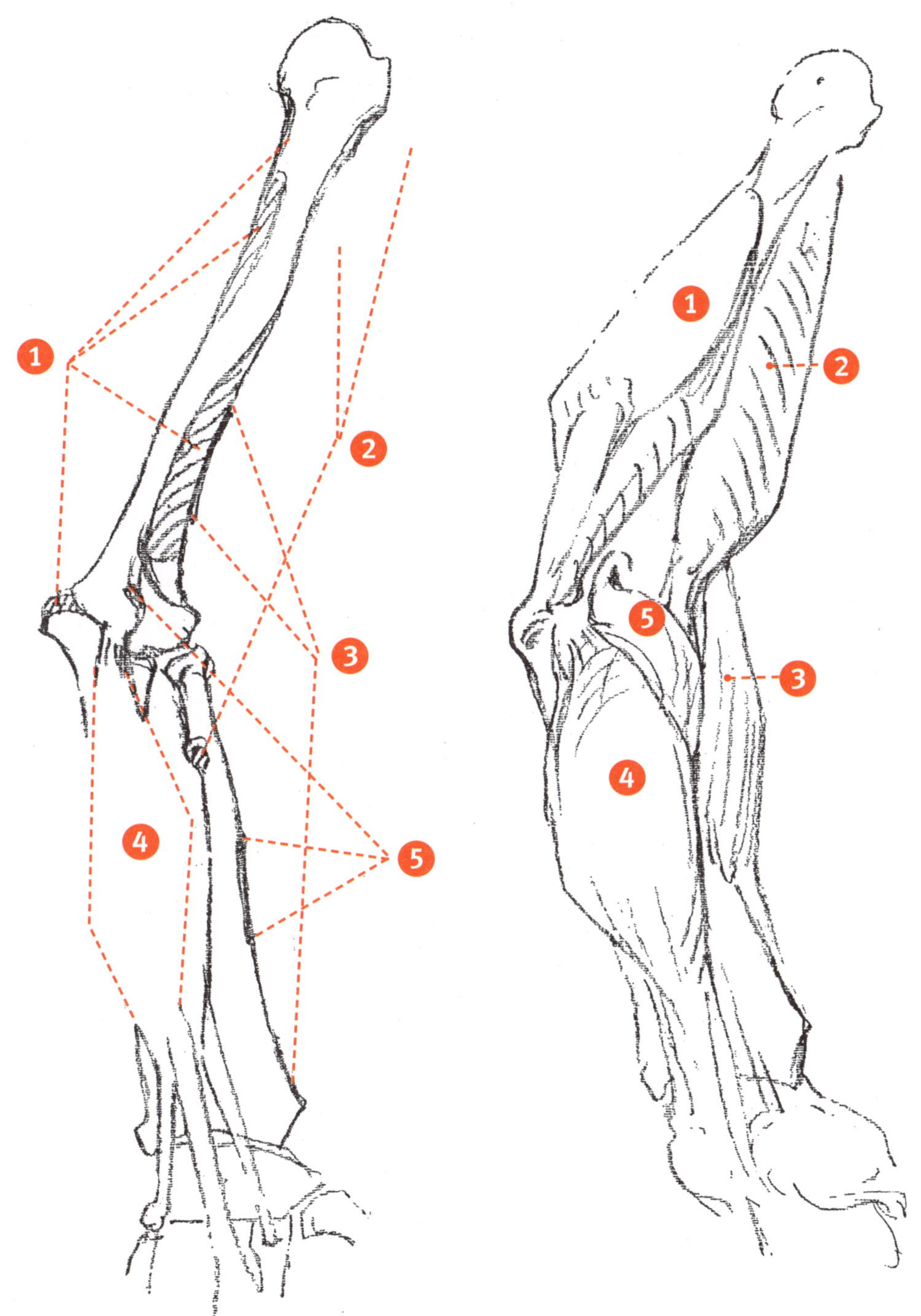
1
2
3
4
5
1
2
5
3
4

THE ARM

Examples for reference and study.

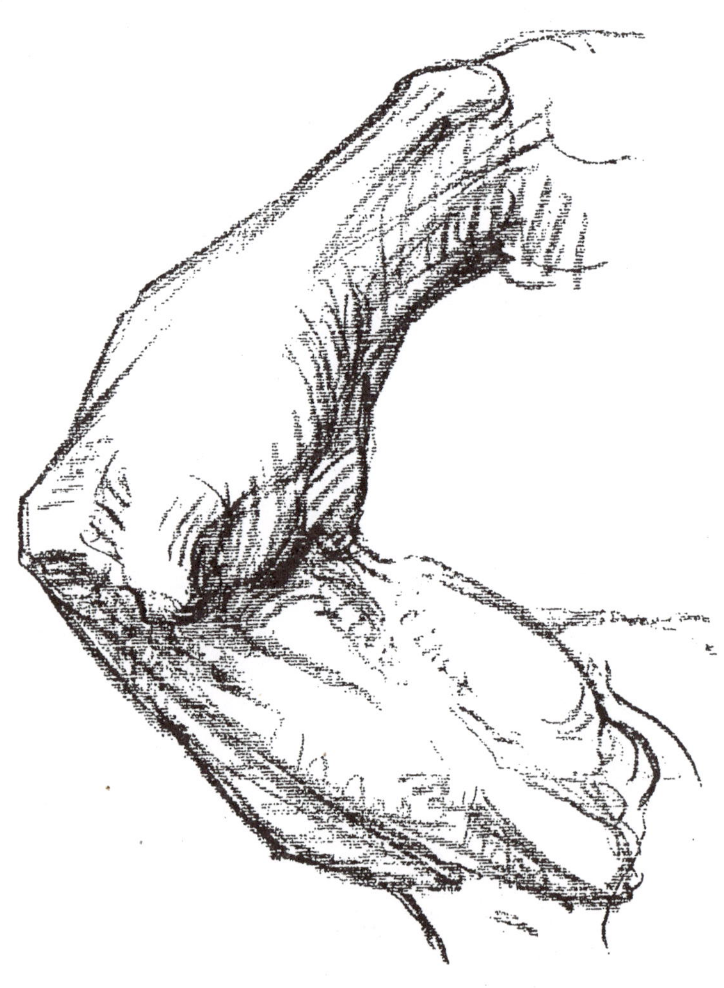

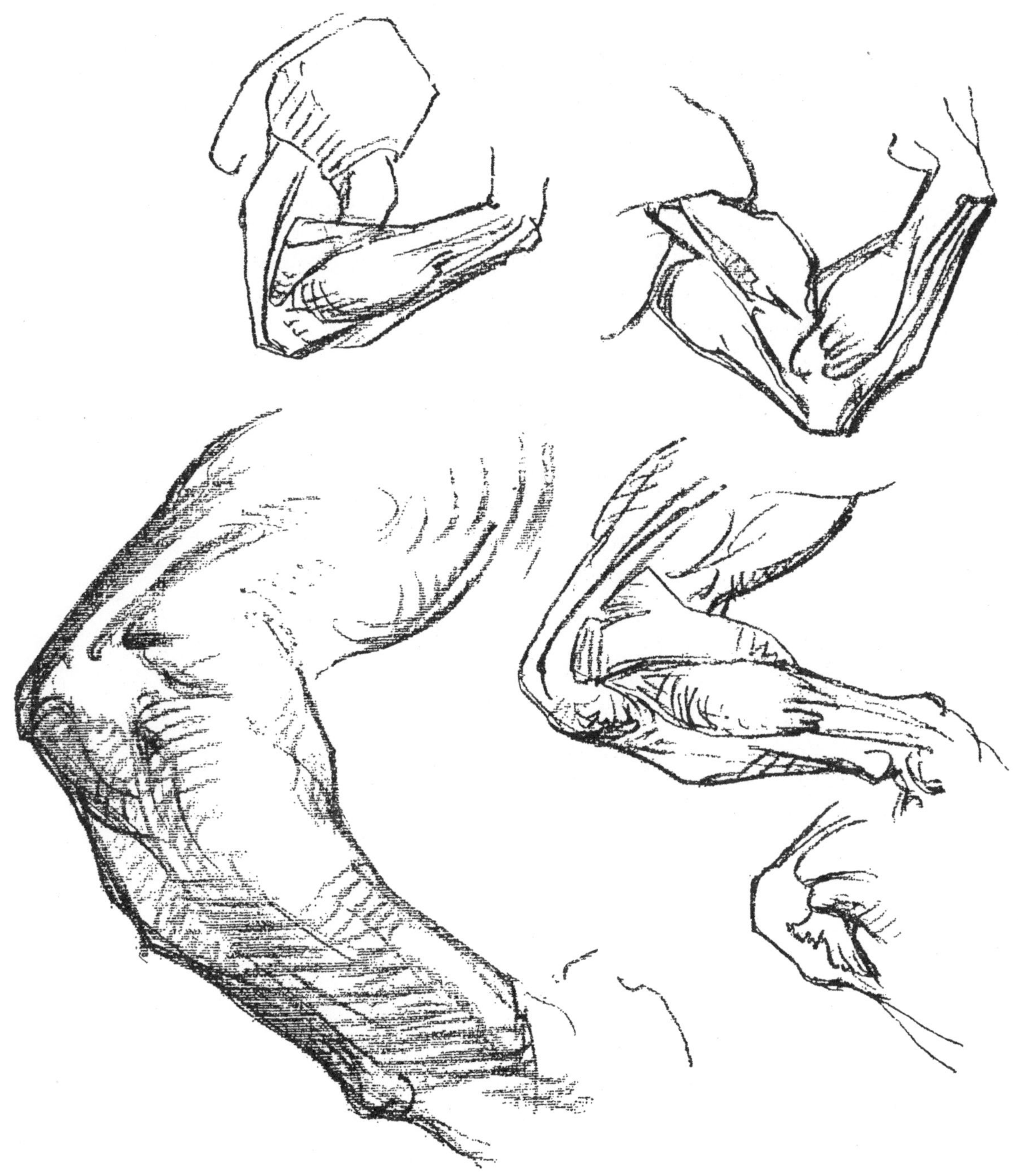

ANATOMY OF THE SHOULDER

Form is given to the shoulder by the *deltoid* (triangle) muscle. An almost perfect triangle is this muscle, its apex downward and wedging into the outer groove of the arm, its base upward and bent around to attach to the shoulder girdle. Just below the base is a ripple which marks the head of the arm bone.

The shoulder girdle is made up of the collar bone and a ridge of the shoulder blade, meeting. They both point outward, the ridge a little lower, but both turn straight forward before meeting. The collar bone is an S-shaped bone, its outer curve and tail made by this forward turning. Over the point of union is a flat space.

From the hollow of this S-curve a groove sinks first downward and then at an angle outward, marking the border between the shoulder and the great breast muscle. Behind the inner two-thirds of the collar bone is a triangular depression between it and the *trapezius* muscle behind; its base to the neck, its apex pointing outward.

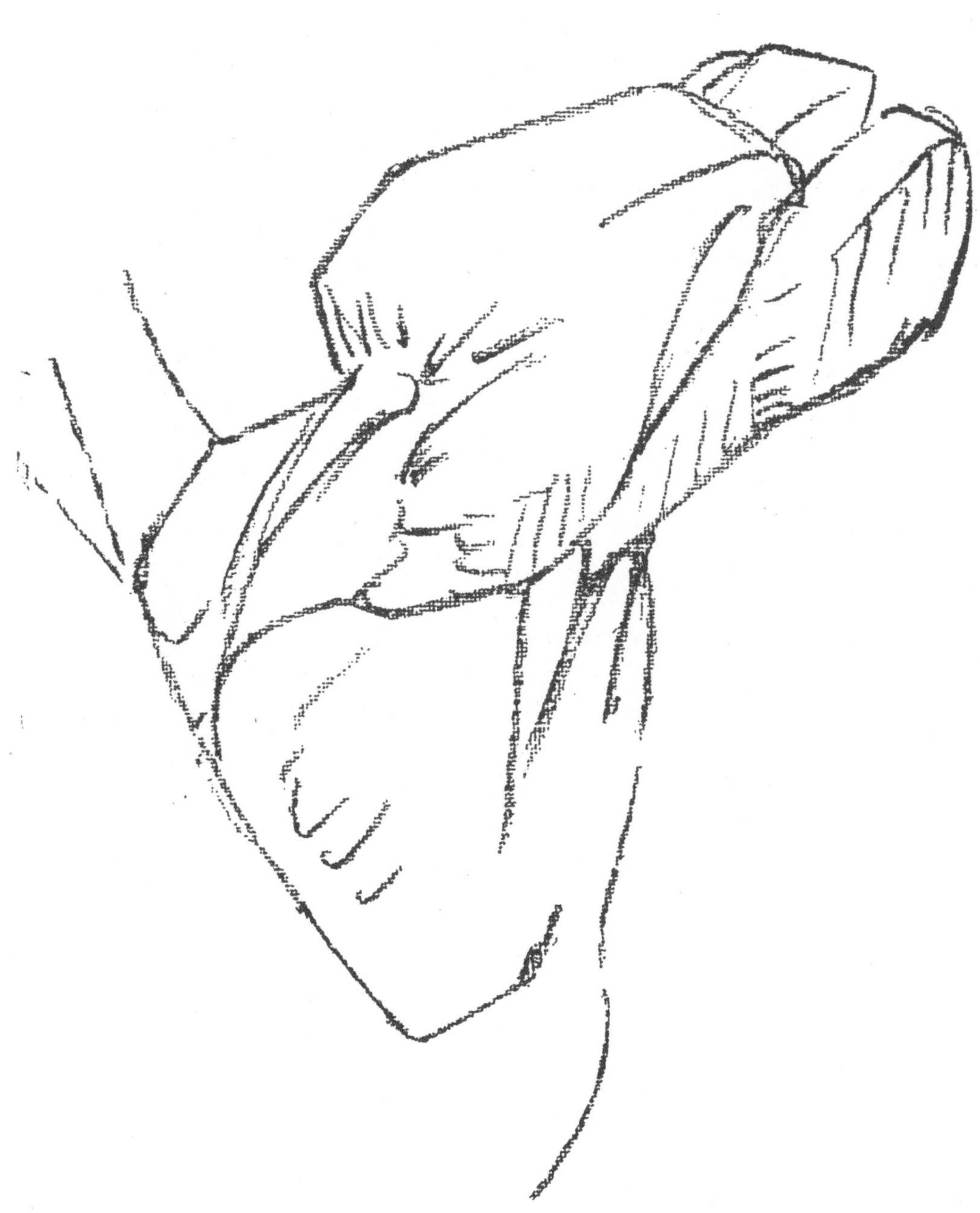

MOVEMENTS

In the shoulder are found two joints. At the point of the shoulder is the joint between shoulder blade and collar bone, a flat hinge pointing straight forward, allowing the shoulder blade to slide freely over the flat surface of the back. Not only may the shoulder blade slide freely over the back, but may even lift from it at the point and inner edge, slightly amplifying its range.

Below it under the *deltoid* is the joint of the shoulder blade with the *humerus* or arm bone, the shoulder proper, facing sideways and a little forward. It is a universal joint, with a right angle and a half of movement in two planes; but its sweep is always increased by the movement of both shoulder blade and collar bone.

At the juncture of the collar bone with the *sternum* or breast plate is a universal joint, with movement in two planes and also twisting, but with very narrow range. Its movements are chiefly lifting forward and up and twisting forward. Its shape expresses an important spring function, it being the only bony union of arm and shoulder with the trunk.

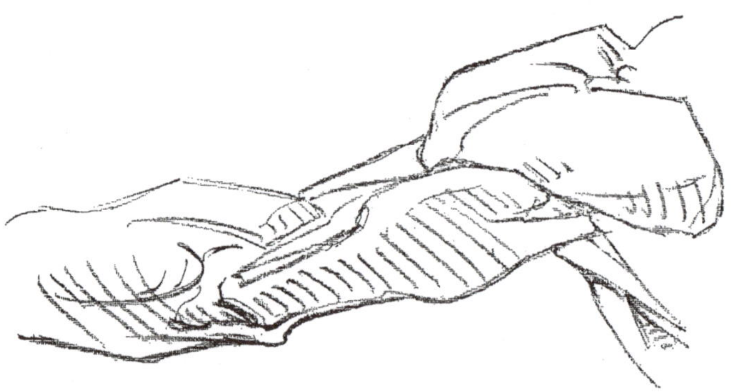

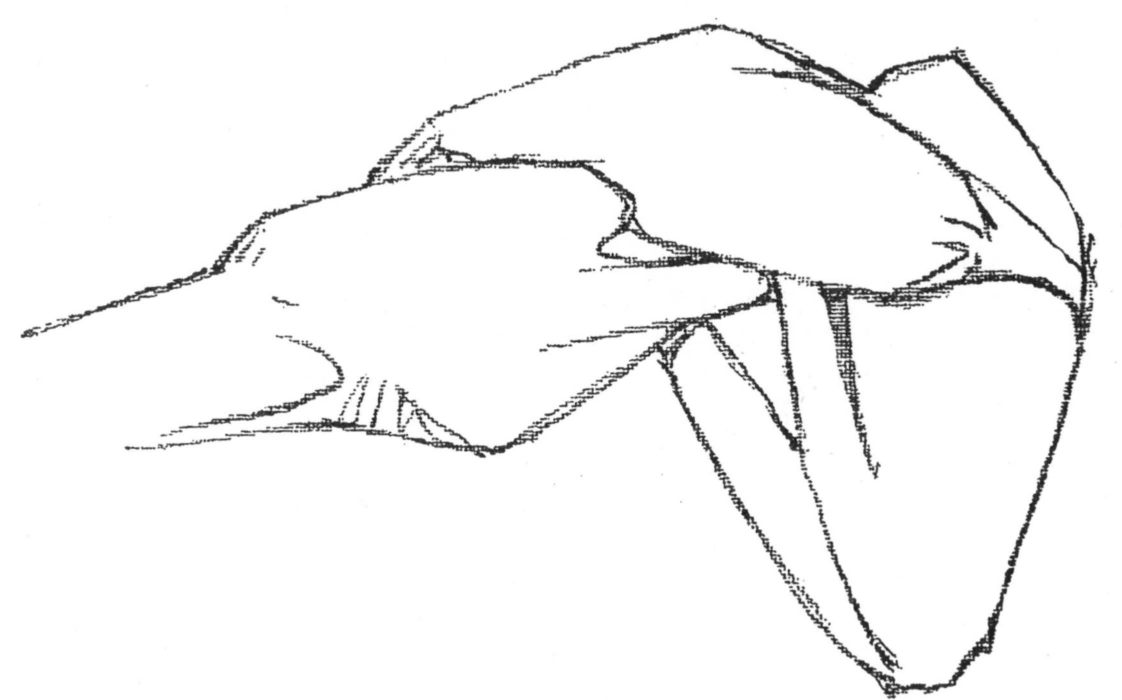

MASSES

The masses of the shoulder, arm, forearm and hand do not join directly end to end with each other, but overlap and lie at various angles. They are joined by wedges and wedging movements. Constructing these masses first as blocks, we will have the mass of the shoulder, or deltoid muscle, with its long diameter sloping down and out, beveled off at the end; its broad side facing up and out; its narrow edge straight forward. This mass lies diagonally across and overlaps the mass of the arm, whose long diameter is vertical, its broad side outward, its narrow edge forward.

The mass of the forearm begins behind the end of the arm and passes across it at an angle forward and out. It is made of two squares. The upper half of the forearm is a block whose broad side is forward, its narrow edge sideways; while the lower half, smaller than the upper, has its narrow edge forward, its broad side facing out (with the hand held thumb up). These blocks are joined by wedges and wedging movements, and to the straight lines are wedded the curved lines of the contour of the muscles.

The *deltoid* is itself a wedge, whose apex sinks into the outer groove of the arm half way down. The mass of the *biceps* ends in a wedge which turns outward as it enters the *cubital fossa*. The mass of the forearm overlaps the end of the arm on the outside by a wedge (*supinator longus*) that arises a third of the way up the arm, reaches a broad apex at the broadest part of the forearm and tapers to the wrist, pointing always to the thumb; and on the inside by a wedge that rises back of the arm and points to the little finger (*flexor-pronator* muscles).

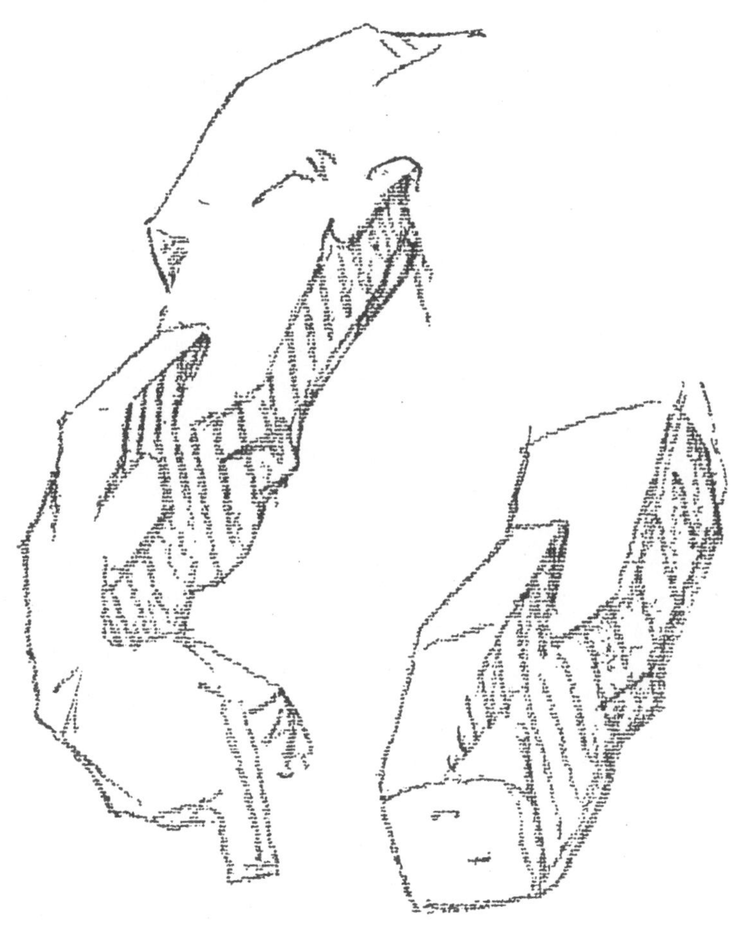

In the lower half of the forearm, the thin edge of the mass, toward the thumb, is made by a continuation of this wedge from the outside; while the thin edge toward the little finger is made by the end of the wedge from the inside. When the elbow is straight and the hand turned in, the inner line of the forearm is straight with that of the arm.

When the hand is turned out, this line is set out at an angle that corresponds with the width of the wrist. The little finger side (*ulna*) being the hub of its movement. The *flexor* tendons on the front of the forearm point always to the inner condyle; the *extensor* tendons on the back point always to the outer condyle. The breadth of the hand corresponds with that of the lower mass; not joining it directly, but with a step-down toward the front.

In the back view of the arm, the mass of the shoulder sits across its top as in the front view. The back edge of this mass is seen to be a truncated wedge arising under the *deltoid* and focusing on the elbow.

The upper end resolves itself into the three heads of the triceps; the lower or truncated end is the triceps tendon, to which is to be added the tiny wedge of the *anconeus* (donkey's foot) muscle bridging from outer condyle to *ulna*.

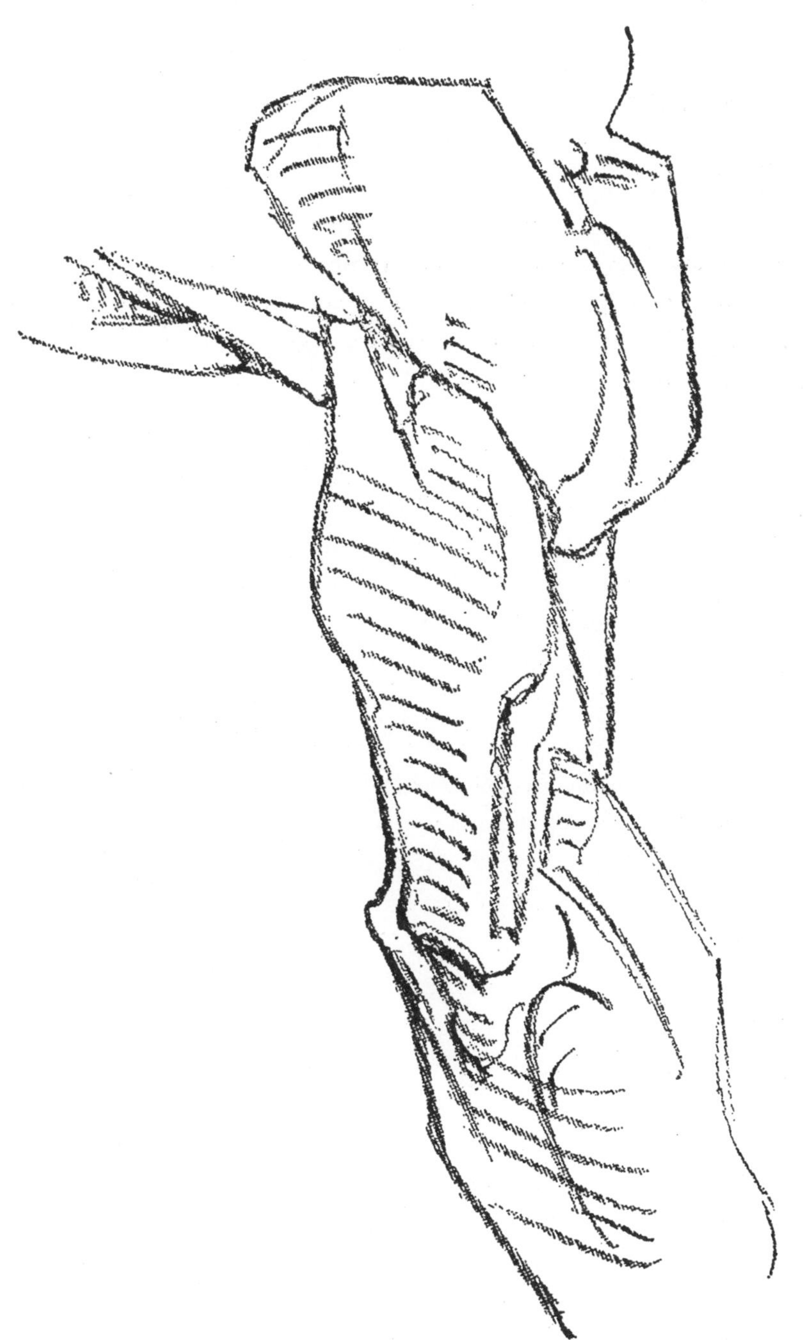

ANATOMY OF THE ARMPIT

The hollow of the arm, filled with its friction hairs, is made into a deep pit by the great breast muscle (*pectoralis major*) in front, and the greater *latissimus dorsi* behind.

The hollow's floor slopes forward, downward and outward, following the slope of the chest wall. Its rear wall is deeper, since the latissimus attaches farther down the back; thicker because made of two muscles (*latissimus* and *teres major*), and rounder because its fibres turn on themselves before attaching to the arm bone.

The front wall is longer because the pectoral muscle attaches farther down the arm. Into this pit the *biceps* and *triceps* muscles plunge, with the *coraco-brachialis* between them. The bottom of the pit may, when the arm is fully raised, be bulged by the head of the arm bone and the lymph glands that lie there.

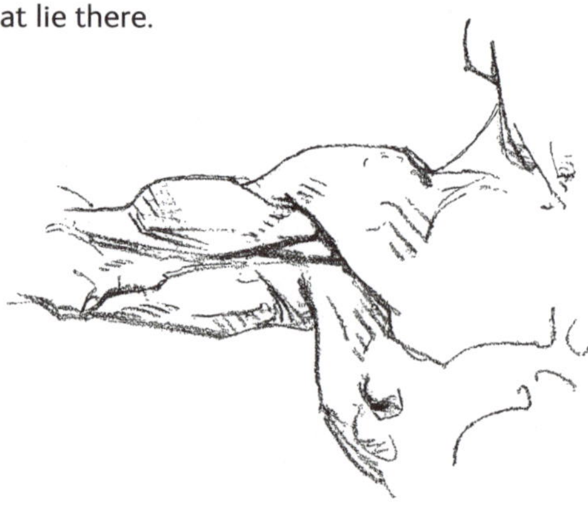

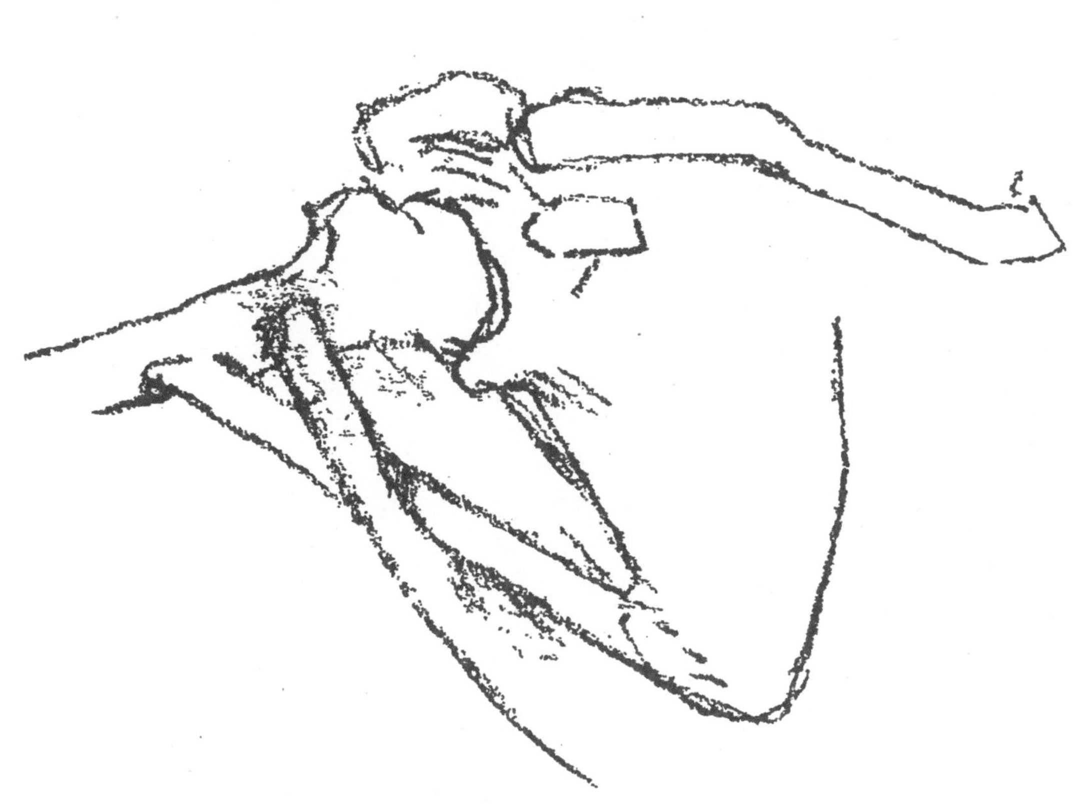

THE SHOULDER

MECHANISM OF THE ARMPIT: FRONT VIEW

① *Biceps.*
② *Triceps.*
③ *Latissimus dorsi.*
④ *Teres major.*
⑤ *Deltoid.*

Latissimus Dorsi:

From spine, sixth *dorsal* to *sacrum* and *iliac* crest; passes inside of *humerus* to fasten to front side near head.

Action: Draws arm backward and inward.

Teres Major:

From lower corner of *scapula* to front of *humerus*.

Action: Draws *humerus* outward and rotates backwards.

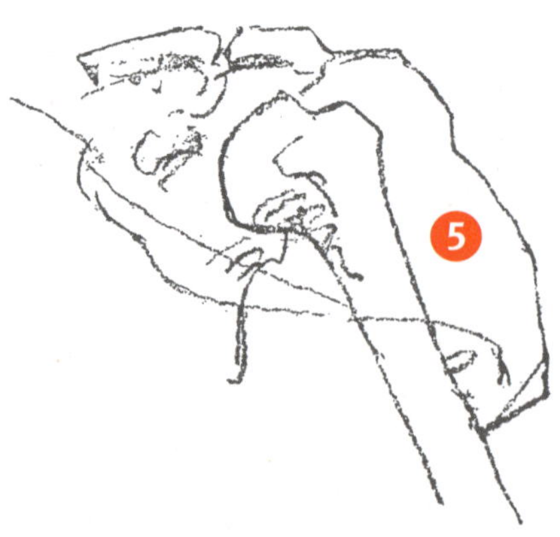

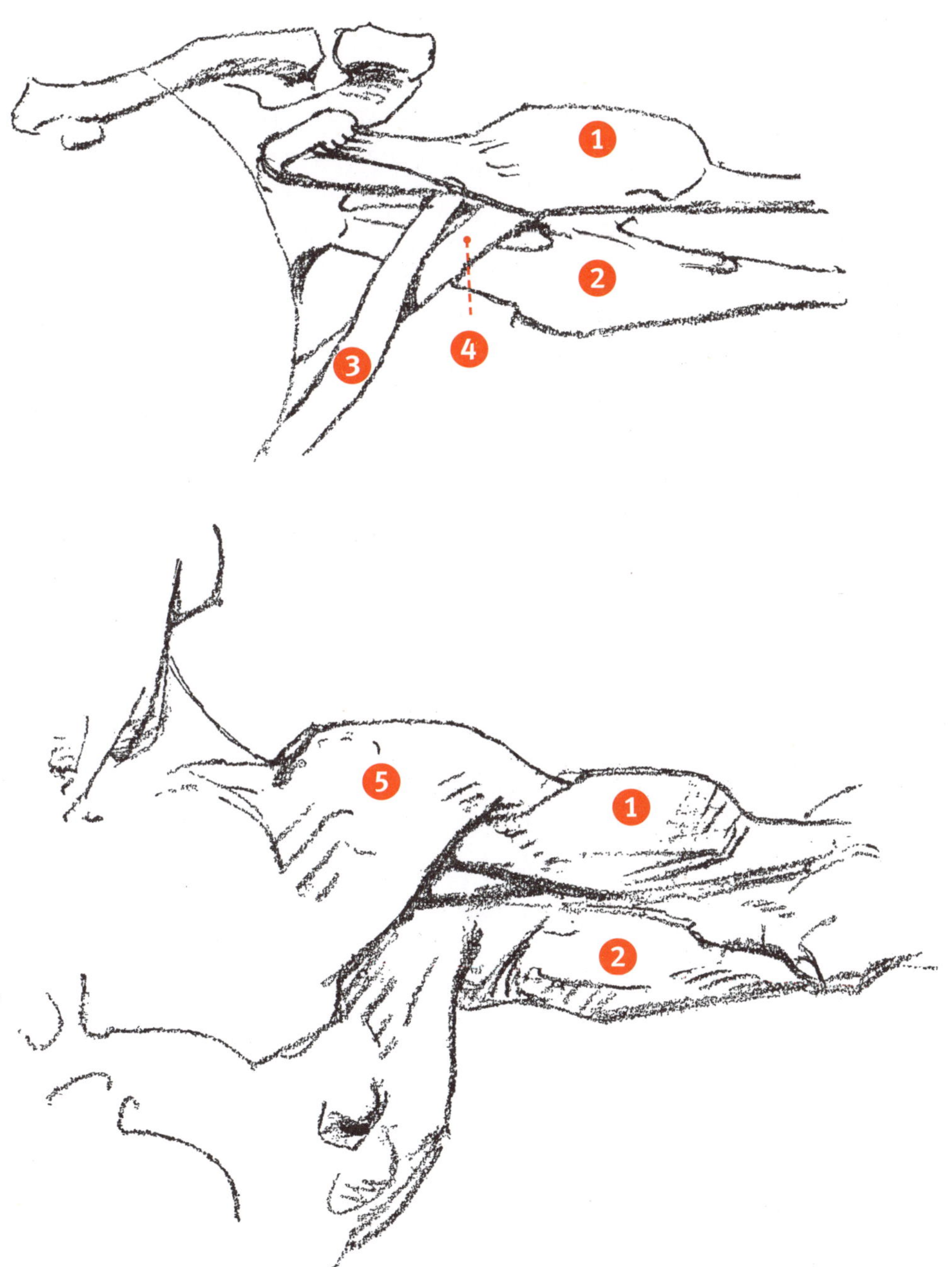
1
2
3
4
5
1
2

THE ARM

WEDGING AND INTERLOCKING OF THE MASSES OF THE ARM AND SHOULDER

(**Masses**, *see* page 116)

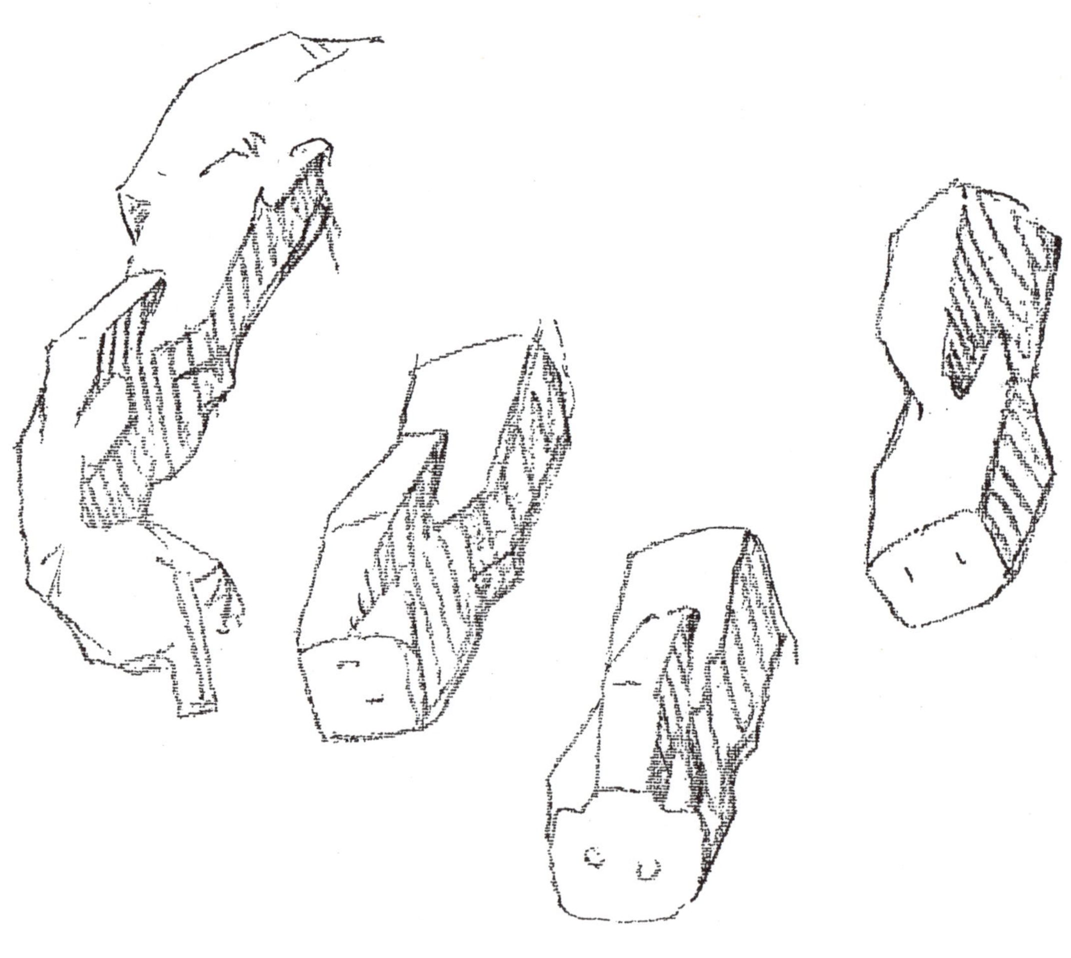

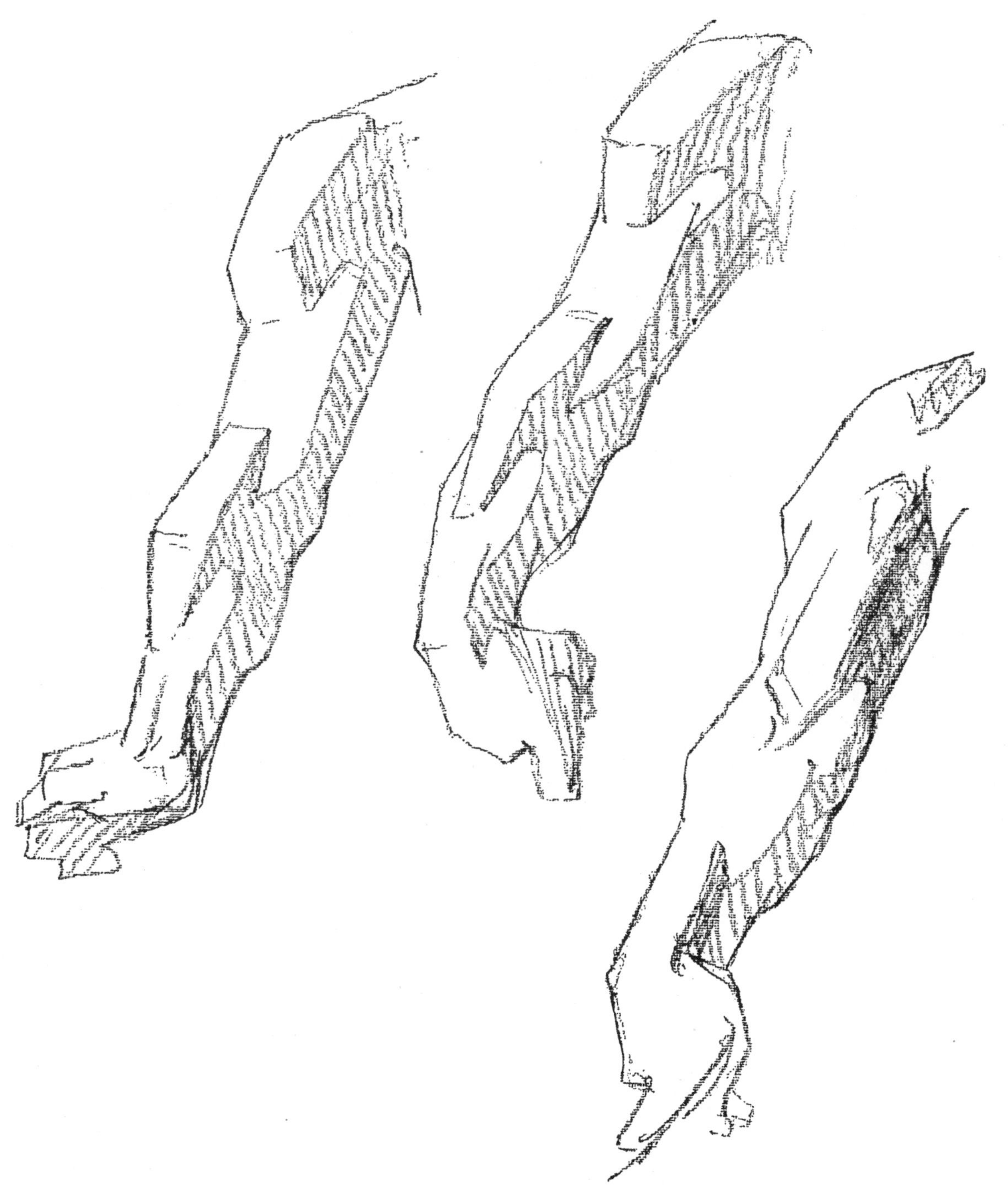

THE SHOULDER

MECHANISM OF THE SHOULDER: BACK VIEW

① *Deltoid.*
② *Triceps.*
③ *Teres minor.*
④ *Teres major.*

Deltoid:
From *clavicle*, *acromion* and ridge of *scapula* to outside of *humerus*.
Action: Elevates, draws forward or backward, *humerus*.

Triceps:
Outer head, back of *humerus* above musculo-spiral groove. Inner head, back of *humerus* below musculo-spiral groove. Middle or long head, shoulder blade below socket to *olecranon* process of *ulna*.
Action: Extends forearm.

Teres Minor:
From *scapula* to inner tubercle of *humerus*.
Action: Draws *humerus* outward and rotates backward.

Teres Major:
From lower corner of *scapula* to front of *humerus*.
Action: Draws *humerus* outward and rotates backwards.

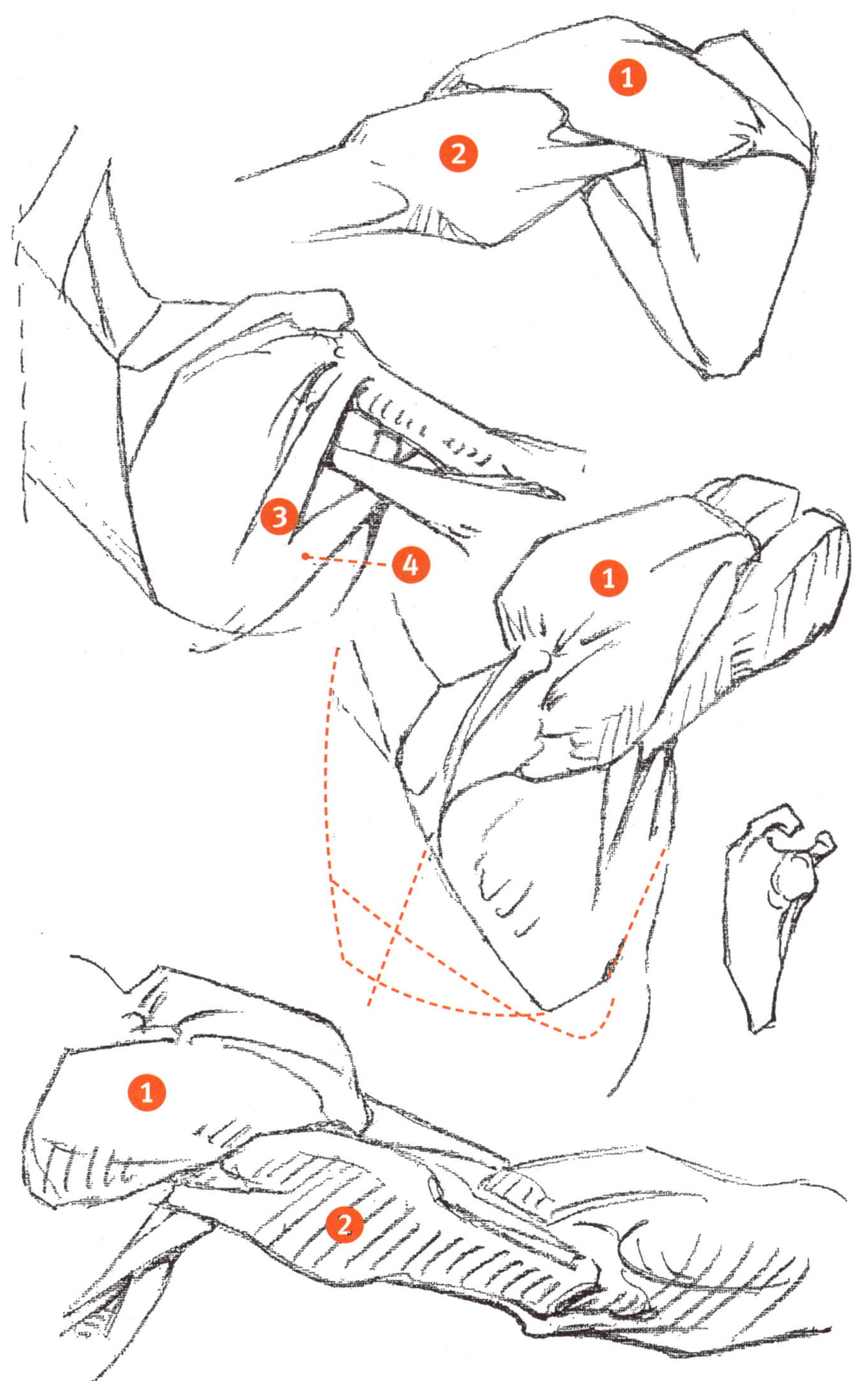
1
2
3
4
1
1
2

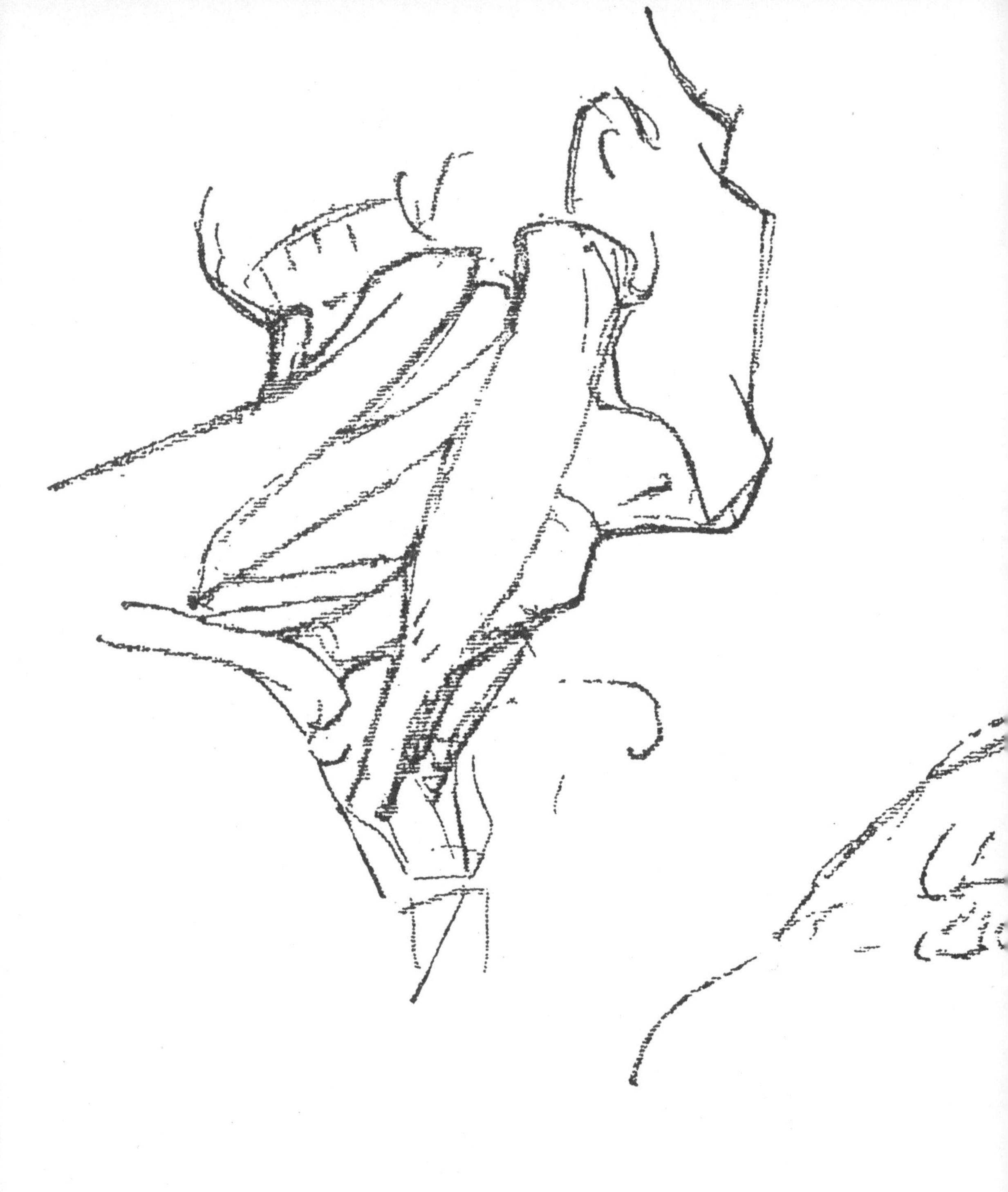

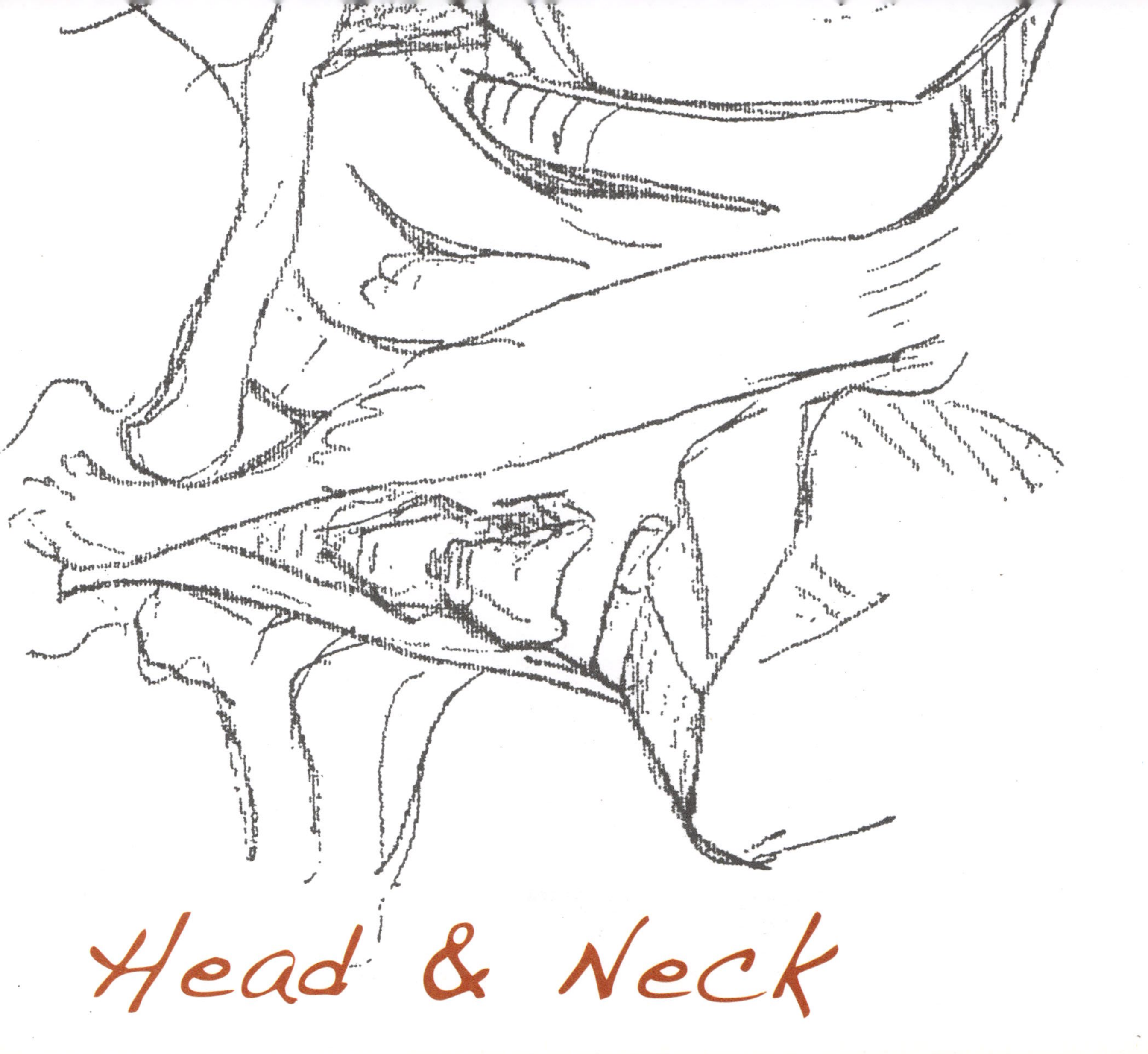

Head & Neck

ANATOMY OF THE NECK

From the sloping platform of the shoulders the neck rises, a cylindrical column, curving slightly forward even when the head is thrown well back. It is canopied in front by the chin. It is buttressed on the sides by the *trapezius* (table) muscle.

The table shape of this muscle appears only from the back, a diamond with lower apex well down the back. Its lateral corners arise from the shoulder girdle opposite the *deltoid*. Rising diagonally upward it braces the back of the head.

The strength of the neck is therefore at the back, which is somewhat flat and overhung by the base of the skull. From bony prominences at the back of the ears, two muscles (*sterno-mastoid*), aptly called the bonnet-string muscles, descend to almost meet at the root of the neck, forming a triangle whose base is the canopy of the chin.

In this triangle below is the *thyroid* gland, larger in women; and above it the angular cartilage of the *larynx*, or Adam's apple, larger in men. Crossing its upper corners outward and downward is a thready skin muscle (*platysma myoides*) which lifts the skin into high folds and draws down the corners of the mouth. It carries the imagination back to the time in evolution when bared teeth were important weapons of defense.

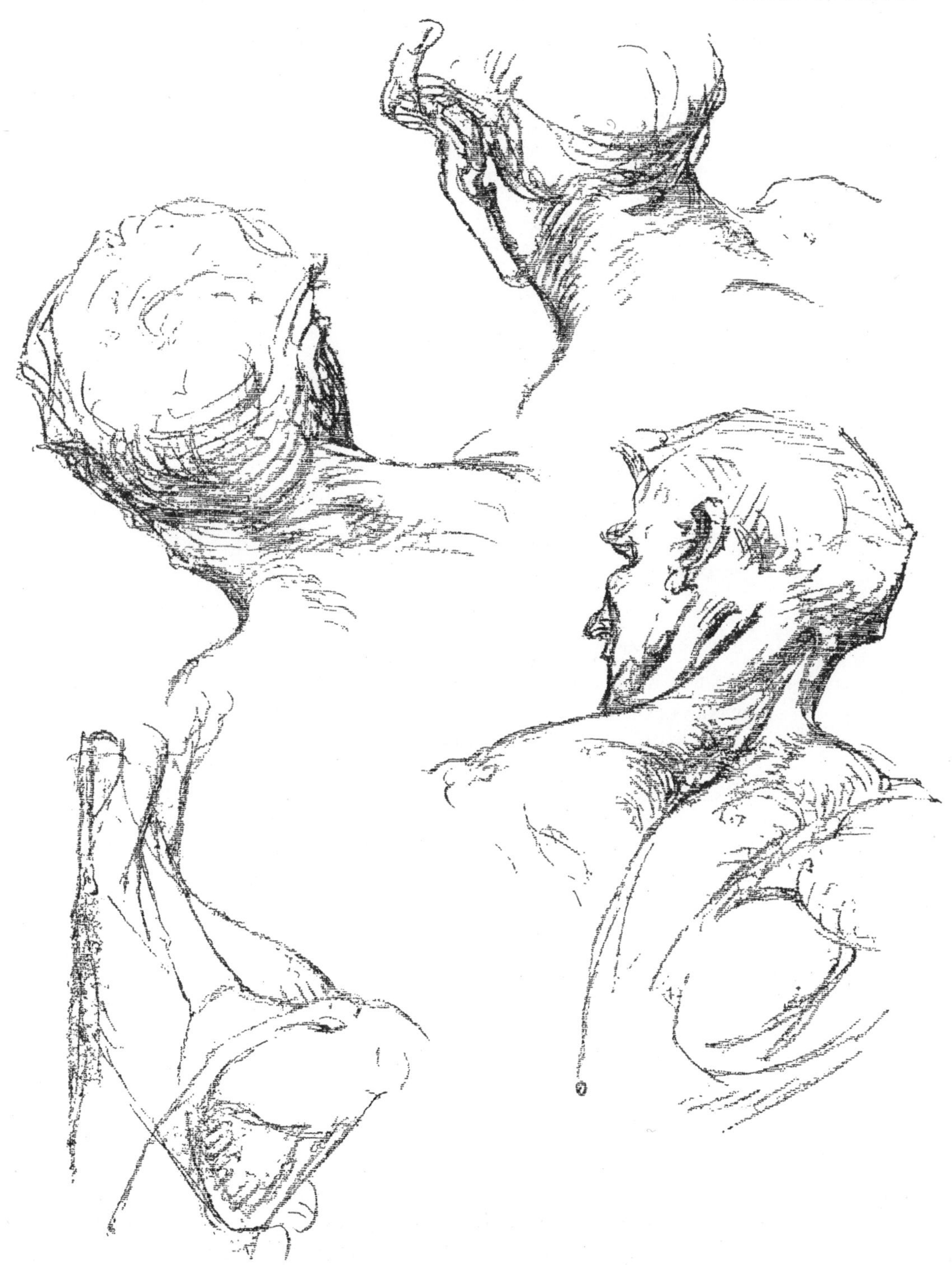

THE NECK

MUSCLES OF THE NECK

① *Sterno-cleido-mastoid.*
② *Levator* of the *scapula.*
③ *Trapezius.*

Sterno-cleido-mastoideus:

From top of *sternum* and *sternal* end of *clavicle* to *mastoid* process (back of ear).

Action: Together, pull head forward; separately, rotates to opposite side, depresses head.

***Levator* of the *scapula*:**

From upper *cervical* vertebrae to upper angle of shoulder blade.

Action: Raises angle of shoulder blade.

Trapezius:

From *occipital* bone, nape ligament and spine as far as twelfth dorsal, to *clavicle*, *acromion* and ridge of shoulder blade.

Action: Extends head, elevates shoulder and rotates shoulder blade.

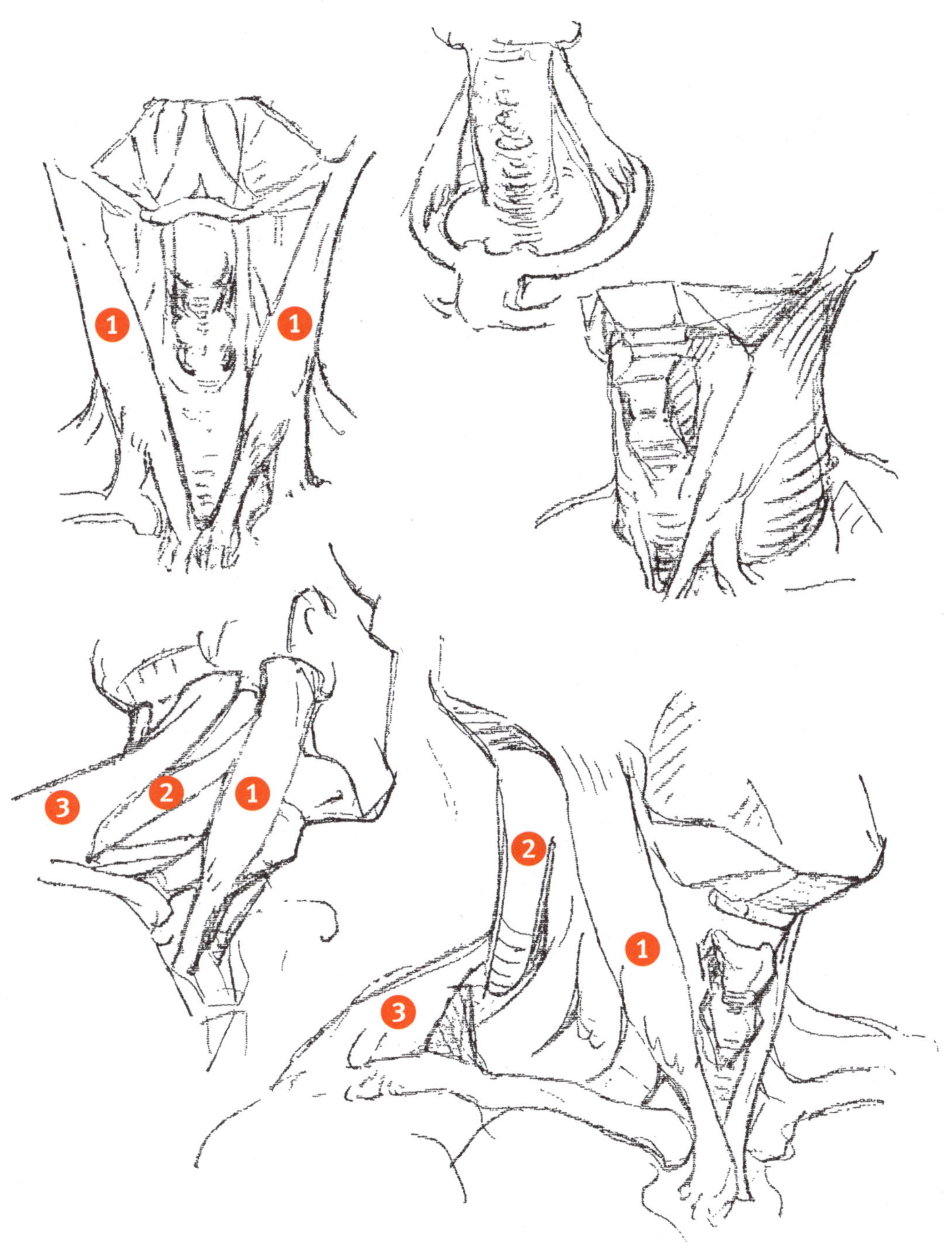
1
1
3
2
1
2
1
3

THE NECK

TONGUE-BONE AND LARYNX

① *Hyoid* bone.
② *Thyroid* cartilage.
③ *Thyroid* gland muscles.
④ *Digastric* (has two portions).
⑤ *Stylo-hyoid.*
⑥ *Sterno-hyoid.*
⑦ *Omo-hyoid.*
⑧ *Sterno-cleido-mastoid.*
⑨ *Trapezius.*

MOVEMENTS OF THE NECK

In the neck are seven vertebrae, each moving a little. When the neck is turned to one side, that side of each vertebra moves back as far as the perpendicular and then the opposite sides move forward, lengthening the neck as they do so. This motion is much freer at the second joint from the skull, which turns on a pivot.

The joint of the skull itself moves only in nodding, in which the rest of the neck may be quite stationary.

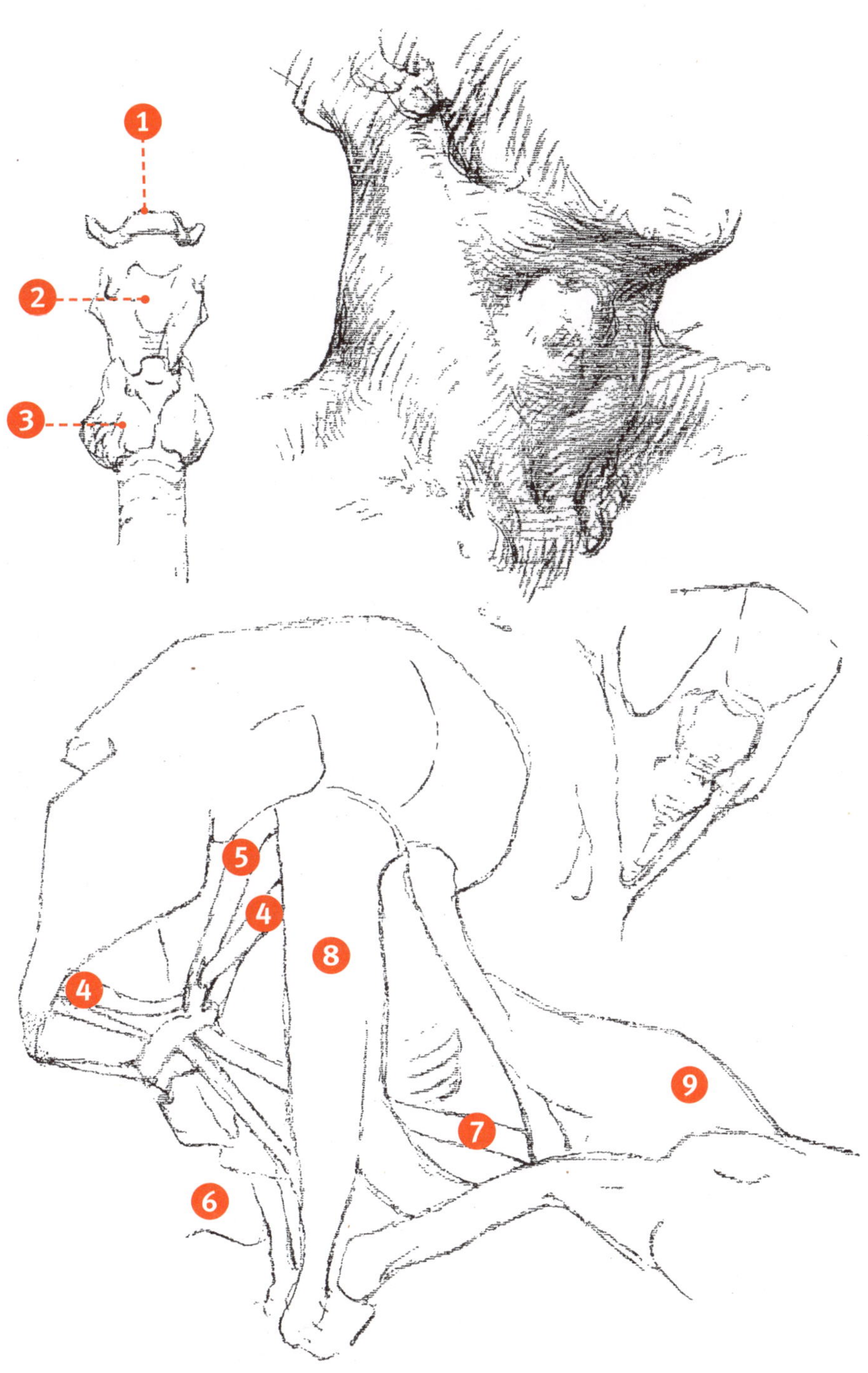
1
2
3
5
4
4
8
9
7
6

THE NECK

MUSCLES OF THE NECK

Platysma Myoides:

A sheathing from chest and shoulder to masseter and corner of mouth.

Action: Wrinkles skin of neck, draws down corner of mouth.

***Digastric* (double-bellied muscle):**

Anterior belly, from *maxilla*, behind chin; *posterior* belly, from *mastoid* process; fastened by loop to *hyoid* bone.

Action: Raises *hyoid* and tongue.

Mylo-hyoid:

Forms floor of mouth and canopy of chin in front.

Stylo-hyoid:

From *hyoid* to *styloid* process.

Action: Draws back *hyoid* and tongue.

Sterno-hyoid:

From *sternum* to *hyoid* bone.

Action: Depresses *hyoid* and Adam's apple.

Omo-hyoid:

From *hyoid* bone to shoulder, upper border of *scapula*.

Action: Draws *hyoid* down and to one side.

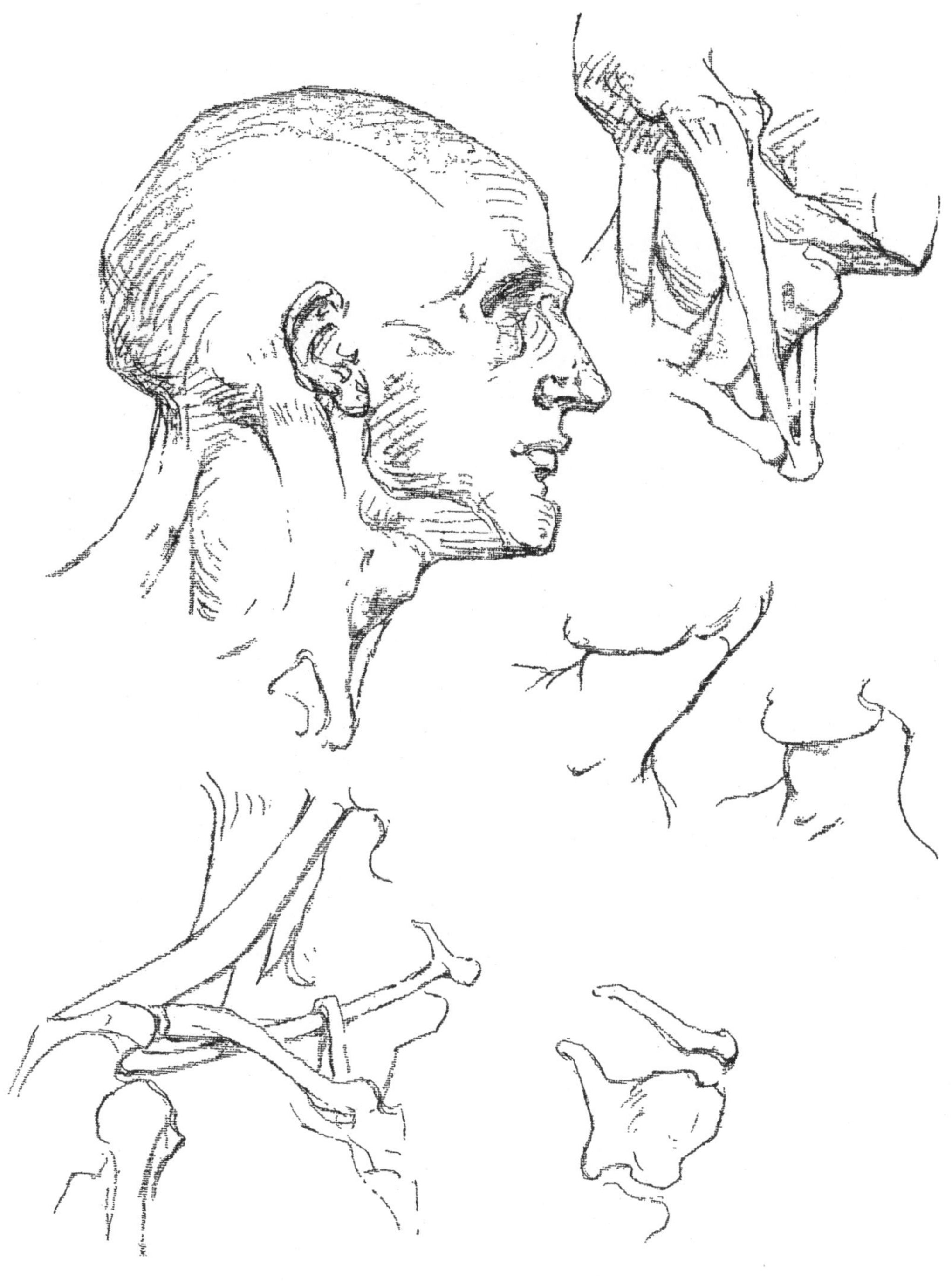

ANATOMY OF THE HEAD

The oval shape has been used for so long as the basis for the construction of the human head that the switch to the block or cube might seem quite revolutionary. Yet for many reasons the cube is more practical.

The oval is too indefinite, and offers no points for comparison, no basis for measurement. The eye does not fix on any point on a curved line. On the ground plan of a square, however, any form may be built. Moreover, the block carries with it from any angle its perspective and its foreshortening, and it carries a solid sense of mass.

Indeed, it carries with itself the important element of the bilateral symmetry of the head – symmetry that is present indeed in all living things. **A vertical line** in the centre **divides the head** or the trunk into parts equal, opposite, and complemental. The right eye is the counterpart of the left; the two halves of the nose are symmetrical; the limbs, except for changes of position, are exact though reversed duplicates of each other. So, what is the best way to construct such a block?

Many medical and anthropological studies on the human skull have been carried out, trying to discover some constant measurement by which to classify them as ancient or modern or according to racial origin. They finally fixed upon two lines with the angle between them. The first passes from the base of the

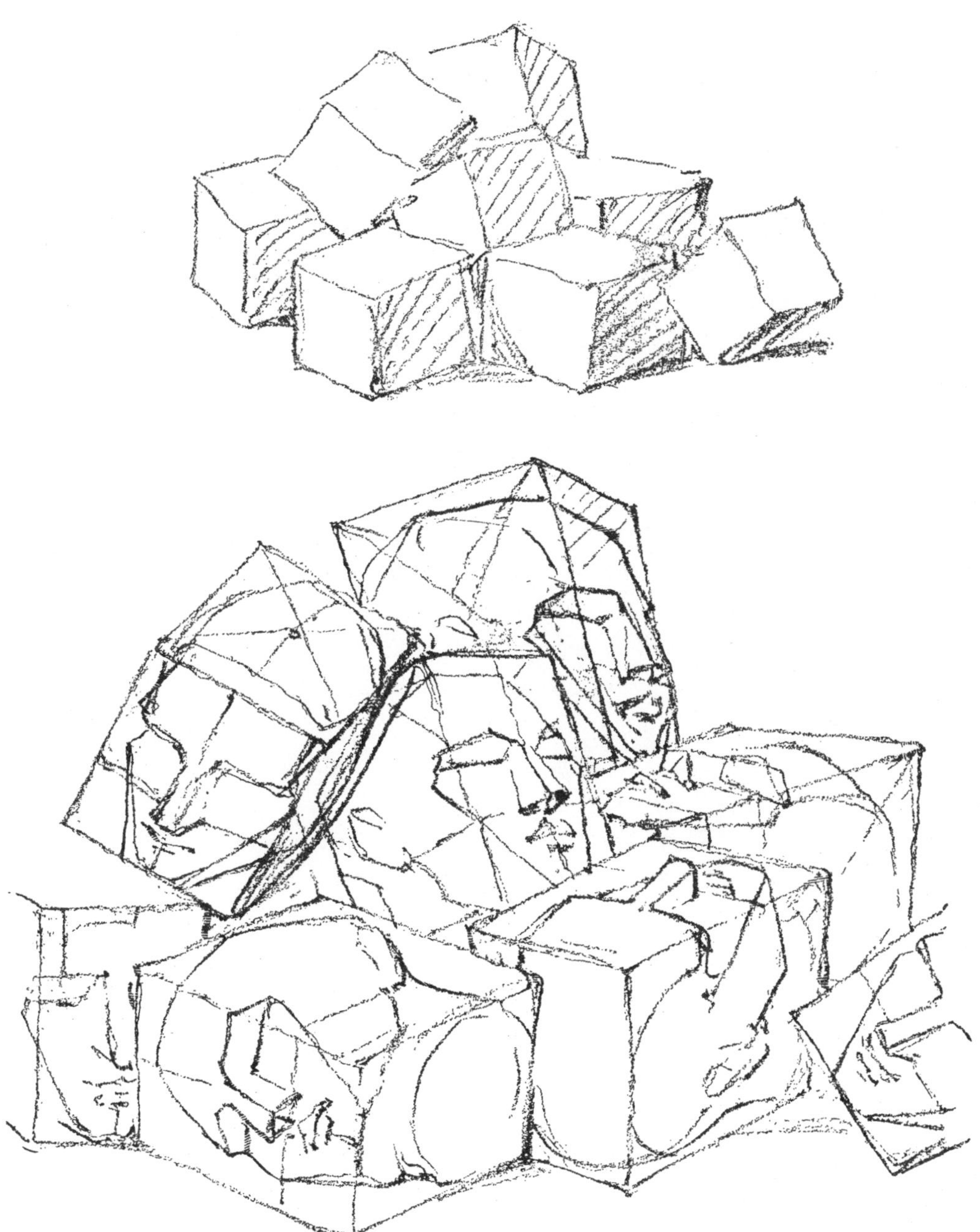

nose to the roof of the ear canal; the second passes from the upper incisor teeth to the prominent part of the forehead.

The angle between these lines is practically constant for a given race or a given age of evolution. Individual variations occur, but they are less than the standard.

This angle is less in the older races, and the vertical line approaches nearer the perpendicular in the newer races, especially the Caucasian. In the classical Greek head it even passes the perpendicular, although no actual Greek skulls in which this is the case have ever been discovered.

This angle, in the Caucasian races, is about 80 degrees. It is not easy to construct a block on such an angle, and it is very desirable to have a right angle. By dropping the horizontal line at its rear end from the roof of the ear canal to the tip of the ear lobe, and by drawing the vertical line from the base of the nose where it joins the upper lip to the bridge of the nose, where it joins the *glabella*, we obtain such a right angle.

If on these straight lines a cage is built, bounding the head and face, it can be found that the front and back are oblong and the sides are square. The top of the cage should be level with the top of the head, the bottom with the bottom of the chin; the border of the cheek should fit the sides. The length of the oblong front will equal one and three-quarters times its width. The cheek bones set back from the front of the cage about one-third of the distance to the ear.

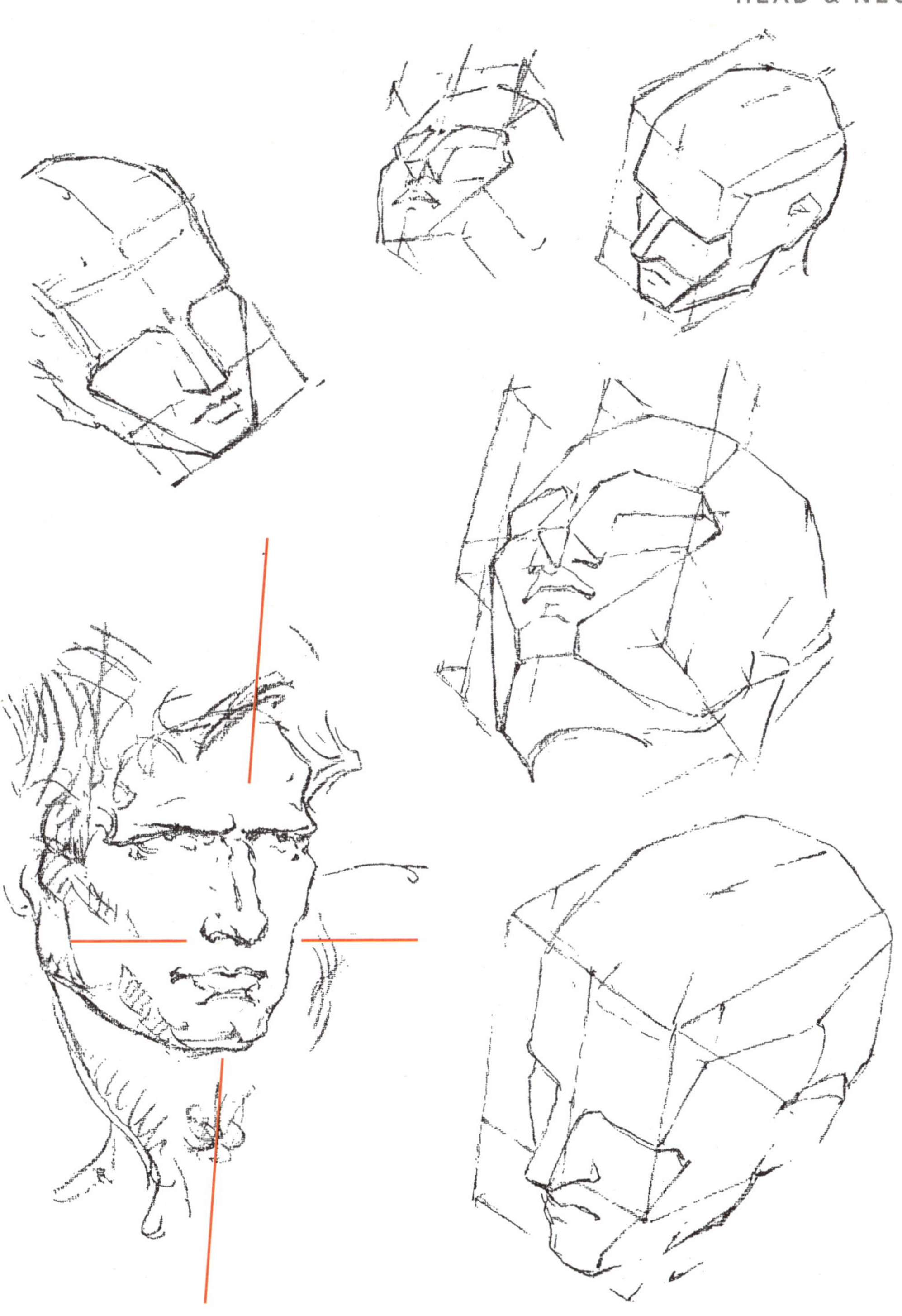

THE HEAD

EMINENCES, RIDGES AND DEPRESSIONS OF THE SKULL

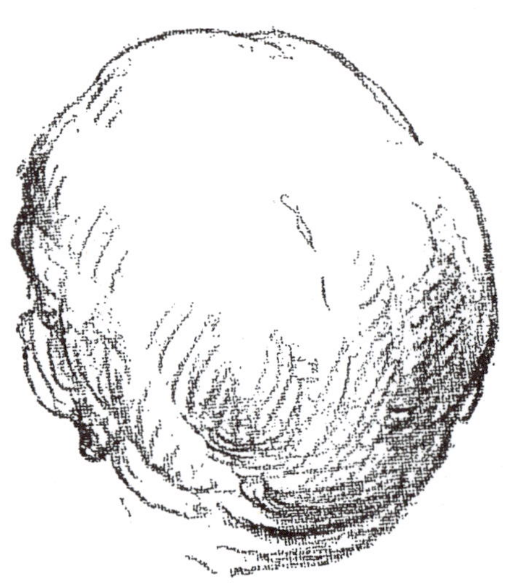

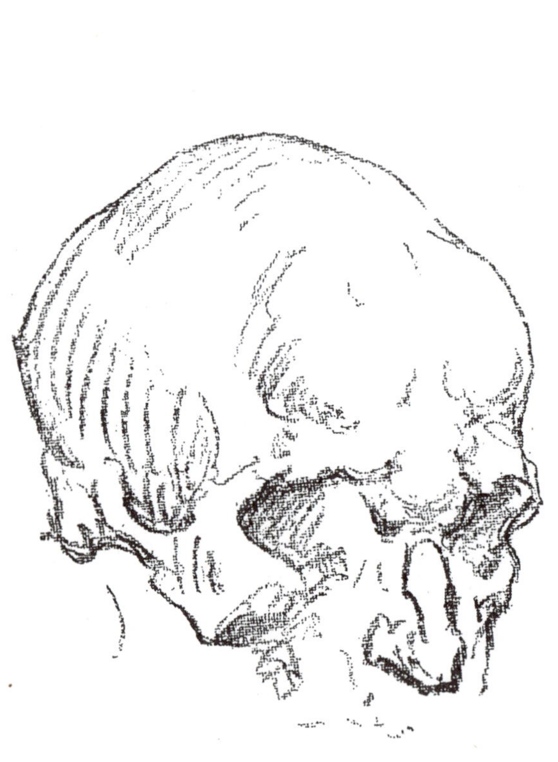

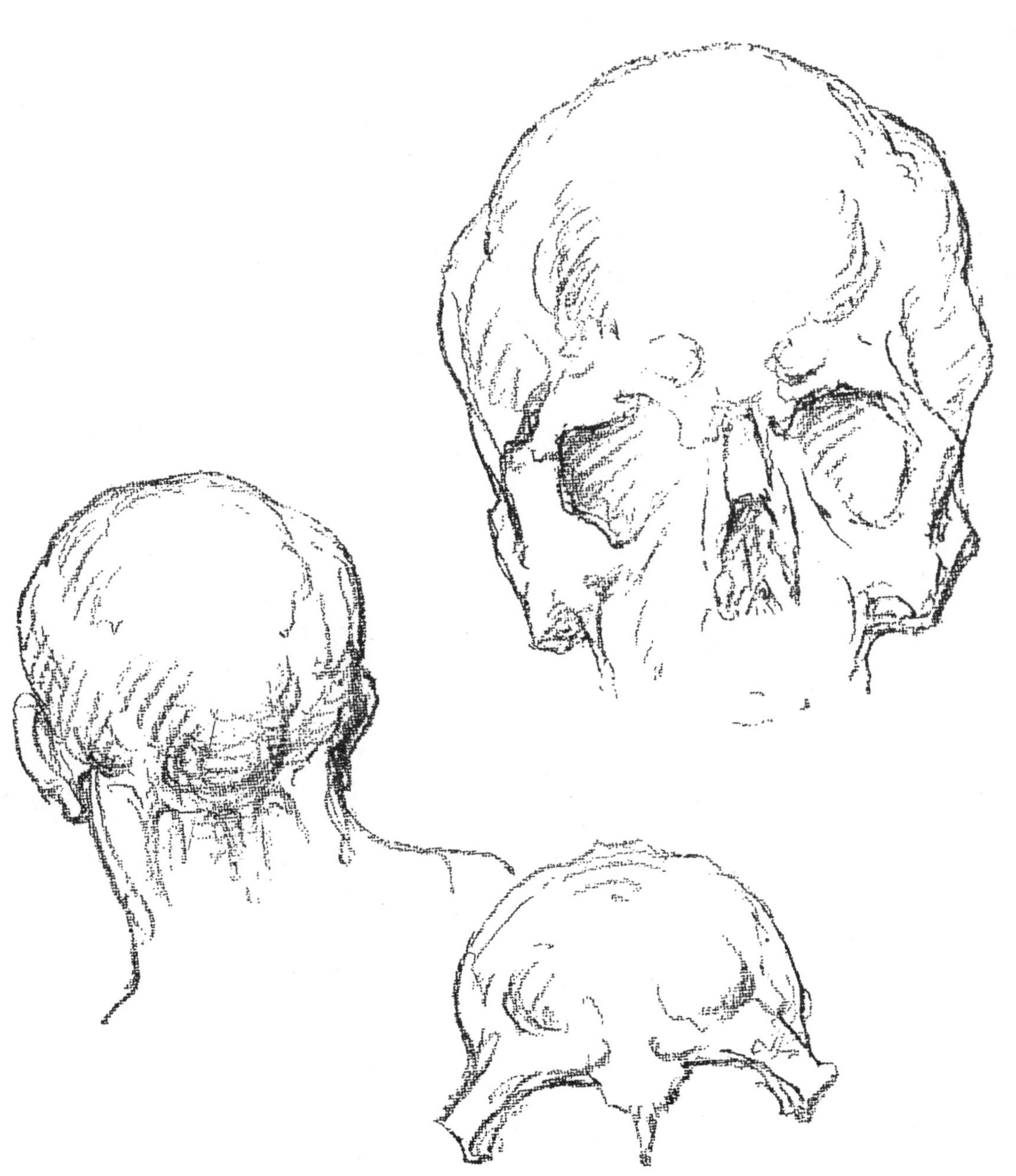

THE HEAD

THE ANGLES OF CONSTRUCTION

(*see* page 138)

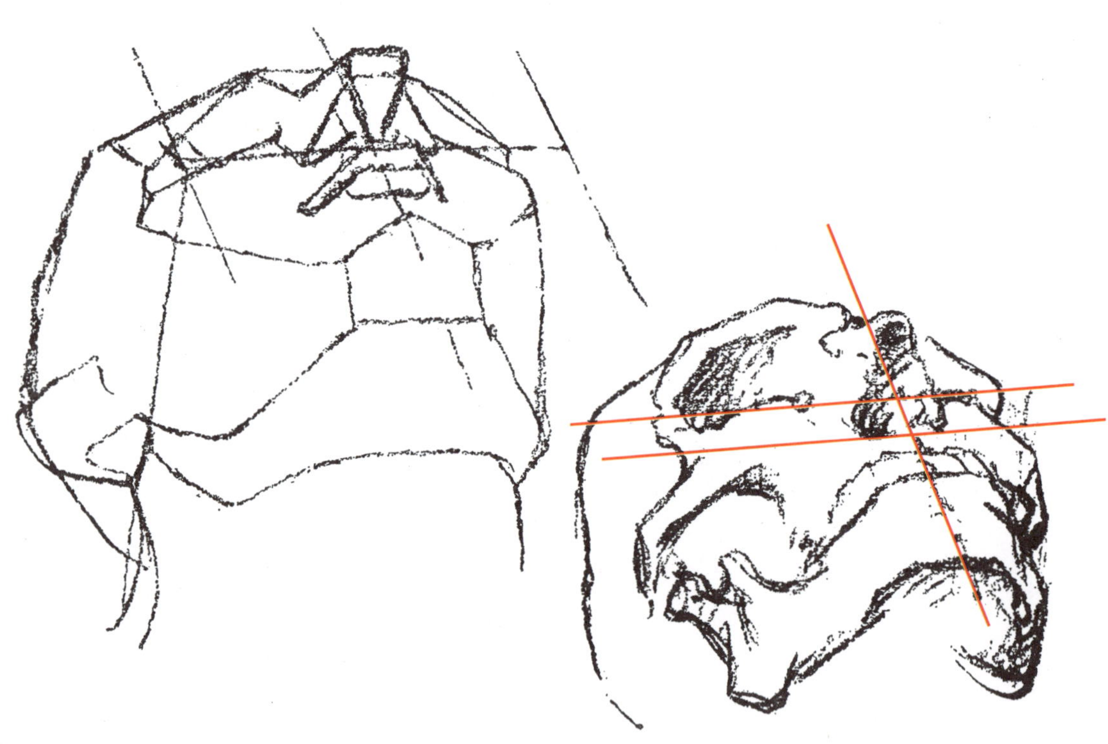

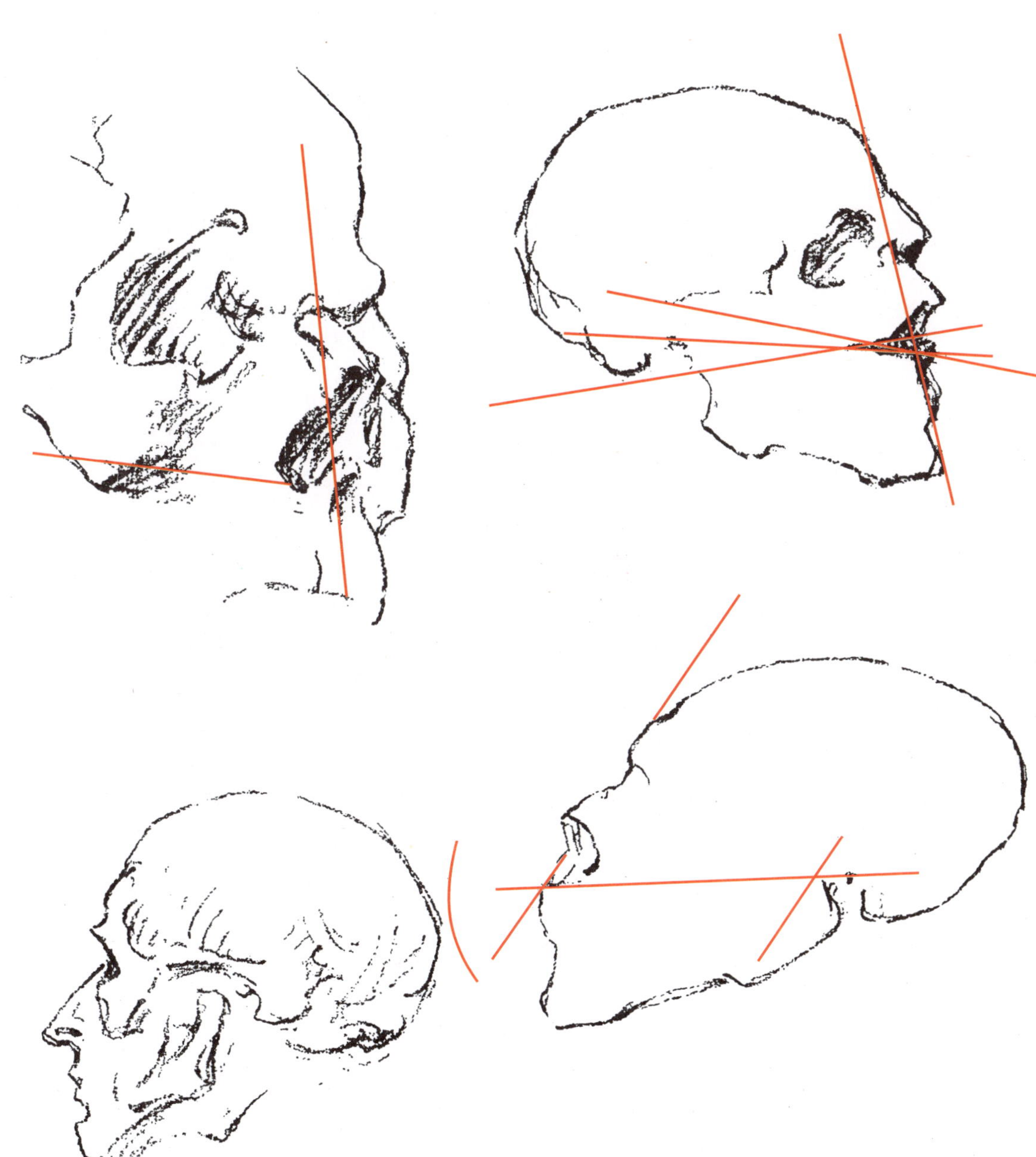

THE HEAD

MUSCLES OF MASTICATION

① *Temporal*.
② *Masseter*.
③ *Buccinator* (cheek muscle).
④ Lesser *zygomaticus* (muscle of expression).
⑤ Greater *zygomaticus* (muscle of expression).

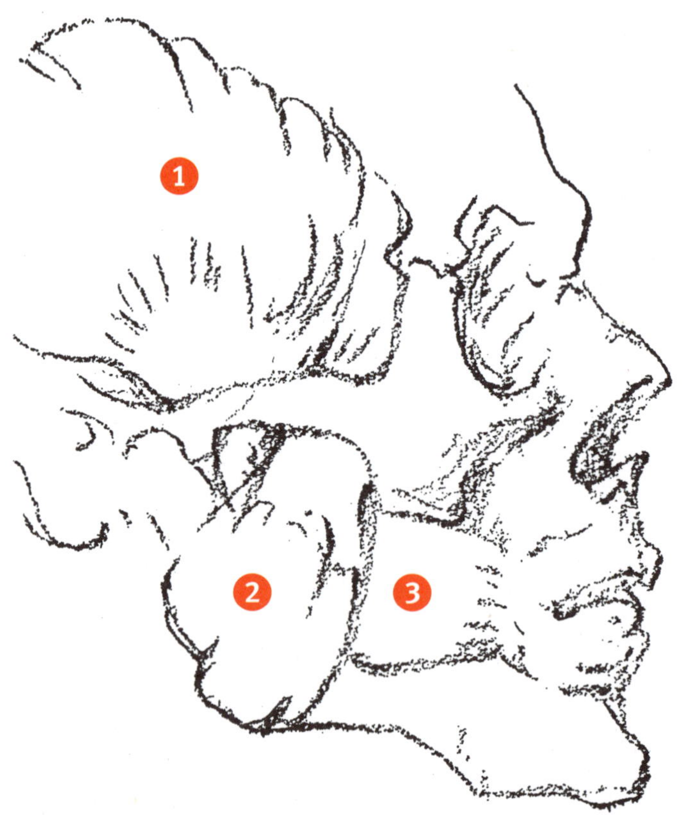

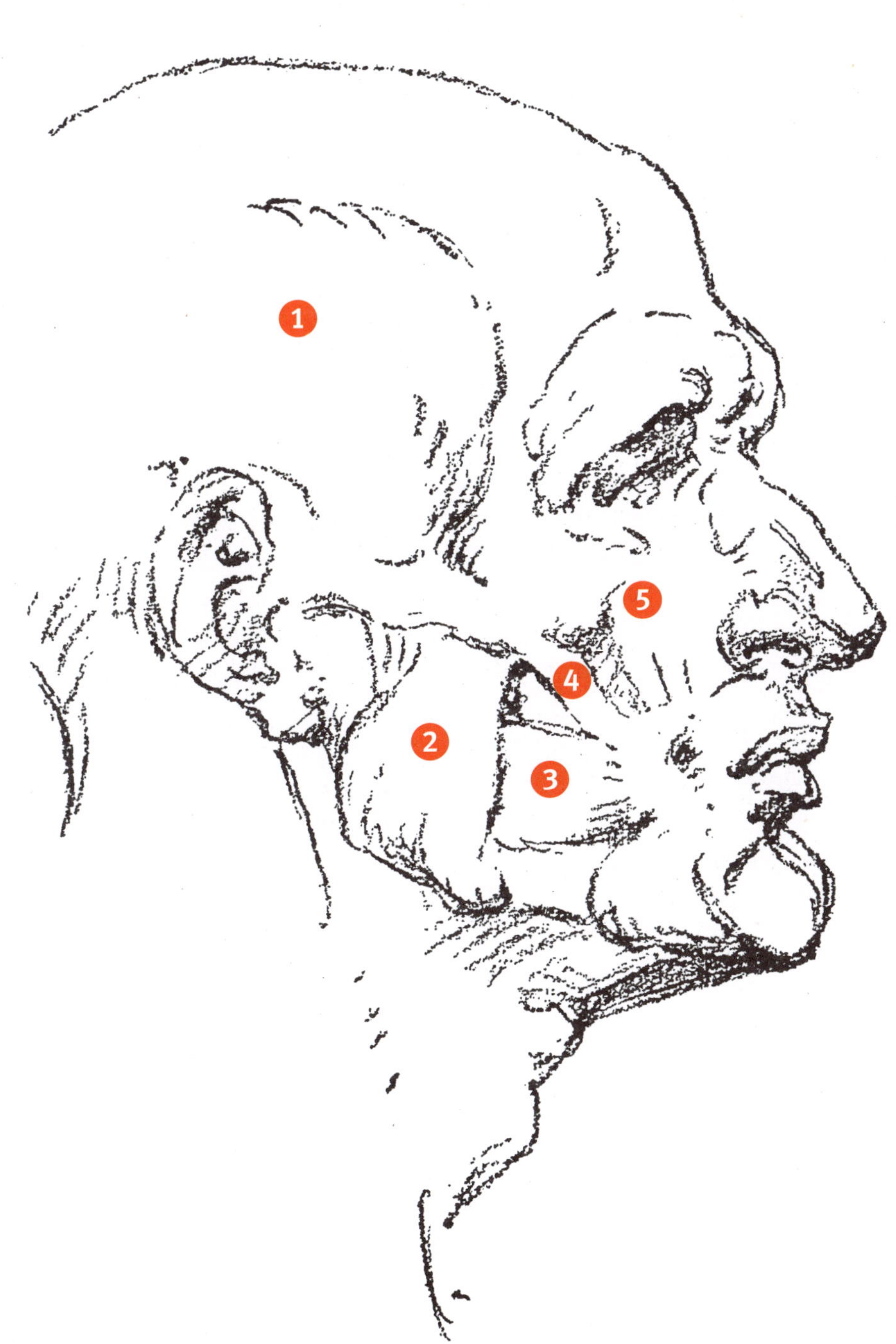
1
2
3
4
5

THE HEAD

CONSTRUCTION LINES IN PERSPECTIVE: MASSES

The **masses of the head** are the cranium, the skeleton of the face, and the jaw. Into the rounded mass of the *cranium* sets the narrower mass of the forehead bounded by the temples at the sides and by the brows below.

From the lower outer corners of the forehead the wedge of the cheek bones begins; moves outward and downward until it just passes the curve of the *cranium*, then down and in, in a long sweep, to the corner of the chin.

Outside of and behind this lower line is another wedge, that of the corner of the jaw, with the line itself for base, and a very low apex.

The two cheek bones form together the central mass of the face, in the middle of which rises the nose.

THE HEAD

PLANES

The plane of the forehead slopes upward and backward to become the cranium; and the sides turn sharply to the plane of the temples. The plane of the face, divided by the nose, is broken on each side by a line from the outer corner of the cheek bone to the centre of the upper lip, making two smaller planes.

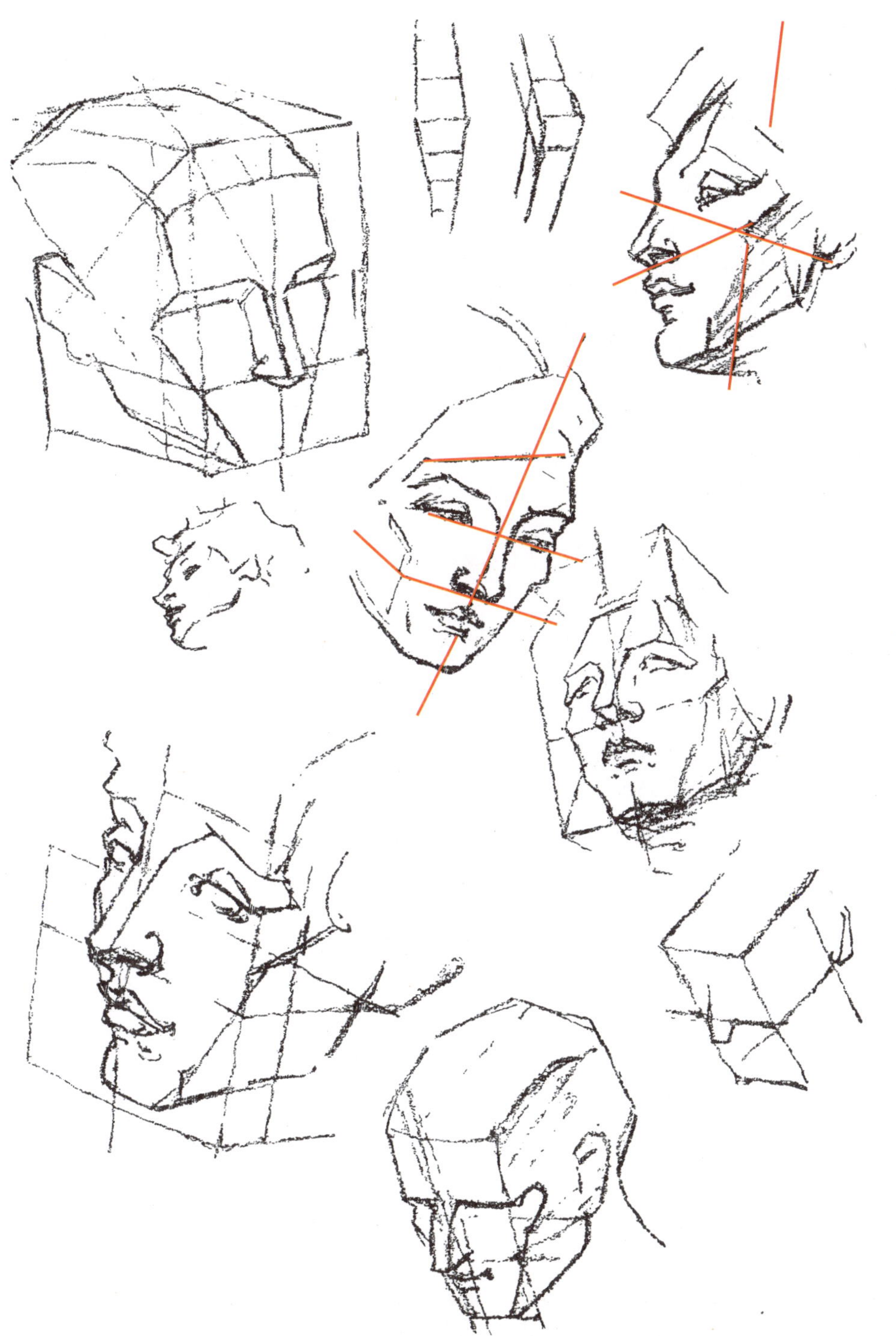

The outer of these turns to become the plane of the jaw, which also is again divided by a line marking the edge of the *masseter* muscle, running from the outer border of the cheek bone to the corner of the jaw; and again making two secondary planes, one toward the cheek and one toward the ear.

The relations of these masses and planes is to the moulding of a head what architecture is to a house. They vary in proportion with each individual, and must be carefully compared with a mental standard.

THE HEAD: PROFILE

In profile the masses of the head are the same – the *cranium*, the skeleton of the face, and the jaw. The front border of the temple is seen to be a long curve, almost parallel to the curve of the cranium. The top of the cheek bone is seen to be prolonged backward toward the ear as a ridge (*zygoma* or yoke) which also marks the base of the temple. It slopes slightly down in front.

From cheek bone and *zygoma*, where they meet, a lesser ridge is seen rising between the temple and the orbit, marking the back of the orbit and the first part of the long line of the temple.

PLANES

The planes and divisions of planes of the face are the same as in the front view, in different perspective.

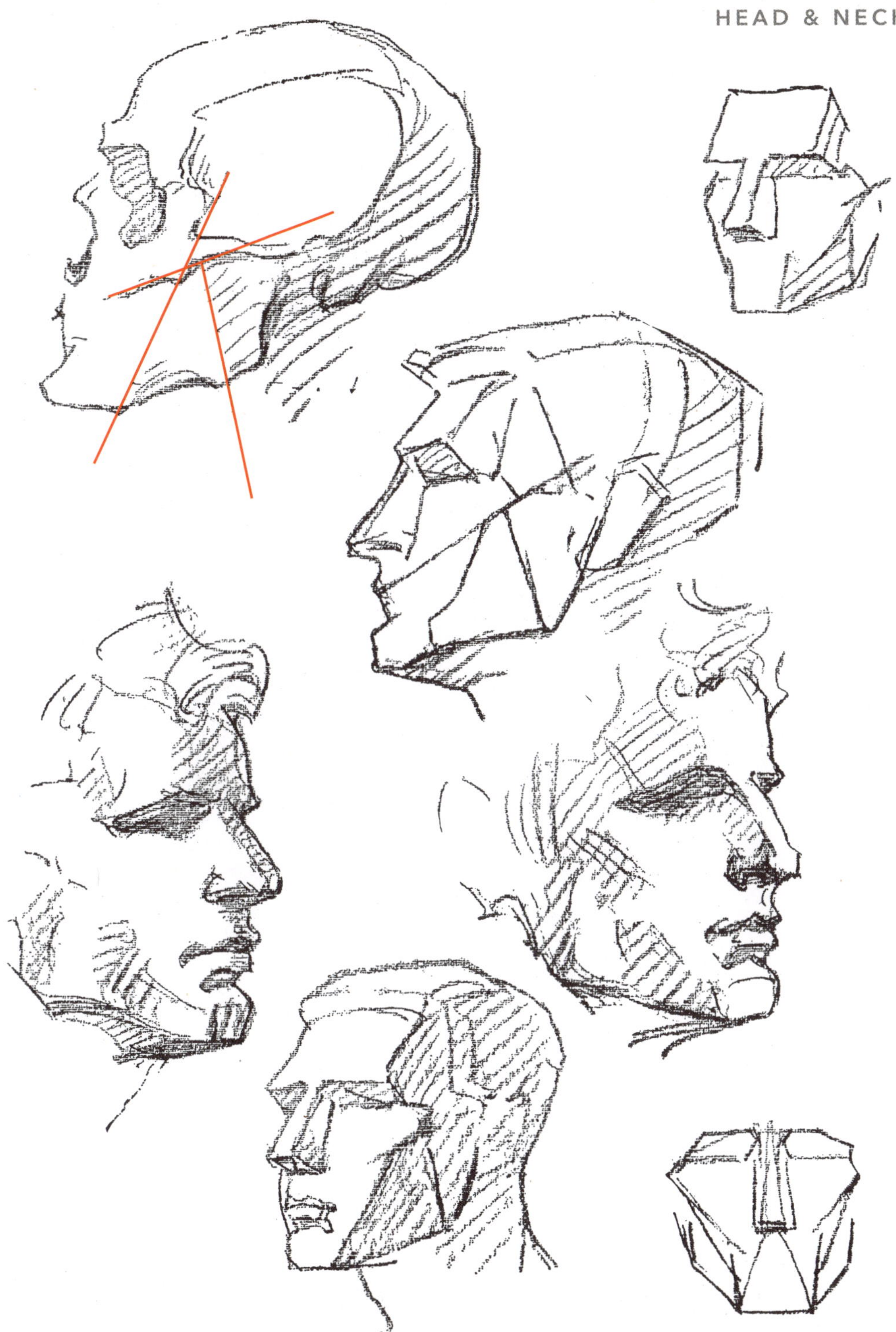

THE HEAD

Examples for reference.

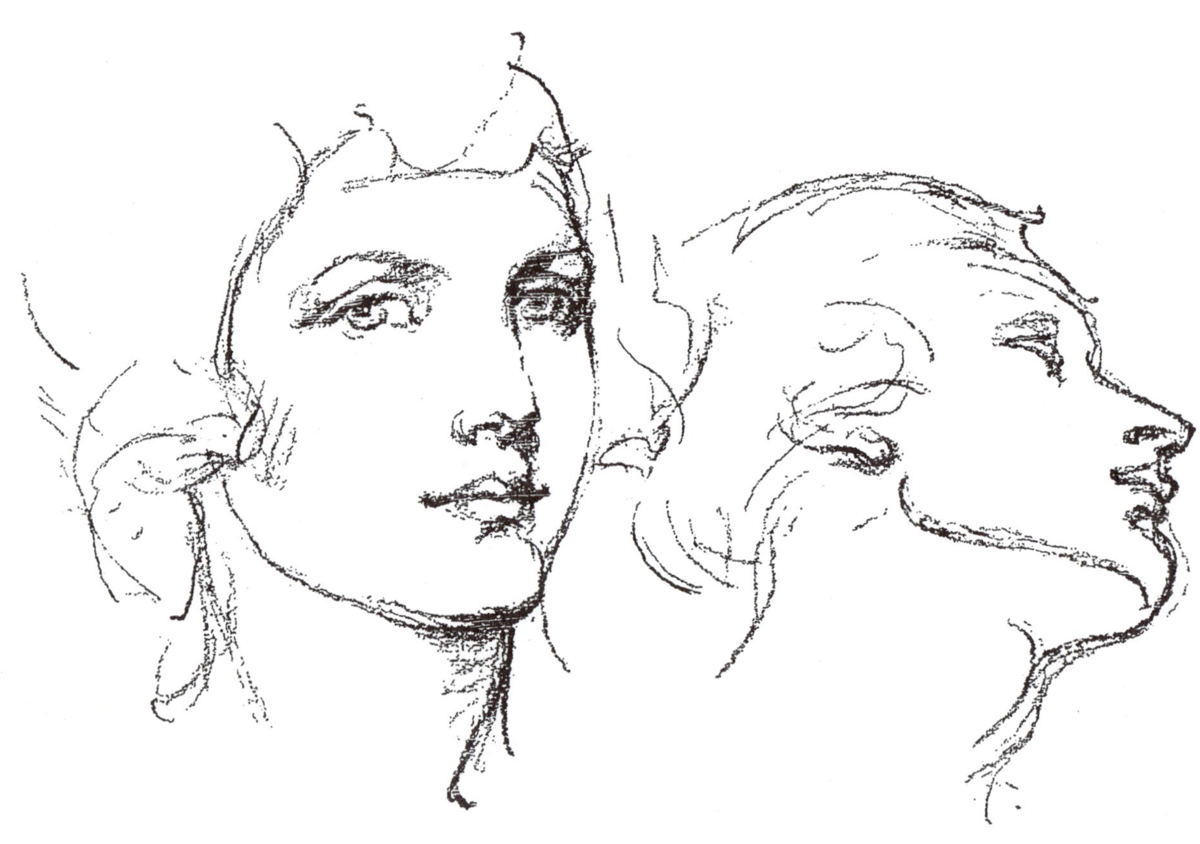

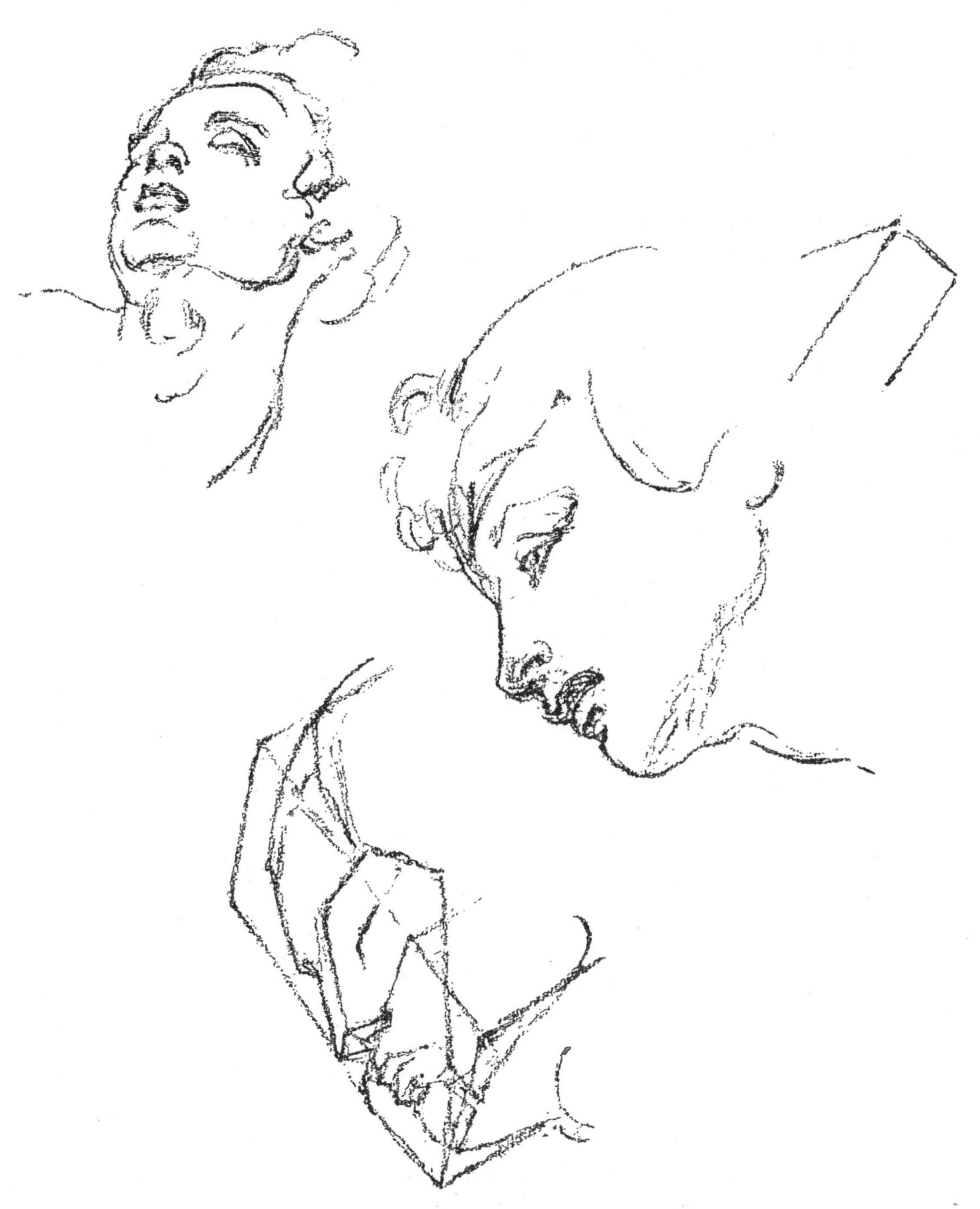

ANATOMY OF THE EYE

The upper part of the eye socket or orbit is marked by the brow, whose bristles are so placed as to divert moisture and dirt outward away from the lid and eye.

Below it on the lid are three planes, wedging into each other at different angles. The first is from the bridge of the nose to the eye. The second is from the brow to the cheek bone; which is again divided in to two smaller planes, one sloping toward the root of the nose, the other directed toward and joining with the cheek bone.

The lower lid is quite stable. It is the upper lid that moves. When the eye is closed, its curtain is drawn smooth; when opened, its lower part follows the curve of the eyeball straight back, folding in beneath the upper part as it does so, and leaving a wrinkle to mark the fold.

The lower lid may be wrinkled and slightly lifted inward, bulging below the inner end of the lid. The transparent cornea or 'apple' of the eye is raised perceptibly, and is always curtained by the upper lid, in part, so that it always makes a slight bulge in the lid, whatever the position, and whether open or closed. The eyeball has about half a right angle of movement in two planes.

At the inner corner of the lids is a narrow pit (*canthus*), floored by a pinkish membrane, which projects some distance beyond the walls of the pit when the eye is turned far out. At the corners of

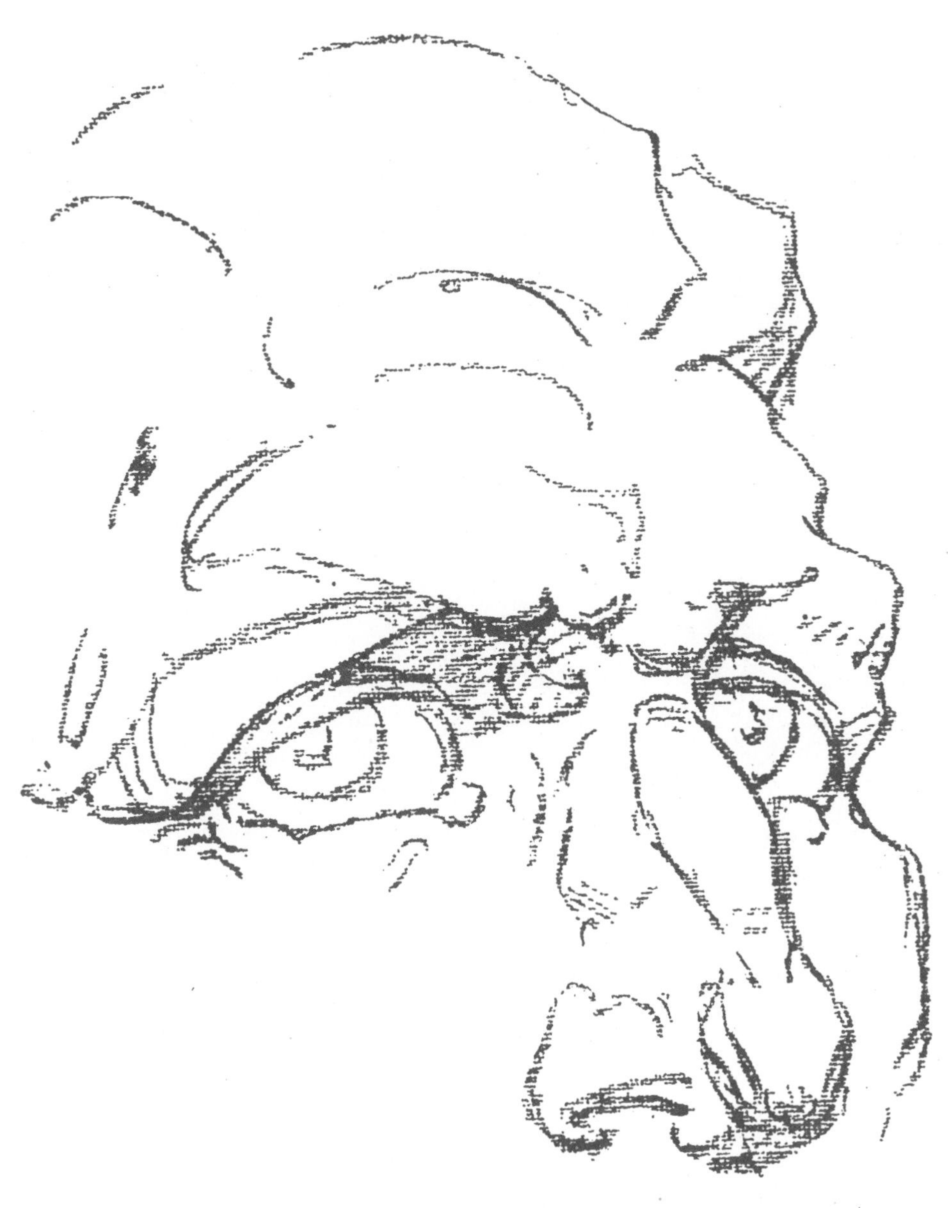

the pit are the openings of the tear ducts, which drain off the excess of *lacrymal* (tear) fluid. There is a continuous light secretion of this fluid, which is spread over the eyeball by the constant winking of the upper lid. The thin film of liquid thus kept there reflects light perfectly from its surface. The lashes, projecting from the margin of the lids, serve both as curtains to shade and as delicate feelers to protect the eye.

The **immovable masses** of the forehead, nose and cheek bones form a strong setting for this most variant and expressive of the features.

COMPARISONS

In looking at any feature one naturally compares it with his concept of the average of such features, or with some mental standard or ideal. The variations of such features will then fall in to classes which represent the more usual variations thereof.

Eyebrows may be level or sloping; straight or arched; short or long; narrow or wide, thick, scanty or penciled.

Lids may be thick or thin, although the upper lid is always thicker along its margin, and always protrudes if the eye protrudes, and is raised over the cornea.

Eye sockets may be far apart or near together; long or short; bulging or shallow. The opening between the lids may be triangular or round, a loop, or a button hole.

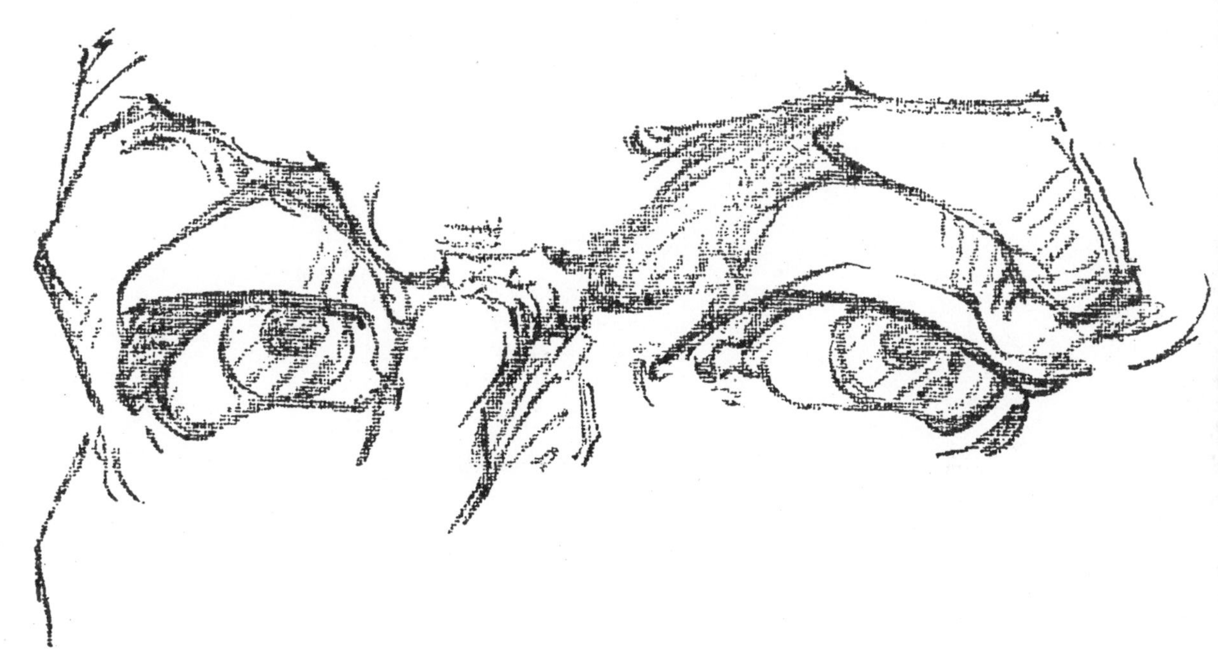

THE EYE SOCKET

WEDGES, PLANES AND THEIR ANGLES

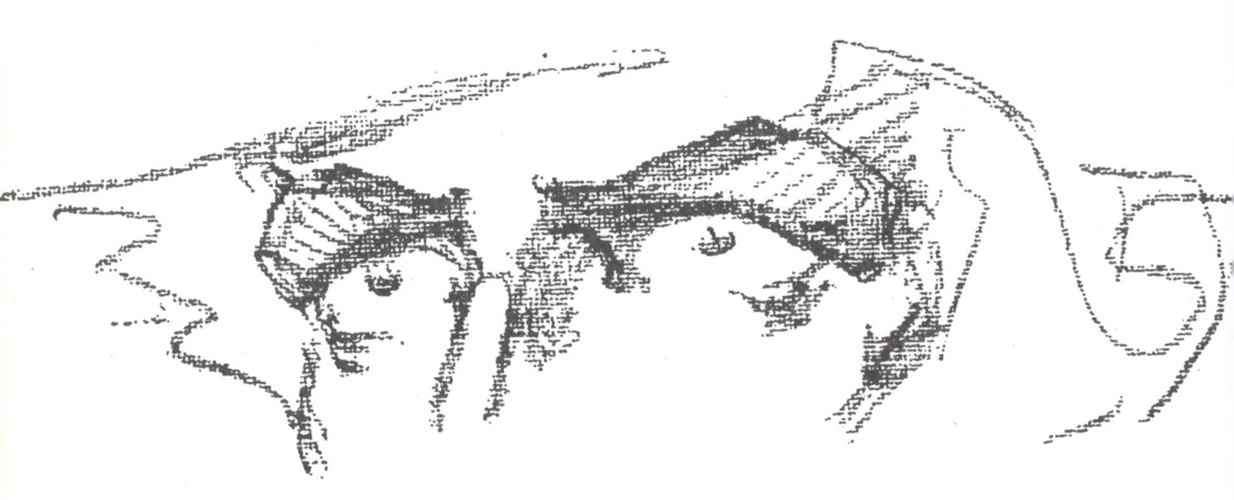

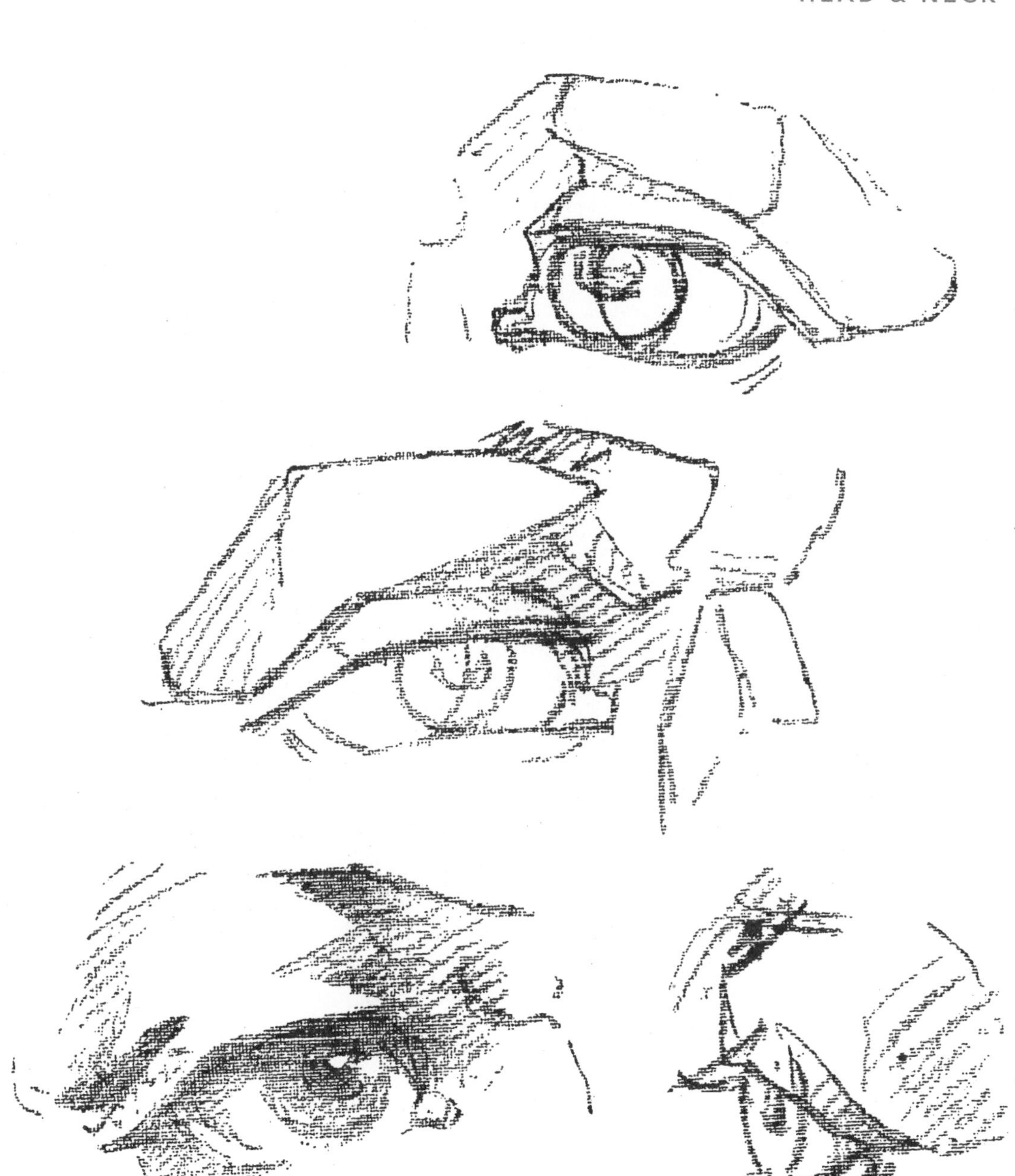

THE EYE

ANGULAR OPENING BETWEEN THE LIDS

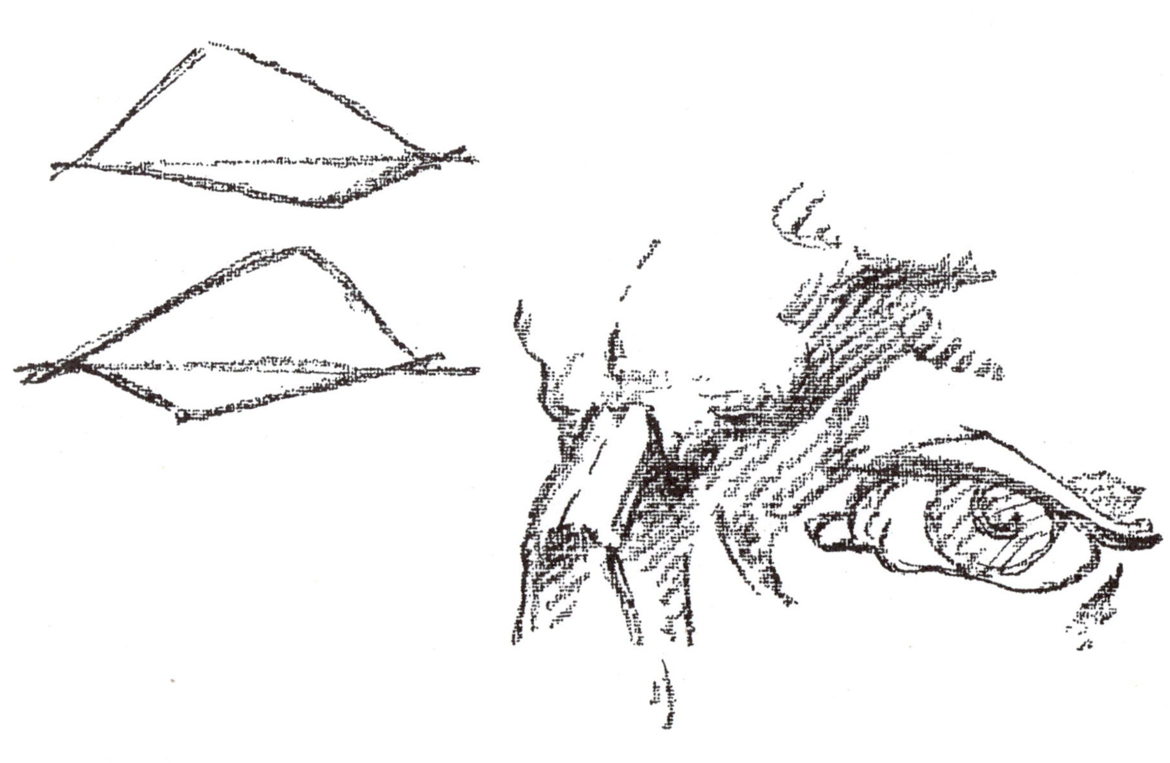

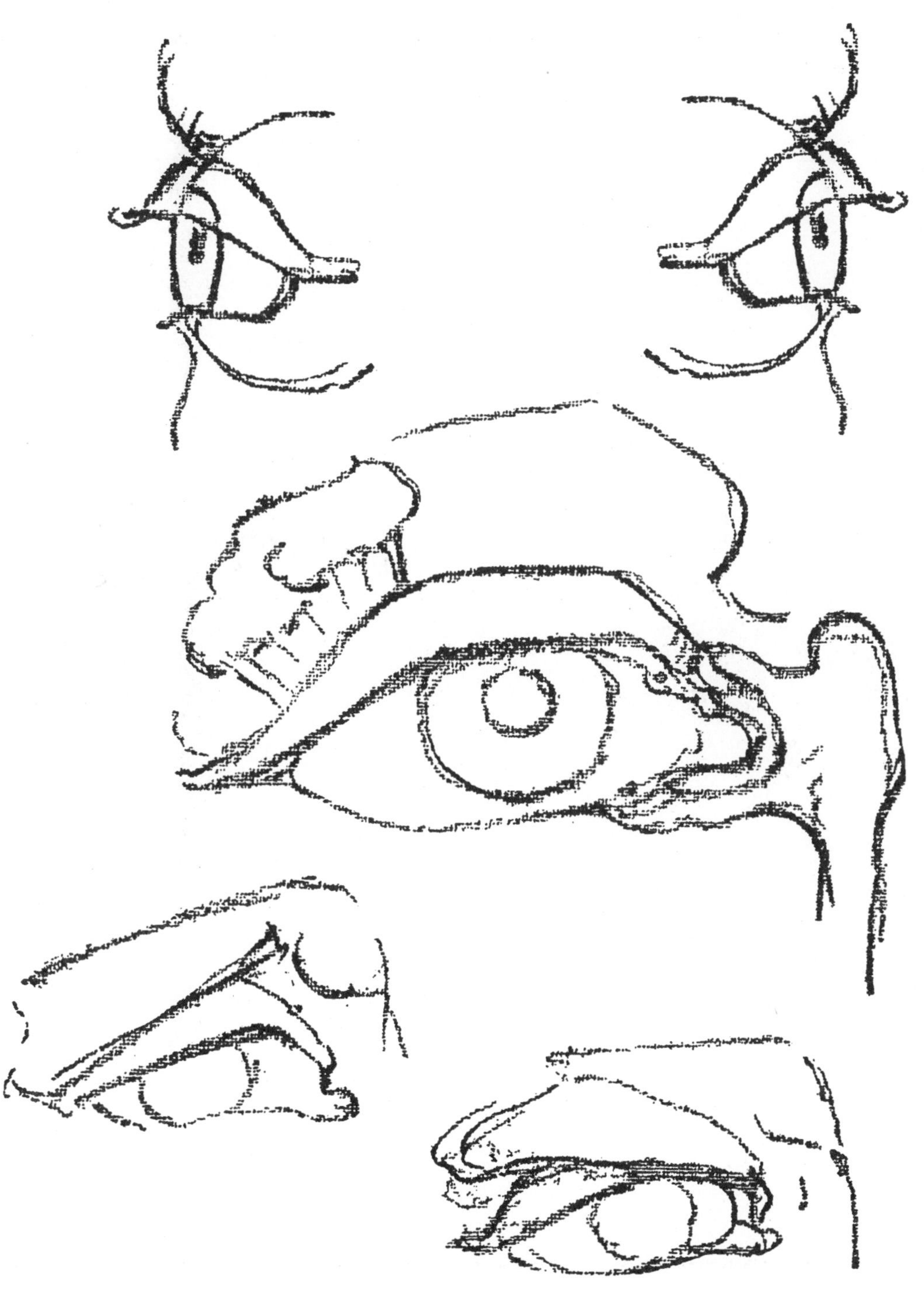

THE EYE

Examples for reference.

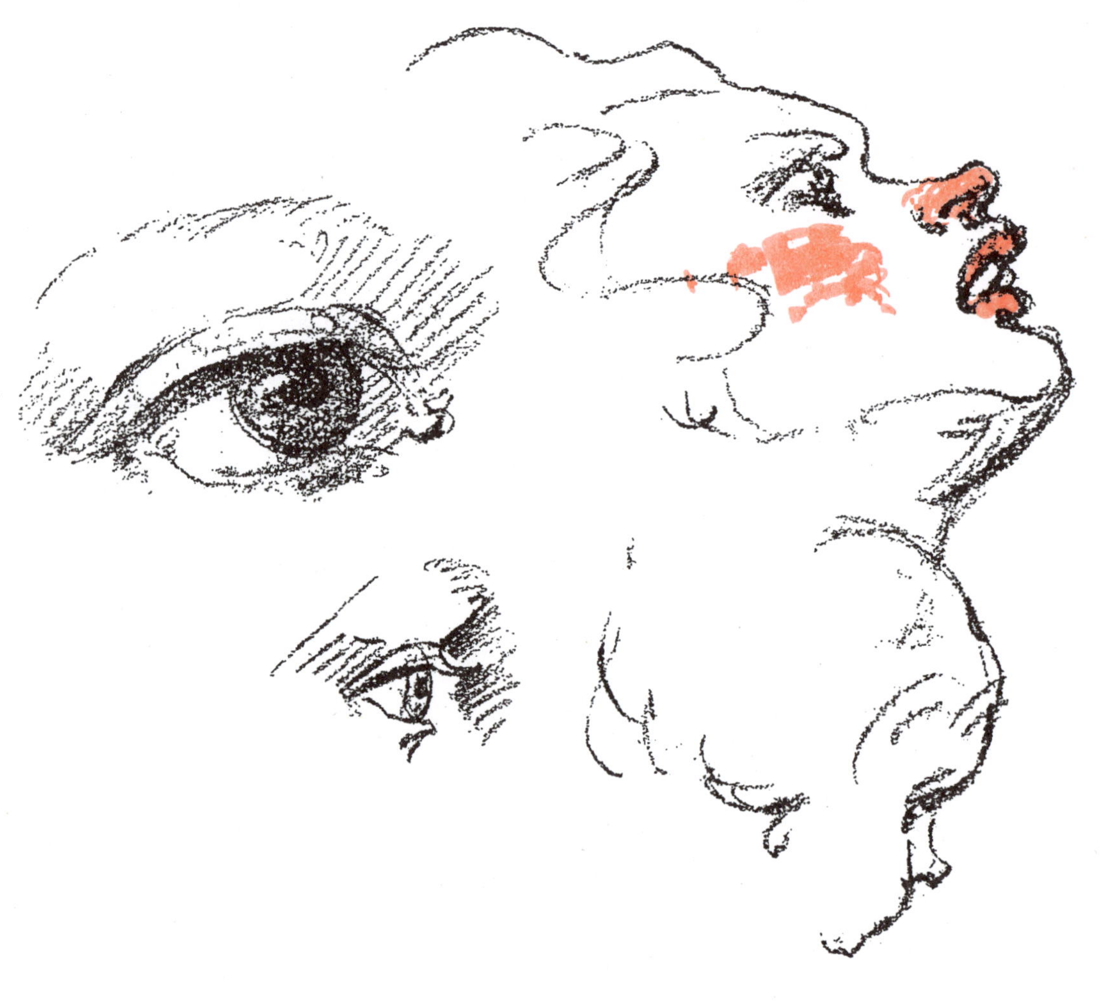

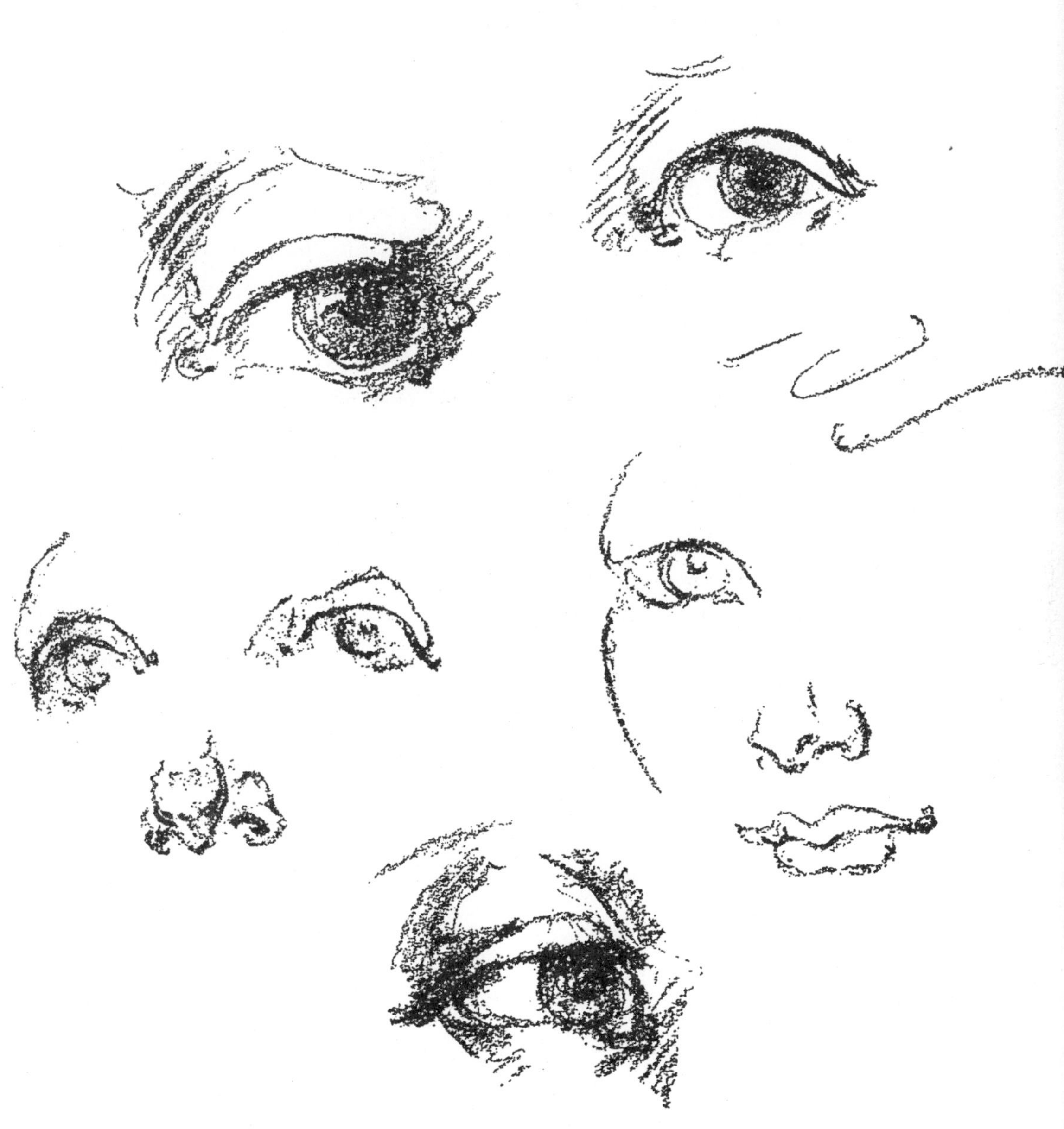

ANATOMY OF THE NOSE

The nose is made of a series of wedges based on its bony structure. Where the bridge of the nose wedges in under the forehead, the two ridges of the *glabella* descend to form a wedge with apex at the bridge. The bony part of the nose is a very clear wedge, its ridge only half the length of the nose, higher as it descends; its base somewhat longer, wider as it descends, making the second wedge.

Beyond the bony part, the nose narrows and the ridge sinks slightly toward the bulb, making a third wedge, base to base with the second. The bulb rises as two sheets of cartilage from the middle of the upper lip (*septum* of the nose), expands into the bulbous tip, flows over the sides, and flares out to form the *alae* or wings of the nostrils.

This cartilaginous portion is quite movable. The wings are raised in laughter, dilated in heavy breathing, narrowed in distaste, and wings and tip are raised in scorn, wrinkling the skin over the nose.

COMPARISONS

Average variations in noses divide them into classes. They may be small, large, or very large; concave or convex; humped, Roman or straight. At the tips they may be elevated, horizontal, or depressed; flattened, tapering or twisted. The wings may be delicate or puffy, round or flat, triangular, square or almond-shaped.

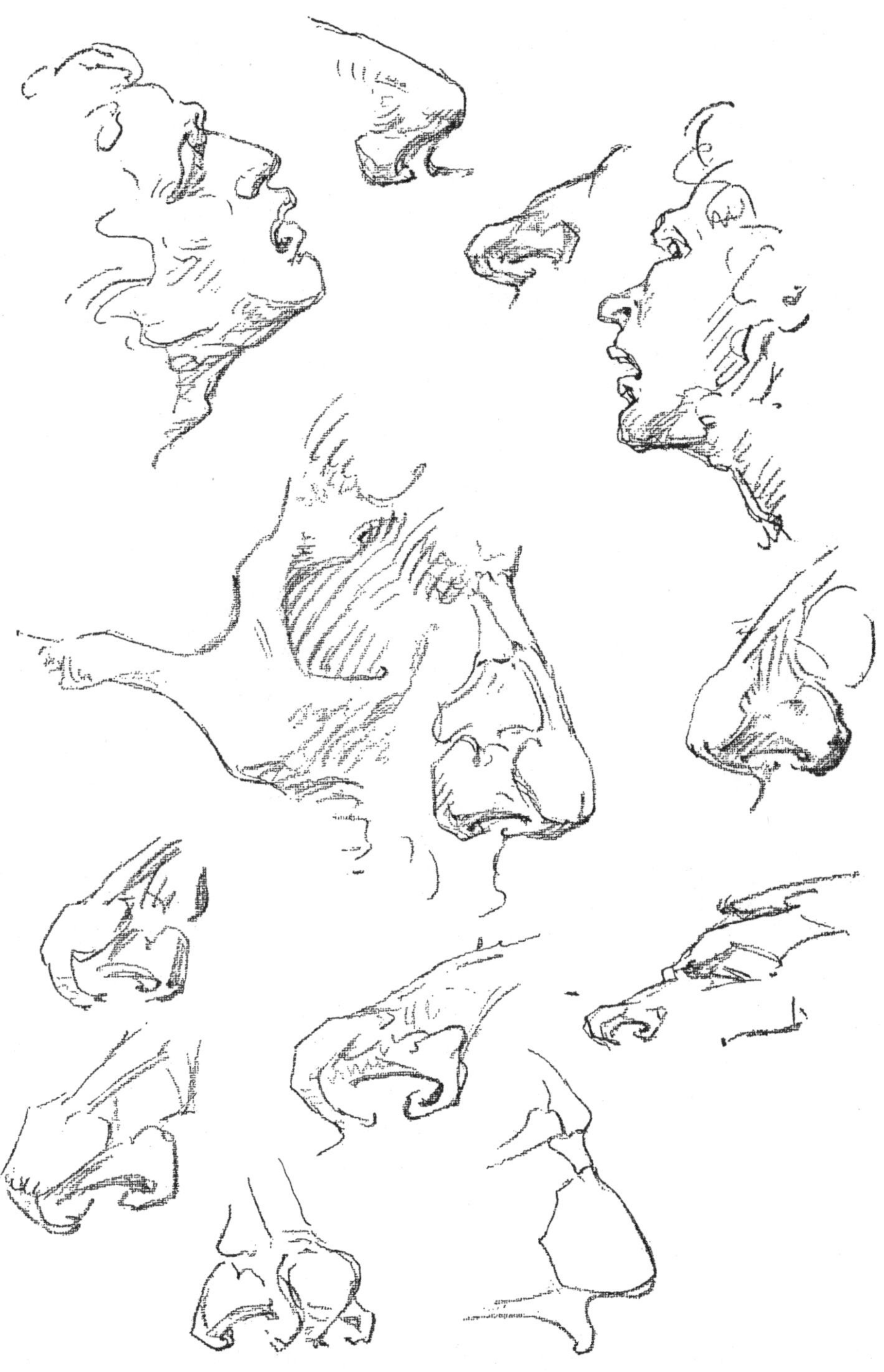

THE NOSE

CARTILAGES OF THE NOSE

① Upper *lateral.*
② Lower *lateral.*
③ Wing.
④ *Septum.*

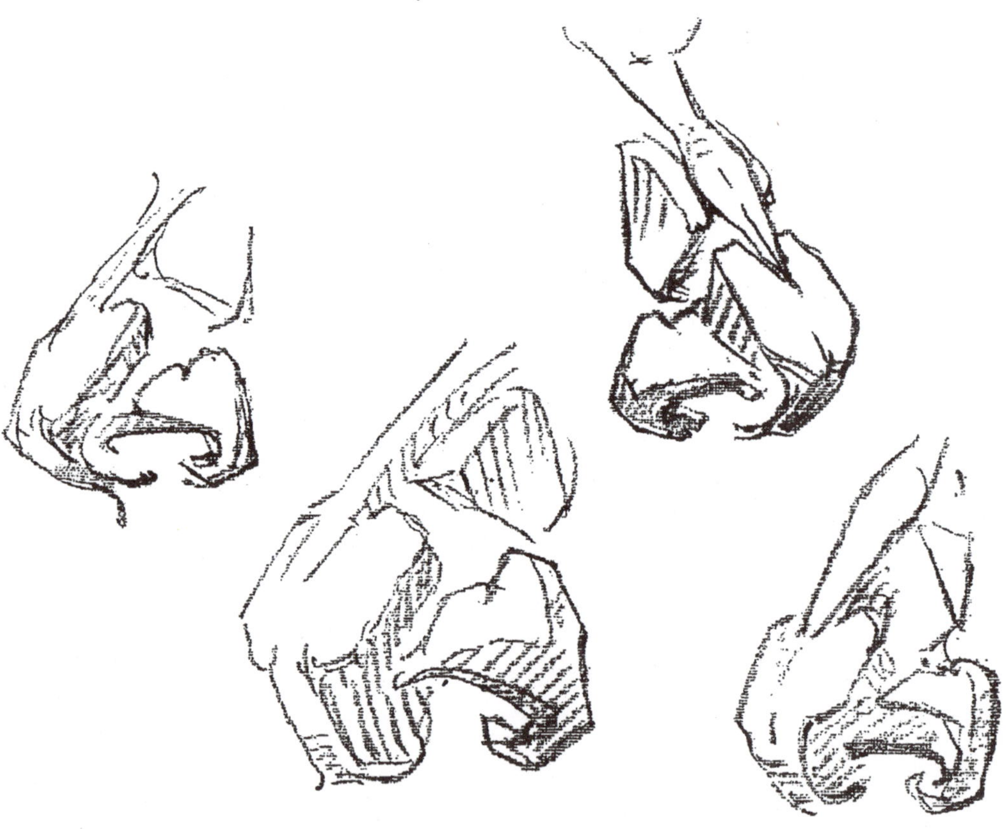

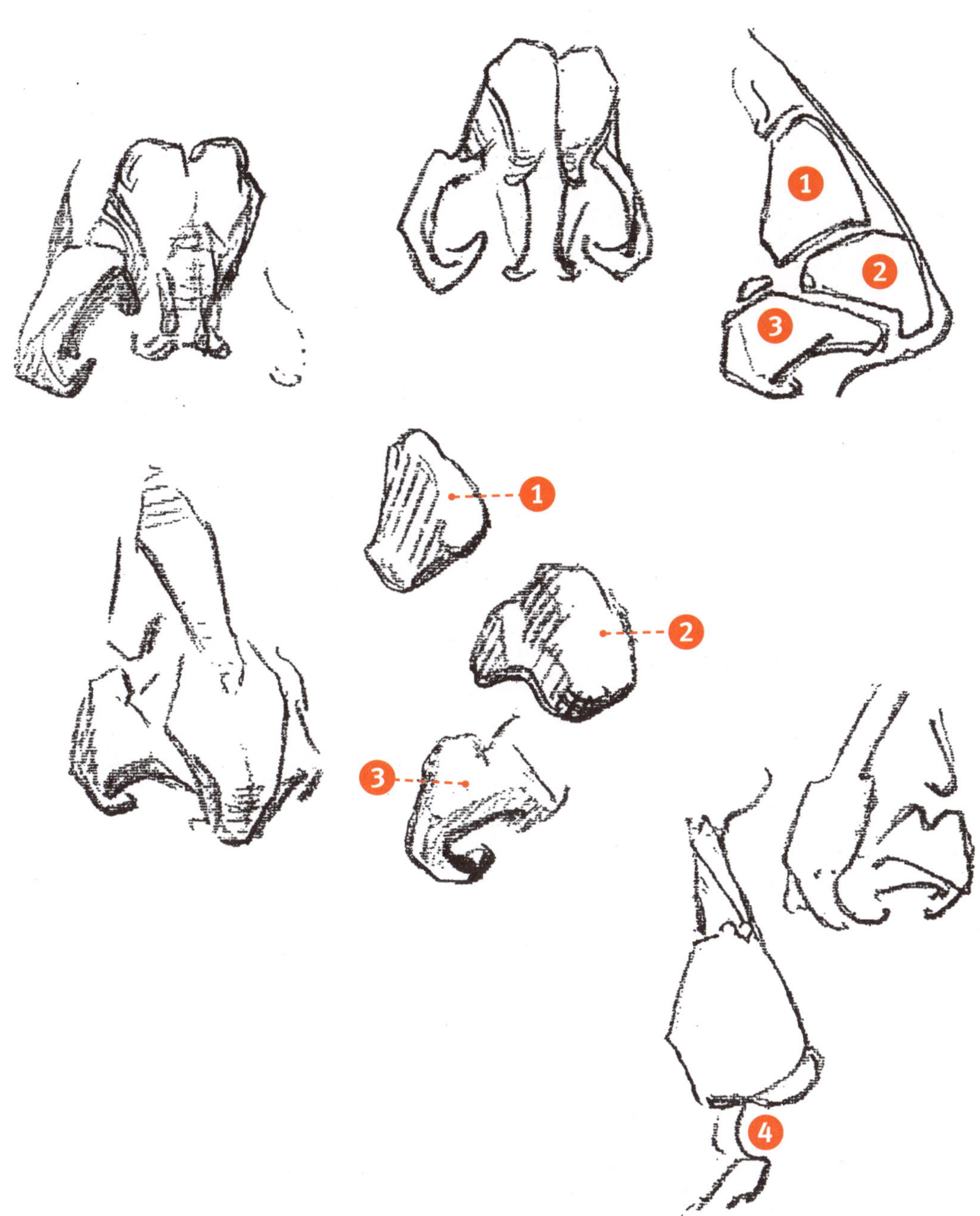
1
2
3
1
2
3
4

ANATOMY OF THE EAR

In animals, the external ear is a smooth cornucopia of cartilage, freely movable, ending in a point. In man it is practically immobile, and its muscles, now mere elastic bands, serve only to draw it into wrinkles.

These vary widely, but there are certain definite forms: an outer rim (*helix*) bearing the remains of the tip; an inner elevation (*anti-helix*), in front of which is the hollow of the ear (*concha*) with the opening of the canal, overhung in front by a flap (*tragus*) and behind and below by a smaller one (*anti-tragus*).

To the whole is appended a lobe. The ear is vertically in line with the back of the jaw, and lies horizontally between the lines of the brow and the base of the nose.

In it three planes are to be found, divided by lines radiating from the canal, up and back and down and back. The first line marks a depressed angle between its planes, the second a raised angle. Average variations in ears present the following classes: large, medium or small; round, oval or triangular. The remains of the point of the ear may be marked or absent.

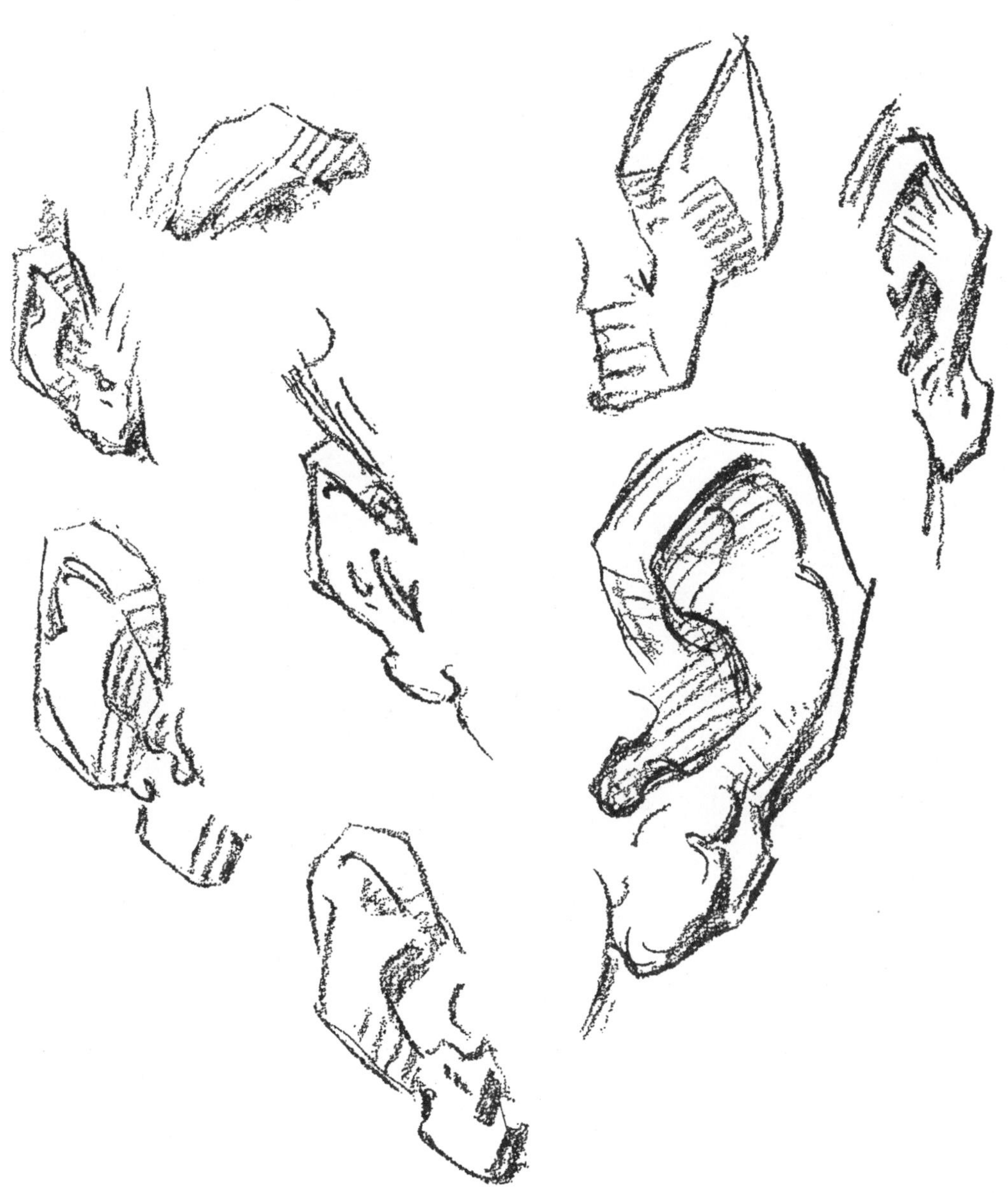

CARTILAGE OF THE EAR

① *Helix.*

② *Anti-helix.*

③ *Tragus.*

④ *Anti-tragus.*

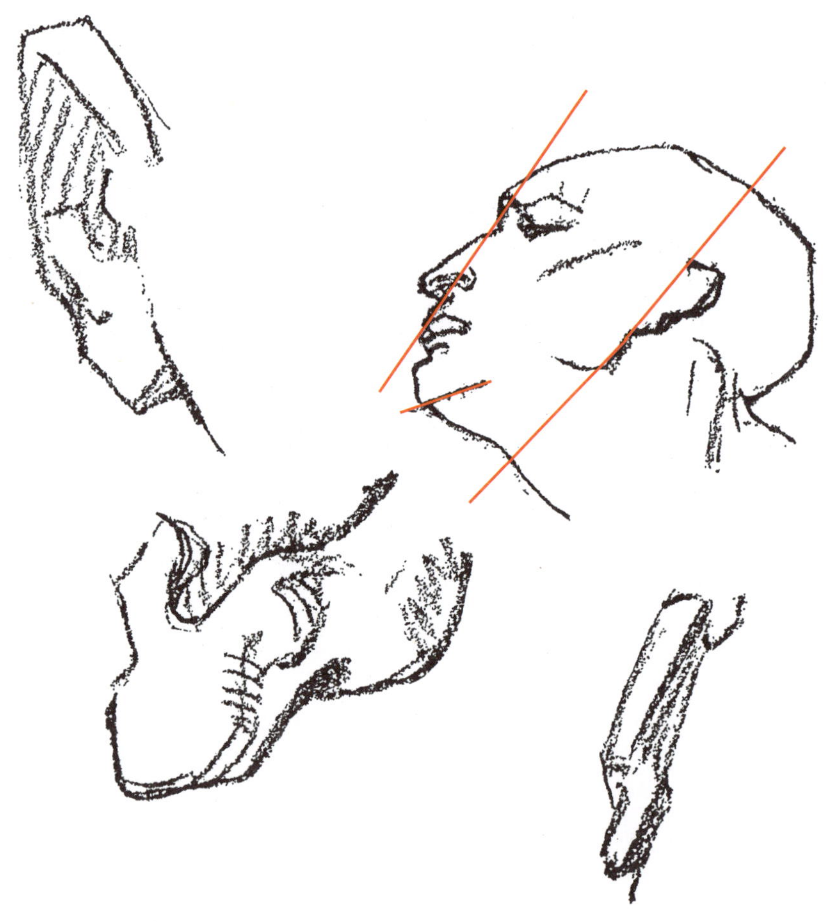

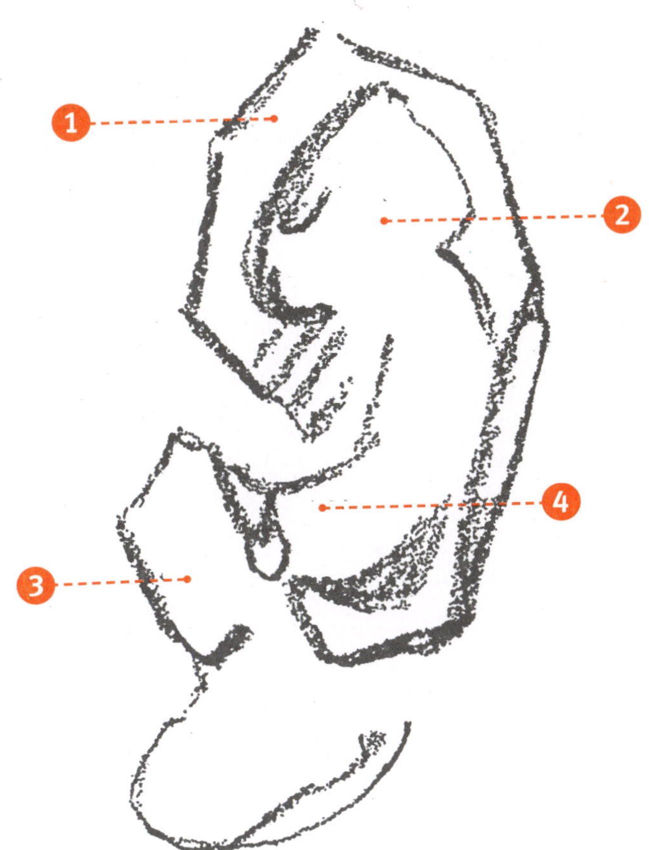
1
2
3
4

THE MOUTH & THE CHIN

The shape of the mouth and lips is controlled by the shape of the jaw. The more curved the jaw in front, the more curved the lips; the more flat it is, the straighter the lips. A much bowed mouth does not occur on a jaw bone that is flat in front nor a straight slit of a mouth on a curved set of upper teeth.

The curtainous portion of the mouth (from nose to margin of red lip) presents a central groove with pillars on either side, blending in to two broad drooping wings, whose terminus is at the pillars of the mouth. The groove ends in a wedge entering the upper lip (red portion). This portion is set at an angle with the curtainous portion.

The **upper and lower red lips**, accurately adapted to each other when closed, are yet quite different in form; the upper being flat and angular, the lower rounded.

The **upper red lip** has a central wedge-shaped body, indented at the top by the wedge of the groove above, and two long slender wings disappearing under the pillars of the mouth. The lower red lip has a central groove and two lateral lobes.

It has three surfaces, the largest depressed in the middle, at the groove, and two smaller ones on each side, diminishing in thickness as they curve outward, not so long as the upper lip. The base or curtainous portion of the lower lip sets at an angle with the

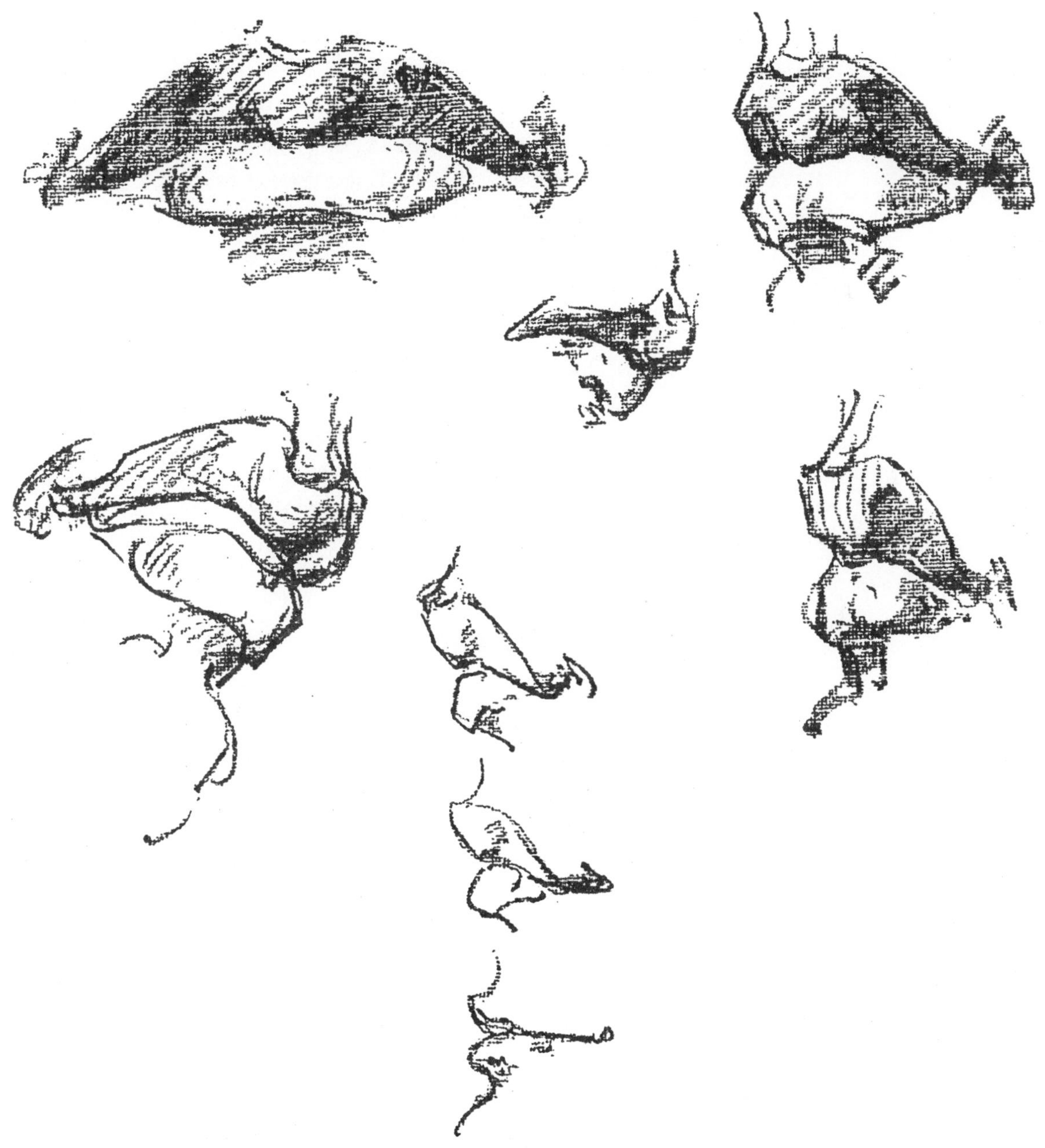

red portion less than that in the upper lip. It slopes backward and ends at the cleft of the chin. It has a small linear central ridge and two large lateral lobes, bounded by the pillars of the mouth.

The **oval cavity of the mouth** is surrounded by a circular muscle (*orbicularis oris*) whose fibres, overlapping at the corners, raise the skin into the folds known as the pillars of the mouth. Its outer margin is usually marked by a crease in the skin running from the wings of the nose out and down to varying distances, paralleling the pillars. Its lower end may blend in to the cleft of the chin. From this muscle radiate various facial muscles of expression.

Average variations in lips present the following comparisons: thick or thin; prominent, protruding or receding; and each may be compared with the other in these respects: straight, curved or bowed, rosebud, pouting or compressed.

THE CHIN

Below the cleft of the chin, the chin itself protrudes. Its breadth at the base is marked by two lines which, prolonged, would meet at the septum of the nose, making a triangle that wedges upward in to the base of the lower lip. It is bordered on each side by two planes which reach to the angle of the jaw.

Variations in chins present the following comparisons: high or low; pointed or ball; flat, furrowed or dimpled; elongated, double, etc.

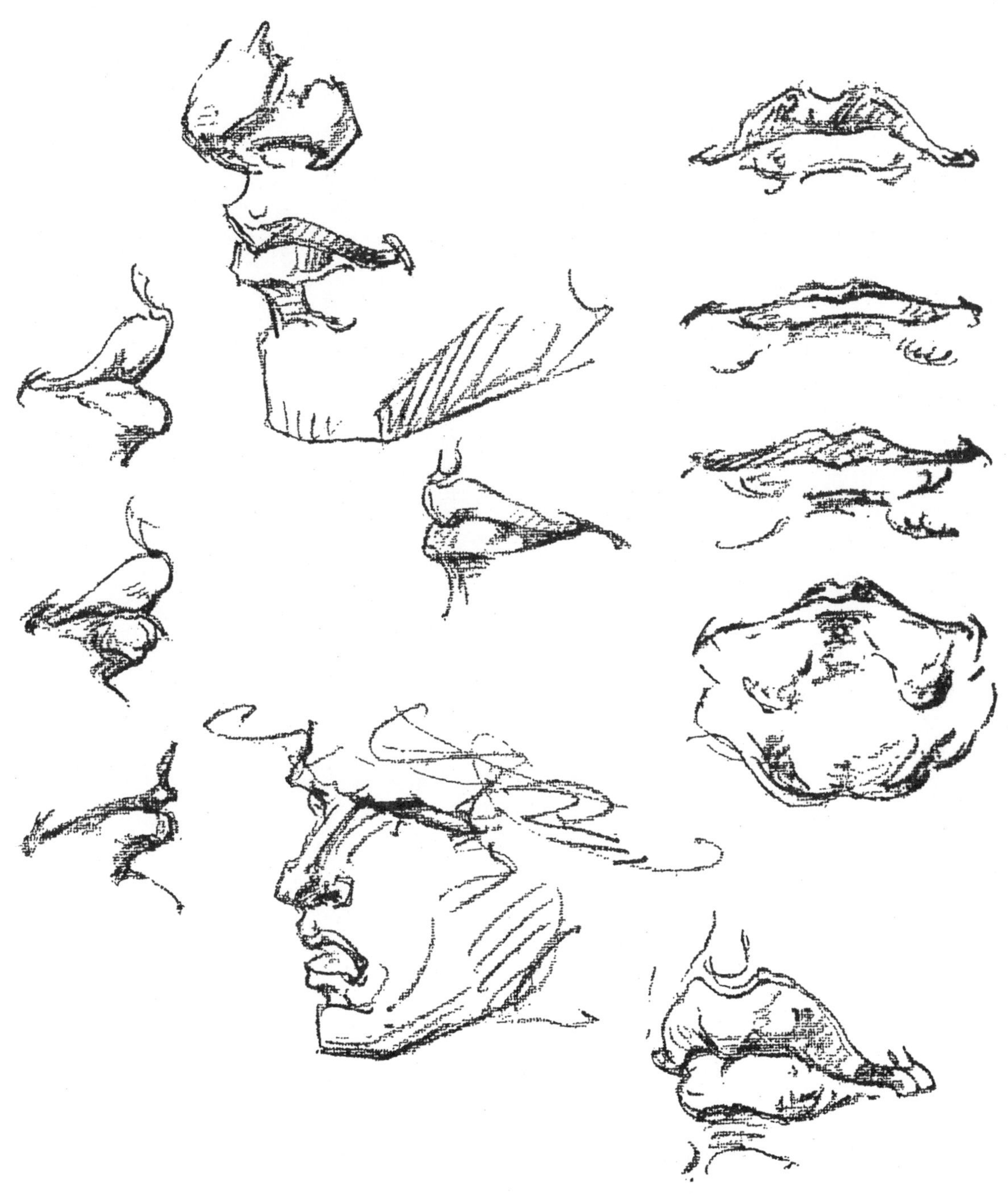

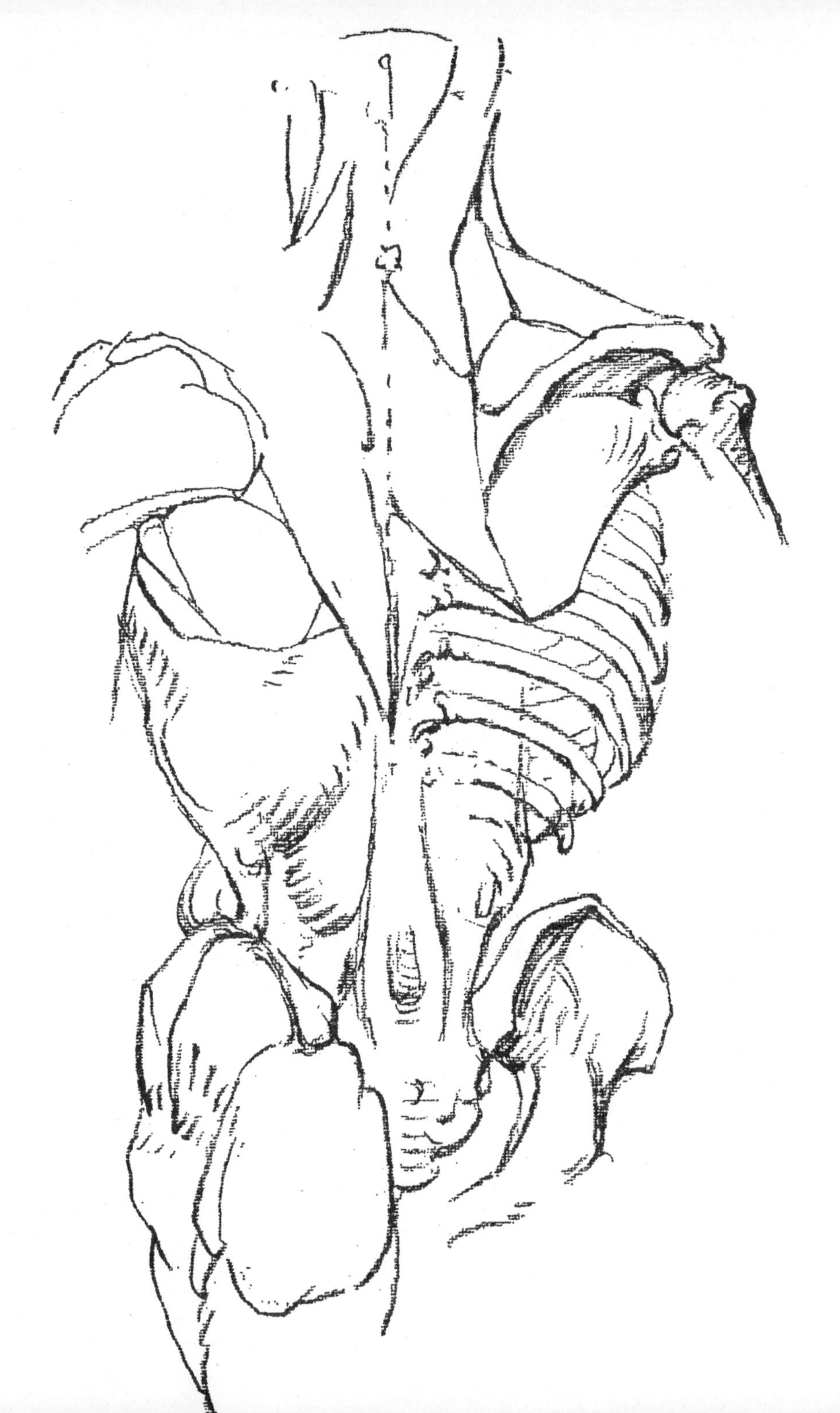

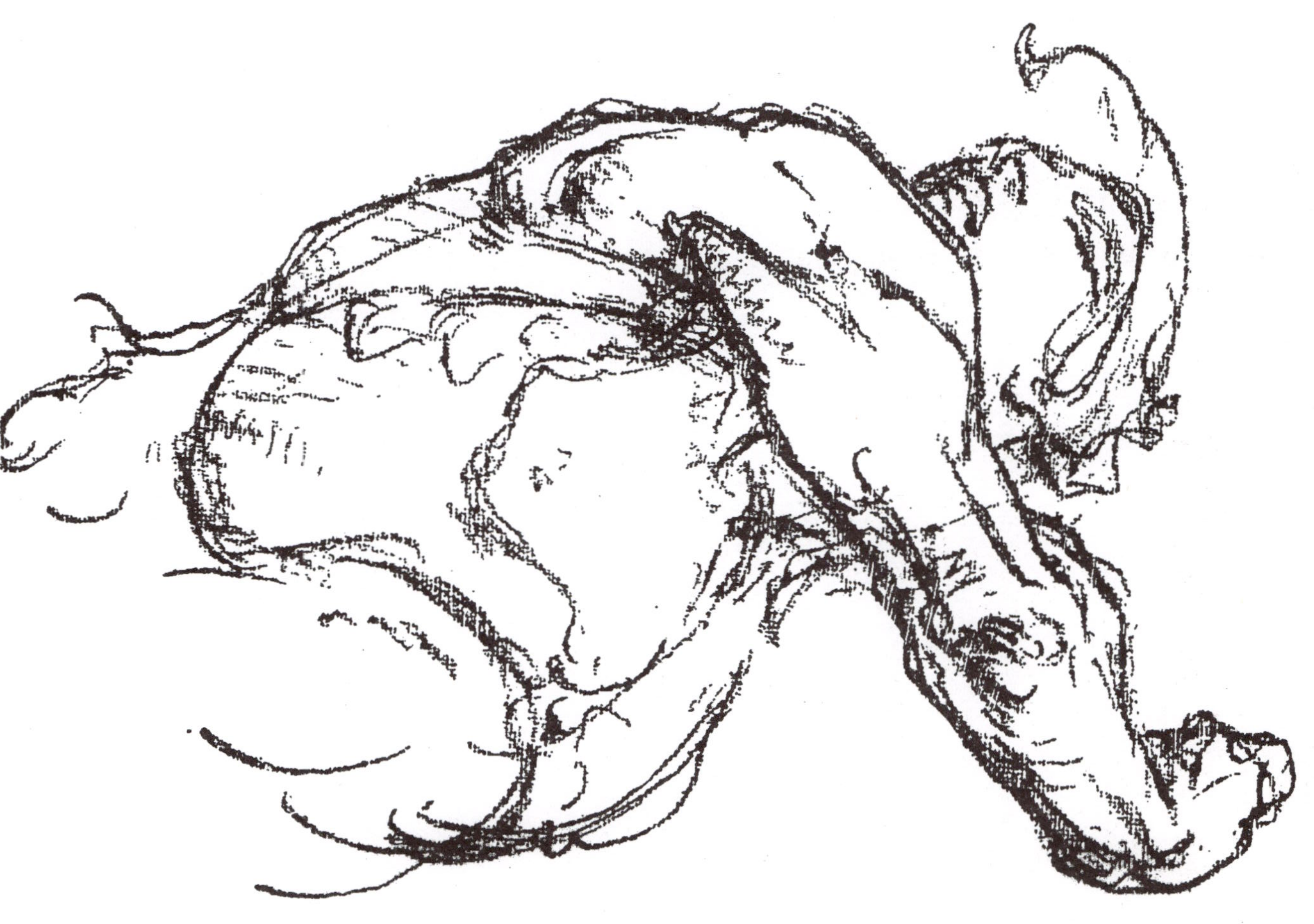

The Trunk

FRONT VIEW ANATOMY

The upper part of the body is built around a bony cage called the thorax, conical in shape, and flattened in front. The walls of this cage are the ribs, 12 on each side, fastening to the spine behind and to the sternum or breast bone in front.

The upper ribs are quite short and make a small circle; they grow longer until the seventh, which is the longest and the last to fasten to the breast bone. The next three grow shorter and shorter, and reach the *sternum* only through a long costal cartilage, which with the projecting end of the *sternum* (*ensiform* cartilage) form the abdominal arch. The last two ribs are quite short and are free at their front ends. The first seven are called true ribs, the next three false, and the last two floating ribs.

COLLAR BONE

To the breast bone at the top of this cone the collar bones are attached, lifting the whole mass away from the cone and making it a flat surface, wedging downward. The inner ends of the S-shaped bone are curved around the apex of the cone, but the outer ends move forward again, bringing the mass of the shoulders with them to form the flat front surface.

MUSCLES

Thus, without the shoulders, the cage of the chest is a cone with the apex upward. Under the muscles this form may easily be seen.

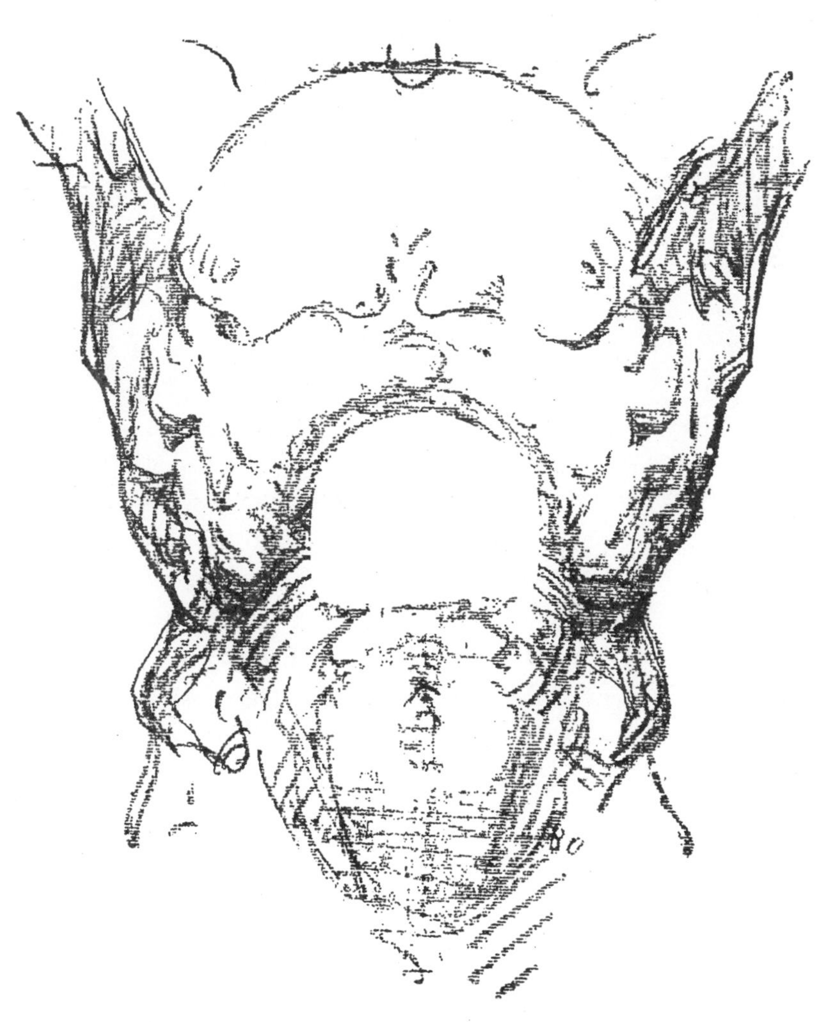

With the shoulders, it is a wedge with the apex downward. The profile of the sides forms a wide wedge, buttressed by a mass of lateral muscles over the *iliac* crest. The front surface, formed mainly by the *pectoral* and *rectus abdominis* muscles, forms a much more slender wedge.

Its upper third bevels more sharply in, as far as the lower border of the breast muscle, paralleling the edge of that muscle, bounded by a line across the bottom of the breast muscle, just below the nipple, through the *epigastric* pit. Its lower two-thirds bevels more sharply down, following the edge of the *rectus* muscle; its lines almost meet at the *symphysis pubis* below.

A **vertical central groove** divides the symmetrical halves of the front, running its full length. It begins in the pit of the neck, between the collar bones. Over the breast it marks the breast bone, and is deepened by the bulge of the pectoral muscles on either side. At the end of this, its upper third, is a pit (*epigastric* pit) marking the divergence of the ribs.

At the end of its middle third is another pit, the *umbilicus* or navel. At the end of its lower third is the mound of the *symphysis*. This line is useful for placing the masses of the chest, the *epigastrium* (over the stomach) and the abdomen.

MASSES

The masses of the torse are the chest, the abdomen or pelvis, and between them the *epigastrium*; the first two comparatively stable, the middle one quite movable. A straight line marking the collar bones defines the top of the first mass; and paralleling it, a line through the base of the breast muscles and pit of the *epigastrium* forms its base.

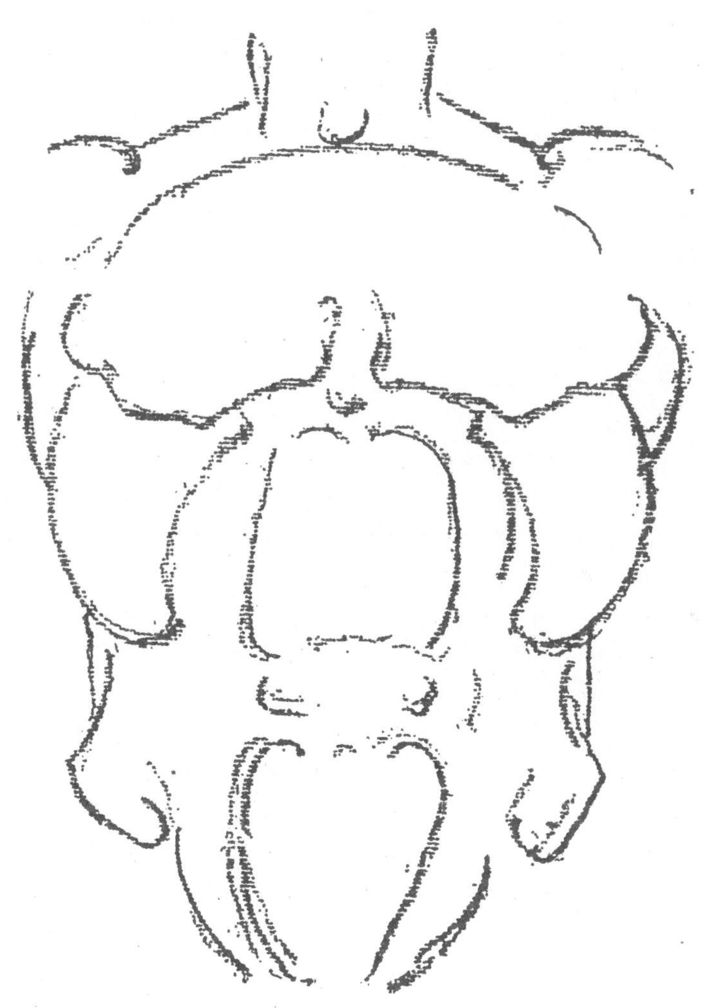

Although the shoulders are freely movable, changing the lines of the first mass, and bulging the pectoral muscles, yet the mass itself changes little except the slight change in respiration. Even in respiration the upper portion, as far as the level of the *epigastric* pit, changes little; the lower ribs perform most of the respiratory movement. Centering on this pit is the abdominal arch, made of the cartilages of the false ribs. At its centre, the end of the breast bone (*ensiform* cartilage) hangs pendent; on either side the arch descends diagonally, variously curved, separating *thorax* from abdomen.

Below this arch is the abdomen, the most movable part of the mobile portion. It is bounded below by a line passing approximately through the anterior points of the *iliac* crests. Its profile shows the lines of the cone of the thorax diverging downward, the lines of the wedge of the chest and shoulders converging downward, and the buttressing of the *lateral* muscles.

In the bending or turning of the body the central line of this portion bends always to the convex side, always paralleled by the borders of the *rectus* muscle.

By this movement the straight wedge of the front is broken. It becomes not a bent wedge, but two wedges; one the upper half of the original wedge, prolonged but not completed downward; the other the lower half, prolonged upward to meet the one above.

More unchanging than either of the above is the mass of the abdomen. The central groove is here shallow and may lose itself below. The long wedge ends in the *symphysis pubis*.

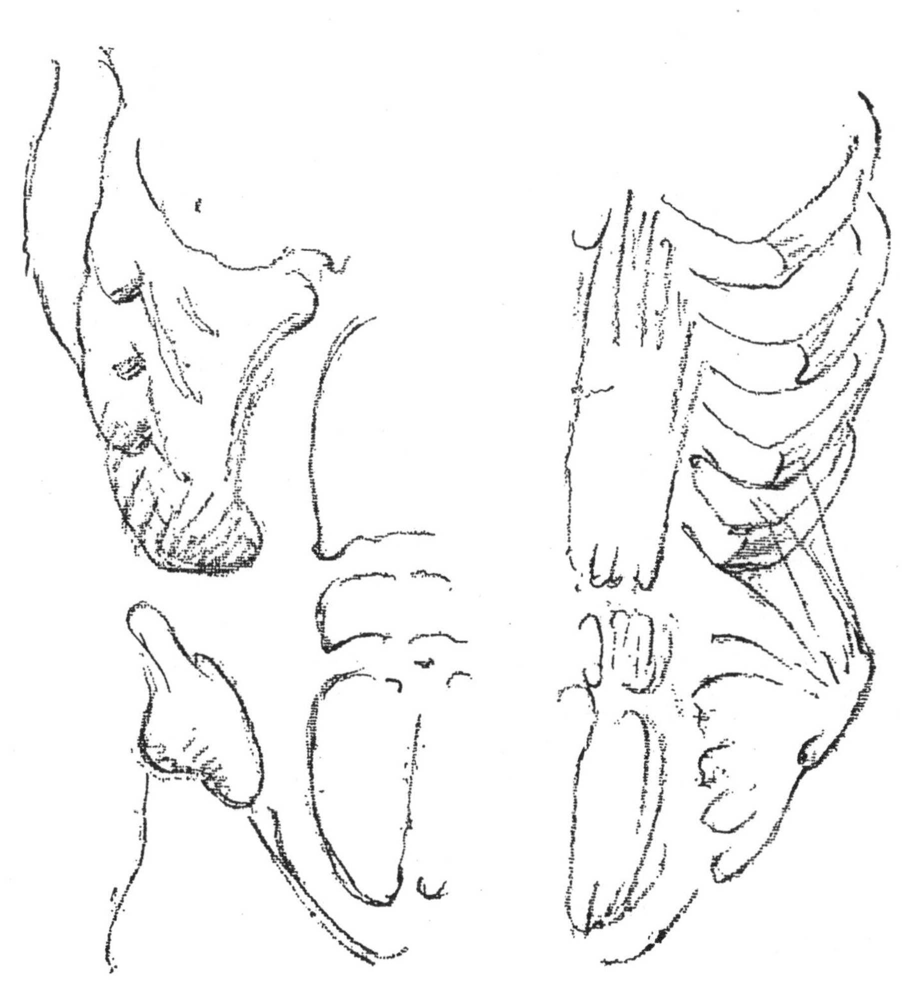

MUSCLES OF THE TRUNK: FRONT VIEW

① *Pectoralis major.*
② *Deltoid.*
③ *Rectus abdominis.*
④ *Serratus magnus.*
⑤ *External oblique.*

(***Pectoralis major***, *see* page 186)
(***Deltoid***, *see* page 126)

Rectus Abdominis:

From *symphysis pubis* to cartilages of ribs, from fifth to seventh.

Action: Flexes *thorax.*

Serratus Magnus:

From eight upper ribs to *scapula*-spinal edge, under surface.

Action: Draws shoulder blade forward, raises ribs.

External Oblique:

From eight lower ribs to *iliac* crest and ligament to *pubis.*

Action: Flexes *thorax.*

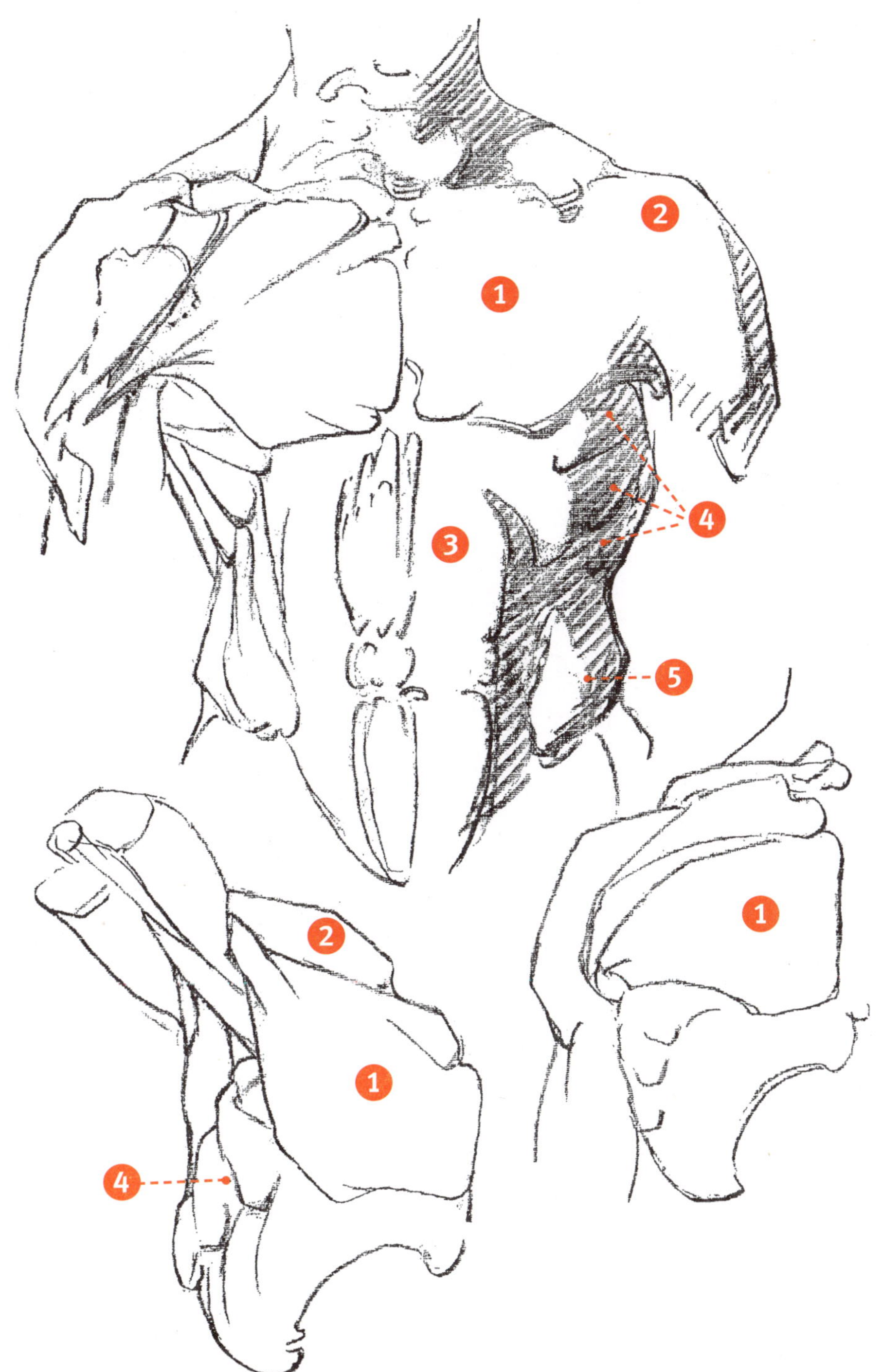
2
1
4
3
5
2
1
1
4

SKELETON OF THE TRUNK

MUSCLES COVERING UPPER PORTION: FRONT VIEW

① *Pectoralis minor*.
② *Pectoralis major*.

***Pectoralis* Minor**:
From third, fourth and fifth ribs to *coracoid* process.
Action: Depresses point of shoulder.

***Pectoralis* Major**:
From inner half of *clavicle*, *sternum*, *costal* cartilages as far as sixth and seventh ribs to *humerus*.
Action: Draws arm downward and forward.

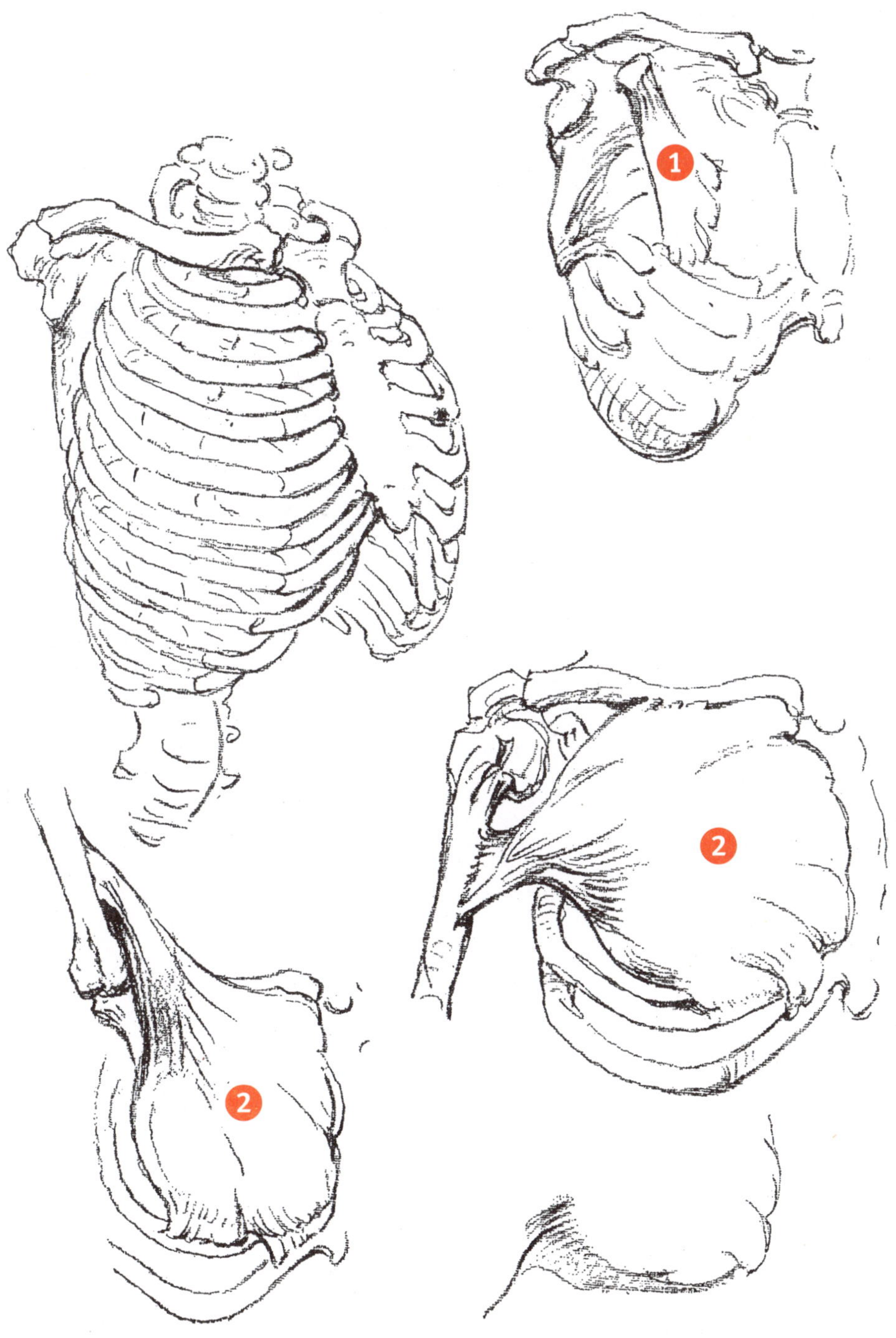
1
2
2

THE TRUNK

TRUNK: FRONT VIEW
ARMPIT AND SHOULDER

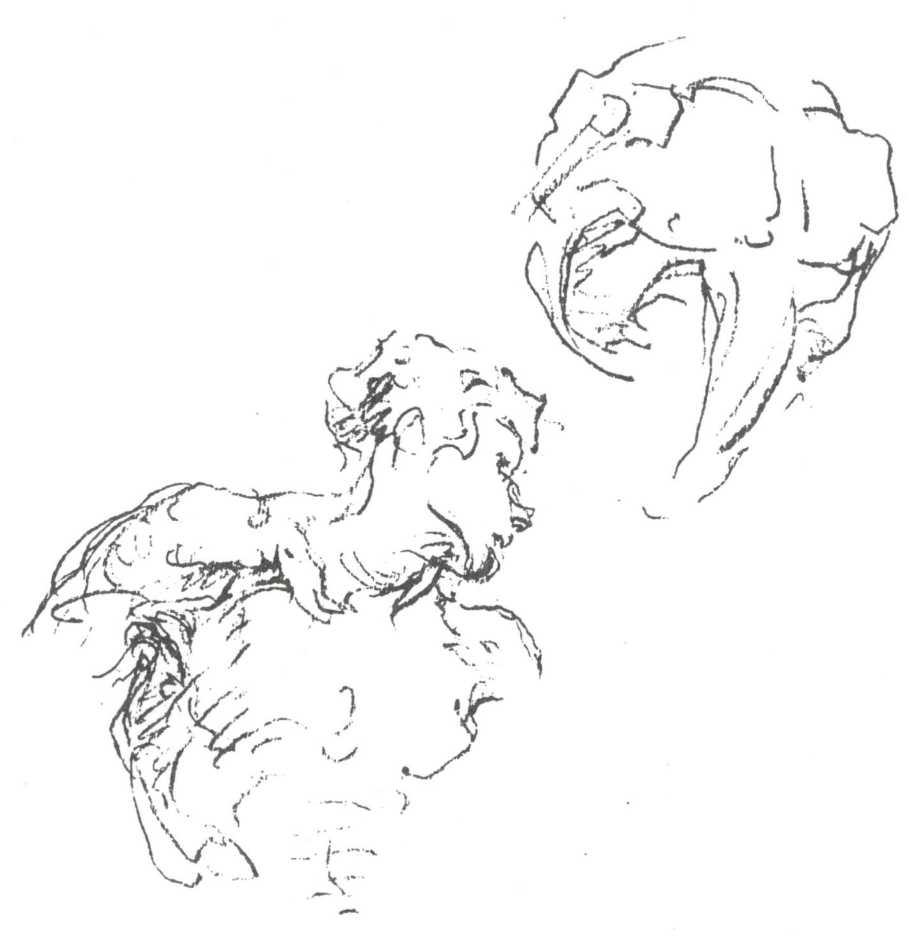

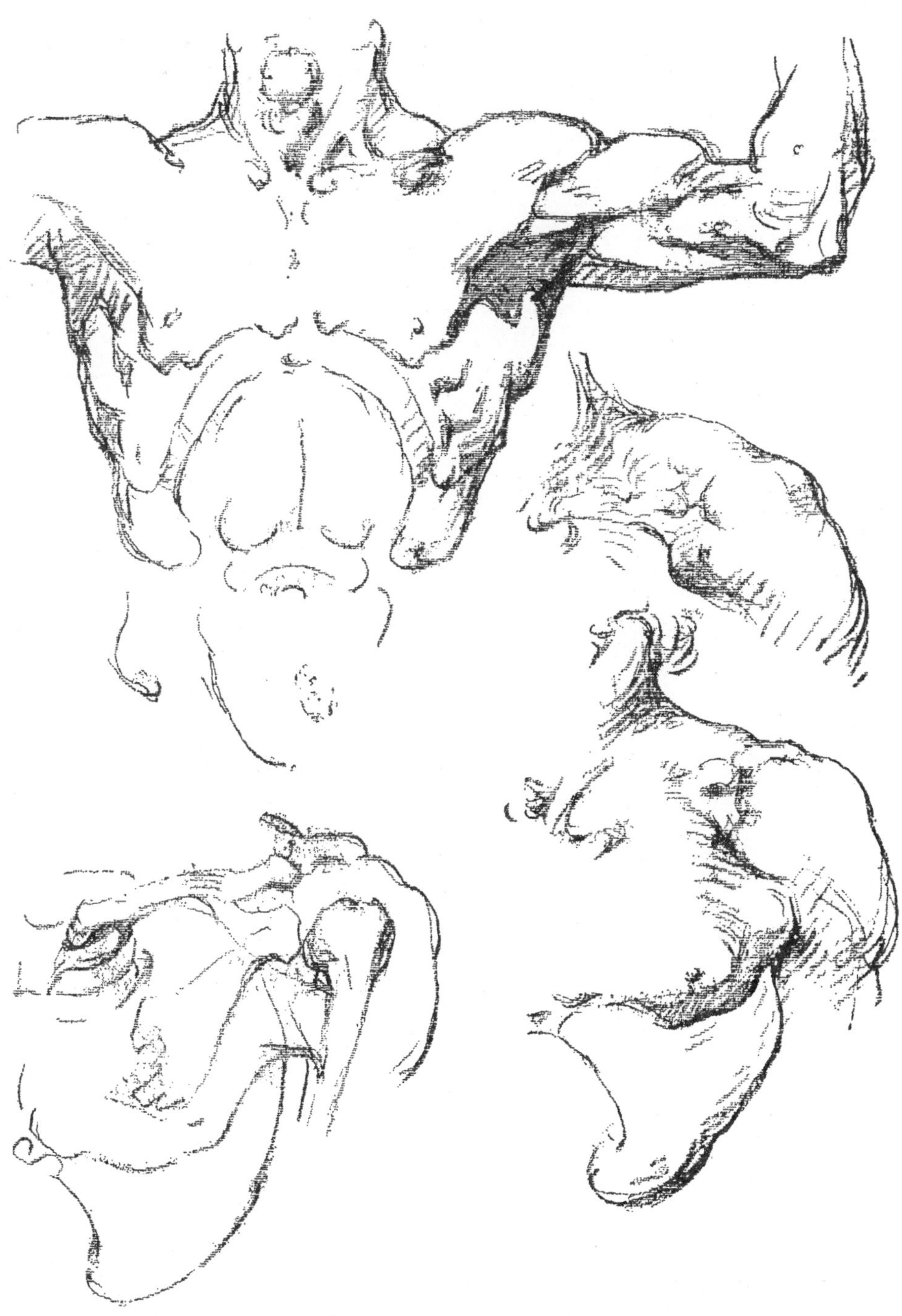

ANATOMY OF THE TORSE

The erect torse presents in profile the long curve of the front, broken by depressions at the border of the breast muscle and at the *umbilicus* or navel into three lesser curves, almost equal in length.

The back presents the sharp *anterior* curve of the waist, opposite the *umbilicus*, bending into the long *posterior* curve of the chest, and the shorter curve of the buttocks. The former, that of the chest, is broken by the almost vertical shoulder blade and the slight bulge of the *latissimus* below it.

In profile the torse presents three masses: that of the chest, that of the waist, and that of the pelvis and abdomen. The first and last are comparatively unchanging. Above, the mass of the chest is bounded by the line of the collar bones; below, by a line following the cartilages of the ribs, being perpendicular to the long diameter of the chest.

This mass is widened by the expansion of the chest in breathing, and the shoulder moves freely over it, carrying the shoulder blade, collar bone, and muscles. It is marked by the ridge of *costal* cartilages that forms its border, sloping up and forward, and by the ribs themselves, sloping down and forward, and by the 'digitations' (finger marks) of the *serratus magnus* (big saw-toothed) muscle, little triangles in a row from the corner of the breast muscle, paralleling the cartilages of the ribs, disappearing under the *latissimus*.

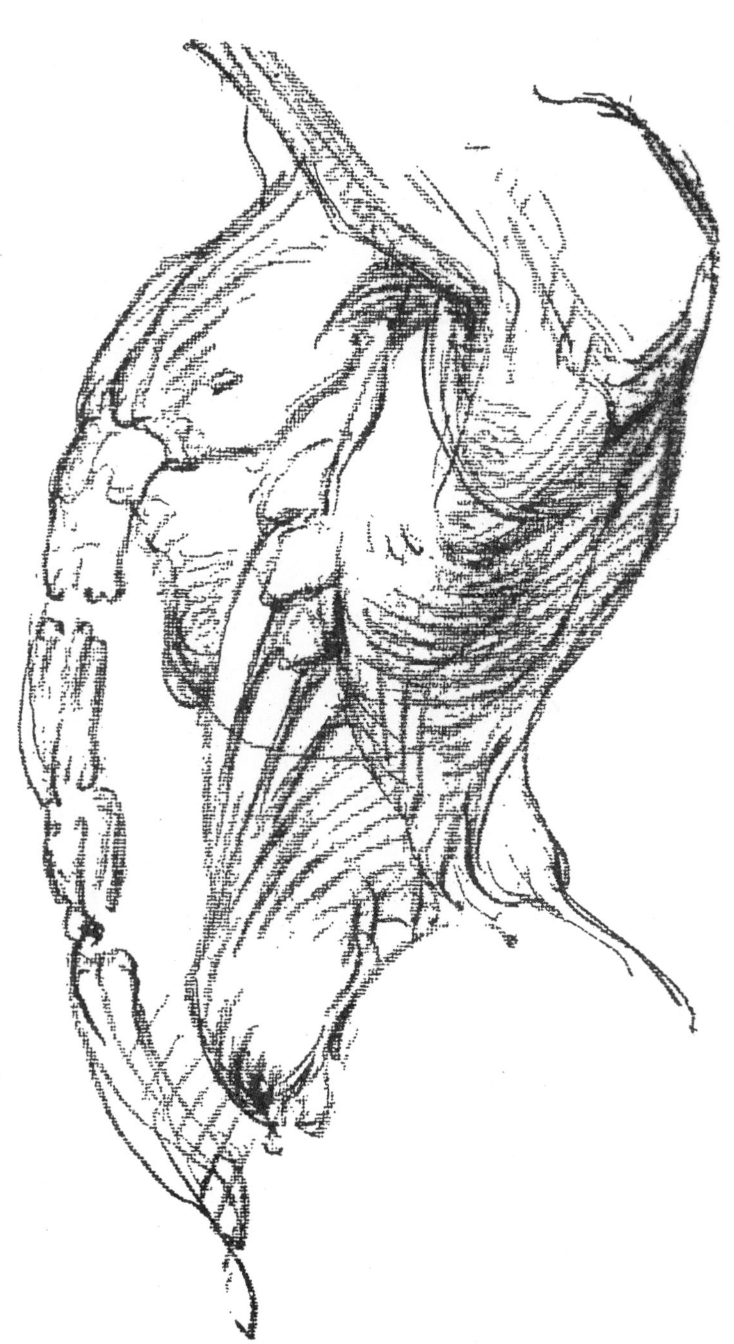

Below, the mass of the pelvis and abdomen slopes up and forward. It is marked by the *iliac* crest and hip, described later. In front it may be flattened by contraction of the abdominal muscles. Over its surface the hip moves freely, changing the tilt of the pelvis.

Between these the central mass contains the waist vertebrae, and is very changeable. Practically all of the movement of flexion and extension for the whole spine occurs here, and much of the side-bending.

This mass is marked by a buttress of *lateral* muscles, slightly overhanging the pelvic brim and bearing inward against the side above. It changes greatly in different positions of the trunk.

TORSE: BACK VIEW

The back presents numerous depressions and prominences. This is due not only to its bony structure but to the crossing and recrossing of a number of thin layers of muscles. It should be borne in mind that the superficial or outside layers manifest themselves only when in action. For this reason, under all changes of position, the spine, the shoulder-blade with its *acromion* process, and the crest of the *ilium*, must be regarded as the landmarks of this region.

The spine is composed of 24 vertebrae. It extends the full length of the back, and its course is marked by a furrow. The vertebrae are known as the *cervical*, *dorsal* and *lumbar*. The *cervical* vertebrae are seven in number, and the seventh is the most prominent in the whole of the spine. It is known as *vertebra prominens*. In the dorsal region the furrow is not so deep as below. Here there are 12

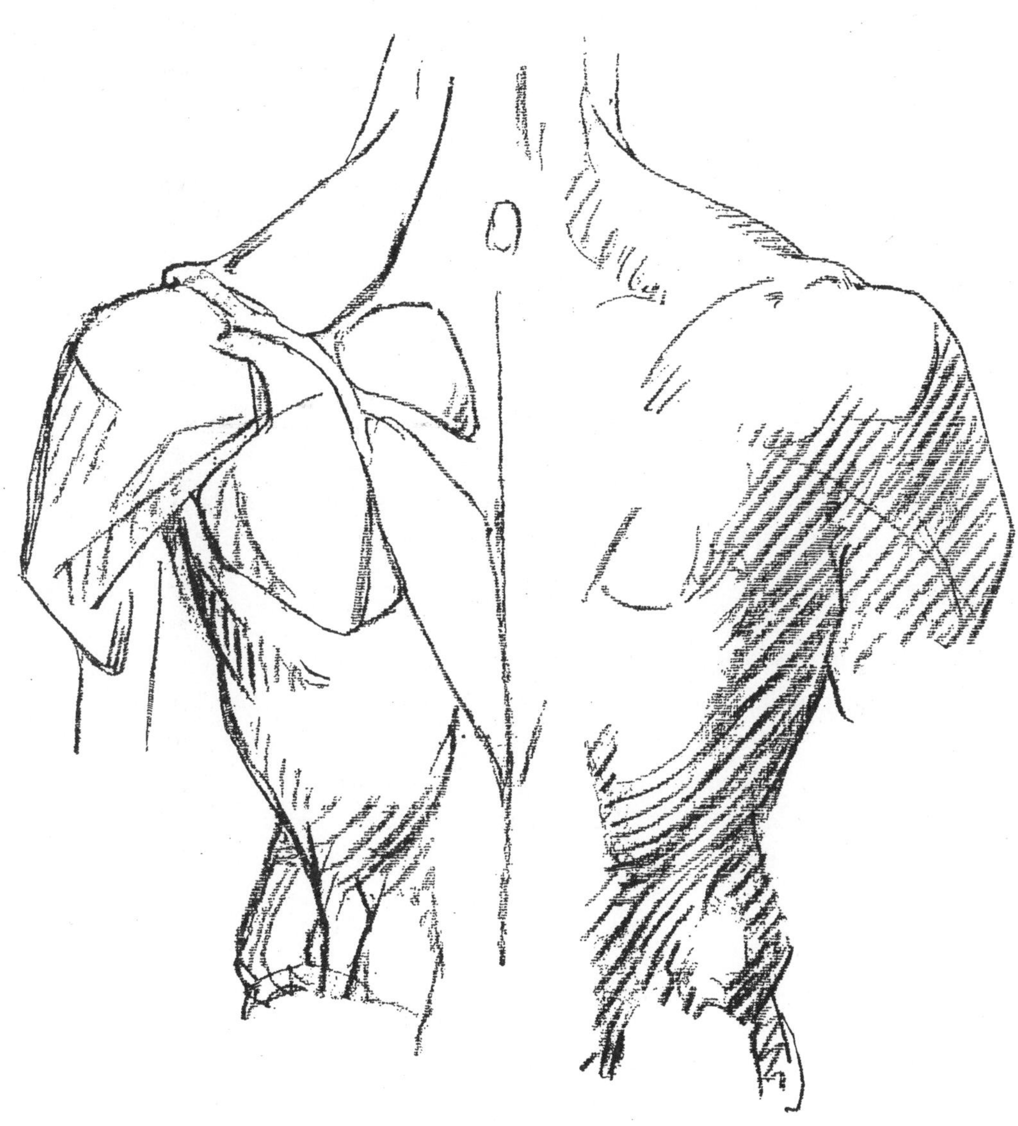

vertebrae. When the body is bent forward, the processes of the vertebrae in this section are plainly indicated.

The spinal furrow becomes deeper as it reaches the *lumbar* vertebrae, where it is marked by dimples and depressions. It widens out, too, in this part of the body, and as it passes over the surface of the *sacrum* to the *coccyx* it becomes flattened. The average length of the spine is about two feet three inches.

The outer corner of the shoulder girdle is the *acromion* process, which is the high outer extremity of a ridge rising from the shoulder blade. The shoulder blade or *scapula* (spade) is a flat plaque of bone fitting snugly against the cage of the *thorax* having a long inner vertical edge, parallel to the spine; a sharp lower point; a long outer edge pointing to the arm pit; and a short upper edge parallel with the slope of the shoulder.

The ridge, or spine of the *scapula*, starts at the spinal edge, about a third of the way down, in a triangular thickening and rises until it passes high over the outer upper corner, where the shoulder joint ties, then turns forward to join with the collar bone at the acromion. The prominent portions are this ridge and the spinal edge and the lower corner. The upper outer corner is thickened to form the socket for the head of the *humerus*, forming the shoulder joint proper.

MOVEMENTS

Movement of flexion and extension occurs almost entirely in the waist or lumbar vertebrae. Movement of side-bending occurs throughout the whole length. Movement of rotation occurs in the *lumbar* vertebrae when the spine is erect, in the middle vertebrae

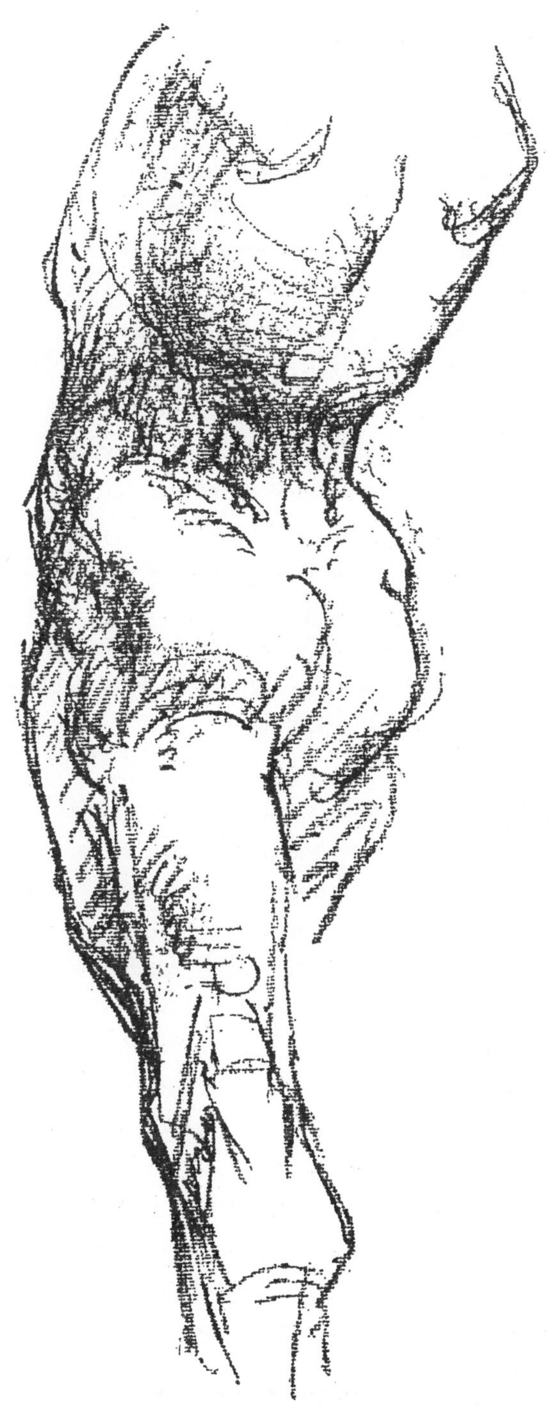

when it is half flexed, in the upper vertebrae when the spine is fully bent. In the *lumbar* vertebrae, the axis of this rotation is behind the spine; in the middle vertebrae it is neutral; in the upper dorsals it is in front of the spine. Each vertebra moves a little, and the whole movement is the aggregate of the many little movements.

The shoulder blade slides against the surface of the cage of the thorax, in any direction, and may be lifted from it so that its point or its spinal edge become prominent under the skin. It produces easily 50 per cent of the whole movement of the shoulder.

MASSES AND MARKINGS

From the rear the mass of the torse presents a great wedge, with apex downward, marked by a complex of lesser wedges and diamonds, and the shoulder blades.

The profile of the sides presents a wide incomplete wedge, whose lines if prolonged would form an apex well below the buttocks. The surface proper of the back presents a great wedge, with base at the corners of the shoulders, with apex driven between the buttocks, buttressed on the sides by the lateral masses of waist muscle.

With the addition of the neck, this becomes a diamond with a very blunt top. From end to end vertically runs the dividing line of the spine; when bent, a series of knobs (tips of vertebral spines); when erect a groove except at the root of the neck, the spine of the seventh *cervical* vertebra. This serves as a sort of ridge pole for muscular tendons for neck and shoulders; and around it therefore is a flat unbroken fascia without muscular fibres, forming a lesser diamond nestling below the upper apex.

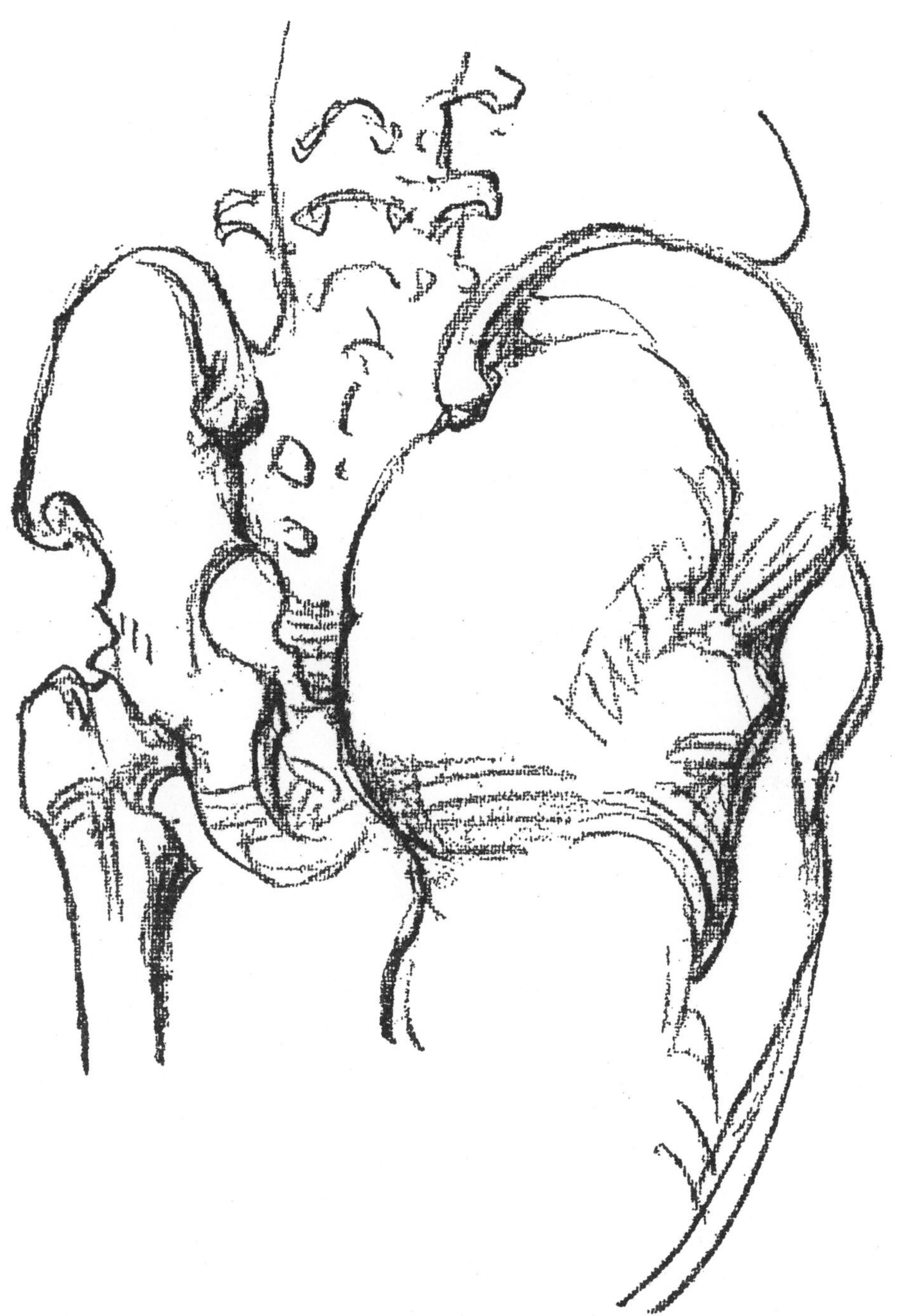

THE TRUNK

SIDE VIEW

① *Latissimus dorsi.*
② *External oblique.*

Latissimus Dorsi:
From spine, sixth dorsal, to *sacrum* and *iliac* crest; passes inside of the *humerus* to fasten to front side near head.
Action: Draws arm backward and inward.

External Oblique:
From eight lower ribs to *iliac* crest and ligament to *pubis*.
Action: Flexes *thorax*.

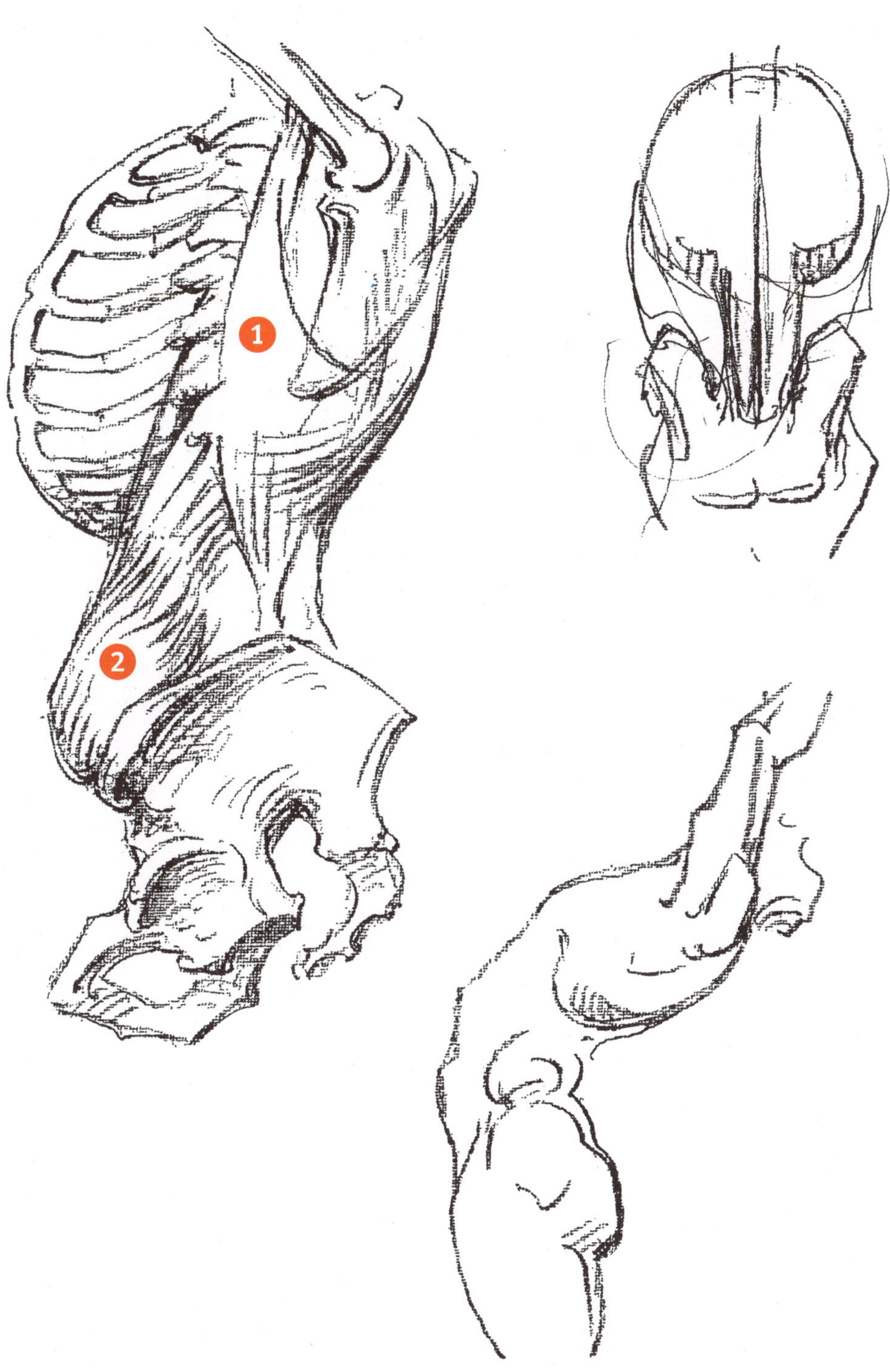
1
2

THE TRUNK

MUSCLES OF THE TRUNK: BACK VIEW

① *Trapezius.*
② *Deltoid.*
③ *Latissimus dorsi.*

Trapezius:
From *occipital* bone, nape ligament and spine as far as twelfth dorsal, to the *clavicle*, *acromion* and ridge of shoulder blade.
Action: Extends head, elevates shoulder and rotates shoulder blade.

(***Deltoid***, *see* page 126.
Latissimus dorsi, *see* page 198.)

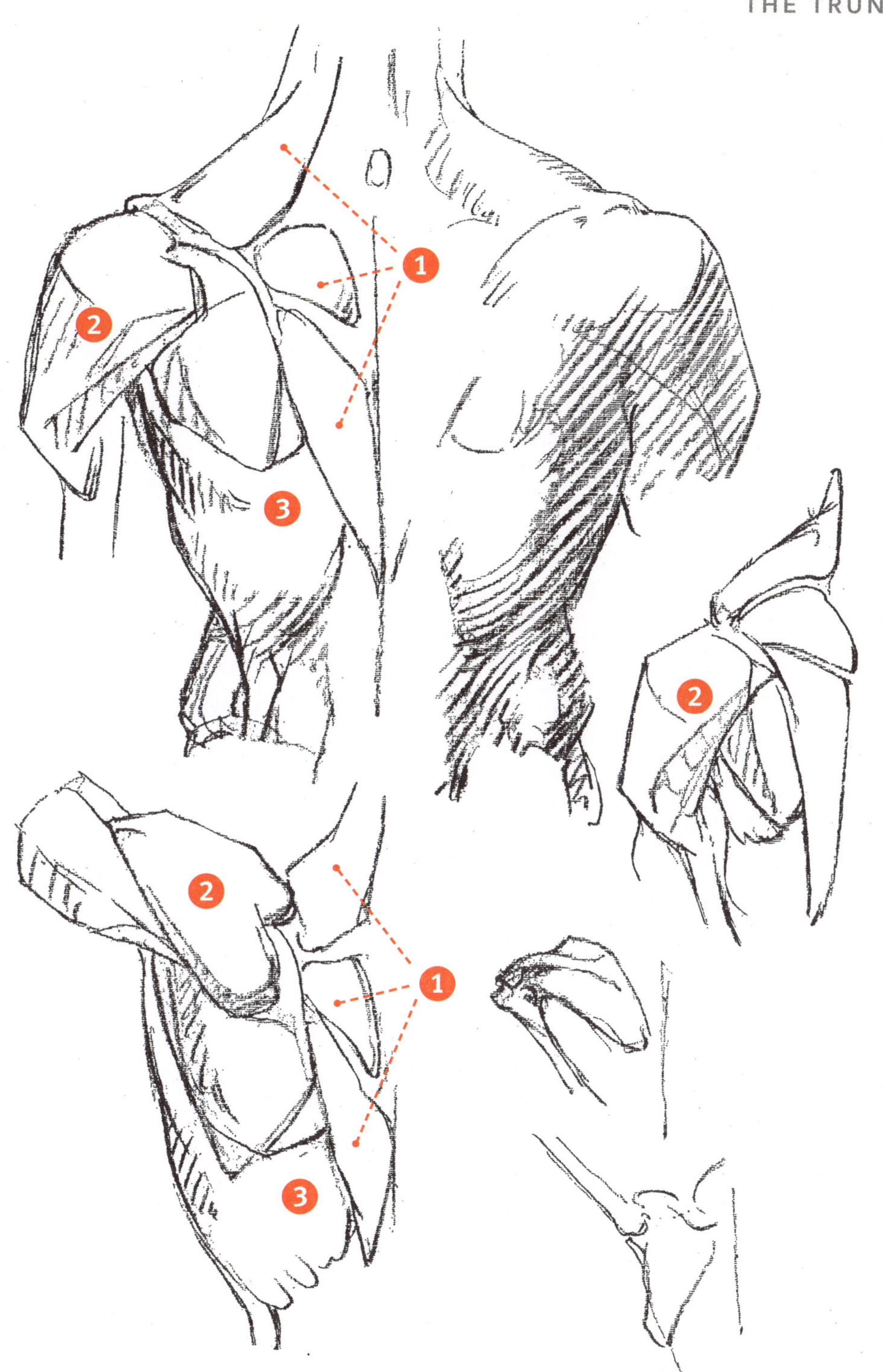
1
2
3
2
2
1
3

THE TRUNK

BACK VIEW

The *trapezius* is a diamond-shaped muscle; with upper apex at the base of the skull, lower apex well below the shoulder blades, and corners at the shoulder girdle opposite the deltoid, as though it were a continuation of that muscle.

From the *sacrum* the muscles diverge upward, while the lower ribs and lower corner of the shoulder blade diverge downward, making lesser diamonds of various definiteness of outline.

The **ridge of the shoulder blade** is always conspicuous, pointing diagonally toward the corner of the shoulder. It sets at a fixed angle with the spinal edge (more than a right angle) and at a right angle with the lower turned-out corner.

In relaxation, both ridge and blade are ridges under the skin, and are converted into grooves by the muscles bulging in contraction.

Of these muscles, those on either side of the ridge are easily recognizable – the deltoid, below and outside, and *trapezius*, above and inside, but the *trapezius* also spreads from the inner end of the ridge to well down the spine. Under this, helping to form the bulge, are the rhomboidei, extending from the blade diagonally upward to the spine, and the *levator angula scapulae*, from its upper corner almost vertically to the top of the neck.

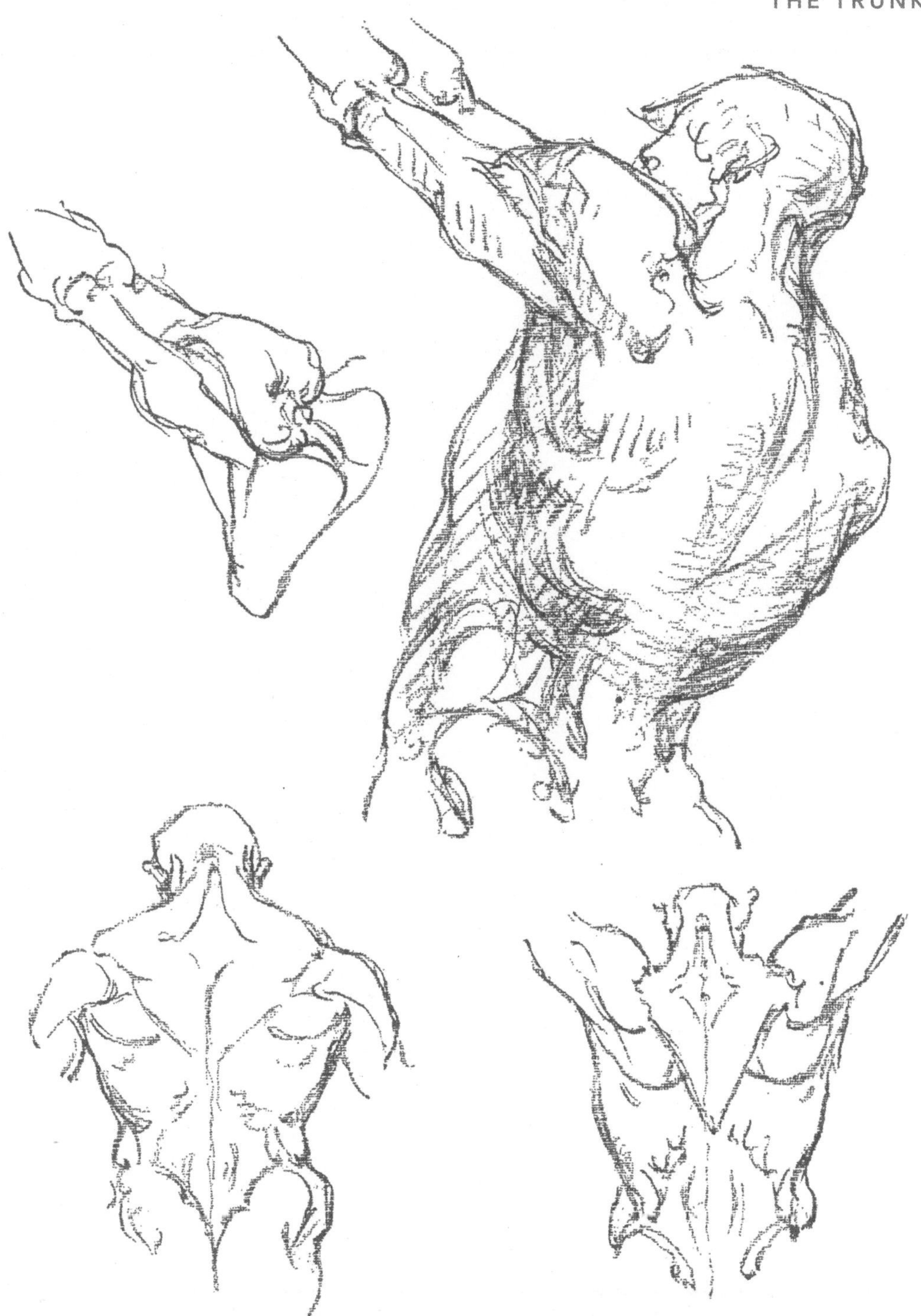

THE TRUNK

MASSES AND THEIR MOVEMENTS. TILTING AND TWISTING: BACK VIEW

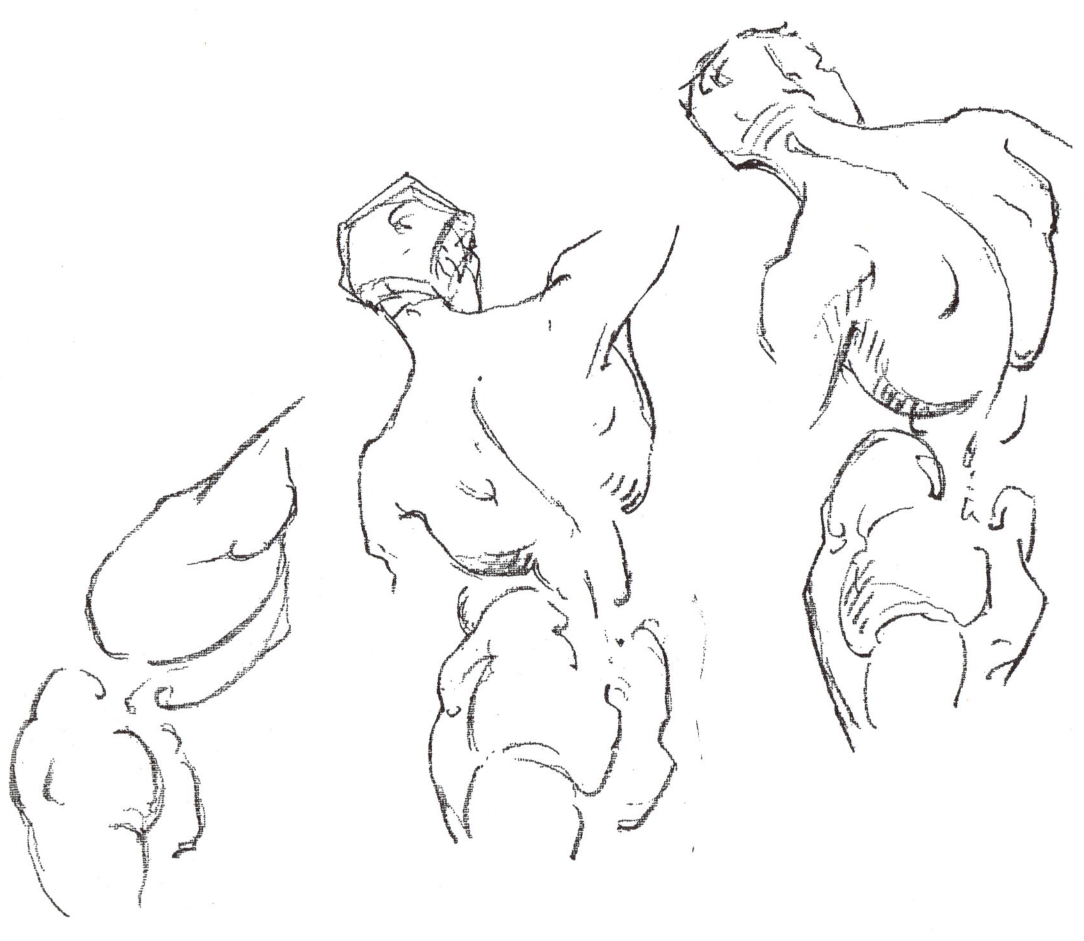

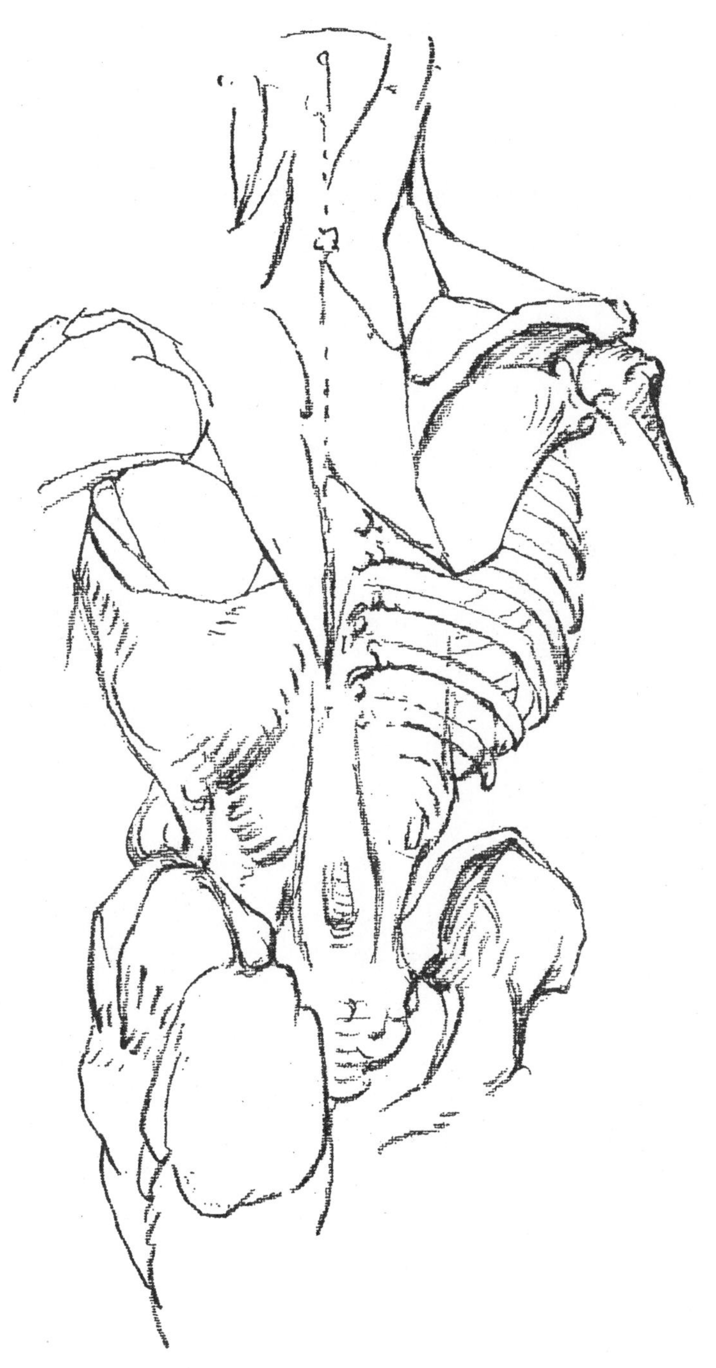

THE TRUNK

THE CAGE OF THE TORSE

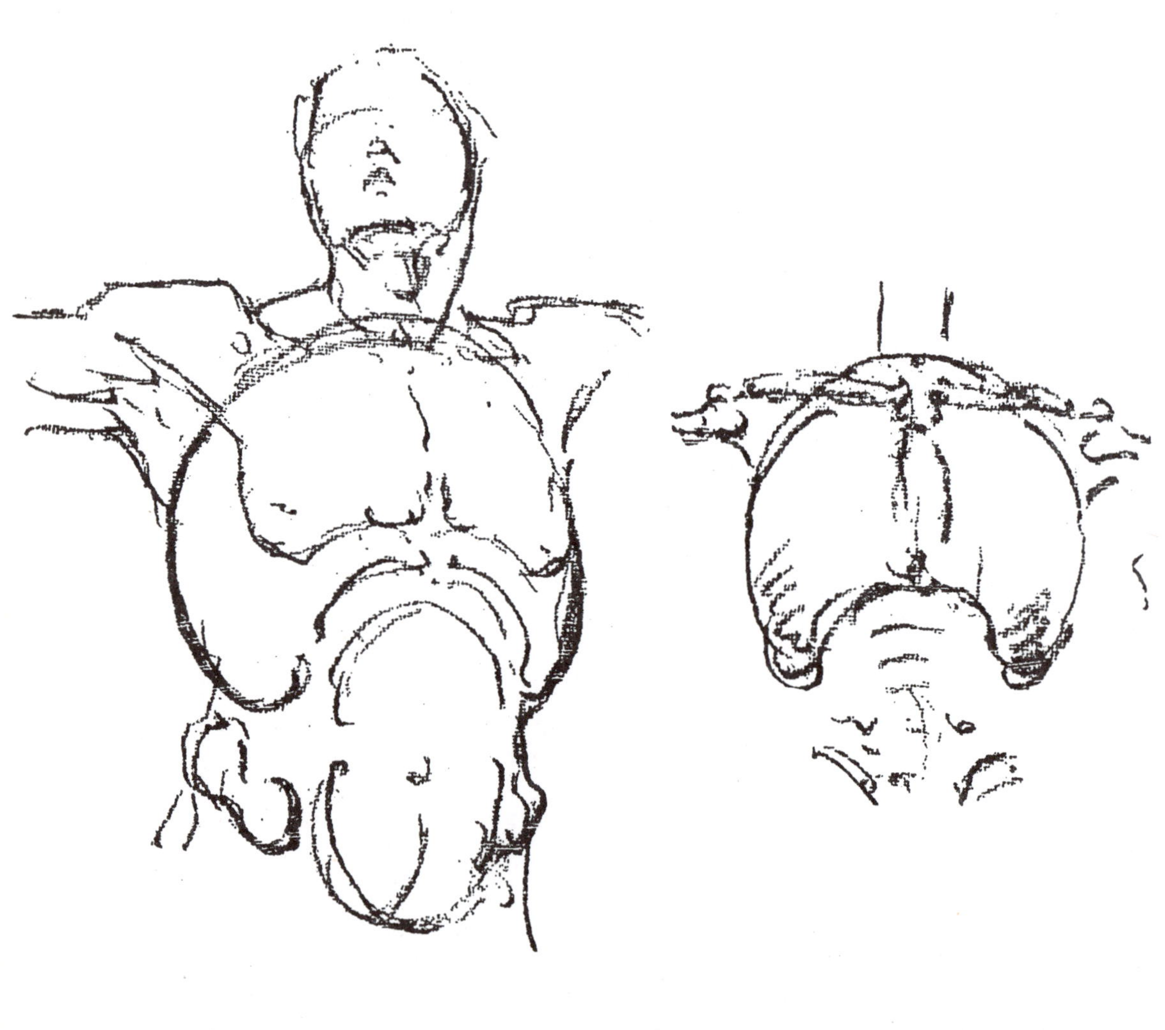

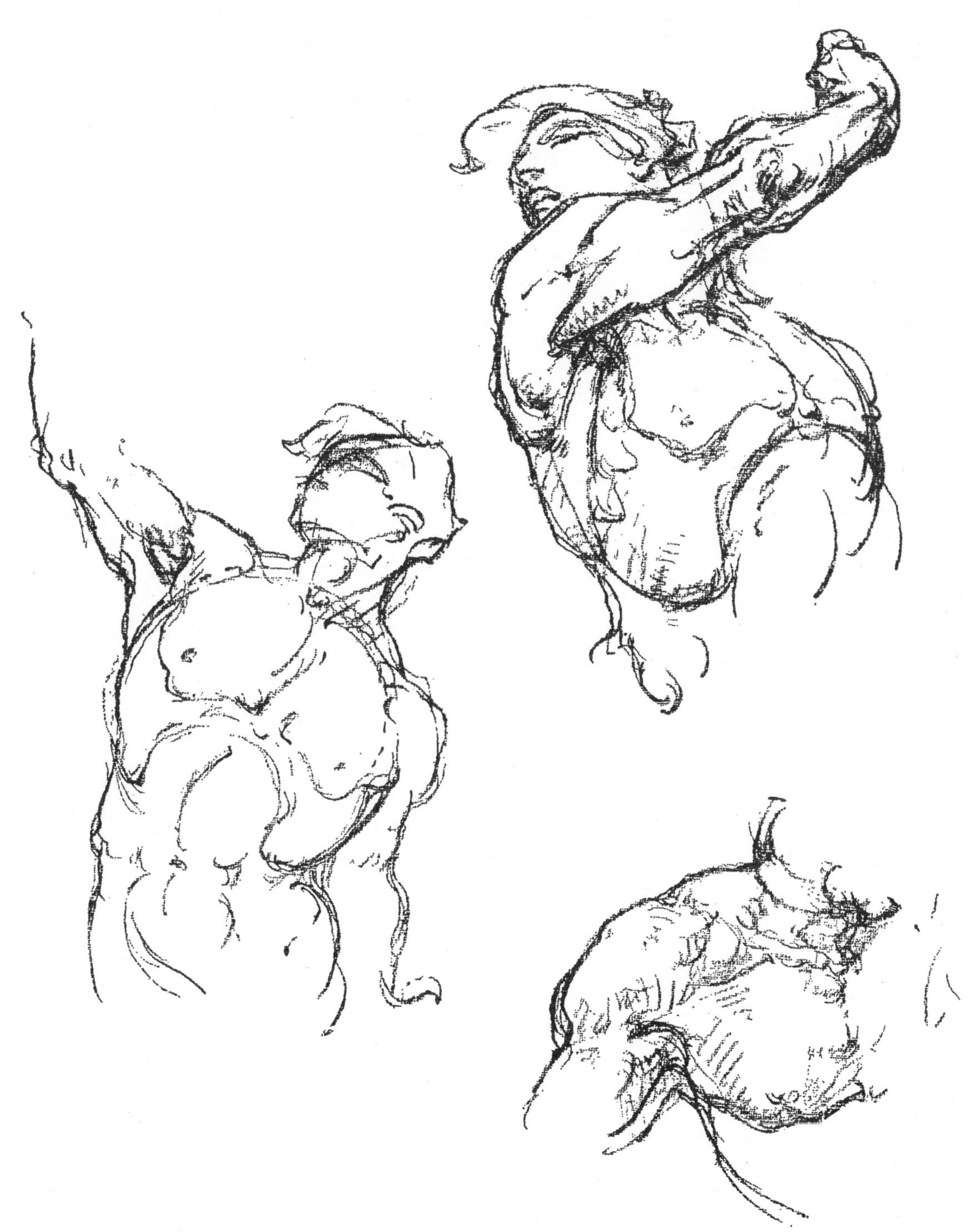

THE TRUNK

WEDGING OF THE CAGE INTO THE HIPS

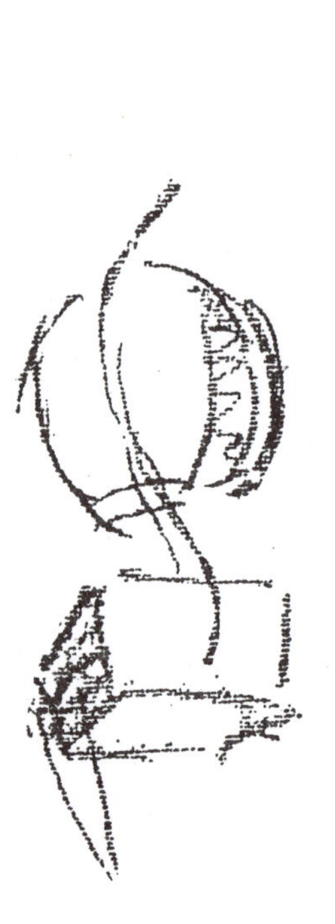

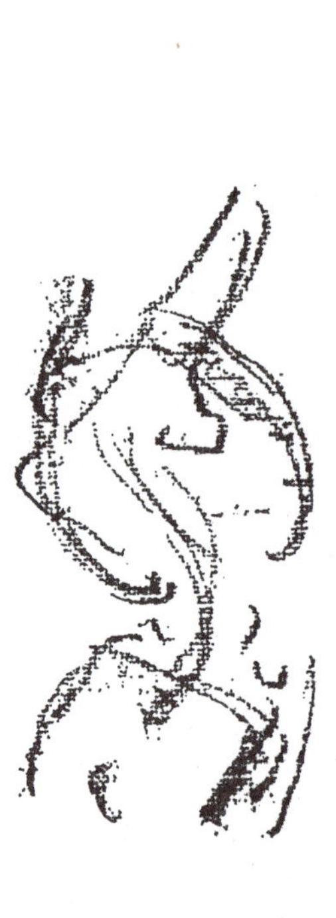

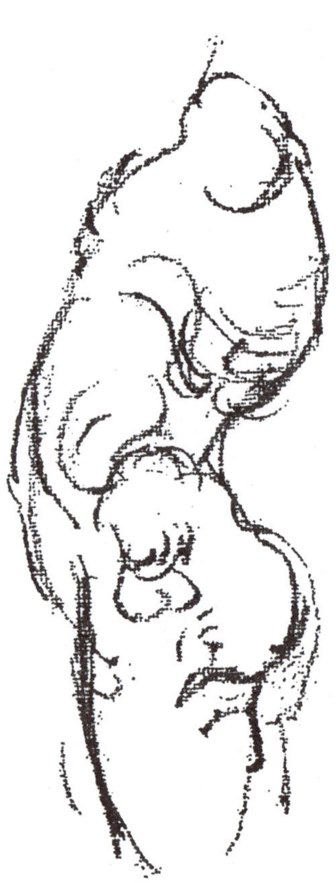

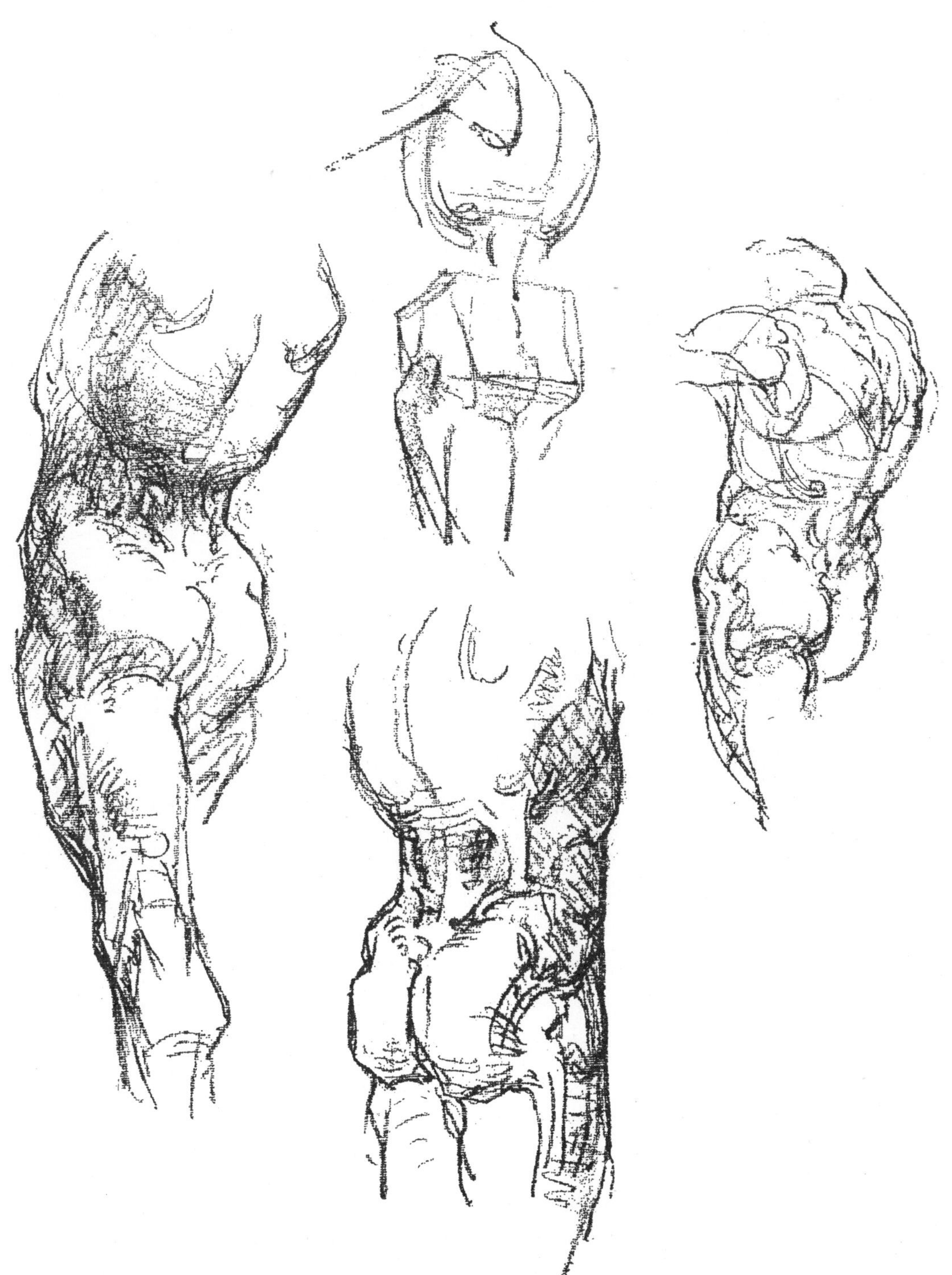

ANATOMY OF THE PELVIS

Three bones make the pelvis; two *innominate* (without a name) bones and one *sacrum* (sacrificial bone).

The *sacrum* is a wedge about the size of the hand but more pefectly shaped, bent like a half-bent hand, and carrying a very small tip about as big as the last joint of the thumb (*coccyx*). It forms the central piece in the back, curving first back and down and then down and in.

The two *innominate* bones are formed like two propellers, with triangular blades twisted in opposite directions. The rear corners of the top blades meet the *sacrum* in the back, and the front corners of the lower blades meet in front to form the *symphysis pubis*.

The hip socket itself forms the central point for the shaft. The two blades stand at right angles to each other. The upper blade is called the *ilium*, the lower is called the *pubis* in front and the *ischium* behind, with an opening between. The only superficial parts are the top of the upper blade (*illac* crest) and the front tip of the lower (*symphysis pubis*).

MASSES AND MARKINGS

The size of the pelvis is due to its position as the mechanical axis of the body; it is the fulcrum for the muscles of the trunk and legs, and is large in proportion. Its mass inclines a little forward, and is somewhat square as compared with the trunk above. At the sides

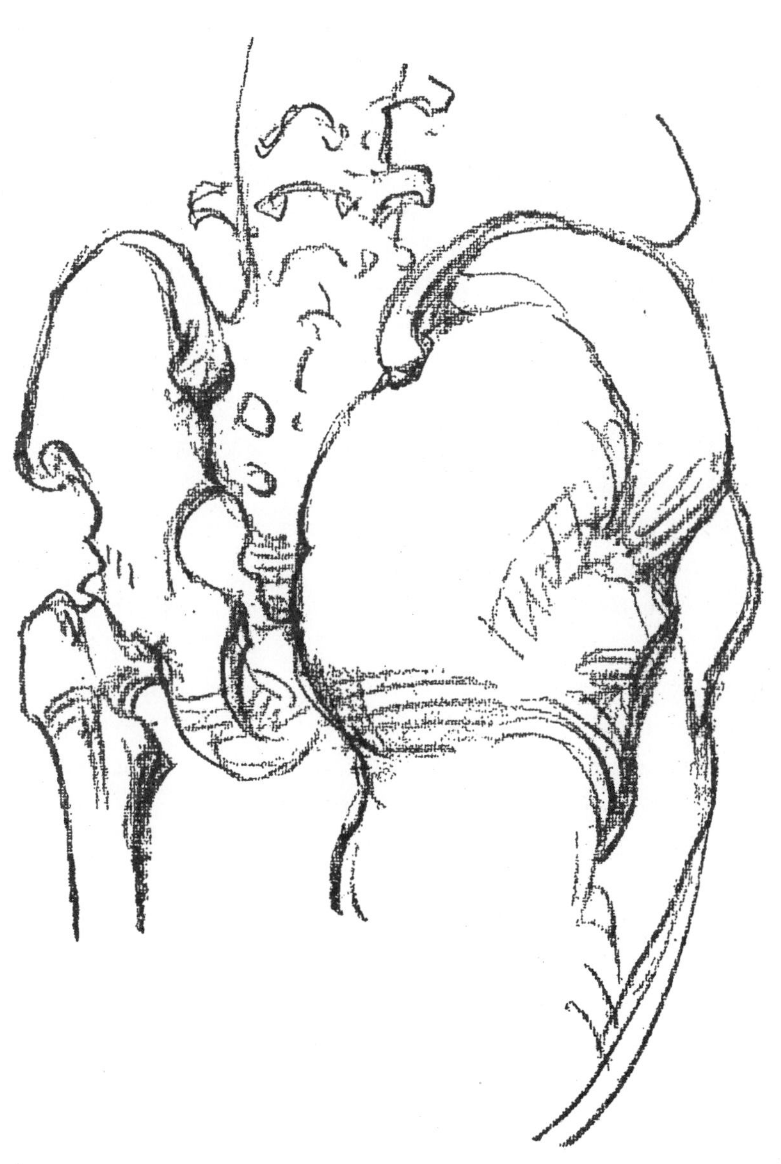

the ridge is called the *iliac* crest. It is the fulcrum for the lateral muscles and flares out widely for that purpose; rather more widely in front than behind.

Above the rim is a roll of muscle belonging to the abdominal wall; immediately below it a groove or depression, made by the sag of the hip muscles, obliterated when these are contracted in action.

THE HIP

So great are the changes in surface form of the muscles in different positions of the hip that the *iliac* crest remains as the one stable landmark. It is a curve, but being beveled backward, it presents to the side view two lines and almost an angle between them at the top.

The posterior line is marked by two dimples where it joins the *sacrum*, and the line continues downward into the fold of the buttocks. From this whole line the *gluteus maximus* muscle passes down and forward, to just below the head of the thigh bone, making the mass of the buttocks and hip. Just in front of this, from the top of the crest, descends the *gluteus medius* muscle, forming a wedge whose apex is at the head of the thigh bone. Between these two muscles is the dimple of the thigh.

Only part of the *medius* is superficial; its front portion is overlaid by the *tensor fascuae femoris* muscle which rises from the edge of the front line of the crest and descends to form with the *gluteus maximus* the wedge filled in by the *medius*. The two fasten to the dense plate of *fascia* that guards the outside of the thigh (*ilio-tibial* band). This muscle is always prominent and

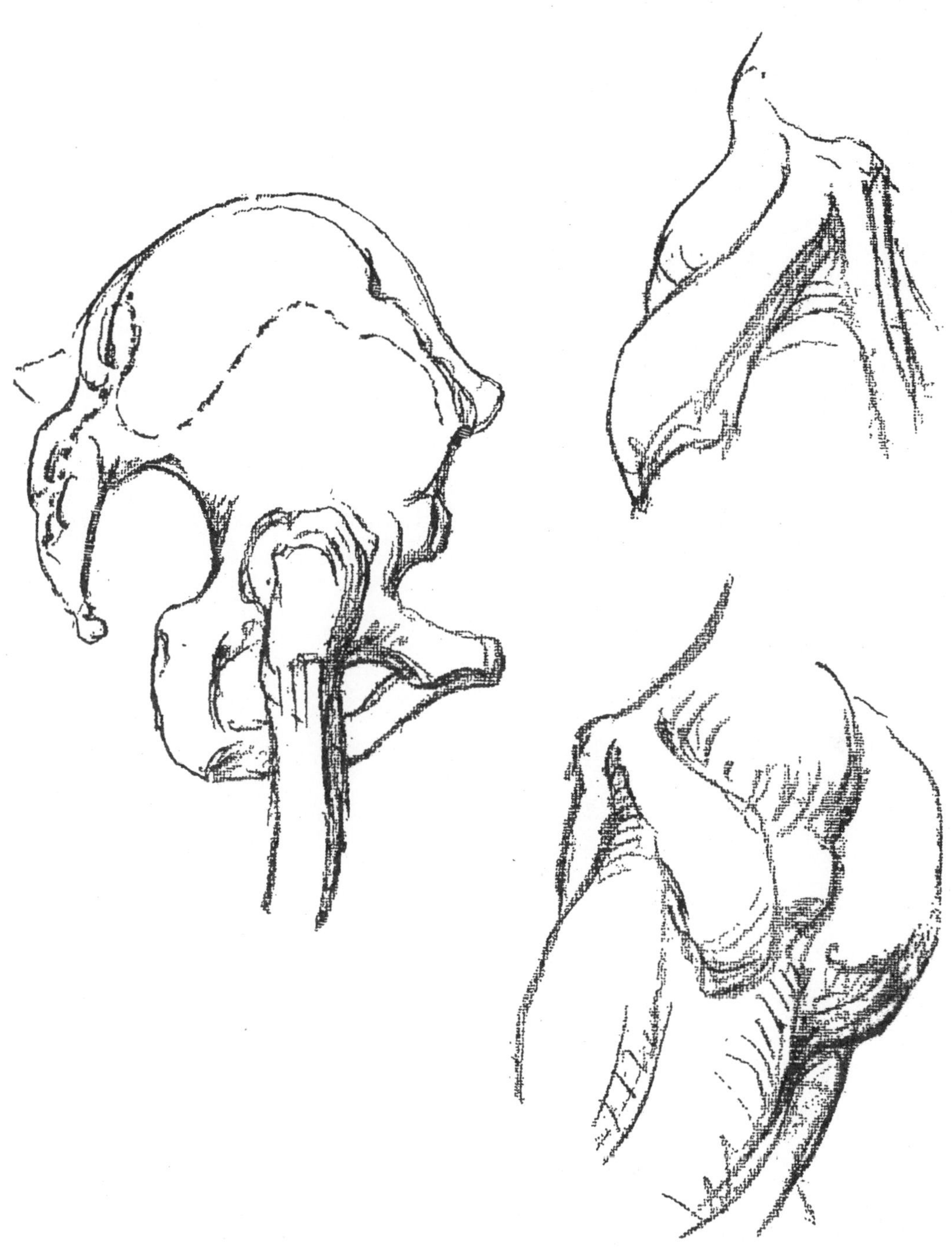

changes its appearance greatly in different positions of the hip, forming a U-shaped wrinkle when the thigh is completely flexed.

On the front end of the crest is a small knob, from which descends the *sartorius* (tailor's) muscle, longest in the body. It forms a graceful curve as it lies in the groove of the inner side of the thigh, passing to under the knee. From just below the knob, overlaid therefore by the sartorius, descends the *rectus femoris* muscle, straight to the knee cap. From the knob, the line continues down and in to the symphysis, marking the boundary between abdomen and thigh.

THE PELVIS AND HIP

① *Tensor vaginae femoris.*
② *Sartorius.*
③ *Rectus femoris.*
④ *Gluteus medius.*
⑤ *Gluteus maximus.*

*(**Tensor; Sartorius; Rectus femoris**, see* page 224)

Gluteus Medius:

From *ilium*, outer surface, to *femur*, greater trochanter.
Action: Abducts and rotates inward thigh.

Gluteus maximus:

From crest of *ilium*, rear portion, *sacrum* and *coccyx* to *femur*.
Action: Extends, rotates and turns out thigh.

4
4
3
5
1
2
3
2
1
3
4
5
1
2
3

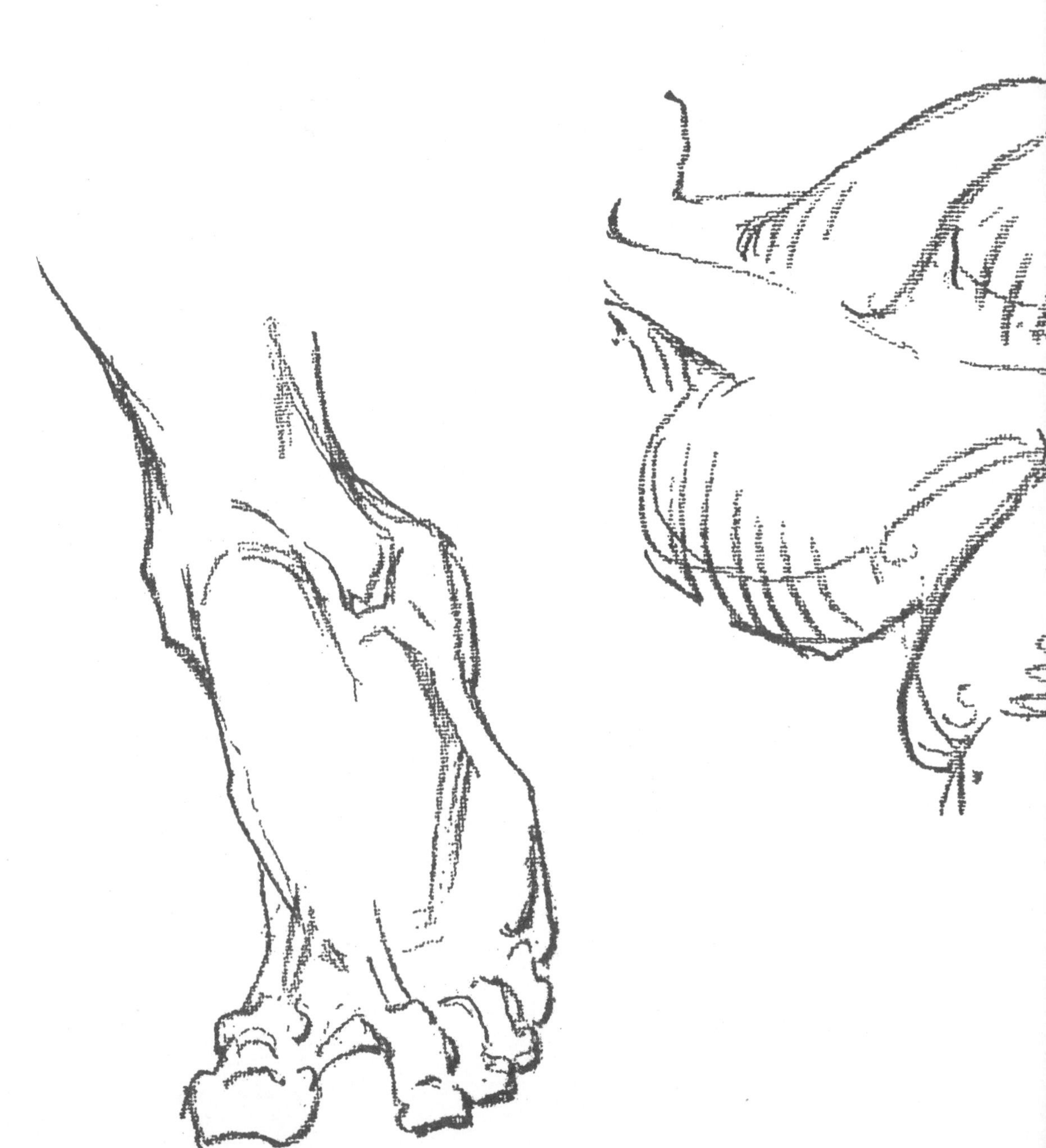

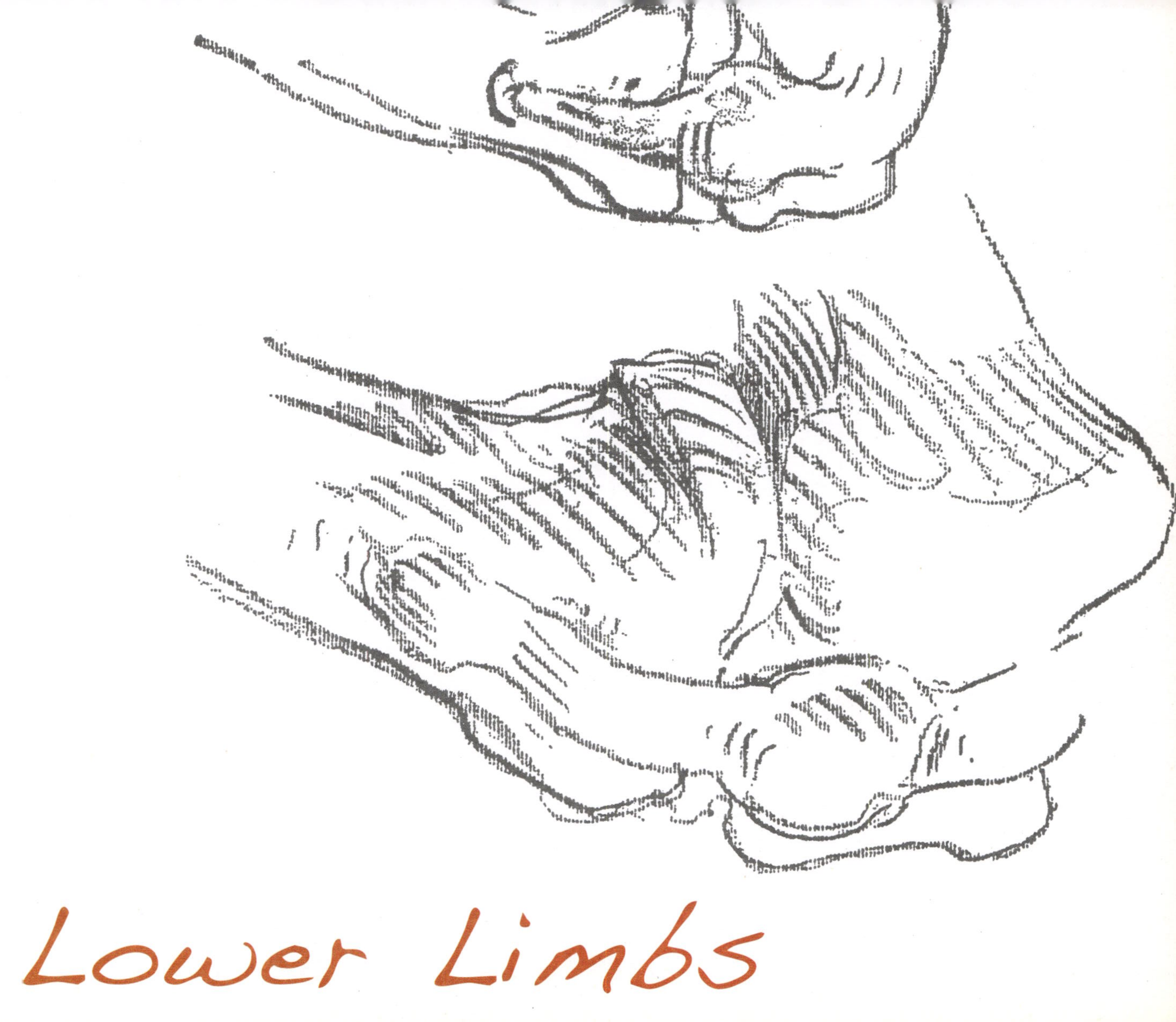

Lower Limbs

ANATOMY OF THE LOWER LIMB

The lower limb is divided into three parts – the thigh, the leg, and the foot. These parts correspond to the arm, the forearm, and the hand of the upper limb.

The thigh extends from the pelvis to the knee, and the leg from the knee to the foot. The longest and strongest bone of the body is the *femur* (thigh bone). It is joined to the bones of the pelvis at the hip socket by a long neck, which carries the shaft itself out beyond the widest part of the crest. From there the *femora* (thigh bones) converge as they approach the knees, bringing the knee under the hip socket.

At the knee, the *femur* rests on the *tibia* (shin bone), the main bone of the leg, and makes a hinge joint. The *tibia* descends to form the inner ankle. Beside it, not reaching quite to the knee, is the *fibula*, the second bone of the leg, which descends to form the outer ankle. It is located on the outside, and is attached to the *tibia* at the top and bottom. These two bones are almost parallel.

Above the juncture of the *femur* and *tibia* lies the *patella* (knee cap). This is a small bone almost triangular in shape. It is flat on its under side, and convex on the surface. The great *trochanter* of the *femur* is the upper tip of the shaft which reaches up slightly beyond where the neck joins. The lower portion of the *femur* widens to form two great hinge processes, known as tuberosities. They are on the outer and inner sides, and they are both visible.

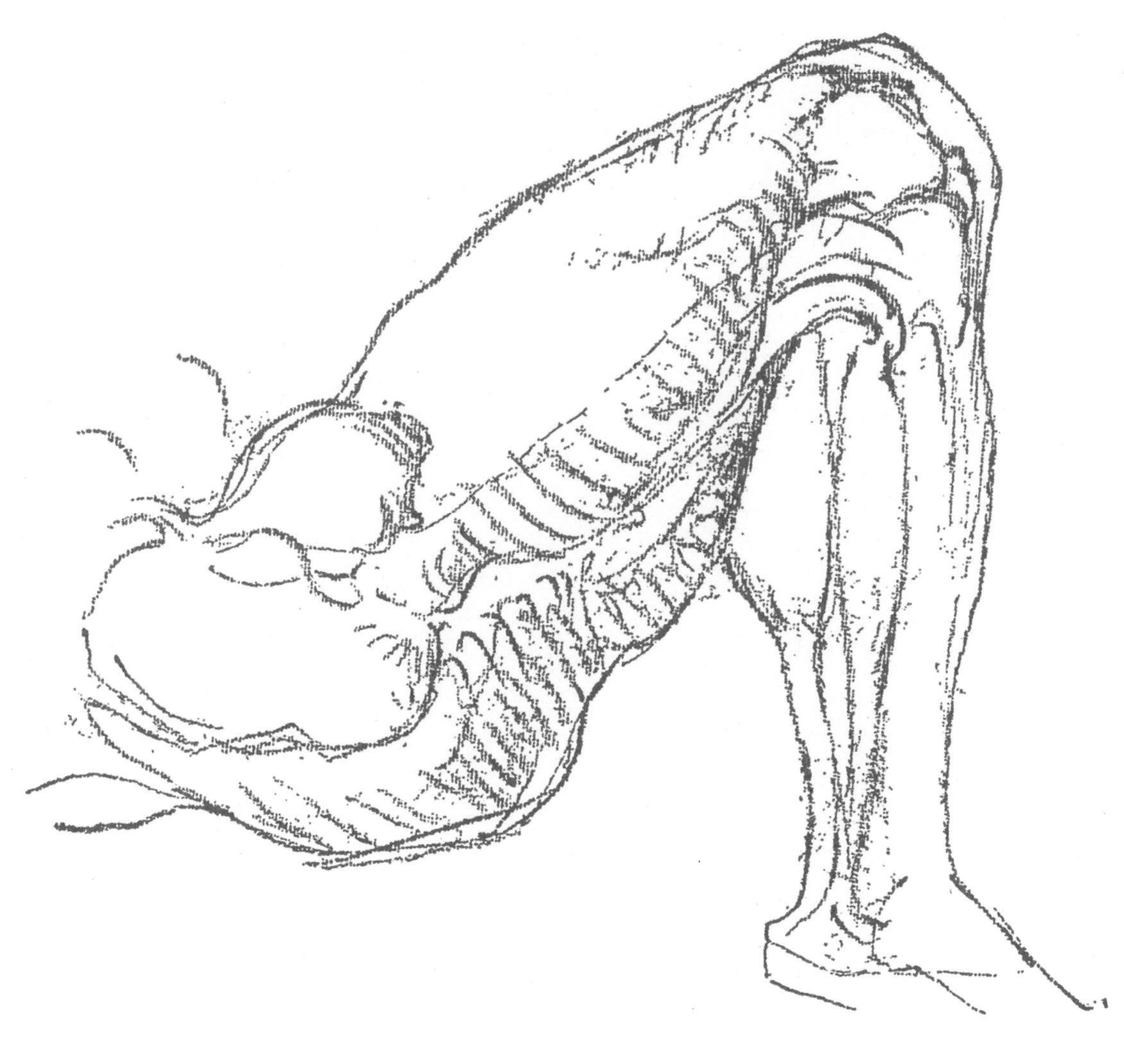

ANATOMY OF THE THIGH

From the head of the *femur* (*trochanter*) to the outside of the knee runs a band of tendon called the *ilio-tibial* band. It makes a straight line from the head of the thigh bone to the outside of the knee. The *rectus femoris* muscle makes a slightly bulging straight line from just below the *iliac* crest to the knee cap. On either side of the latter is a twin mass of muscles.

That of the outside (*vastus externus*) makes one mass with it, and slightly overhangs the *ilio-tibial* band outside. That of the inside (*vastus internus*) bulges only in the lower third of the thigh, and overhangs the knee on the inside. Behind and inside of this is the groove of the thigh occupied by the *sartorius* muscle, passing from the *ilium* above to the back of the knee below. Behind the groove is the heavy mass of the *adductors*, reaching two-thirds of the way down the thigh.

Behind groove and *adductors*, around the back of the thigh and to the *ilio-tibial* band outside, is the mass of the ham-string muscles, whose tendons are found on either side of the knee at the back. It is a dual mass of muscle, dividing above the diamond-shaped popliteal space at the back of the knee, whose lower corner is formed by the *gastrocnemius* muscle; similarly divided.

MASS

The mass of the thigh is inclined inward from hip to knee, and is slightly beveled toward the knee from front, back and outside.

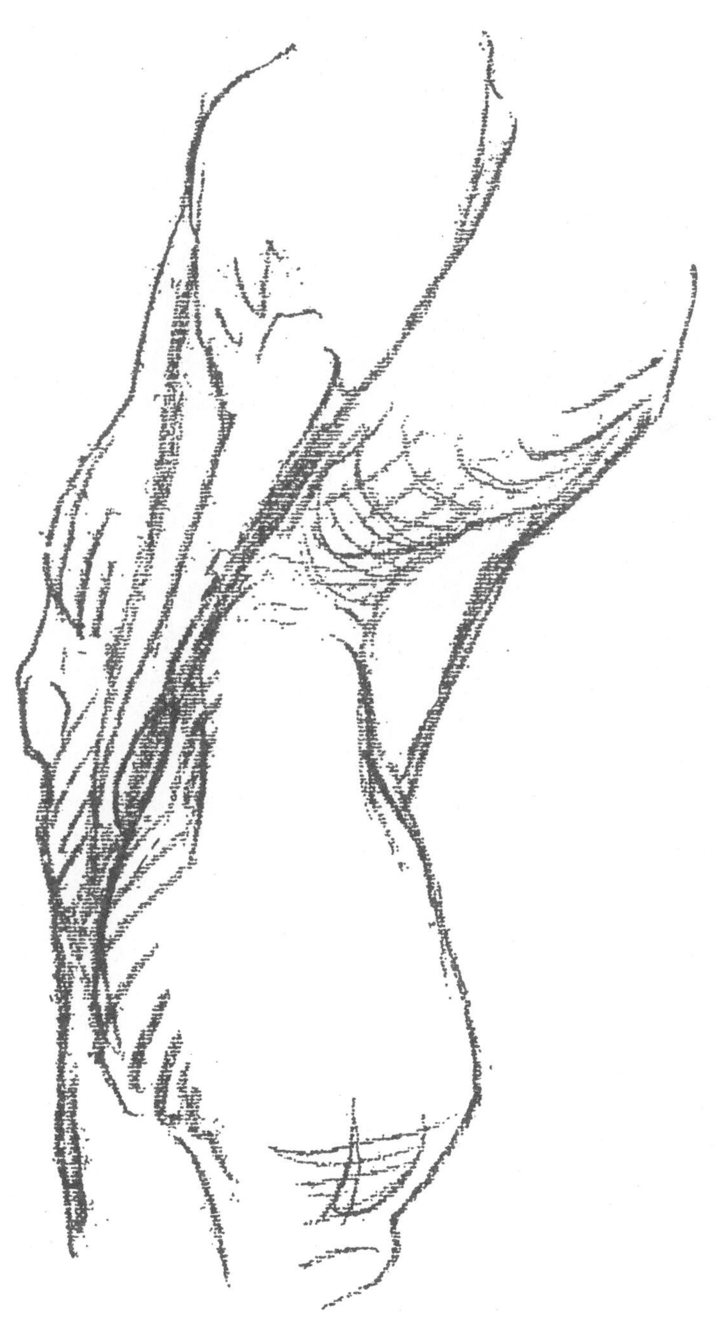

ANATOMY OF THE LEG

Of the same width as the end of the thigh bone is the head of the *tibia*, or shin bone. Immediately below the head the shaft narrows on both sides, but on the outside and a little to the rear is the head of the *fibula* (which corresponds with the *ulna* of the forearm) more than filling out the narrowing on that side.

The ridge of the shin bone descends straight down the front of the leg, a sharp edge toward the outside, a flat surface toward the inside, which at the ankle bends in to become the inner ankle bone. The outer bone of the foreleg (*fibula*) soon overlaid by a gracefully bulging muscular mass, emerges again to become the outer ankle bone.

On the back of the leg are two muscles. Beneath is the low, flat and broad *soleus* (sole fish) muscle; on top of it is the double-bellied calf muscle (*gastrocnemius*, frog's belly), covering its upper half, but crossing the knee joint above and helping to make the two knobs there. These two muscles unite to form the tendon of Achilles at the heel.

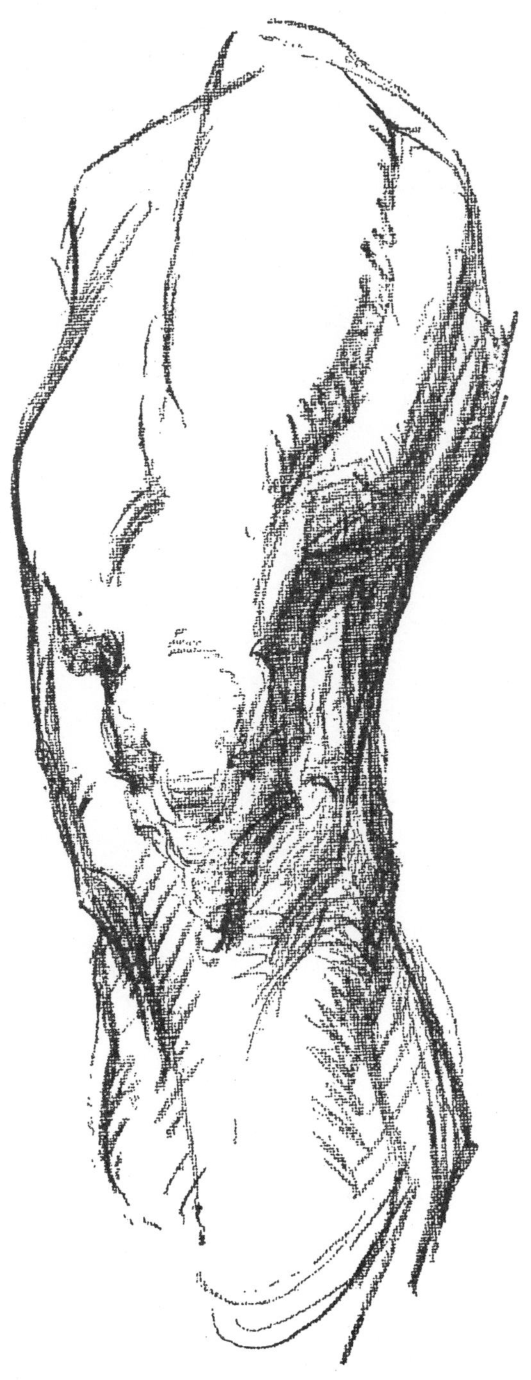

LOWER LIMBS

BONES OF THE LOWER LIMB

- Hip – Pelvis.
- Thigh – *Femur*.
- Leg – *Tibia* and *Fibula* (outside).

MUSCLES OF THE LOWER LIMB: FRONT VIEW

① *Tensor* of the *fascia lata.*

② *Sartorius.*

③ *Rectus femoris.*

④ *Vastus externus.*

⑤ *Vastus internus.*

⑥ *Tibialis anticus.*

⑦ *Peroneus longus.*

⑧ *Extensor longus digi torum.*

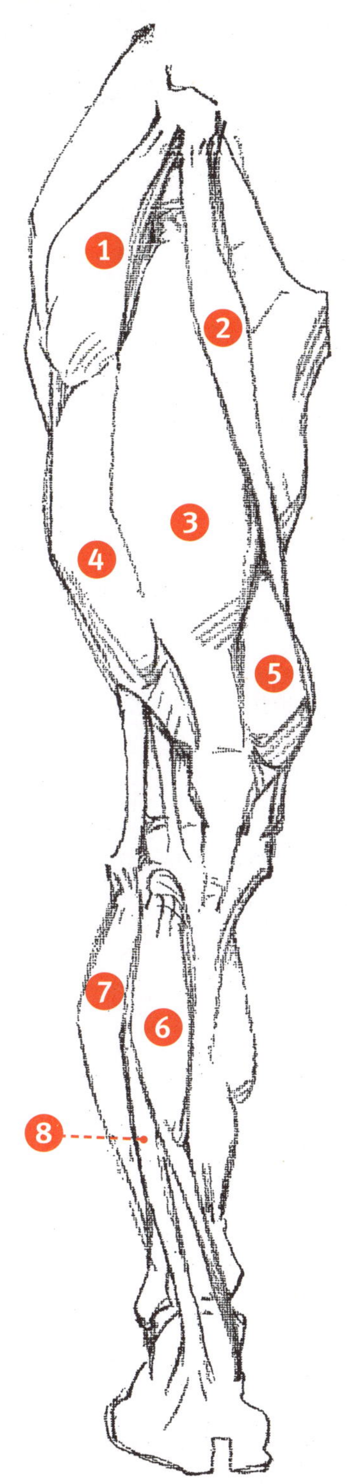
1
2
3
4
5
7
6
8

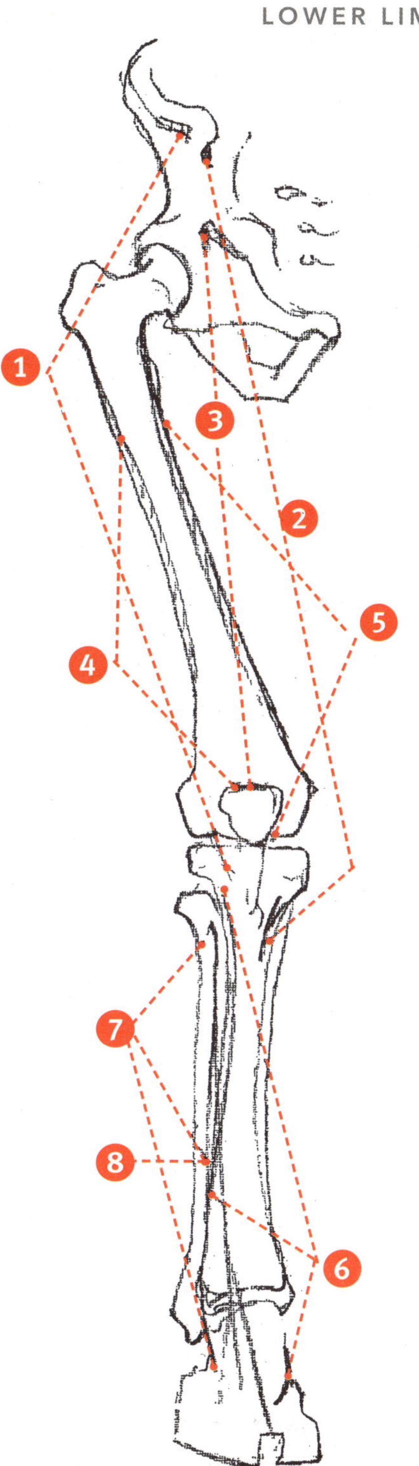
1
3
2
5
4
7
8
6

***Tensor Vaginae Femoris* (*tensor fasciae femoris*):**
From crest of *ilium*, front end, to *fascia lata*, or *ilio-tibial* band.
Action: *Tenses fascia* and rotates inward thigh.

Sartorius:
From spine to *ilium* in front to *tibia* inside.
Action: Flexes, abducts and rotates inward thigh.

Rectus Femoris:
From *anterior inferior* spine of *ilium* to common tendon of *patella*.
Action: Extends leg.

Vastus Externus:
From outer side of *femur* to common tendon of *patella*.
Action: Extends and rotates outward leg.

Vastus Internus:
From inner side of *femur* to common tendon of *patella*.
Action: Extends and rotates inward leg.

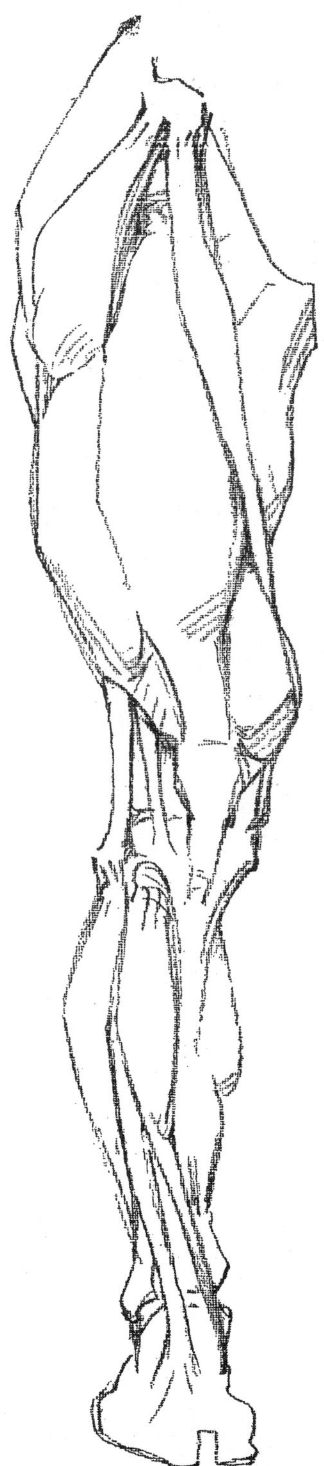

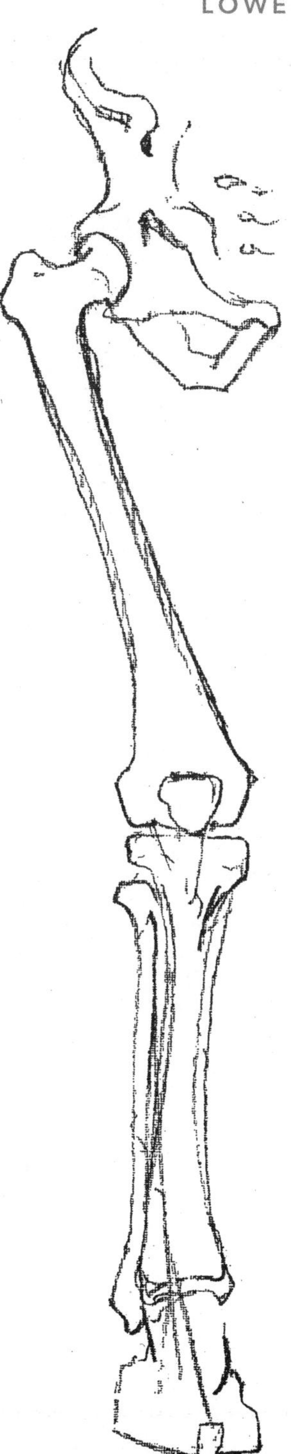

LOWER LIMBS

MUSCLES OF THE LOWER LIMB: BACK VIEW

① *Gluteus medius.*
② *Gluteus maximus.*
③ *Semi-tendinosus.*
④ *Semi-membranosus.*
⑤ *Biceps femoris.*
⑥ *Gastrocnemius.*
⑦ *Soleus.*

(***Gluteus medius; Gluteus maximus*** see page 214)

Semi-tendinosis:
From *ischial* tuberosity to *tibia*.
Action: Flexes knee and rotates inward leg.

Semi-membranosus:
From *ischial* tuberosity to *tibia*.
Action: Flexes knee and rotates leg inward.

Biceps Femoris:
Long head from *ischial* tuberosity; short head from *femur*, to head of *fibula*.
Action: Flexes knee and rotates thigh outward.

(***Gastrocnemius***, see page 232)
(***Soleus***, see page 236)

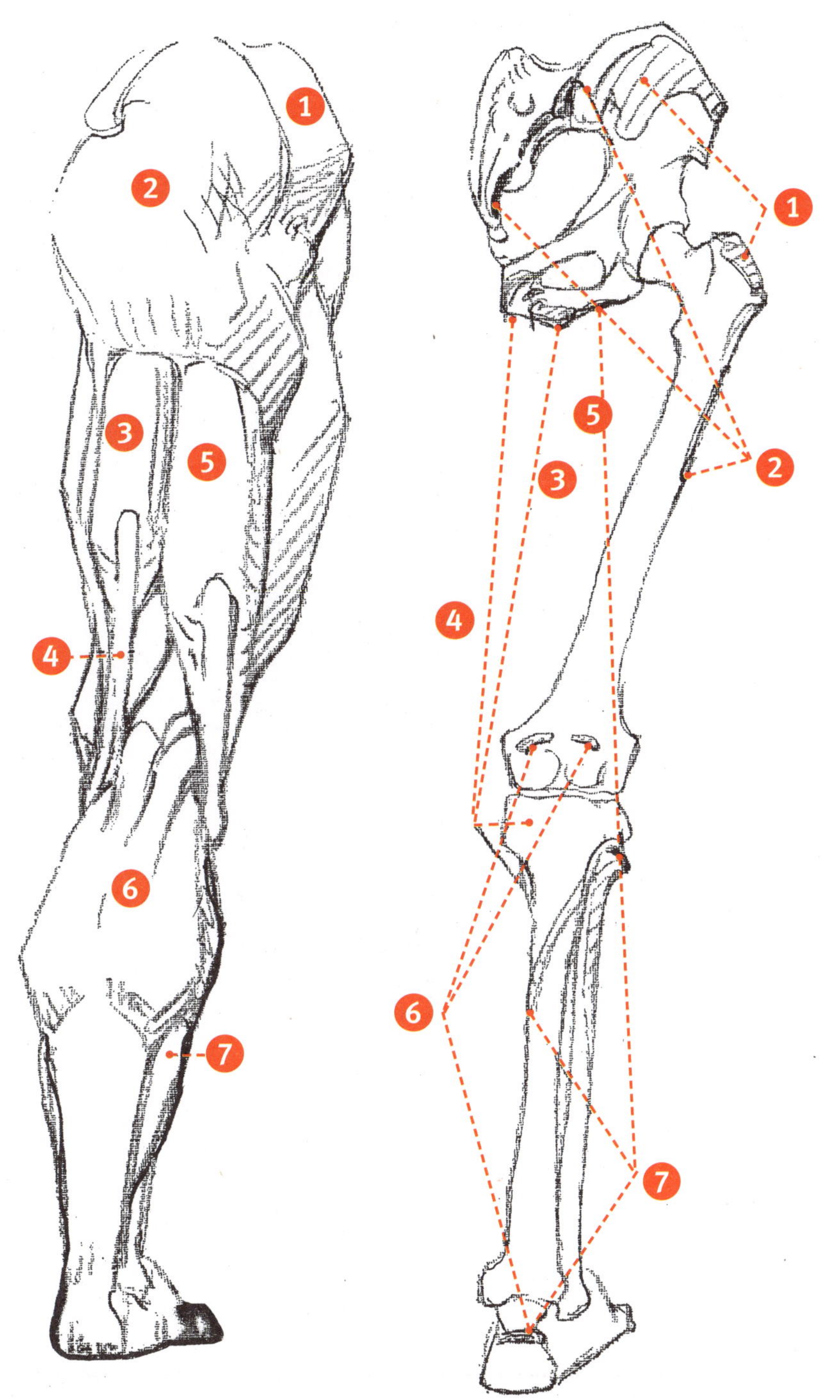
1
2
3
5
4
6
7
1
2
5
3
4
6
7

LOWER LIMBS

KNEE JOINT: BACK VIEW

HAM-STRINGS, GASTROCNEMIUS AND POPLITEAL SPACE

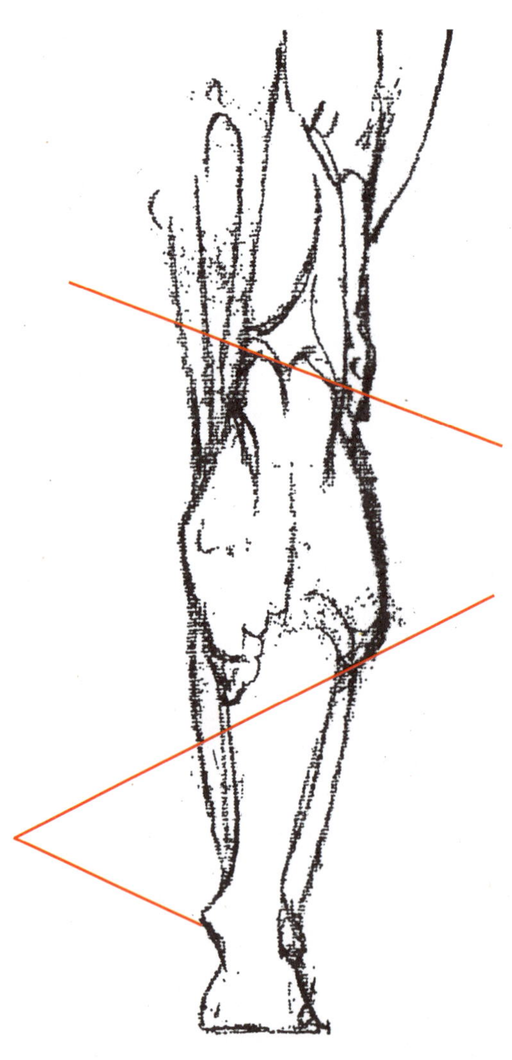

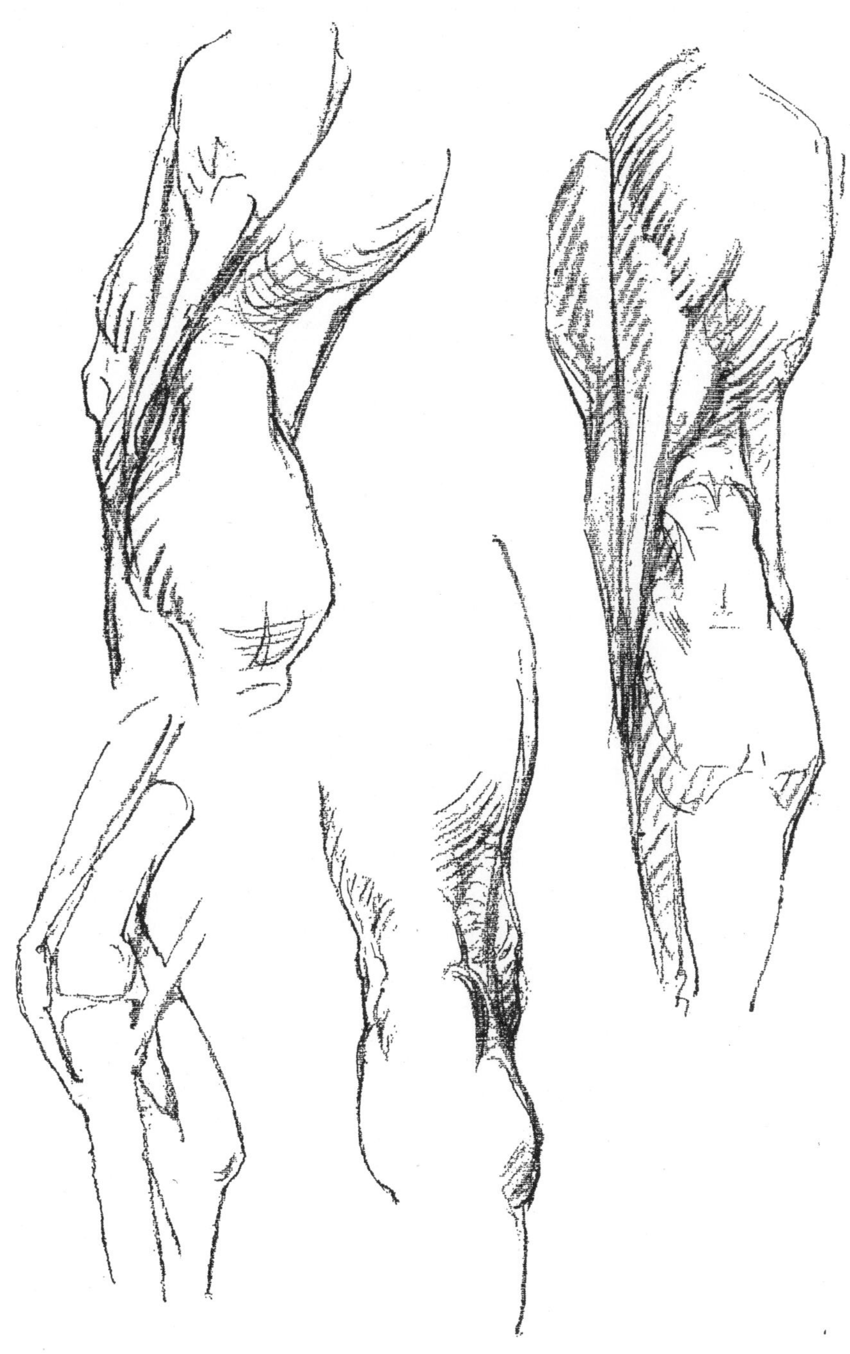

LOWER LIMBS

MUSCLES OF THE LOWER LIMB: OUTER VIEW

① *Gluteus maximus.*
② *Gluteus medius.*
③ *Biceps femoris.*
④ *Vastus externus.*
⑤ *Gastrocnemius.*
⑥ *Tibialis anticus.*
⑦ *Peroneus longus.*

BELOW THE KNEE

Gastrocnemius:

From tuberosities of *femur* to tendon of Achilles.

Action: Extends foot, raises body in walking.

Peroneus Longus:

From head and upper part of *fibula* passes beneath foot from outside, to base of big toe.

Action: Extends ankle and raises outer side of foot.

Tibialis Anticus:

From upper and outer two-thirds of *tibia* to inner side of foot.

Action: Flexes ankle and raises inner side of foot.

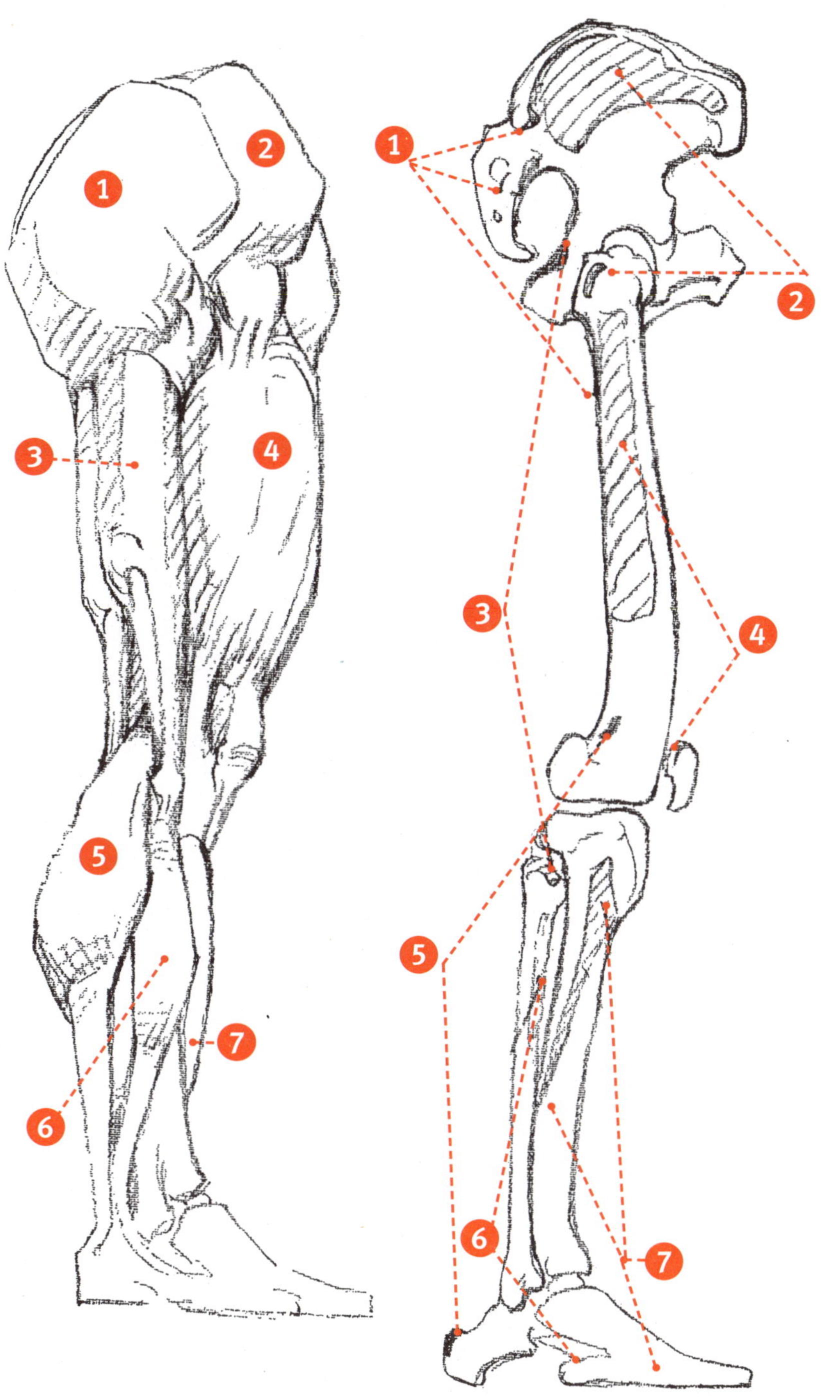
1
2
3
4
5
6
7
1
2
3
4
5
6
7

LOWER LIMBS

Examples for reference.

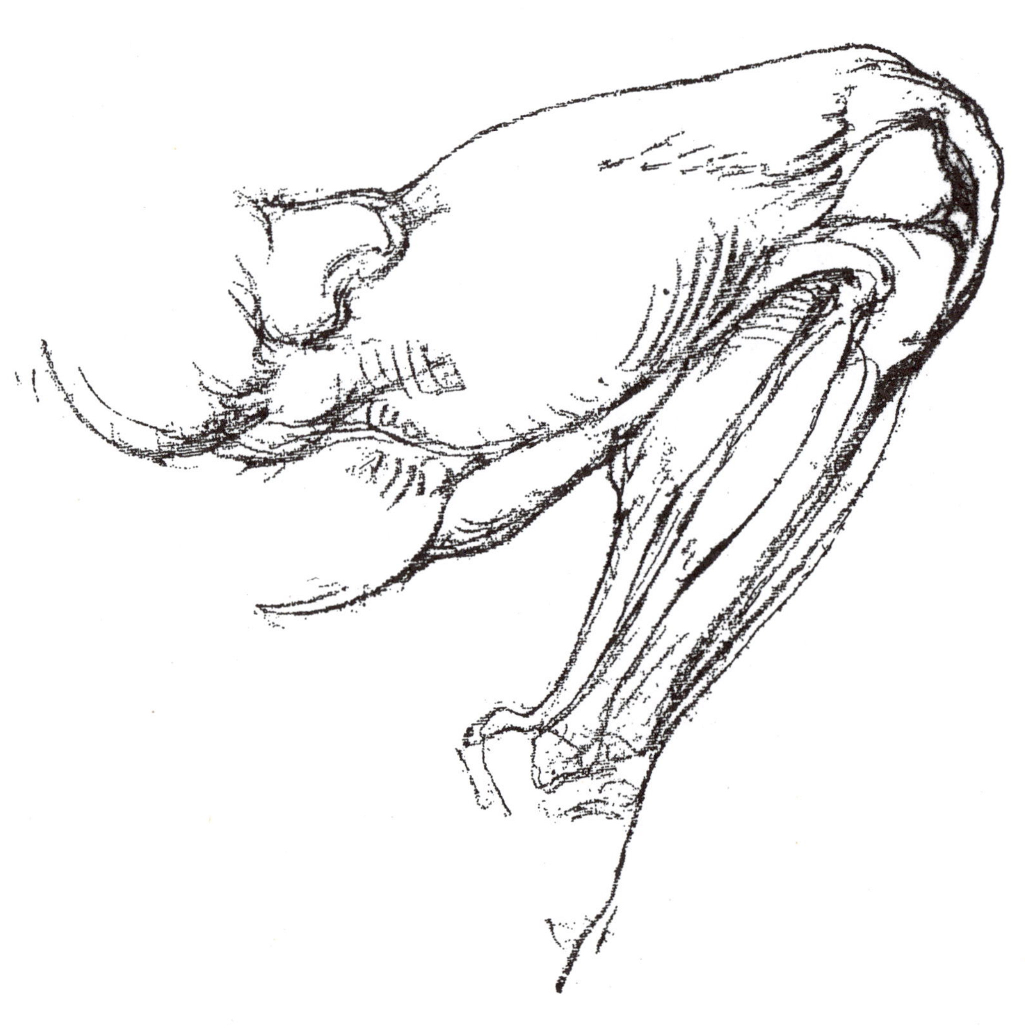

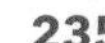

LOWER LIMBS

MUSCLES OF THE LOWER LIMB: INNER VIEW

① *Rectus femoris.*
② *Vastus internus.*
③ *Sartorius.*
④ *Gracilis.*
⑤ *Semi-tendinosus.*
⑥ *Semi-membranosus.*
⑦ *Gastrocnemius.*
⑧ *Soleus.*

BELOW THE KNEE

Soleus:

From upper part of *fibula* and back of *tibia* to tendon of Achilles.

Action: Extends foot and lifts body in walking.

Extensor Communis Digitorum (extensor longus digitorum pedis):

From *tibia* and front of *fibula* to second and third *phalanges* of toes.

Action: Extends toes. *See* diagram, page 225.

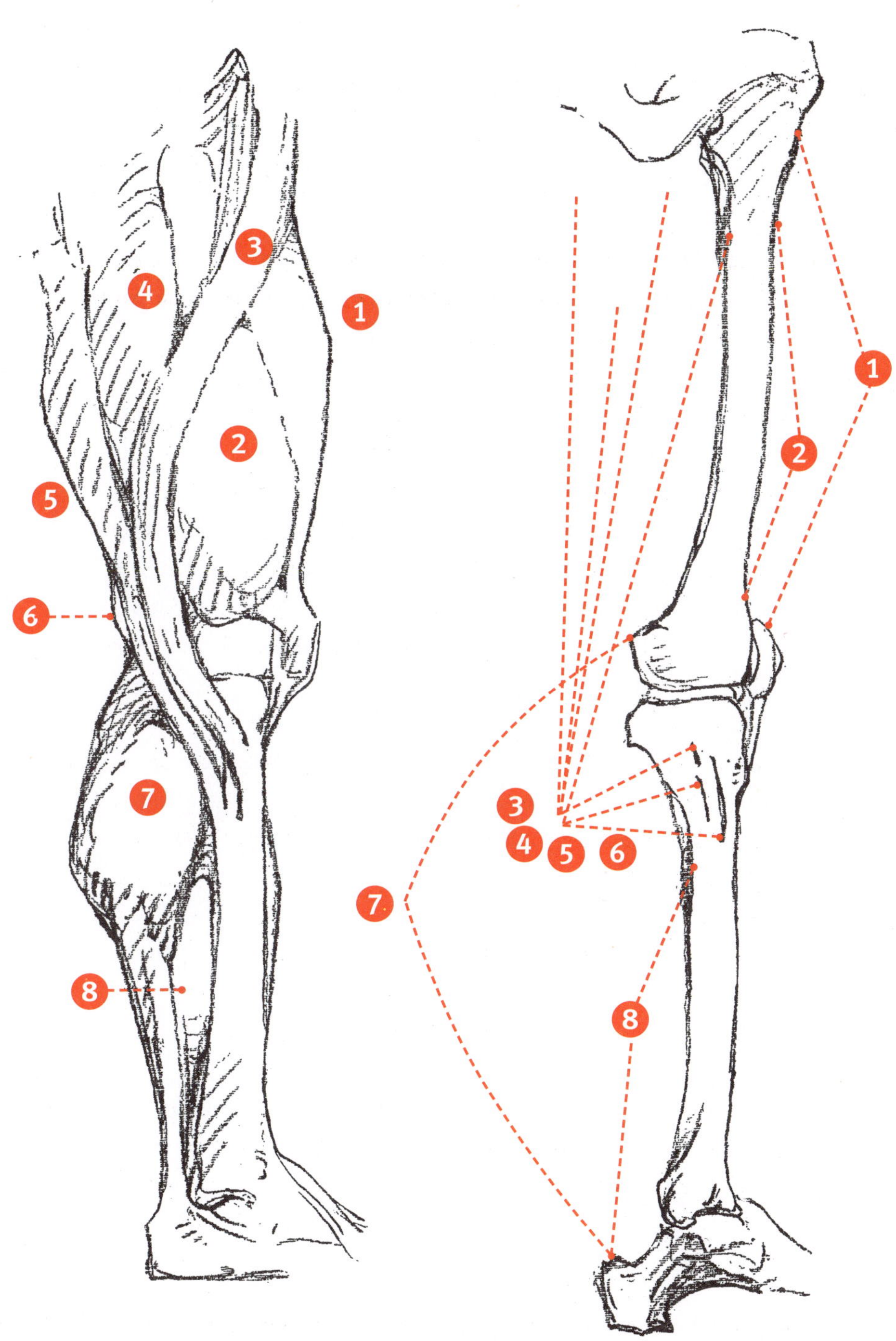
3
4
1
2
5
6
7
8
1
2
3
4
5
6
7
8

ANATOMY OF THE KNEE

The knee must be thought of as a square with sides beveled forward, slightly hollowed at the back, and carrying in front the knee cap; like the stopper of an ink well.

A powerful ligament connects the cap with the high ridge of the shin bone below, the two sliding together on the end of the thigh bone, which is therefore exposed in flexion. The cap is always at the apex of the angle made by thigh and leg. From the knee cap at the top rise the three muscles already described, the rectus by a tendon narrowing upward; the *vastus externus* by a tendon angling slightly out; the vastus internus bulging prominently from the corner of the cap.

When the knee is straight, its bursa, or water mattress, forms a bulge on either side in the corner between the cap and its tendon, exactly opposite the joint itself; the knee cap being always above the level of the joint.

The back, when bent, is hollowed out by the ham-string tendons on either side; when straight, the bone becomes prominent between them, making, with these tendons, three knobs.

The inside of the knee is larger; the knee as a whole is bent convex toward its fellow. The hip socket, the knee and the ankle are all in line; but the shaft of the thigh bone is carried some distance out by a long neck, so that the thigh is set at an angle with the leg.

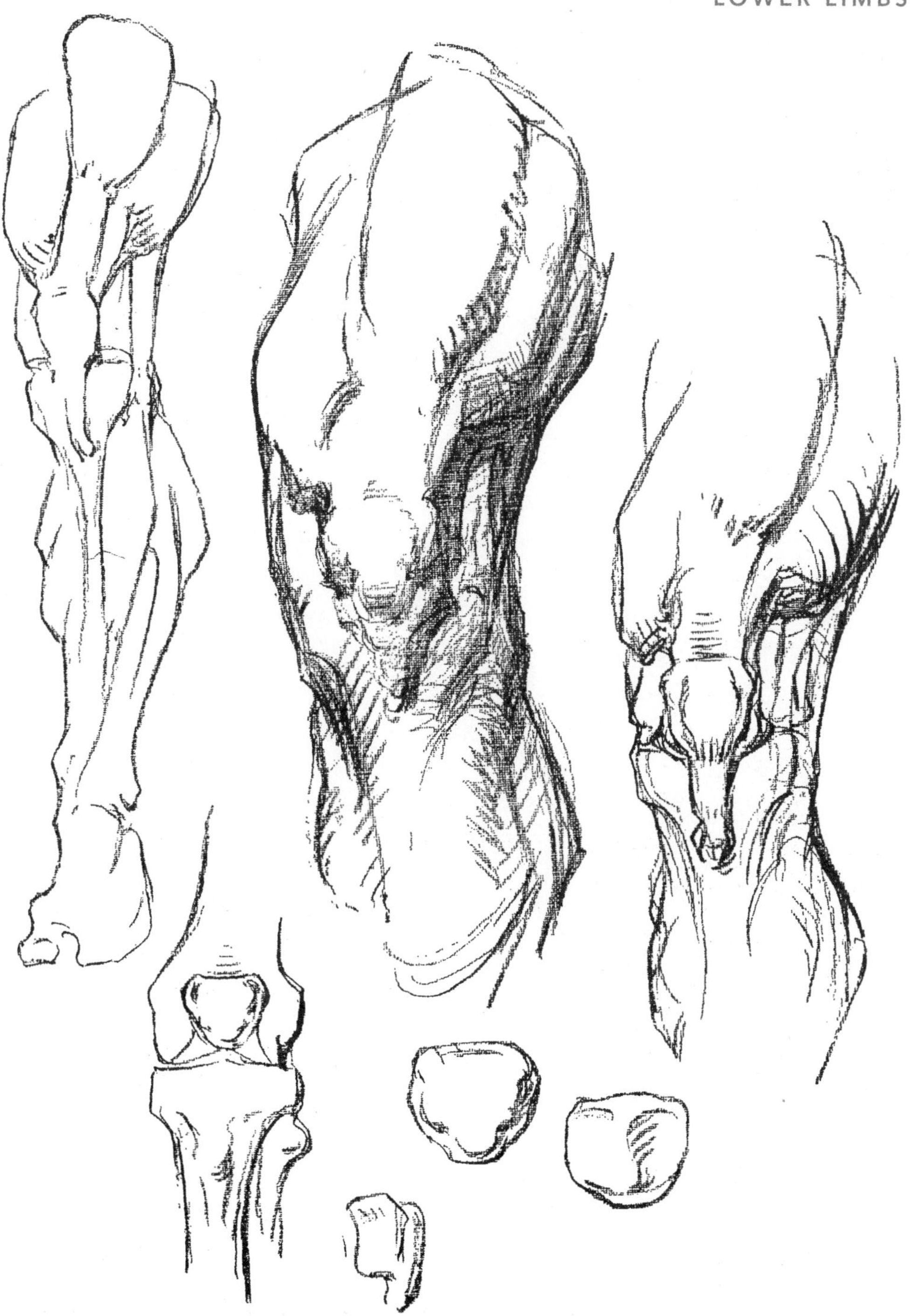

THE KNEE

KNEE: OUTER VIEW

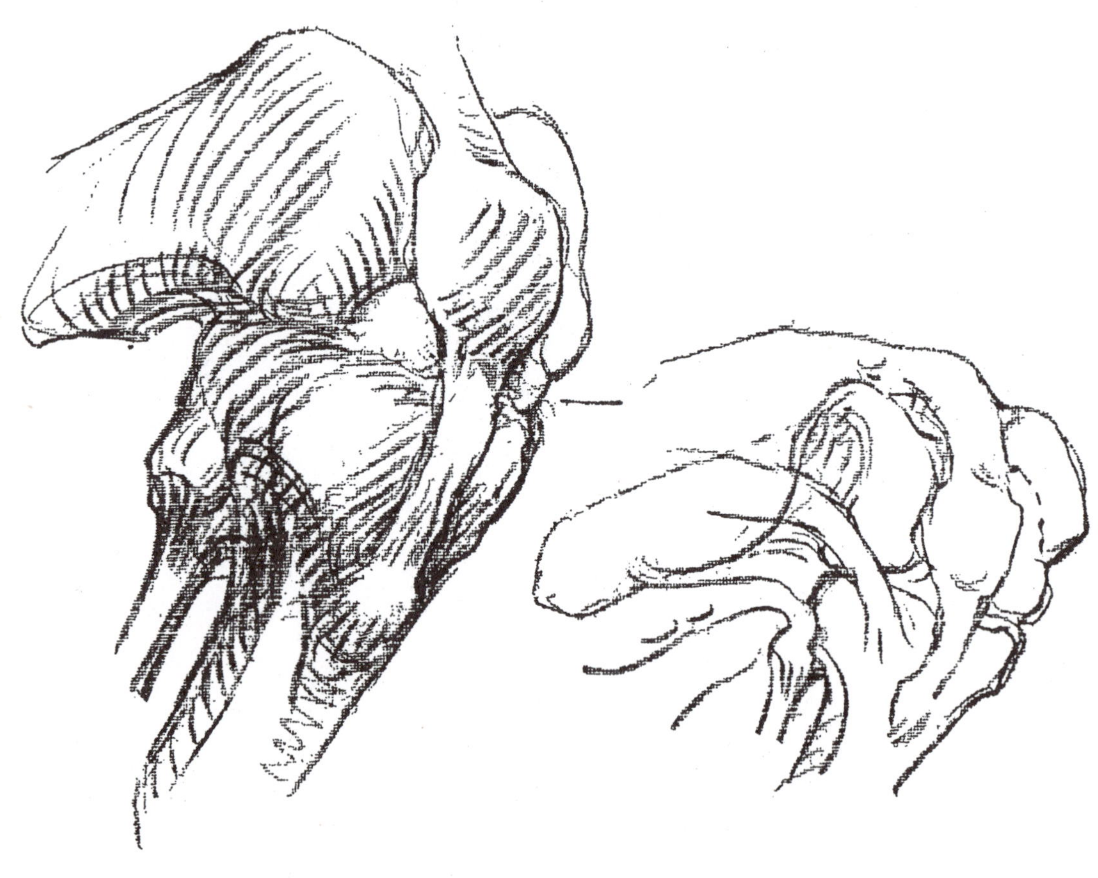

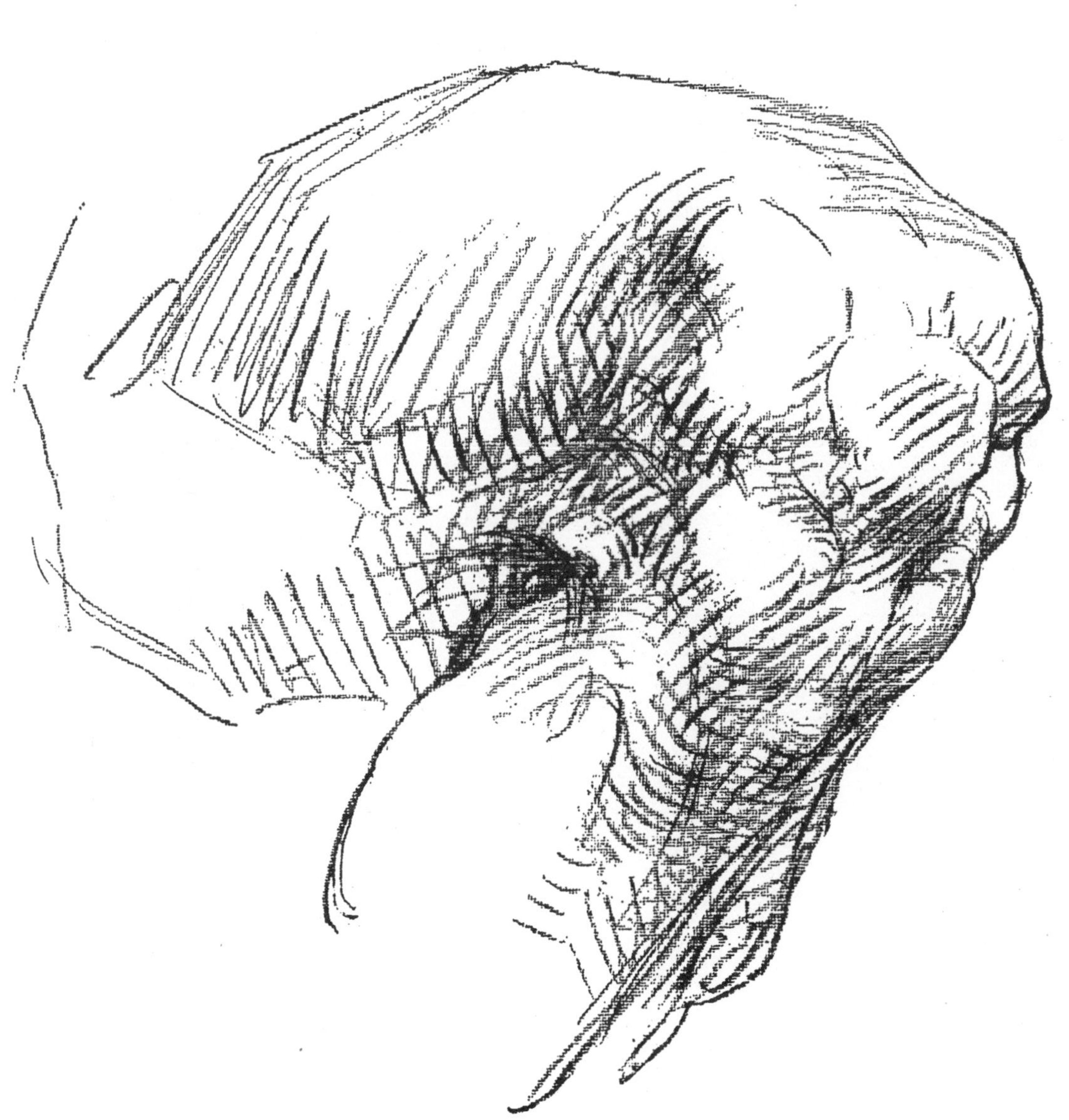

THE KNEE

KNEE: FRONT VIEWS

① Pad or sack.
② Common tendon.
③ *Patella* or knee-pan.
④ Ligament of the *patella*.

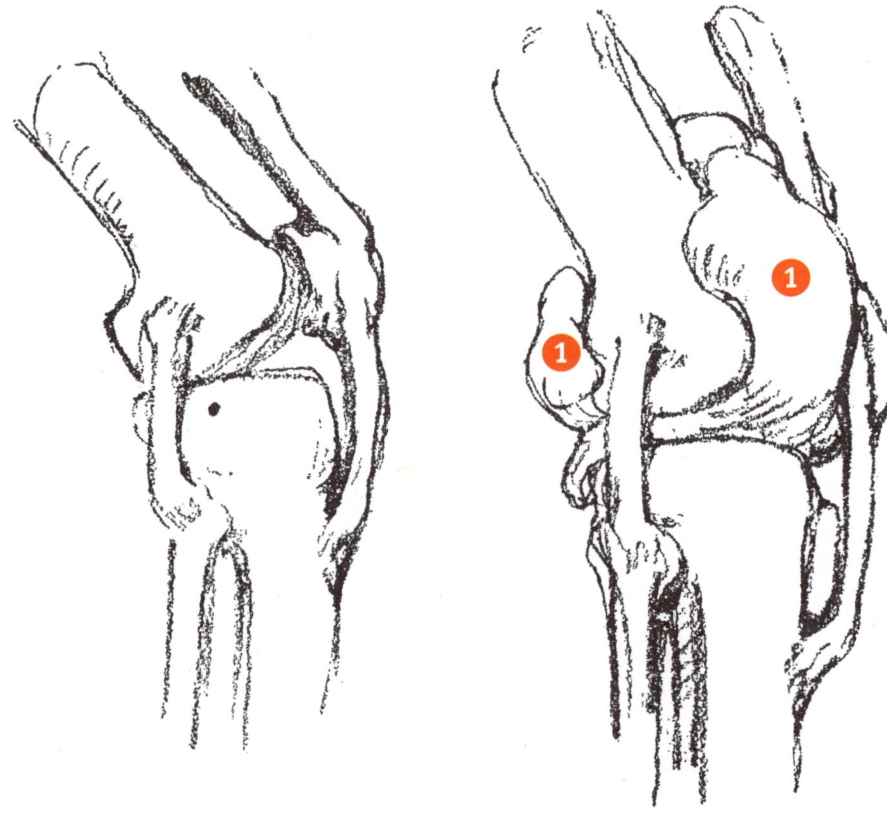

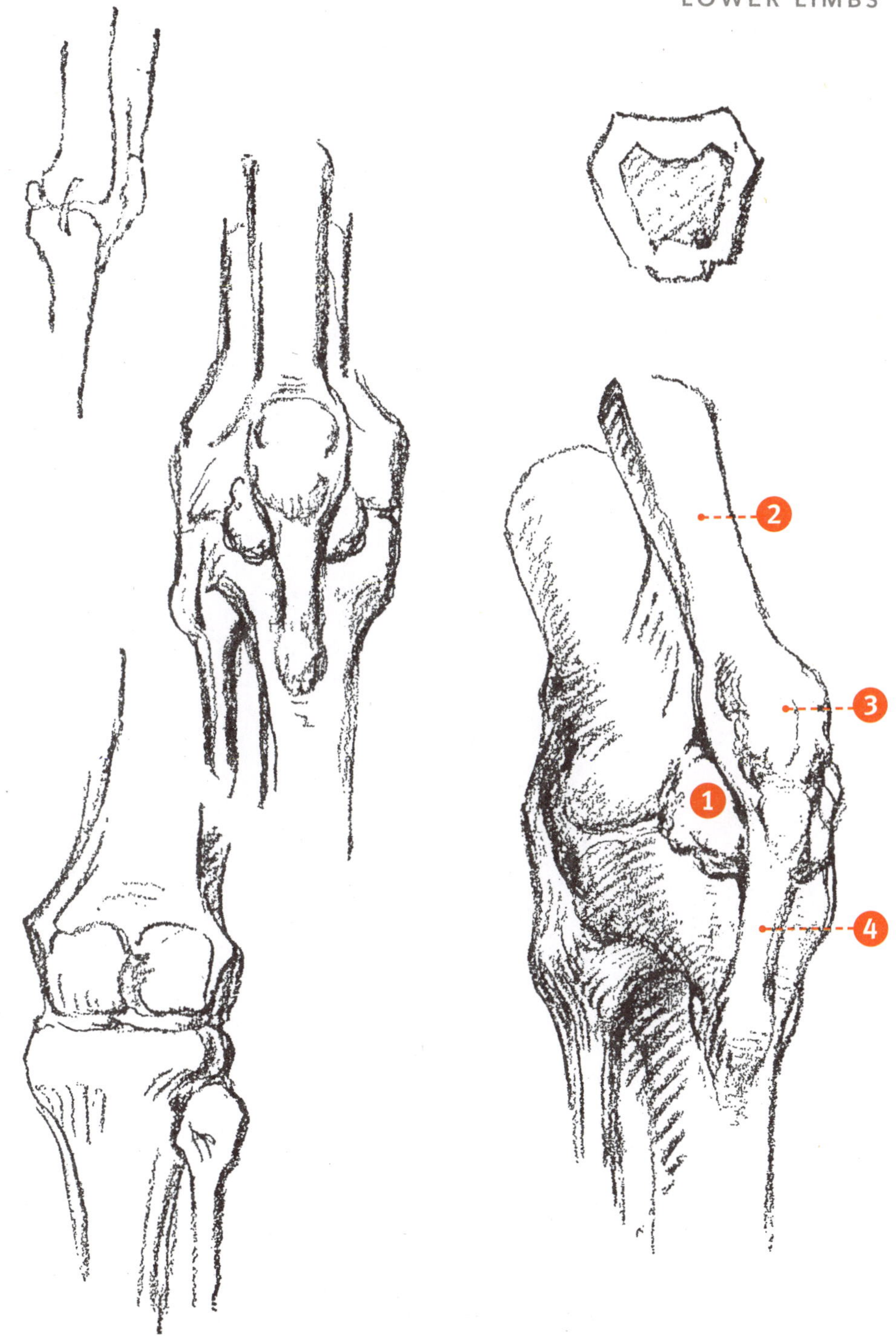
2
3
1
4

THE KNEE

KNEE: INNER VIEW

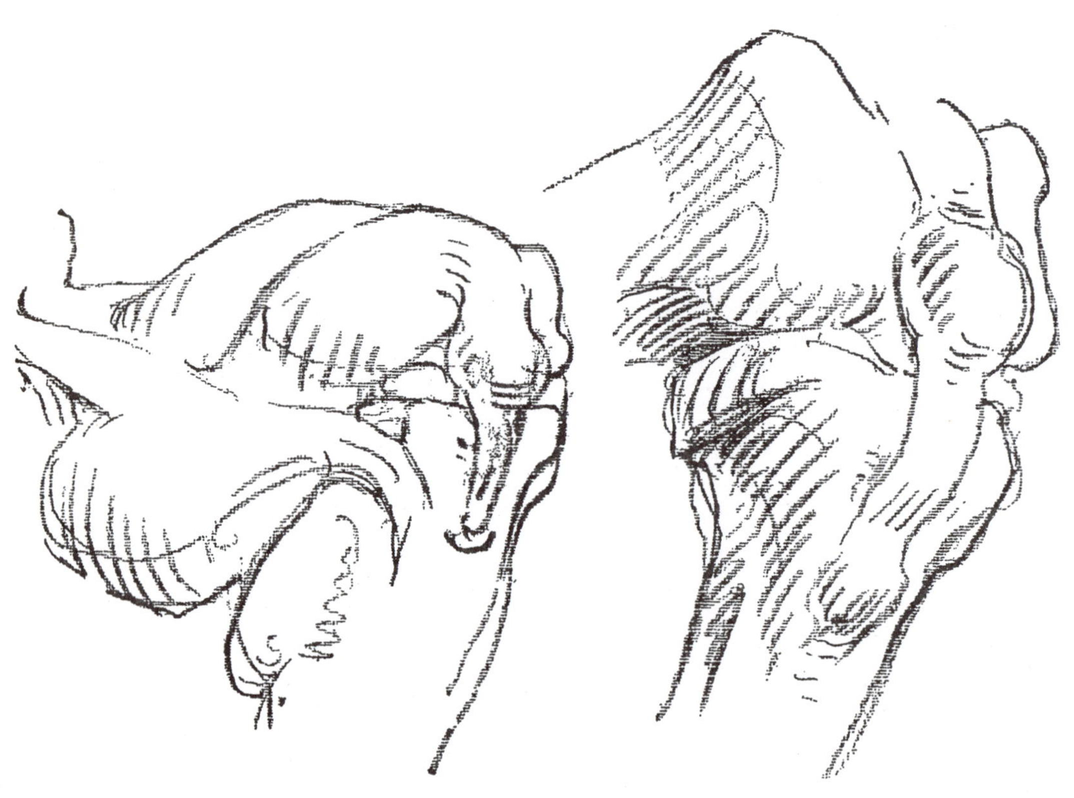

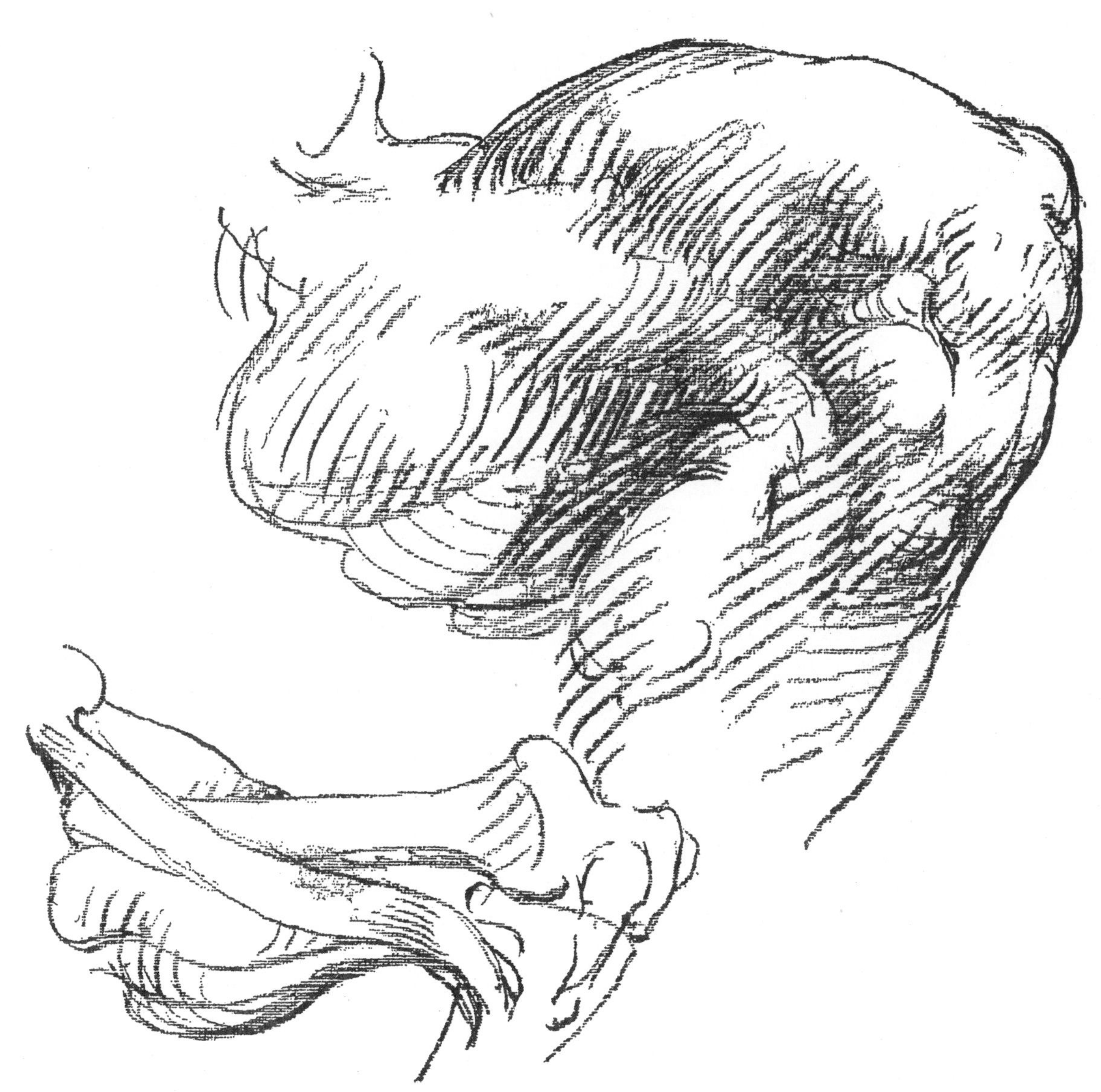

ANATOMY OF THE FOOT

As the little finger side is the heel side of the hand, so the outside of the foot is the heel side. It is flat upon the ground, continuous with the heel; it is lower than the inside – even the outer ankle bone is lower – and it is shorter.

The inside, as though raised by the greater power of the great toe and the tendons of all the toes, is higher. To the front of the ankle is the knob that corresponds with the base of the thumb. Opposite it, on the outside, is a similar knob corresponding with the base of the little finger.

In the foot this symmetry adapted to the function of weight-bearing, has developed into a wonderful series of arches. The five arches of the foot converge on the heel; the toes being flying buttresses to them. The balls of the foot form a transverse arch. The inner arches of the foot are successively higher, forming half of a transverse arch whose completion is in the opposite foot. Opening gradually toward the ankle, this arching movement finally culminates in the two columns of the leg and the arch between; wherefore the leg is placed somewhat to the inside of the central line of the foot.

MOVEMENTS

In all positions, the foot tends to keep itself flat with the ground; the arches of the foot changing accordingly. In action, the foot comes almost into straight line with the leg, but when settling upon the ground, the outer or heel side strikes first and the whole foot settles toward the inside.

THE FOOT

THE FOOT: OUTER VIEW

INTERLOCKING OF THE ANKLE WITH THE FOOT

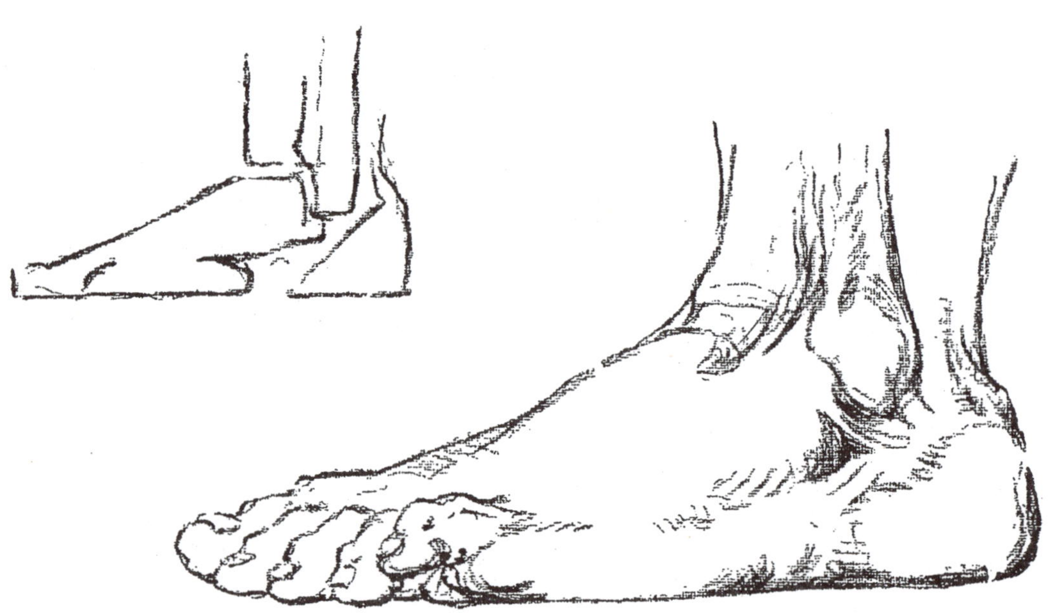

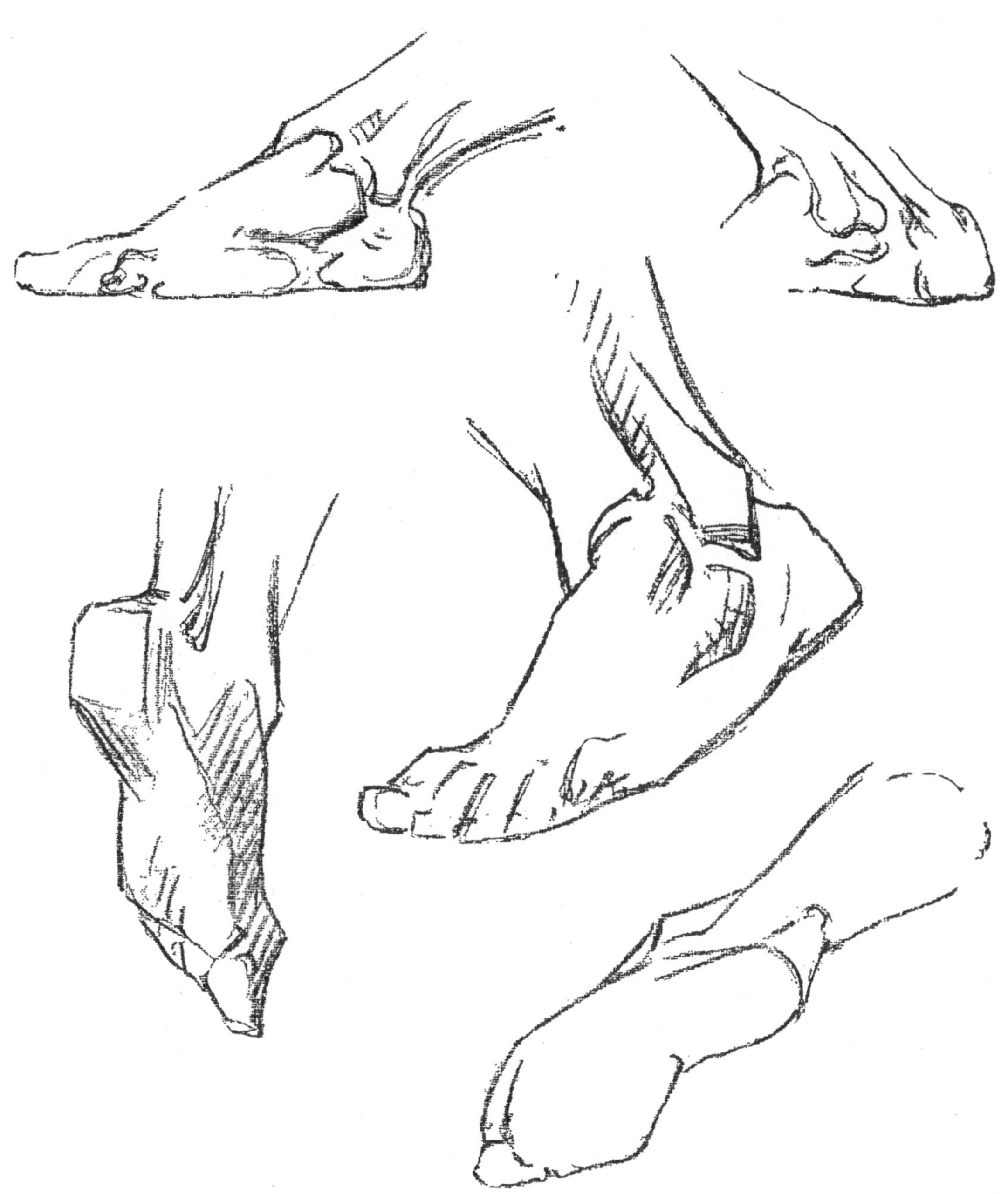

THE FOOT

THE FOOT: INNER VIEW

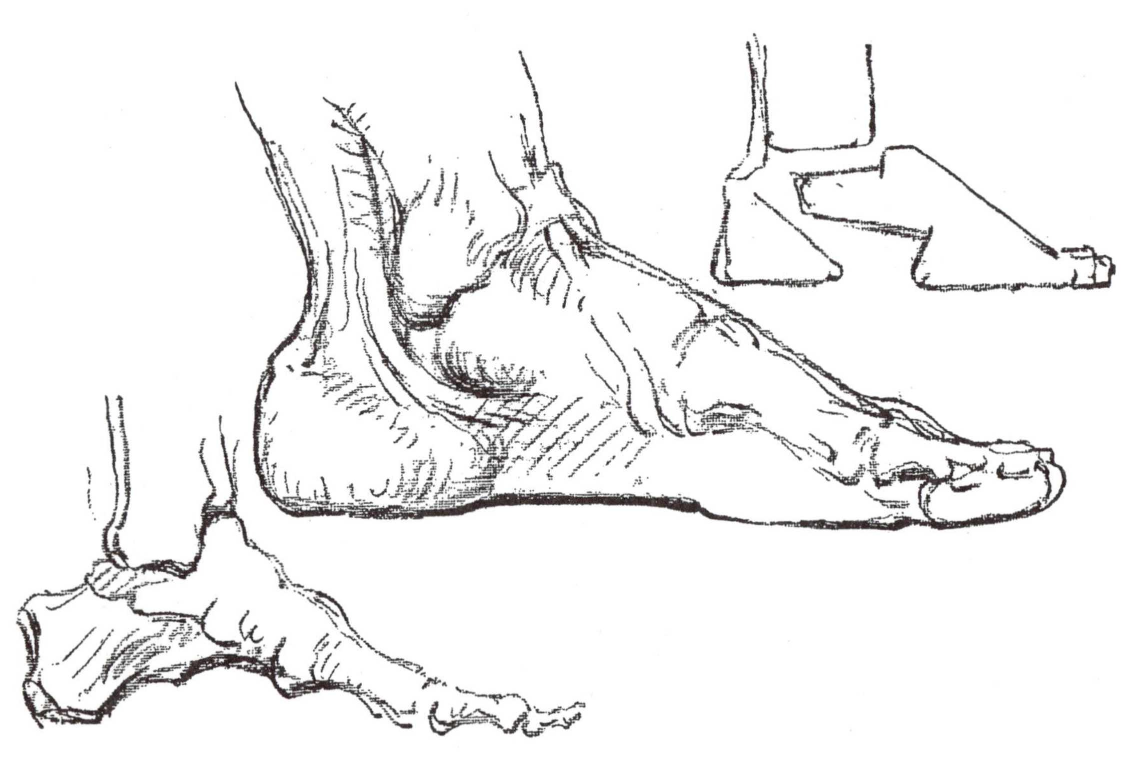

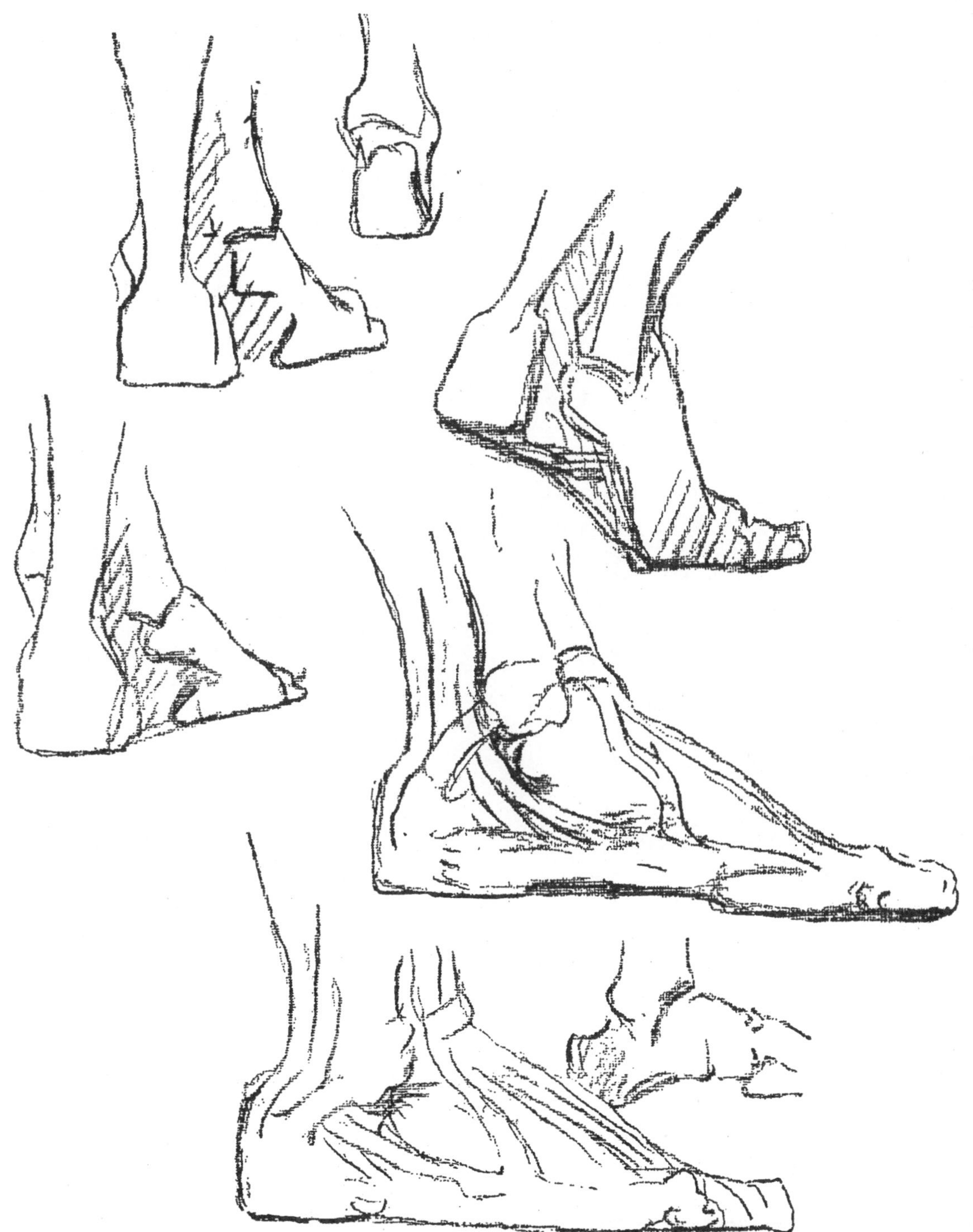

TOES

THEIR PADS AND WEDGING

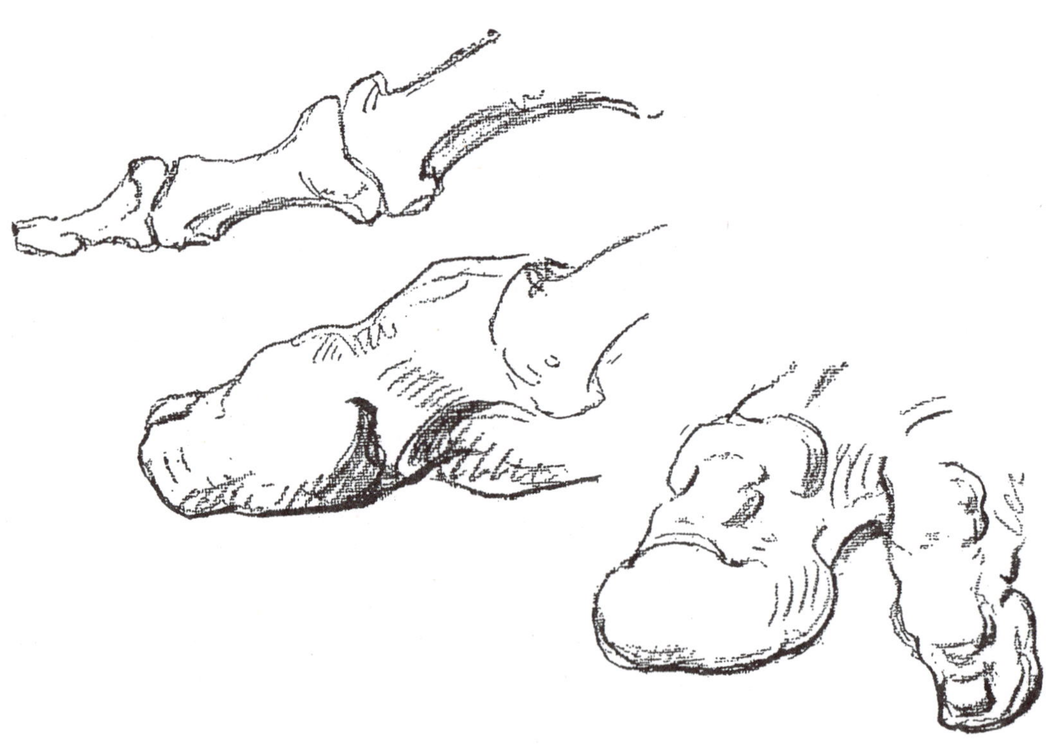

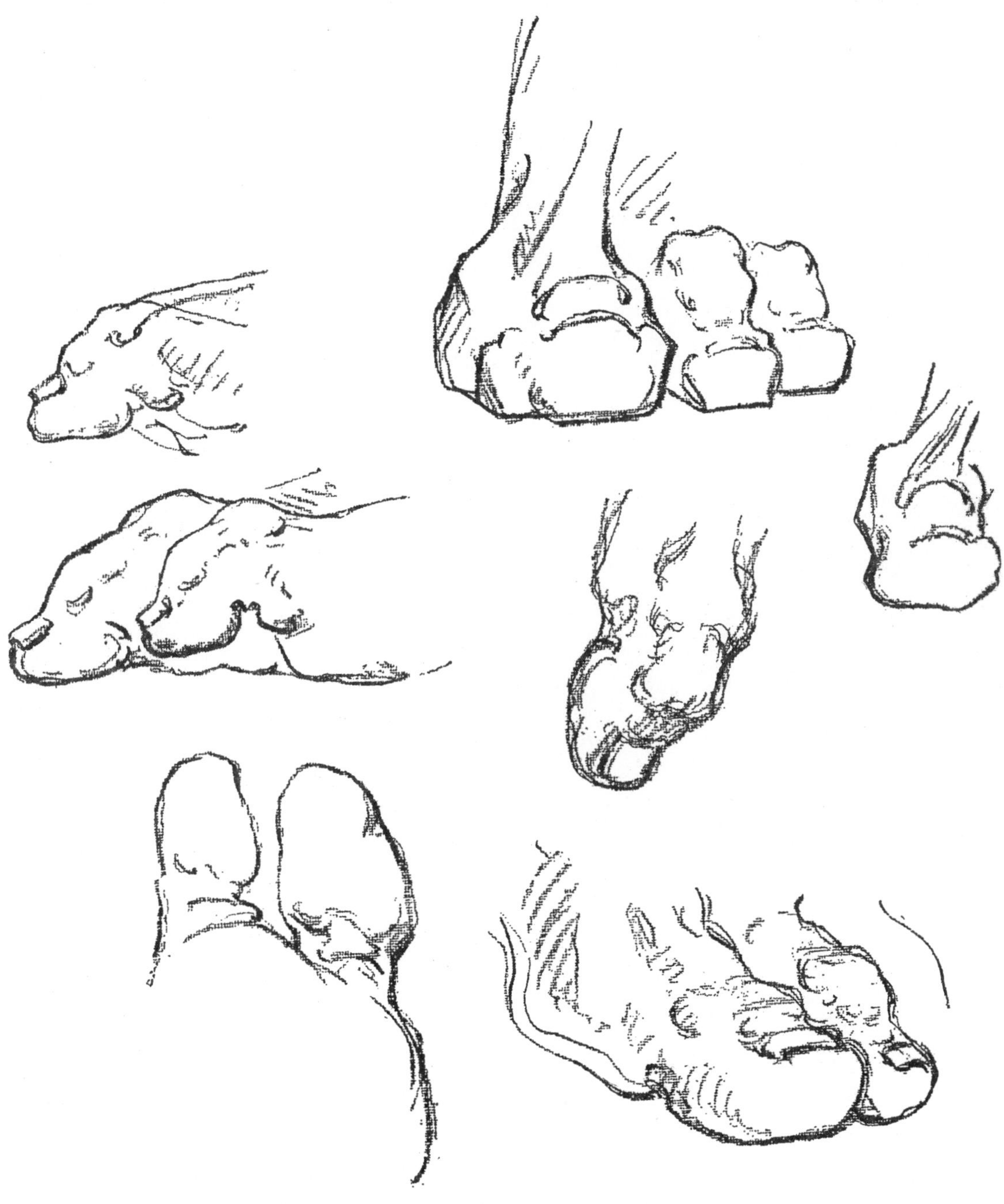

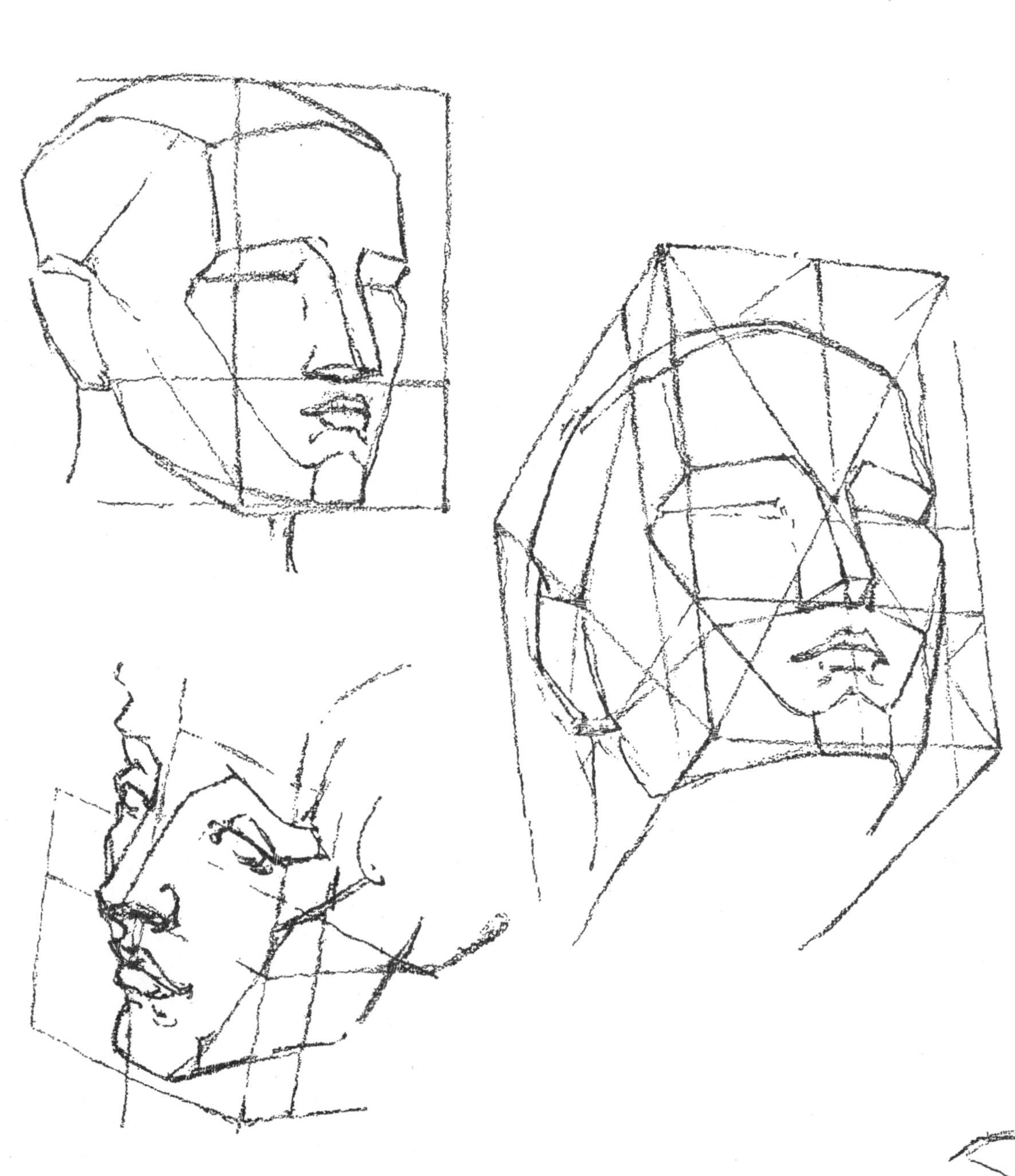

INDEX

Technical terms used

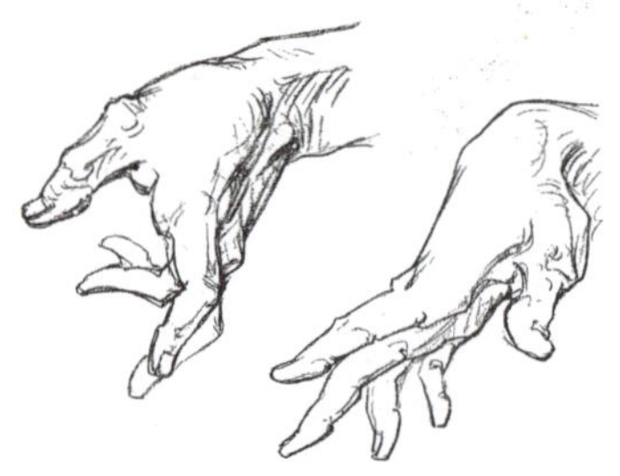

ARTISTS' WEBSITES

We work with a number of incredible artists on our art, gothic and fantasy titles, including:

Yu Cheng Hong: www.yuchenghong.com
Michael C. Hayes: www.artofmike.com
John Howe: www.john-howe.com
Jason Juta: www.jasonjuta.com
Abigail Larson: www.abigaillarson.com
Alan Lathwell: www.alanlathwell.cgsociety.org
Todd Lockwood: www.toddlockwood.com
Daryl Mandryk: www.mandrykart.com
Cris Ortega: www.crisortega.com
Natalie Shau: www.natalie-shau.com
Tiago da Silva: www.tiagodasilva.com
Dino Tomic: www.atomiccircus-tattoo.com
Josephine Wall: www.josephinewall.co.uk